Warriors, Witches, Whores

Contemporary Approaches to Film and Media Series

A complete listing of the books in this series can be found online at wsupress.wayne.edu

General Editor
Barry Keith Grant
Brock University

Advisory Editors
Robert J. Burgoyne
University of St. Andrews

Caren J. Deming
University of Arizona

Patricia B. Erens
School of the Art Institute of Chicago

Peter X. Feng
University of Delaware

Lucy Fischer
University of Pittsburgh

Frances Gateward
California State University, Northridge

Tom Gunning
University of Chicago

Thomas Leitch
University of Delaware

Walter Metz
Southern Illinois University

Warriors, Witches, Whores

Women in Israeli Cinema

Rachel S. Harris

Wayne State University Press
Detroit

© 2017 by Wayne State University Press, Detroit, Michigan 48201. All rights reserved. No part of this book may be reproduced without formal permission. Manufactured in the United States of America.

ISBN 978-0-8143-3967-1 (paperback); ISBN 978-0-8143-3968-8 (ebook)

Library of Congress Cataloging Number: 2017949052

Wayne State University Press
Leonard N. Simons Building
4809 Woodward Avenue
Detroit, Michigan 48201-1309

Visit us online at wsupress.wayne.edu

Parts of chapter 1, "A Woman's War: The Gulf War and the Israeli Chick Flick," were published in a previous version as "A Woman's War: The Gulf War and Popular Women's Culture in Israel" in *Narratives of Dissent: War in Israeli Arts and Culture*, ed. Rachel S. Harris and Ranen Omer-Sherman (Detroit: Wayne State University Press, 2013), 317–35.

An earlier draft of chapter 2, "Women in Conflict: The Impact of Militarism and Male Hegemony on Women's Lives," was published as "Parallel Lives: Palestinian, Druze, and Jewish Women in Recent Israeli Cinema on the Conflict: Free Zone, Syrian Bride, and Lemon Tree in *Shofar* 32, no. 1 (Fall 2013): 79–102.

A section of chapter 5, "Witches and Wailers: Mizrahi Women's Power," was published in an earlier draft as "Ahoti Hayafa (2011): Magical Realism and Marginalisation in the World of the Mizrachi Woman," in a special issue of *Symbolism* 12/13, Jewish Literature and Magical Realism, guest edited by Axel Stahler.

For Randy Deshazo
כשאני כאן לבד
תני לי יד

"When I am here alone
Give me your hand"

Tni Li Yad by Boaz Sharabi
Lyrics Shimrit Orr
Melody Nurit Hirsch

Contents

Acknowledgments — ix

Introduction — 1

Part 1. Women on the Front Lines: Reconceptualizing War, Militarism, the Conflict, and the Female Soldier

1. A Woman's War: The Gulf War and the Israeli Chick Flick — 31
2. Women in Conflict: The Impact of Militarism and Male Hegemony on Women's Lives — 49
3. Women Waving Guns: Does Feminism Meet the IDF on the Israeli Screen? — 65

Part 2. Women in the Home Guard: Religion, Ethnicity, and Sexuality

4. "A Woman of Worth": Who Sees the Religious Woman? — 91
5. Witches and Wailers: Mizrahi Women's Power — 123
6. Hot and Fertile: Sex, Sexuality, and Prostitution — 149

Part 3. Feminism, Postfeminism, and New Directions in Israeli Feminist Filmmaking

7. A Question of Rape: Feminism, Postfeminism, and Issues of Representation — 187
8. A Move to the Center: Foreign Workers, Arab Women, and the Shift from the Margins — 221

Afterword: The Effects of Feminist Activism on the Changing Cinematic Landscape — 239

Notes — 249
Filmography — 277
Bibliography — 283
Index — 293

Acknowledgments

This book is the result of serendipitous encounters and fortunate timing, though I could as easily say that it began by accident. In 2010, fewer than five hundred Israeli feature films had been made, many of which had been lost, were available only through film and television archives, or were in old video formats that could be viewed only in Europe or on antiquated equipment. I had seen several Israeli films and taken a short Israeli film course at the Rothberg School of International Studies at the Hebrew University, a basic foundation for a new course I was planning on Israeli cinema. With a concerted effort, I imagined that I could probably watch about two hundred films, which was most of the readily available material, a task that would probably take several years. Limited to my local video store's rental options, the increasing offerings of Netflix, which had begun streaming Israeli films with about twenty-five listed at any given time, the occasional listing on my cable provider, and purchases made from stores in Israel, I thought that this number would provide me with a strong impression of the range of Israeli cinema and its history, and certainly offer enough material from which to build an undergraduate course.

Soon after moving to Chicago, at a dinner with close friends Ruth Lipman and Jerry Warren, I mentioned my plans. Their son Josh, who had recently graduated and moved to the area, revealed his passion for Israeli film and expressed an interest in embarking on this adventure with me. So, every Wednesday for about a year, Josh and I met, ate dinner, and watched an Israeli film or two. Our viewing was indiscriminate. We sometimes followed actors or directors. We sometimes chose films for their subject matter or the period in which they were made. We attended new film releases and followed stories in the newspaper. Increasingly we researched the films, and when browsing the internet no longer sufficed I invested in books and scholarly articles, turning our casual entertainment into extended, often theoretical, discussions. Periodically we were joined by roommates, neighbors, and friends. Eventually Meytal Ozeri, the emissary for Young Judea and herself a source of Israeli films we couldn't otherwise find, became a long-standing viewing companion, finally taking over Josh's role and continuing to discuss films with me long after her return to Israel.

The digitalization of the Spielberg Archives, with its online portal that has made older documentary footage and early feature films freely available, aided my work. The special efforts made by Israeli film funds to digitalize long-forgotten Israeli classics, an effort that means that films that would otherwise have been lost in the archives are now for sale in good media stores in Israel, also helped me. I particularly want to thank Eitan Senna in the film department of Haozen Hashlishit in Tel Aviv and the staff at Eighth Note at Ben Gurion airport for directing me to many of these newly released classics.

As this project expanded, I began to advise film festivals on Israeli cinema. I am grateful to Cindy Stern for making me the Chicago Festival of Israeli Cinema representative at the Jerusalem International Film Festival, enabling me to view the newest cinematic offerings, and for sourcing copies of freshly released films on my return home. Hedva Goldschmidt at 2GoFilms was extremely generous with screener copies, and the Israeli consulate in Chicago, through Nitza Gilad, Maya Karmely, and Nir Eilon, and the Chicago International Film festival have also helped me gain access to new films and connected me with actors and filmmakers. Through the Israel Project at the University of Illinois I have been able to screen films and invite filmmakers to campus, and I thank the Program in Jewish Culture and Society at the university and the Jewish Federation of Chicago for making this possible, and particularly the late Michael Kotzin, whose vision and enthusiasm so often shaped the scope of what was possible. Thanks also go to the Chicago Humanities Festival, which graciously invited me to interview some of the leading cultural figures in Israel, and to Eran Riklis for permission to publish the image from *The Syrian Bride* on the front cover of this book.

Many colleagues have been extraordinarily kind, particularly Yael Munk, Amy Kronish, Elliot A. Ratzman, and Dan Chyutin, who attended screenings with me, provided hard-to-find films, and directed me to topical scholarship and journalism. Dan has served as a sounding board and important intellectual companion, particularly in the later stages of the book's evolution, reading manuscript drafts and bringing me suitcases full of recently released films on his visits. I am so grateful for this meeting of the minds. Thanks go to Alexis Pogolreskin, Adriana Jacobs, and Carol Zemel, who read late drafts of selected sections and helped me to find clarity of mind as well as expression. Mya Guarinieri Jaradat generously shared her published and unpublished research on the foreign workers and refugees in Israel. I also want to thank Michal Aviad, Anat Shperling, Netalie Braun, Smadar Zamir, Lior Elephant, Israela Shaer Meoded, and the women of the Forum for Women Filmmakers and Television Artists for their insightful observations about women's activism in the film industry, and I commend them for their ongoing fight for equality of access, treatment, and representation for women.

While I have seen many more than the two hundred films I set out to view, the Israeli film industry itself has changed radically in the last decade. From the handful of films made annually during the 1980s and early 1990s, this relatively obscure industry has undergone a dramatic transformation. The quality and number of films (shorts, documentaries, and features) being produced has grown significantly, and Israeli films are repeatedly finalists and award winners at major international film festivals all over the world. No matter how current the films I reference in this book, new releases and new developments continue to make this an ongoing topic of interest and study.

With the help of a summer spent at the Brandeis Summer Institute for Israel Studies in 2011 I did prepare a course on Israeli Cinema, which I have taught for several years, and I have gone on to build a film collection at the University of Illinois library through the support of the Program in Jewish Culture and Society and the Jewish Federation of Chicago and the interest and perseverance of Laila Hussein Moustafa, the Middle East librarian who allotted the Hebrew budget for this project. A semester release from my department, the Program in Comparative and World Literature, and a generous sabbatical leave from the university enabled me to complete the writing of this book. I want to recognize my editor Annie Martin, as well as Kristin Harpster, Sandra Judd, and all the staff at Wayne State University Press for their patience and tireless support of this project.

Of all the unexpected pleasures that this project has engendered, it was a conversation about the representation of women in Israeli films depicting the religious ultra-orthodox Jewish community that I had with a man on our second date, as I explained the book project to him, that was to become the most significant and life-changing impact of this work. Not only did he name the films I was describing, he suggested several more I hadn't yet seen and a few I didn't even know. Five weeks later we were engaged and a year after our first date we were married. Randy Deshazo, who brought his own film collection and encyclopedic knowledge of Israeli actors, filmmaking, and culture of the 1960s, 70s, and 80s to our relationship and our home, has been a true companion while I wrote this book. Though his tolerance for some of the better forgotten Israeli films is far lower than mine, and he will flee when a film is truly unwatchable, our endless conversations, his searching questions, and his careful reading of this book's many drafts have made this project particularly special. Though I might have managed this book alone, it wouldn't have been half as much fun! It is for this reason that I dedicate it to him.

Introduction

In the final scene of *Hill 24 Doesn't Answer* (Thorold Dickinson, 1955), after a night of heavy fighting the UN observers tour Hill 24, tasked with assigning territory in the truce between Israel and its Arab enemies. A female soldier tumbles forward, dead, with an Israeli flag tightly clasped in her hand. The UN observer holds it up and declares the hill for Israel; he then lays it over the dead woman. Her death serves as the ultimate symbol of national sacrifice, earning the respect of the men on-screen, who salute her. The audience is moved by this martyrdom in which a life is exchanged for a country; the swelling chorus builds climactically, and the camera pans out across the desolate landscape that will become the State of Israel.

This bombastic nationalistic expression was the finale for Israel's first full-length feature film. With dialogue predominantly in English, *Hill 24 Doesn't Answer* was made for an international audience with the express purpose of communicating a historical narrative about the ideological motivations and the practical endeavors that led to the creation of the new country. Entered into the Cannes Film Festival, it made a favorable impression as a tense war thriller. Through a series of flashbacks the plot weaves together the stories of four soldiers shown in the opening sequence dying while defending the hill to which the finale returns. Each narrative traces the origins, motivations, and relationships of one of the male soldiers, who serve as heroic typologies within cinematic representations of Israel's national

Hill 24 Doesn't Answer: Esther (Margalit Oved) lies at the feet of the UN forces adjudicating the apportionment of land after the battle.

narrative: a Holocaust survivor who overcomes his trauma, an assimilated Diasporic Jew who reconnects with his people, and a non-Jew inspired by the righteousness of creating a Jewish nation. The fourth member of the unit, Esther (Margalit Oved), appears in each of the men's story lines, but there is no dedicated flashback that focuses on her life.

Notwithstanding the symbolic representation of her death, Esther's role as a supporting character throughout the film signifies her position in the story of Israel as a helpmate for male heroism. Ella Shohat has claimed, "Her (hi)story begins here, with the Zionist act, not before it, and will only be told through the agency of male Western, Jewish and non-Jewish, narrators."[1] Like Esther, the film's other two major female characters, Miriam Mizrahi, played by Haya Harareet, and her friend, the unnamed Druze woman played by Shoshanna Damari, are emblematic of the roles available to women in this period. Harareet, originally of Polish-Jewish extraction, plays a woman of Middle Eastern descent, exemplified in her name "Mizrahi" and her exchanges with the Druze woman in Arabic. Working with the underground, she meets the Irish James Finnegan, and their passionate romance conjures an orientalist sexual fantasy, as a result of which, after being discharged from the British police, he joins the fledgling Israeli army. Damari, a popular Jewish-Yemenite singer, is cast as the primitive Druze who sings in Arabic while stirring the boiling pot in the makeshift kitchen. With her traditional dress, manner, and actions, she exemplifies the invisible subaltern as her disembodied voice lyrically floats over the pastoral scenes of Finnegan moving among village children. Later Esther will also sing in Arabic, as the four soldiers drive in a truck toward the base of the hill that is the starting point for their final mission. Only at the last minute is she assigned to the mission after the men vouch for her, and the commander is explicit that her inclusion depends on her superior knowledge of the terrain. These expressions of her indigeneity connect her allegorically with the other women in the film, who share her inherent connection to the land by virtue of their Jewish-Arab ethnicity, as well as being metonyms for it. This figurative connection situates men as protectors of the land and of women, thereby denoting women as passive figures in this fight for nationhood. Esther, Miriam, and the Druze woman are paradigmatic of female representation in Israeli cinema for the next four decades, and their roles are characteristic of the limited and symbolic purpose women have on screen. They may serve as lovers, nurses, helpmates, and even soldiers, but their presence is tangential to the central story of male heroism.

Israeli film's tendency to employ the imagery that helped foster the Zionist national narrative that, in Yael Zerubavel's words, creates "a particular periodization and evaluation of the past" that turns "certain events into political myths" was a critical tool in the creation of national memory and, by extension, a national identity.[2] Patriotism was central to the new film industry developing during the 1950s and 1960s, positioning men at its forefront. Cinema consecrated the image of the New Jew, exemplified in themes of war, heroism, and masculinity: a physically strong, ideologically motivated Zionist whose very essence served as a rejection of an internalized conception of European Jewry that was built on anti-Semitic tropes. Rooted in the new land, this image of the *sabra* was characterized by native proficiency in Hebrew, intimate acquaintance with the land of Israel, and embodiment of the Labor Zionist ethos and became the most iconic representation of the social and political values of the new country.[3] These themes were particularly evident in Israeli filmmaking, whose masculine trajectory and central male protagonists had already been shaped by the early Zionist documentaries and the handful of films made during the 1930s, almost all of which focused on militarism and agrarian labor. Nurith Gertz has traced the Hebrewist ideology that Israeli cinema further defined:

> The geography that unfolded beneath his feet and gaze denoted his connection with the homeland and his power to control it, and this power was shaped and aggrandized by the camera and by cinematic language. The camera adhered to his point of view and identified with it, and the best cinematic techniques of the time amplified his image and displayed his control of space. This hero determined history, the structure of the plot, and the masculinity of the Zionist order. He defined the space he controlled, a space from which all others were excused, or within which they were made subordinate.[4]

Positioning a masculine ideal at the center of Israeli cinema met with widespread success, and films that built on this imagery created several film stars, including Yehoram Gaon, Haim Topol, Arik Lavie, and Assi Dayan. Directors and producers who recycled these images—Menachem Golan, Ephraim Kishon, and Uri Zohar—acquired international prestige among audiences who celebrated both the cinematic efforts and the plucky little country's existence in the face of enemies calling for its annihilation.

Hugely popular, cinema "was cheaper than other forms of entertainment, such as the theater, the opera, or a concert, and could be afforded by even the poorest members of the population,"[5] and there was widespread consumption of foreign imports, particularly Hollywood escapist fantasies, which offered a distraction from the harsh realities of life under war and a strict austerity regime. The local film industry was influenced by these foreign productions and was also in competition with them for audience attention. Thus Israeli cinema's tendency to employ a Western cinematic language reflected its broader relationship to international productions, the fact that many of the industry's early operatives were foreign born and trained, and the industry's hope that exporting cinema would communicate the history and development of the Zionist enterprise and generate revenue. The highly nationalist environment meant that local audiences were predisposed toward films about Israel, while international audiences were curious about the transformation of the sabra. Thus the adoption of international models, even ones filtered through the ideals of Labor

Zionism, made the exports accessible. Israeli films that wished to compete for viewers both at home and abroad reinterpreted Hollywood's popular images of heroism, creating Israeli versions of cowboys and soldiers that transmuted the American conventions into images of Israeli pioneering. These early productions cast Arabs as antagonists in roles that Hollywood had reserved for Native American Indians, reimagined the Western frontier landscape in the Negev Desert, and evoked the national spirit.[6]

These imports also inundated Israelis with the stock figures of Hollywood's vision of womanhood—nurses, wives, mothers, and girlfriends. As Molly Haskell argued of Hollywood's Golden Age (1930–60), the mere physical presence of an attractive woman in an action or adventure film suggested sexual allure. This heightened the drama and emphasized the heroes' bravado, the meaning of sacrifice, and the responsibility of protecting hearth and home as the villains sought out every means by which to destroy her and, by extension, the hero.[7] Haskell's rudimentary approach to feminist film scholarship in light of second-wave feminism chronicled the representation of women on screen, challenging embedded stereotypes. Drawing on sociology and situating film texts within the historical contexts in which they were produced, she considered basic questions about the amount of time women spend on-screen, whether they are active or passive agents, and their exploitation and objectification.[8] In Israeli cinema, which was driven by its nationalist agenda, women spent limited time on-screen; female characters were tangential to the plot, narrative, and action, while paradoxically their presence remained *necessary* for organizing meaning within the film's patriarchal diegesis.

Israeli critics opposed the frivolity of Hollywood films, viewing them as ideologically barren and likely to corrupt the public's moral values. They preferred local productions with a nationalist fervor, deeming them virtuous and viewing even fiction films as educational because they inculcated viewers in the Labor Zionist ethos. This crafted message, often at a remove from historical or social reality, served as an important tool in nation building. Nevertheless, though Labor Zionism espoused an egalitarian ideology, local films positioned nation building as a masculine practice in which female pioneers played a secondary role, which subverted at least the illusion of women's equality. As such, the strong nationalist message disguised the mimetic adoption of Hollywood's tendency to marginalize women and inadvertently exhibited most women's discriminatory experience of Zionism. The separation between the textual subject (the character on-screen) and the social subject (the cultural construction of womanhood) that feminist film scholarship identifies as a way for a female viewer to insert her subjectivity into her cinematic experience collapsed in the early years of Zionist filmmaking because the dominant cinematic and social models were aligned in Zionism, and both situated women at the margins of the national discourse.[9]

Camera work reinforced a worldview that situated men in a controlling position, typified in Finnegan's first encounter with Miriam. Walking against a streaming crowd, he towers

Hill 24 Doesn't Answer: James Finnegan (Edward Mulhare) finds Miriam (Haya Harareet) sheltering the wounded.

over the illegal Jewish immigrants caught by the British authorities as they attempted to immigrate into Palestine clandestinely. His fair hair and clean shirt are brightly lit, emphasizing his authority and creating a powerful contrast with the bedraggled survivors in deep shadow. He finds Miriam huddled over a body protected by large rocks and pulls her away, shining the torch on her face. Thus our first encounter with Miriam is entirely controlled by him. He moves her into the frame and shines the light that shows her face. When he moves the torch away from her to look at the body she is protecting, she moves out of our vision as the camera closes in on the prostrated, injured male.

The scene demonstrates that the way women are presented on-screen already undermines their subjectivity, providing an exemplar of what Laura Mulvey termed the male gaze. In "Visual Pleasure and Narrative Cinema" (1992) she looked beyond material depictions of the roles women played to consider the inherent nature of cinema as a gendered medium. Drawing on Christian Metz's application of Freudian and Lacanian theories to cinema, she set out a feminist attack arguing that the pleasure derived from cinema was predicated on the interest of a male spectator. Mulvey claimed that in the conventions of classical cinema women were placed in a position of "to-be-looked-at-ness" for male gratification.[10] In this reading, men found sexual pleasure in a mode of looking (scopophilia) that eased their inherent castration anxiety—either in a fetishistic way that built up the woman's beauty (and all that might represent her) or in a voyeuristic way that is, according to E. Ann Kaplan, "linked to disparagement, has a sadistic side, and is involved with pleasure through control or domination and with punishing the woman."[11] Mulvey outlined the tyranny of the male gaze: (1) the characters looking at the woman on screen, (2) the camera (and the man behind the lens) looking at the woman, and (3) the viewer looking at the woman. The overwhelming positioning of the male gaze meant that it was always in a position of power, leaving few options for the woman being gazed at, thereby forcing her into a position of objectification. By dictating the terms, patriarchy dominates and represses women. Even if a woman can change her position or return the gaze, her response is limited by a male hegemony, "through its controlling power over female discourse and the female desire."[12] Mary Devereaux refined Mulvey's analysis by noting that "[t]he male gaze is not always male, but *it is always male-dominated.*"[13] Here Finnegan not only serves as the character looking at the woman who will become the object of his romantic desire, he also represents the power structure that has her hiding in the rocks. In addition, his sympathy for her and the cause that she represents positions him as a surrogate for the audience who supports her renegade behavior, seeing her model quintessential heroic values that would ultimately be pivotal for the creation of the State of Israel within the boundaries of a femininity that never threatens his masculinity or authoritative status.

Esther's and Miriam's lead roles in *Hill 24 Doesn't Answer* cannot overcome the film's fundamental displacement of women from the film's more central concerns about militarism, the reunification of the Jewish Diaspora in a process that constructed Israeli identity, or overcoming the image of Jewish victimization that the Holocaust signified. The women are never viewed outside of a male narrative; thus they are always constituted in relation to the men who describe them. Orly Lubin addresses the feminist problematics of these kinds of cinematic construction, arguing that it is not only the representation of woman, or even of woman's experience, that creates a feminist text. Rather, it is a woman's construction of her own history and meaning that serves as an articulation of women's experience and, hence, subjectivity. As she notes:

> A text can also be subversive. While establishing a hegemonic set of norms, it can simultaneously, through the same words, expose their hegemonic character. Thus, by exposing the norms as humanly constructed rather than naturally given, it can provide the female reader with the means to resist them. Similarly, a text that purports to be feminist can actually be hegemonic. While seeming to position women at the center, it can subvert this positioning through negative judgements and negative consequences.[14]

Early Israeli cinema never conceptualized an independent feminine experience, and there was no history of a separate female-audience-focused cinema such as the conventional woman's film. For Judith Mayne, Claire Johnston, and other scholars exploring women's relationship to cinema, "woman's films"—emotional melodramas that focused on women's lives as they intersect the domestic and the romantic and that were addressed specifically for female audiences—demonstrate the complexity of defining a female viewer's experience of a film in simple positive or negative terms. Despite being informed by patriarchal ideology, woman's films offer a space in which female spectators can identify with a female reality. Linda Williams argues that the female spectator's pleasure is not purely derived from the catharsis of the "weepy" but can also be found in identification with the depicted patriarchal oppression and the ways in which the women on-screen respond to it.[15] The absence of such locally made films in Israel meant that women had no independent cinematic experience. This is not surprising during an era that sanctified and sustained depictions of the collective, driven by male-dominated themes and experiences. The hegemony of this national ethos instilled a shared national vision, in which women were also expected to participate. While people's realities were certainly different, this dynamic creation of a Jewish national identity trumped individualism and fed into a notion of shared togetherness (*beyahad*).[16]

Despite the absence of the woman's film, female audiences enjoyed Israeli cinema no less than men. The criticisms leveled against Mulvey's work that challenge her failure to account for the female spectator's enjoyment of cinema even when it appeared to objectify and demean her might have been specifically conceptualized for the Israeli case. But as E. Ann Kaplan argues, patriarchal systems have socialized women, teaching them to see their marginalized place in the film's hierarchy and accept it.[17] Israeli cinema projected on-screen a cultural language that pervaded all avenues of Israeli society, and women no less than men could either see themselves as national heroes engaged in pioneering activities and serving in the major socialist enterprises represented in the early years of Israeli cinema or alternatively choose to identify as women in feminine (though marginal) roles supporting others in these Zionist endeavors. Mary Ann Doane explains (in relation to Hollywood cinema) that female viewers have few options and can either identify with the male protagonist, thereby sacrificing their gender, or identify with the female victim, trapping them in a masochistic relationship with the figure on the screen.[18] In a response article, Mulvey claimed that female spectatorial pleasure came from a transgender identification with the male viewing position and its regimes of fetishism and voyeurism, compromising the "relationship between the image of woman on the screen and the 'masculinization' of the spectator position, regardless of the actual sex (or possible deviance) of any real live movie-goer."[19] This definition served to cohere the semiotic position that there is a difference between "woman" as signified and women as they exist. While this is true, even with regard to Israeli cinema, the socialization of women as part of the Israeli collective discouraged the desire to challenge the normative representation. Doing so would have stood against a clearly defined and coherently articulated national narrative that fueled a patriarchy that inscribed not only what was on-screen but the experience of spectators, thereby creating male viewers even of females.[20] In Israel, the cinematic reality denied any female spectator position other than one that identified with the national project and women's assigned position within it.

The dominance of this cultural conditioning also inscribed nationalist (and hence masculine) conceptions of women's beauty that played out in appropriate cinematic display. Hair, speech, comportment, dress—or undress—aligned with the fashion for a "new stereotype of modern womanhood as a cross between housewife and model, princess and passionate lover."[21] Unlike other cinema of the Middle East in this period, in Israeli cinema there were no constraints on women's presence or the degree of modesty required on-screen, and for many the opportunity to act propelled women to stardom if not through the film then through women's magazines and beauty contests and as cultural ambassadors for the country. Like Haya Harareet, female actresses in Israeli films of the early period served as exemplars of sabra beauty ideals that combined a regional exoticism with a Western aesthetic. This was a look that proved popular internationally, and many would make the transatlantic journey to have short-lived careers as Hollywood starlets, never emerging out of the limiting shadows of this cinematic history.[22]

Gila Almagor (b. 1939), the most famous and most filmed Israeli woman of her generation, had a limited international career while maintaining a rigorous schedule as a theatre actress and film star in Israel. Her film work spans six decades of Israeli cinema, from her first appearance in *Blazing Sands* (*Holot Lohatim*, 1960) to her most recent appearances, which include *Fire Birds* (*Tziporey Hol*, 2015), the Hungarian *Fever at Dawn* (*Hajnali làz*, 2015), and the German crime television series *Der Tel-Aviv-Krimi* (2016). Her career serves as a model for women's changing experience within Israel's film industry. During the 1960s and 1970s Almagor was often the only female among a cast of mostly male characters. The illusion of equality was exemplified by her inclusion in "the gang" in films such as *Blazing Sands, What a Gang* (*Havura SheKazot*, 1962) and *Don't Tell Morgenstein* (*Af Milah L'Morgenstein*, 1963) and was symptomatic of the socialist ideals of group togetherness in these early years. This ideological creed was frequently undermined, however, by her character's positioning within the film. Almagor generally appeared in conventional female functions, serving as a helpmate, and her roles were almost always incidental to the plot, offering color, even romance, but seldom driving the narrative action and rarely if ever interacting with other women of equal position on-screen during this early period.

In these founding decades of Israeli cinema, Almagor, as the token woman in a male world, hardly ever represented a woman's perspective, only a man's perspective of her, thereby reinforcing patriarchal hegemonic norms. This Zionist ethos spilled over from the screen into the film industry. Here, too, women's contributions received less recognition and validation. Frequently working for little or no pay and the promise of future returns (which never came), Almagor would later describe the contradictions that existed during this period in which the national ethos encouraged her to view the hardships she experienced as an artistic form of pioneering in a shared collective, while as a woman she was often treated differently from the men, yelled at on set, sexually harassed, and excluded from a male fraternity.[23]

Within the nationalist-heroic genre, Zionist ideals not only reflected the country's military and political priorities but also shaped subtler forms of nationalism by depicting the hero as Ashkenazi (a Jew from European origins). By contrast, the Mizrahi (Jews from Islamic countries, a translation of the term "Oriental") could expect to be portrayed as fools or gangsters in films about thugs, crime, prostitution, and drugs. Films such as *Eldorado* (1963) and *Kazablan* (1973) were few in number, but they clearly established the Mizrahi as a criminal element.[24] Playing Mizrahi prostitutes and gangster's molls in *Eldorado*, *Fortuna* (1966), and *Queen of the Road* (*Malkat Hakvish*, 1971), for which Almagor also had her first screenwriting credit, she denoted the corrupting influences that marginal segments—particularly Mizrahi Jews—could have on the utopian, heroic, and European Zionist project. In these films, she was not only abandoned or raped, she rarely lived to the films' end, further emphasizing her marginality both as a female and as a Mizrahi.[25] Almagor's own ethnicity as an Ashkenazi woman aside, these roles emphasized Zionist expectations that women would conform and threatened women with social ostracism if they failed to do so—a powerful instrument in a society that privileged belonging.

Trading in stereotypes for comic and dramatic effect, a local ethnic-melodrama genre emerged. These *bourekas* films were nicknamed by Boaz Davidson after an Ottoman Jewish street pastry, a parody of the "spaghetti" western moniker. Directed, produced, and frequently acted in by Ashkenazi Jews, they created farces about Mizrahi Jews. *Bourekas* films mocked the new immigrants and satirized their encounter with the establishment. Though considered trashy by critics, they were popular successes, sometimes even achieving international recognition, as with the Golden Globe–winning comedy *Sallah* (*Sallah Shabbati*, 1964). The more serious tearjerkers, such as *Fortuna*, *Sarit* (1974), *Nurith* (1972), *Queen of the Road*, and *A Little Bit of Luck* (*Tipat Mazal*, 1990), frequently featured female characters at the center of the narrative, yet the pattern of female disempowerment remained the same. The expectation that women deserved equal treatment communicated the films' Western sensibility, but these women were nonetheless trapped in primitive and patriarchal Mizrahi homes, mistreated, abandoned by lovers, or forced into a life of prostitution. The traditional family these films depicted re-created ethnic stereotypes, positioning Mizrahi women as chattel. Thus, while the films highlighted the women's oppression, they also reinforced female social and cultural inferiority, thereby subverting any potential feminist message. Adding to this irony, the very people the films were castigating for their primitivism were their biggest fans. Apparently oblivious to this cultural insult, audiences enjoyed the replication (in Israeli terms) of the cinema with which they had been raised in Turkey, Egypt, Iraq, Morocco, Algeria, Syria, Tunisia, and Lebanon.

These films often turned on the presence of an Ashkenazi male who could rescue the Mizrahi maiden from a society portrayed as oppressive and primitive. The new local form failed to account for a difference in the viewers' experience between their current situation and the one they had enjoyed pre-emigration. In Middle Eastern cinema, oppressed heroines were Muslim (occasionally Christian), allowing Jewish audiences a degree of removal and cathartic schadenfreude; a disidentification that eluded them in the Israeli exploration of the genre. But filmmakers and audiences seemed to accept the cognitive dissonance between being attacked and being entertained, as well as the ways in which the films featured female actresses in plots that focused on women's negative treatment, and the antifeminist stance that those films ultimately represented. Women functioned as the indirect object of the debate about the superiority of Ashkenazi patriarchy to Mizrahi patriarchy, without ever occupying its central stage, thereby displacing women and issues of gender power with masculinity and issues of ethnic power. The arrival of several directors, such as the Iraqi George Ovadiah, the Moroccan Ze'ev Revach, and the Kurdish Joseph Shiloach, who pursued a local variant of Middle Eastern–Jewish filmmaking with more sympathetic roots within Mizrahi culture challenged the Ashkenazi representation of Mizrahi males without recovering the position of Mizrahi females. Later this pattern would serve as a template as other groups began to be represented in Israeli cinema. Repeating discrimination across an axis of nationality and gender, films representing Arab society would use female characters as a device with which Israeli masculinity could criticize Arab masculinity, feigning to do so in the name of women and eviscerating Arab patriarchy while continuing to marginalize the female characters the films were pretending to defend.[26] Subsequently this paradigm also would play out on an axis of religion and gender, in which the religious female was oppressed by religious patriarchy and could be saved only by the secular gaze, which raised her from her life of drudgery and obscurity while exposing her to a Western liberal value system that feasted on her objectification.

Despite an increasing number of films that cast female leads during the 1960s and 1970s, such as *Nini* (1962), *Dalia and the Sailors* (*Dalia VeHamalahim*, 1964), *I Love You Rosa* (*Ani Ohev Otach Rosa*, 1972), *My Michael* (*Michael Sheli*, 1974), *Aunt Clara* (*Doda Clara*, 1977), *My Mother the General* (*Imi HaGeneralit*, 1979), *Noa at 17* (*Noa bat 17*, 1981), and others, Israeli cinematic depictions repeatedly situated women within traditional domestic and romantic roles, thereby playing out conventions of maternal or sexual women in ways that reinforced negative gender categorization. Somewhat aberrant amidst these traditional roles, the figure of the war widow allowed women to occupy a more central and heroic position in the narrative, as in films like *The Hero's Wife* (*Eshet HaGibor*, 1963), *Siege* (*Matzor*, 1969), *Repeat Dive* (*Tzlila Hozeret*, 1982), and *Atalia* (1984).[27] Chaste and noble, these women functioned as symbolic memorials for their dead husbands, becoming heroic by association. For the bereaved, personal suffering was sublimated into a collective national suffering, a paradigm that persists in Israeli cinema. Yet even in these films, representations of the women's sexual reawakening threatened their position within the nation's mourning culture and implied women's dangerous capacity for subversion, thereby undermining any possibility that these films might be read as feminist texts, because though they positioned women at the center, this positioning was subverted through its negative depiction.[28]

After the 1967 war there were more psychologically fragile female characters, such as Hannah Gonen, Efrat Lavie's iconic role in *My Michael* (Dan Wolman, 1974). The mental isolation that she experiences as a wife and mother triggers despair that exacerbates tension within her marriage, while her melancholia is redirected into primal sexual fantasies toward the Arab twins she once played with as a child. These changes may have reflected a shift in the political climate, particularly as a comment on the trauma of war and the country's division before it, but they did so without demarcating any transformation in the position of women. Rather than offer a compelling contrast to the stoic war widow, vulnerable females merely served as her extension and were regarded as emotional time bombs that threatened to disrupt a nationalist heroic narrative that both valorized repression and depended upon it.

The increased representation of women on-screen did little to confront the earlier images of women as physically and mentally vulnerable with limited agency in a male world. Instead, filmmakers simply developed new characters, stories, and cinematic vehicles that reinforced the patriarchal, misogynistic, and highly exploitative ideas about women that pervaded Israeli society. While the films of the 1960s presented brief displays of female nudity, mainly in comedies or to heighten the drama in independent films, by the 1970s the sexual exposure of females on the Israeli screen had become commonplace in high and low culture and was paradigmatic of women's status as sex symbols. As Lubin has argued, nakedness had become a contingent prop that positioned women as inferior.[29] Women were objectified and sidelined, and a decade of films used women's bodies as a way to represent homosocial bonding, usually in the context of Tel Aviv's permissive and decadent society. Throughout the 1970s and 1980s, serious and comedic films, in popular and artistic genres, tended to present women as hysterical, sexually available (if not always to the suffering protagonist), or bustlingly maternal, and sometimes all three![30]

It would take a while for feminist values to change the Israeli cinematic male gaze. One principle reason for this is the delayed arrival, by Western standards, of second-wave feminist politics. Ironically, the country's socialist underpinnings, the appointment of Golda Meir as Israel's prime minister in 1969, and an economic boom in the 1970s that led a large number of women to enter the workforce entrenched the myth of equality while disavowing a reality of female oppression and marginalization.[31] In the 1970s, Marcia Freedman and Marilyn Safir, American Jewish feminist faculty members at the University of Haifa, and Shulamit Aloni, a citizen rights activist and politician, began raising awareness about feminist issues like teenage prostitution, rape, sexual abuse, domestic violence, and breast cancer. They advocated for women's rights within the larger discourse of the civil rights movement, fighting for equal pay; equal access to employment, education, protection, and resources; and freedom from sexual harassment and physical violence. The movement was also shaped by local feminist concerns such as the peace movement, women's treatment by the religious authorities, and women's equality within the military and defense establishment. Even as feminists worked toward many of their primary goals in the following decades, they not only were attacked by a male hegemony for distracting attention and resources from national security but also faced a backlash for focusing on issues that predominantly affected white, middle-class women.

During the 1990s, Mizrahi feminists began to define separate agendas that recognized the intersection of ethnicity (and class) with gender, fighting against their double marginalization within Israel. They felt betrayed by Ashkenazi feminists, whom they accused of ignoring the particularity of their discrimination. This third wave of feminism, with its multicultural approach, opened the doors to a variety of feminisms that included religious feminists, Arab feminists, and queer politics, exposing the lack of consensus within Israel's feminist movement. As the movement grew and fragmented, elements began to move from the rarefied environments of politics and academia into the mainstream, including cinema.

At the heart of this shift in Israeli filmmaking was the attempt to push back against a cinematic culture that assumed women's narratives were synonymous with male narratives. Yet, while the rise of feminist politics has resulted in a greater sensitivity by filmmakers toward considering feminist thematics in their works, the integration has not necessarily resulted in "feminist films." Furthermore, films that explicitly profess the goal of "feminist filmmaking" have not always yielded a strong or positive representation of women. As Israeli filmmakers grapple with what E. Ann Kaplan has described as "the problem of defining the feminine in a situation where women have no voice, no discourse, no place from which to speak"[32] and, like feminist filmmakers in other contexts, "examine the mechanisms through which women are relegated to absence, silence, and marginality in culture," they have done so within the cultural heritage particular to Israeli cinema.[33] Simultaneously, the surfacing of other identity politics, including class, race, and sexuality, yields a hybridity of identifications that can often complicate and even work against feminist ideology, exposing multiple layers of prejudice and patriarchal Ashkenazi heterosexual hegemonic control. Thus a picture emerges of a complex cinematic landscape that engages with feminist thematics to different degrees of interest and achievement.

Without a tradition of films specifically made for women that could have served as a counter-cinema representing female experience and, as Johnston argues, provided an opportunity for women to construct their own subjectivity, feminist filmmakers in Israel lacked the conventional paths that American and British cinema followed. In addition, the narrative of collectivism that dominated the Israeli public sphere was radically different from the focus on individualism that informed the development of feminist film theory in the West.[34] Together with the absence of female-gendered cinematic spaces, and the tabula rasa that feminist filmmakers faced when creating female centered, ideologically feminist texts, it is problematic to directly map Western feminist film theory onto a discussion of Israeli film. Nevertheless, this theoretical framing has had an impact on more recent Israeli filmmaking and on its concomitant scholarship.

The move toward the creation of a female-centric language for film studies that emerged from Gaylyn Studlar's rebuttal of Mulvey's "Visual Pleasure," in which, using Deleuzian theory, she substituted the oedipal relationship (where the woman is displaced in order to connect with the dominant male) for a desire to unify with the mother figure, led to an increasing reliance on female psychoanalytical theorists such as Hélène Cixous, Julia Kristeva, and Luce Irigaray, who have been more invested in conceptualizing female experience.[35] In turn, these discussions destabilized the fixed position of the female spectator, who was once assumed to be trapped by cinema's dominant mode of address, by fracturing the notion of a singular and stable female viewing position. Moving beyond the essentialist perspectives that feminist film theory had developed in its reliance on psychoanalytic models, which ignored real-life distinctions and undermined readings of "female experience" writ large as the Western-white-bourgeois-heterosexual experience of its female theorists, led to culturally dependent criticism.

This third-wave feminist form of film criticism exposed the need to account for a range of viewing experiences whereby the spectator's viewing is shaped by the baggage that he or she brings to the text.[36] This line of inquiry revealed spectators' ability to watch films *against the grain*, "a strategy designed by out of power groups to counterbalance the dominant textual traditions by offering alternative interpretations of works within those traditions."[37] In a return of the repressed, viewers outside of the ruling elite have learned to read the codes of classic Hollywood (and Western) cinema and find meaning and identification in unexpected places: gay males embraced strong female actresses and musical camp (rather than effeminate marginalized males), black women identified with white romantic heroines (rather than domestic servants), office workers identified with soldiers and laborers, et cetera, and so theorists found attempts to demarcate the multiplicity of viewers' experiences unraveling even as they tried to explore women's engagement with film.[38] If the subculture ultimately serves to shape the particularity of viewer experience, then scholars must read film with a culturally conditioned sensitivity.

The decision to make *Hill 24 Doesn't Answer* in English and to adapt Hollywood iconography for its regional context offers an opportunity to consider the fracture between Hebrewism, which was a dominant ethos in the country, and the desire to engage with an international audience in order to showcase the strong nationalist message on a world stage. This apparent clash can be understood only through a reading of the cultural nuances of the period generally and the nascent film industry's anxiety over funding and reception in particular. Using Stuart Hall's conception of the two major dynamics at play in the creation of meaning in the media, we can separate the experience of filmmaking into distinct categories, which for our purposes here may be regarded as the fundamental split between the making of film and the viewing of film. In the first case, the film's message is encoded at four different stages (production, circulation, use, reproduction) and thus the film's nationalist message was framed to be appropriately identified and received by drawing on recognizable conventions. But it was framed for two different, yet overlapping audiences: an international audience that knew little about the country and could be offered a civics lesson that framed the ideological dimension of the national discourse, and residents within Israel who wanted affirmation that military sacrifices would not be forgotten. The discursive processes Hall outlined for framing ideas draw upon society's dominant ideologies even as they interact with other influences such as taste, entertainment, and modes of transmission, in order to communicate meaning. Yet the evolving nature of this process depends on feedback and is therefore subject to changes in taste, in the industry, and in society's dominant ideologies as new forms (and films) are created. By the end of the decade only foreign films made in Israel used English, and Hebrew had become the dominant language, reflecting the hegemonic influence of Hebrew socialization. The film's historical gaze provides a snapshot of the sociopolitical climate in which it was made, but seventy years later it seems a time capsule for a cinema that has since become self-reflexive in its representation of militarism, Arab and Mizrahi minorities, and women.

In the second part of Hall's equation the audience decodes the film, a process that is shaped by the audience's own situation and cultural biases and to some degree remains in flux, as even a single viewer may experience a film differently with changes in experience or time. For *Hill 24 Doesn't Answer*, international audiences had different expectations of the film than Israeli audiences, even when the film first appeared. In the twenty-first century, viewed in light of the rise of Palestinian nationalism, identity politics, and feminism, the film's celebration of masculinity can no longer pass unquestioned, and the film's decoding is filtered differently by contemporary viewers than it once was. Hall's theory of encoding/decoding offers three positions (dominant/hegemonic, negotiated, oppositional) to account for the spectator's *desire* and *ability* to identify with the original intended (and encoded) message, to partially negotiate it, or to reject it entirely to fit "an alternative framework of reference."[39] Israeli cinema's monolithic control to a large degree ensured audiences decoded the originally intended message following the dominant/hegemonic paradigm. However, the disruption between the artistic community's sensibilities and the governing political ideologies, as well as cinema's own diversification in light of identity politics in recent decades, has interrupted this traditional relationship without undermining the historical legacy that forms the country's cinematic cultural memory. Thus the shared past serves as foundational terrain even as feminist film theory can point to a disruption between the originally encoded message and its decoding by contemporary audiences. Furthermore, feminist filmmakers can use the cinematic past as raw material in a critical discourse that now allows for a diversity of female and feminist audiences, defined by a host of distinct social forces and their respective competing discourses (based on race, class, sexuality, ethnicity, and political ideology), that process and decode in a myriad variety of ways.

This model of British cultural theory depends upon the contextualization of films both in their creation and in their reception. It also provides a way to consider audiences' capacity to subvert films' intended messaging, thereby removing control from filmmakers and producers in an act of feminist empowerment.[40] As Israeli cinema aligns itself with the ideas of American and British feminist film scholars, even though they write about other kinds of films made in wildly different contexts, an awareness of the cultural and historical differences that have informed both Israeli society and its cinema nuances Israeli film's feminist politics and aesthetics.[41] At the same time, it is worth noting that the cultural context in which Israeli cinema is produced, and the feminist directions it is exploring, represent a distinct phenomenon, given its historical and cultural background, rather than being emblematic of universal forms of directions in feminist filmmaking.

Women Making Films

Recent archival work by feminist filmmakers and scholars has recovered the lost history of Israeli cinema's foremothers, identifying key early figures such as Margot Klausner, the founder and president of Herzliya studios; Lia Van Leer, who developed a *cinemateque* culture; and Elida Gera, Israel's first female feature director (of the 1969 film *Before Tomorrow* [*Lifnei Mahar*]); until recently mostly forgotten by audiences and critics alike. This elision of female contributions to Israeli cinematic history reflects the tendency to subsume individual pathways into the national collectivity of the shared Zionist past. But I suspect this lacunae also reflects male gatekeeping of cinema's historiography. In the two-part series *The History of Israeli Cinema*, which featured interviews with academics, and the Channel 1, ten-part series *A Feast for the Eyes: The Story of Israeli Cinema*, built around interviews with actors, directors, producers, and musicians, which offered Israeli audiences a historical and cultural contextualization for viewing that past, only brief mention was made of Gera's landmark contribution. Even this inclusion occurred only after her film had been recovered by Israela Shaer Meoded and screened at the Rehovot International Women's Film Festival with her introduction. By contrast, other key male figures such as Menachem Golan, Uri Zohar, and Ephraim Kishon were singled out for extensive consideration.

When the actress Michal Bat-Adam directed her first film, a French-Israeli coproduction, *Moments* (*Moments de la vie d'une femme*), in 1979, she did so at a time when the dominant paradigms of the Israeli national narrative were facing increasing challenges and the country was more accepting of individualism. Feminism had become apparent, at least in select sectors of Israeli society, such that though her film was not actually a feminist milestone, it was celebrated for being so. While Gera preceded her, this contribution had been written out of the industry's historiography. By contrast, a decade later Bat-Adam's timing fit contemporary expectations about feminism and women's contribution to previously male-dominated fields, and her work was thus viewed as a landmark. She later produced, wrote, and directed a number of films, though her work was rarely a commercial success. Bat-Adam's move into directing may be partly attributable to the prominent role of her husband, Moshé Mizrahi, as a filmmaker. In an industry in which male privilege was accentuated, Bat-Adam was supported and actively encouraged to direct by Mizrahi, who was himself already well placed to provide mentorship and facilitate her entry (indeed, he served as producer on *Moments*). Yet even this pedigree could do little to help Bat-Adam on set in her early years as a director, and she reported difficulties with crews reluctant to take orders from a woman.[42]

Bat-Adam was one of the very few female filmmakers during the 1980s, and her films were little known outside of a rarefied highbrow cultural circle, as Israeli cinema had taken an artistic turn that was unpopular with audiences, who could now choose the more populist television programming instead. Bat-Adam demonstrates clear attempts in her work to represent female experience independently from that of men's worlds, but frequently falls back on conventions that depend upon a male presence within the film. Lubin has criticized this necessity, which she claims serves to consummate women's potential desire and affection for one another, returning a phallus to what might have been a potential feminist space.[43] Yet the idea that a woman's story could be told, written by a woman, directed by a woman, and featuring female actresses at the center of the drama, would have a profound effect on future generations of female filmmakers and would open a psychological doorway for many by demonstrating that filmmaking was not only a male occupation.

Inspired by Bat-Adam, Almagor wrote her autobiography *Aviya's Summer* in 1985, which became a one-woman play and then was adapted as a film in 1988 (*HaKayitz Shel Aviya*, Eli Cohen). Having grown up in poverty with only her mother (her father had been shot by Arab snipers five months before she was born), Almagor re-created the claustrophobia of 1950s Israel. The film charts the incompatibility between the pressures of the national narrative, with its mythic regard for physical strength and heroism, and her mother's debilitating mental illness. Traumatized by her Holocaust experiences and the death of the rest of her family, Henya (played by Almagor) oscillates between being a fiercely independent, kind, and loving mother and being a woman destroyed by madness. Aviya, meanwhile, struggles between the love and responsibility she feels for her mother and her desire for acceptance by the collective. The film's dynamic depends on the women's constantly evolving relationship, creating a powerful female subjectivity that explores the legacy shared between mothers and daughters. Despite deviating from the traditional masculine narrative by situating the film as the story of a woman overcoming her Holocaust past, even at the remove of a generation, it fed back into the nationalist discourse, whereby Aviya's embrace of Hebrewism saves her from, in this case, inheriting her mother's madness. Critical responses to the film have particularly focused on the nationalist aspects of the narrative and its engagement with the Holocaust, sidelining any discussion of the film's gendered nature.

A year later *Braids* (*Tzamot*, Yitzhak Halutzi, 1989), a made-for-television historical drama set in 1947 and based on the true-life story of So'uad, a fourteen-year-old Jewish girl imprisoned by the Iraqi government for her involvement with Zionism, created a female narrative of heroism within the confines of traditional Zionist discourse. As with *Aviya's Summer*, the film's focus on a young girl enabled it to move away from a Diasporic history and toward a Zionist redemption in which the girls are finally brought into the nation's arms and reborn Israelis.

Other efforts during the middle of the decade to create female-centered or female-led films included *Banot* (Nadav Levitan, 1985), which is about a women's unit in the military and is focused on women's worlds and women's experiences, and *Nadia* (*Amnon Rubinstein*, 1986), the story of an Arab-Israeli girl who longs to be a doctor and studies at a Jewish boarding school, adapted from a novel by Galila Ron-Feder. This latter film reflected cinema's increasingly leftist leanings and an interest in the possibility of Arab/Jewish integration—evident in the highly masculine *Beyond the Walls* (*MeAhorai HaSoragim*, 1984) and *Fictitious Marriage* (*Nisui'im Fictivim*, 1988).

The move to tell female-focused stories with leading female characters included efforts to showcase the unique nature of women's relationships, including the mother-daughter dynamic in *Aviya's Summer*, the mentorship of the other female prisoners in *Braids*, and the camaraderie and competition in *Banot*. Despite the women's limited agency, the determination to make films with marginal male characters while women dominated the screen revealed the beginnings of a feminist awakening and was indicative of the heightened awareness of women's previous absence. The nationalist overtones of these films meant that they were frequently screened on television, were popular with youth movements, and were often shown in conjunction with commemorative events on public holidays. By contrast, art films by women filmmakers had less exposure, and though several experimental films offering proto-feminist depictions of women's sexuality were made during the 1980s, they are almost entirely unknown except among scholars and aficionados. Idit Shehori's *Circles* (*Ma'agalim Shel Shishi Shabat*, 1980) followed four sexually liberated single women (including a lesbian character) on a night out, providing a glimpse into female relationships. Ayelet Menahemi's *Crows* (*Orvim*, 1988), about a young woman's big-city adventures facilitated by a group of gay homeless teens, appeared in a double bill with *Big Girl* (*Yalda G'dola*, Nirit Yaron), a short coming-of-age film about women's sexual exploration and sexual exploitation. These films, which were mostly screened at film festivals, depicted an alternative and hedonistic

Tel Aviv and were little known outside an artistic scene, occupying a marginal space in the lexicon of Israeli filmmaking. Between these extremes of alienated experimentation on one hand and female engagement with major Zionist conventions on the other, we can see the emergence of a protofeminist phase in Israeli filmmaking that shows a concerted effort (by male and female directors) to rethink female representation, even in a limited way. Yet, other than *Aviya's Summer*, one of the first Holocaust films made in Israel, these films remain little known and rarely screened today.

It was only in the 1990s that a dramatic evolution became evident in the roles and depictions of Israeli women in cinema. Exhaustion with Israeli male chauvinism, and the sense of a female social revolution, resulted in films offering strong female protagonists.[44] Concurrently, the advent of new television stations and particularly cable programming, alongside transformations in viewing patterns during the 1990s, created opportunities for fledgling talent, fostered in the incubators of the new film schools and studios of the channels that emerged. Moreover, the role of film had changed. It had fulfilled the work of popular entertainment in the 1950s and 1960s, when no television existed in Israel, while during the 1970s and 1980s, as art film it had served as the nation's conscience at a time when other organs of entertainment had moved away from the serious nationalist and Zionist considerations of the past and become increasingly invested in light, popular, and commercial programming. With the proliferation of television channels and networks, radical improvements in technology, and changes in funding structures, film became a space for innovation, offering new kinds of stories, new modes of representation, and previously unimaginable diversity.

The arrival of *Tel Aviv Stories* (*Sipurei Tel Aviv*, 1992) served as a watershed moment. Written and directed by two women, Ayelet Menahemi and Nirit Yaron,[45] the film was composed of three shorts edited as a single film that positioned female leads as the films' subjects and consciously explored the modes by which women were being objectified by playing with plot, characterization, and camera work. The film's poster consciously drew on male imagery of the lone hero, characteristic of the Rambo franchise popular at the time, thereby drawing on male archetypes that were revised in an Israeli feminist context.[46]

The film's mainstream popularity moved feminism from the cinematic margins and in a single moment provided Israel with a new conception of women on-screen. This triptych portrayed female heroines empowered over the course of their respective narratives. Their awakening often occurs as a response to male aggression, expressions of male desire, and male efforts to enact control over the female. Each of the films considered a different kind of woman, and each presented the complexity of women's lives as well as the moderating and controlling influences of Israeli society and particularly the institutional disadvantages that women experienced, including the inability to divorce. The use of leading and secondary women created a diverse array of female characters that positioned women as antagonists

Tel Aviv Stories: The cover of the English DVD release. The three lead actresses are shown but neither they nor the female film directors are named on the front of the box.

and protagonists, heroes and anti-heroes. The women were young and old, naïve and hard bitten, single and married. They also came from different classes, ethnicities, and professions, including a model, a writer, a theatrical actress, a boutique owner, a veterinarian, and two policewomen, at least one of whom was characterized as Mizrahi. As a defining moment in the development of Israeli cinema, the film created a new language for female representation and for women's participation within the film industry.

Tel Aviv Stories also exemplified the diversity of feminist politics. It did not offer a particular solution or defined image of womanhood. Rather, it recognized women's individuality and unique personal concerns, while the three shorts collectively spoke to a shared female experience of discrimination, exclusion, and objectification. The film is emblematic of the diverse ways in which Israeli cinema has been informed by both international and local feminism. There is no single strand or single trajectory that can be linked to a specific feminist legacy. Instead, the film demonstrates a complex negotiation with Israeli cinematic history, feminist ideology, and local Israeli feminist concerns. It is this model that would come to represent feminist filmmaking in Israel. The tightrope between the Israeli cultural legacy, with its masculinist view, and feminist ideology, which sought to create alternative paradigms, developed in myriad directions, but time revealed that feminist-themed films were not always progressive, as the weight of Israel's cinematic history continued to overshadow the industry.

For Mizrahi feminist filmmakers, the cultural weight of Middle Eastern films and their association with the domestic spaces of the filmmakers' childhoods has served as a point of departure within what Yaron Shemer has termed *New Mizrahi Cinema*. Creating a nostalgic landscape in which gender and ethnicity intersect, New Mizrahi Cinema encapsulates the conflict Mizrahim faced between the need (and desire) to assimilate and their *othering* by an Ashkenazi hegemony. In light of Hamid Naficy's discussion of accented cinema, it is possible to identify an associative relationship between the celebration of an ethnic Arab/Turkish/Iranian culture and the domestic space within which it found freer expression in Israel of the 1950s through 1980s. This cultural experience was denied in the public sphere, where the Labor Zionist ethos with its Ashkenazi inflection continued to dominate. Thus Mizrahi feminist filmmakers gender Israeli ethnic filmmaking, as is evident in *Three Mothers* (*Shalosh Imahot*, Dina Zvi-Riklis, 2006), *Sh'chur* (Shmuel Hasfari, 1994), the short *Shuli's Boyfriend* (*Ha Bachur Shel Shuli*, Doron Tsabari, 1997), *Aviva My Love* (*Aviva Ahuvati*, Shemi Zarhin, 2006), and the recent *Orange People* (*Anashim Ketumim*, Hannah Azoulay Hasfari, 2013).

Moreover, since 2007, several women filmmakers born in Israel who identify as Palestinian, including Annemarie Jacir (*Salt of this Sea* [*Milh Hadha al-Bahr*], 2008), Suha Arraf (*Villa Touma*, 2014, *Women of Hamas* [*Nashot Hamas*], 2010), Abeer Zeibak Haddad (*Dolls* [*Duma*], 2011, *3000 Nights* [*3000 Layla*], 2015), Ibtisam Salh Mara'ana (*3 Times Divorced* [*Shalosh Pe'amim Megureshet*] [*Talaq bil-thalath*], 2008, *77 Steps* [*77 Dragot*], 2010, *Lady Kul El Arab*, 2008, *Write Down, I am an Arab* [*Sajil Ana Arabi*], 2014), and Hiam Abbas (*Inheritance* [*Héritage*], 2012), have gained international prominence with films that consider the particular experience of Palestinian women.[47] These films explore a range of feminist and human rights issues, including sexual abuse, divorce, and patriarchal oppression, but also address the distinct particularity of Palestinian-female experiences of discrimination by the Israeli authorities, dispossession, and the impact that becoming a transnational diasporic community has on Palestinian legacy. Palestinian women filmmakers based in Israel straddle the intersection between Western and Middle Eastern cinema and on occasion experience the same lack of access to historical family sites that has informed Mizrahi cinema's nostalgic identification with the Arab world. To a limited degree they are more embedded within a Middle Eastern feminist filmmaking discourse that has begun to develop across the Islamic world and that features an interest in the impact of class divides on women's emancipation, the conflict between feminism and traditionalism, and the control of religious authorities on women's lives.[48] Like the Lebanese filmmaker Nadine Labaki, whose first film, *Caramel* (*Sukkar Banat*, 2007), set in a women's hairdressing salon, was critiqued for failing to engage with the political and military conflict, Palestinian women are often challenged for representing female narratives outside the nationalist discourse when the conflict persists.[49] Employing Timothy Walsh's notion of a structured absence, the failure to directly address conflict within the films may be an artistic effort by the filmmakers to convey the potency and ever-present dominance of militarism on the local reality. Yet, the critical expectation that war be represented as a central feature of much of this regional filmmaking also reflects a desire by the hegemonic filmmaking establishment to reassert masculine control on women's filmmaking by reinserting conflict, a fundamentally male concern. Thus there is an assumption that women's experience is always governed by the same real and existential anxieties as male experience, rather than allowing for the possibility that women's narratives have other concerns, or that the national narrative fails to represent women's different experience of local and national forces on their lives. Palestinian women's filmmaking can thus be examined in relation to that of other feminist filmmaking in the Arab world, but also shows parallels with the work of Arab-Jewish women filmmakers, with their shared narratives of displacement and experiences of discrimination from an Israeli Ashkenazi hegemony. In addition, a line can also be drawn between religious Jewish feminist filmmakers in Israel and their counterparts in the Middle East, who face similar intracommunity censorship and oversight by religious authorities. As a feature article on Middle Eastern women filmmakers in *Variety* observed, Haaifa Al-Mansour, Saudi Arabia's first woman filmmaker, admires the Ultra-Orthodox Israeli director Rama Burshtein for her shared female experience of negotiating religious feminist artistic expression in film within patriarchally sanctioned limitations.[50]

These points of comparison are nevertheless limited. Feminist filmmaking cannot be viewed as monolithic even within the Islamic world. There are wide degrees of variation predicated on several factors, including the health of the film industry, the degree of censorship present, the development of feminist movements generally, and the sociopolitical realities that inform the context and the content of cinema. Thus Israeli-Palestinian feminist filmmakers often share more (culturally, educationally, economically, and in the process of funding, producing, and screening film projects) with Jewish-Israeli feminists than with other feminist filmmakers within the Islamic world. Women within most contemporary Middle Eastern cinema continue to reflect a dichotomy between career and family life, a dynamic that suggests the empowered woman has paid a high price for her independence. By contrast, feminist cinema in Israel has internalized the Western ideal that women can have it all, and the films often create female characters who enjoy multifaceted resolutions that include happy homes and rewarding work lives.

The barriers to entry in this male-dominated profession mean that women have experienced limited access to resources. Yael Munk notes that the affordability of documentary filmmaking offers women a route into the Israeli film industry, which, in turn, enables women to create a narrative voice of their own. Women's involvement in nonfiction filmmaking influenced new trajectories, leading to more personal and autobiographical modes for depicting the Israeli reality. This has created a new sensitivity "that has helped to clarify the delicate positioning of the oppressed and of the victim as a whole, as well as denouncing the latent and therefore frequently unrecognizable violence in many aspects of Israeli life."[51] This feminist gaze meant the camera turned toward previously marginalized figures: "women, children, the elderly, and those defined by the hegemony as enemies"[52] and has informed the broader feminization of documentary filmmaking by both male and female directors. As a medium, it has also paved the way to feature filmmaking for several female directors, including Michal Aviad and Suha Arraf.

Controlling the modes of cinematic production has facilitated new kinds of stories, but it is also the increasing cultural capital of several actresses that has resulted in paradigm shifts in female representation. Hannah Azoulay-Hasfari and Ronit Elkabetz have transformed the Mizrahi female from the marginal figures in *Hill 24 Doesn't Answer* to a multidimensional character with a complex history and a future beyond that of living memorial or dead symbol. Evgenya Dodina has shown the integration of the Russian female into Israeli society, and her roles may be contrasted with the roles in which for decades Russian women were shown as prostitutes in a white slave trade. Hiam Abbas and Reymond Amsallem have reimagined the position of the Palestinian (and Druze) woman, and in the latter case also created a wide range of female characters across the spectrum of Israeli society. Others, such as Dana Ivgy, Yaël Abecassis, Hannah Lazslo, Evelin Hagoel, and Anat Waxman, have pushed against sexist conventions, renegotiating not only the range of characters that women can play but the ways in which they are displayed. Female directors such as Aviad, Menahemi, Keren Yedaya, and Dina Zvi-Riklis, alongside a number of actresses turned directors, including Bat-Adam, Azoulay-Hasfari, Abbas, and Elkabetz, are influencing new feminist perspectives through films that critically challenge sexism, patriarchy, and women's marginalization. These works tackle feminist intersections with race, offer a variety of perspectives on women's issues, and consider the local context of religiosity. Female actresses now drive the plot, control the screen and the gaze, and refuse to be defined as good or bad, virtuous or corrupt, wife and mother or career woman. Instead they have taken on all of these roles and more. They have complicated the notion of what a woman might be and the world she might occupy, carving out a position in Israeli cinema that has reshaped the industry.

Directions in Israeli Film Scholarship

Israeli film scholarship has become increasingly cognizant of these changes, tending to explore many of the feminist currents as they interplay with other thematic questions. Regine-Mihal Friedman and Yael Zerubavel have written on the widow archetype in Israeli cinema, and Friedman has also explored the relationship between women and Holocaust films, a topic taken up by Nurith Gertz and Anat Zanger, who have further investigated the representations of women in cinema dealing with memory and trauma.[53] To this area of study, Raz Yosef has added questions of gender, sexuality, and ethnicity, building on Ella Shohat's work in the field, which has also impacted Yosefa Loshitzky and Yaron Shemer's writing considering women within the broader arena of identity politics and ethnic studies, while Dan Chyutin is most prominent among a number of recent scholars exploring the role of women in films about the religious community.[54] Yael Munk and Orly Lubin have engaged most extensively with women-led films, considering cinematic treatments of women in light of psychoanalytical-influenced feminist film theory.[55] This book owes a great deal to the legacy of these different studies and builds on the scholarship's disparate trajectories to formulate a syncretistic understanding of the ways in which Israeli cinema has approached feminist questions.

The emergence of serious feminist filmmaking during the 1990s, despite hints in the protofeminist filmmaking of the 1980s, has depended on the coalescence of several factors: changes within the film industry, the rise of feminism within the public sphere, filmmakers' education within the language of feminist film theory, and a decline in the hegemony of the Zionist ethos both on-screen and within the profession. By teasing out the ways in which a feminist filmmaking agenda increasingly occupies Israeli cinema, the roots on which this cinema draws, and its realization from the late 1990s onward, *Warriors, Witches, Whores: Women in Israeli Cinema* offers descriptive models for approaching Israeli film criticism from a feminist perspective. Thus the climate in which contemporary filmmaking operates, while increasingly sensitive to female concerns and feminist theory, is not always free of the male bias that has driven Israeli society since the country's inception. With this in mind it is Lubin's proposition about the context in which texts position women and present feminist ideas that underpins my reading of women in Israeli cinema.

Warriors, Witches, Whores: Women in Israeli Cinema explores women's reimagination on-screen since *Tel Aviv Stories*, examining new categories and tropes that have emerged in the representation of women. It seeks to present an examination of the genres and film styles that characterize this turn in Israeli cinema and to analyze the particularity of Israel's industry as a way of reflecting upon the multiple levels at which feminism is enacted within any regional cinema. The dominance of Israel's male-centric cinematic legacy has encoded a recognizable language of tropes, images, characters, and conventions. At the same time, political, cultural, and aesthetic evolutions offer direct challenges to the established hegemony, thereby creating meaning through a discursive play between past and present. Hall's model of cultural specificity allows me to consider the multiple dynamics at play in the creation of feminist filmmaking in Israel. Through close reading, I consider ways in which women's involvement within the industry has changed the messages encoded within the text, and how feminist themes in Israeli cinema can now be decoded from a variety of perspectives that rewrite women into the country's cinema. This enables me to reflect upon Israel's gender, ethnic, and social diversity, through which I recover the previously invisible female, and allows for a nuanced approach that recognizes the constantly shifting borders of identity categories, the impact of the climate in which films are made and screened, and the ways in which film itself becomes a medium for influencing and shaping the discourse of feminist politics, thereby creating the very circularity of communication that Hall envisaged. Thus my theoretical approach filters feminist film scholarship through a cultural studies frame in order to engage with the cultural and political particularism of feminism in Israeli cinema.

In adopting a cultural studies approach, I consider the creation of a female-centered and thematically feminist film culture in light of structural and ideological shifts in Israeli society. These changes are situated in dialogue with the cinematic history that preceded them and the ongoing social inequalities that perpetuate women's marginalization within Israeli society. This book considers questions of social and political power, the ways these have impacted the representation of women on-screen, and the ways in which feminist filmmakers have fought against these inequities behind the camera, in the stories they tell, and in the ways women are represented in cinema.

The book is divided into three major sections. Each once considers a different form of feminist engagement. The first part explores films that situate women in traditionally male spheres of militarism, considering the impact of interjecting women within hegemonic spaces or reconceptualizing them in feminist ways. The second part recovers the narratives of women's experience that were previously marginalized or silenced, thereby creating a distinct female space that offers new kinds of storytelling and cinematic aesthetics that reflect feminist expressions of identity. The third part offers examples of feminist activism that reach beyond the boundaries of the film to comment on social issues, particularly those that affect women. This section demonstrates the ways in which feminists use film (and work within the film industry) in order to affect change to women's position in society. While there are thematic overlaps between the chapters, each section marks structural differences in the modes of feminist response.

The first section examines the ways in which Israeli films began to integrate women into representations of war, militarism, the Israeli Defense Forces, and the Arab-Israeli conflict, areas traditionally the province of men and masculinity. The incursion of leading female characters, feminist themes, and the spotlighting of institutionalized chauvinism, alongside the undermining of war as a male province, directly attacked Israeli film history, thereby redefining its status quo. This section begins with an examination of the Gulf War in chapter 1. Instead of a traditional battlefield, Israel's Gulf War was experienced on the home front. Rooms in homes were sealed against gas attacks and equipped with emergency lights, radios, groceries, toys, and board games. These images contrasted with the usual symbols of war: army fatigues and boots, call-up notices, tanks, guns, barbed wire, military bases, and masculine camaraderie. This domestic space served as the backdrop for a female-centered consideration of the experience of war in films like *The Song of the Siren* (*Shirat HaSirena*, 1994) and *Yana's Friends* (*HaHaverim Shel Yana*, 1999). Examining the cinematic adaptation of *The Song of the Siren*, which was previously a best-selling novel, also provides an opportunity to reflect on the issues that arise in translating a feminist text onto the screen.

Chapter 2 examines the ways in which *The Syrian Bride* (*HaKalah HaSurit*, 2004), *Free Zone* (*'Ayzor Hofshei*, 2005), and *Lemon Tree* (*Etz Limon*, 2008) use the cinematic gaze, liminal spaces, and the domestic environment to parallel Arab and Jewish women's experience of the conflict, thereby feminizing a traditionally male discourse. These films create a sisterhood of shared experience that transcends national boundaries through positive depictions of motherhood and wifely duties or negative portrayals of women's subjugation under patriarchal hegemonies. At the same time they offer a critical consideration of the particularity of Palestinian women's oppression, because of both the ongoing conflict and the traditionalism of their society. Hiam Abbas, the leading Palestinian actress who features in all three films, offers a case study for considering the ways in which a woman can also function as an agent of change within the industry, working offscreen to change on-screen representation.

Chapter 3, the final chapter in this section, considers films that feature women in the Israeli Defense Forces. This chapter raises questions about the limited efficacy of attempting a feminist challenge in traditionally male-dominated spheres. A conflict exists between placing women in a traditionally masculine space as an act of feminist empowerment, such as in *Banot* (1988) and *Zero Motivation* (*Efes BeYahasei Enosh*, 2014), and the problem of signifying masculine space as the norm, a challenge that *Close to Home* (*Karov La Bayit*, 2005) and *Room 514* (*Heder 514*, 2012) attempt in their representations of women as a disruption to the normative order. Similarly, a feminist dichotomy exists in depicting armed women (in the IDF films or in thrillers) that lies between women's physical empowerment through the weapon and masculine sexual fantasies that demean and subordinate women, thereby removing the supposed and implied agency of women that the presence of guns might suggest in *The Assassin Next Door* (*Kirot*, 2009) and *The Debt* (*HaHov*, 2007).

The second section of the book examines women within spheres considered traditionally feminine, such as the home, marriage, and sexuality, but views these from the perspective of ethnicity and religion, which have become some of the hallmarks of recent Israeli cinema. A feminist film analysis reveals that these films, which were often the first films to feature female leads and suggest women's subjectivity and were frequently made by men, used the opportunity to invade female spaces. Made under the guise of feminist progressive agendas, they exposed women to a lascivious and pornographic lens interested in rewarding male sexual fetishes and male fantasies of mothering and sexual desire. Feminist filmmakers have responded by reconceptualizing women's traditional spaces considering the intersection of gender and ethnicity and gender and religion. They have also constructed a feminist language for exploring female subjectivity and sexuality, which has led to many of the most avant-garde feminist film projects.

Chapter 4 focuses on representations of the religious community in Israel. Secular filmmakers viewed the religious laws of modesty as part of the religious establishment's patriarchal obsession with women's capacity to sexually corrupt men. Joseph Cedar's treatment of sexual abuse in *Campfire* (*Medurat HaShevet*, 2004), and the violent rape of a drunk woman in *The Wanderer* (*HaMeshotet*, 2010) create a paradigm of sexual violence. Amos Gitai (*Kadosh*, 1999), Avi Nesher (*The Secrets* [*HaSodot*, 2007]), and others attempted to recover religious women's experience by depicting their oppression, marginalization, and suffering. However, their efforts led to voyeuristic and pornographic displays that exposed their own fetishization of religious women as an exotic forbidden fruit. By contrast, *Ushpizin* (*HaUshpizin*, 2004), made by a Jewish Orthodox filmmaker, depicts a warm and loving marriage, the husband's complicated relationship with faith, and the couple's clear affection even in the face of infertility, thereby recovering respect for the Jewish woman within the confines of religious law. *Bruriah* (2008) engages in a more explicit feminist project. Emerging out of a hybrid religious/secular cinematic space, it works to reclaim the Talmudic narrative of an unfaithful wife known for her intellect. The film's respectful framing of an Orthodox marriage, and its blurring of traditional gender roles within it, universalizes romantic partnerships, moving beyond an othering of the religious community. Most recently, *Fill the Void* (*Lemaleh et HaHalal*, 2013) attempts to disrupt the established tropes that have come to represent Ultra-Orthodox women by demonstrating female agency within religious society's strictures.

Chapter 5 examines the feminization of ethnicity through folk religion (rather than the formal religion of the previous chapter) in ethnic-feminist filmmaking. Women's engagement with religion and the supernatural is often cast as witchcraft, but whereas this is shown as a perversion in *The Secrets*, in films like *Sh'chur*, *Turn Left at the End of the World* (*Sof Ha'Olam Smola*, 2004), *My Lovely Sister* (*Ahoti HaYafa*, 2011), and *A Late Marriage* (*Hatuna Meuheret*, 2001) it becomes a form of female resistance. These practices, depicted most often within the framework of women's communities, within female domestic relationships (mothers, daughters, sisters), and among ill-educated women within ethnic communities, raise questions about hierarchies of knowledge and power.

Chapter 6 concludes this section with an exploration of women's representation as sexual objects and the reclaiming of women's sexuality in recent feminist cinema. Nationalistic films focused on male conquest of the land and sublimated male desire into this pioneering project, casting their sexual domination of women as an extension of this labor. Woman qua woman was expected to be chaste, representing her virtuosity for Zionism. But this depiction did not include Mizrahi women, who frequently appeared as prostitutes, a representation that sustained the conflict between Ashkenazi and Mizrahi patriarchy, as in *Dead End Street* (*Kvish L'lo Motzah*, 1982). The rise of feminist filmmaking in the twenty-first century has particularly addressed women's subjectivity through films that explore women's sexuality from a female perspective, including *The Slut* (*HaNotenet* 2011), *She's Coming Home* (*Hahi She Hozeret HaBayta*, 2013), *Or, My Treasure* (*Or*, 2004), and *Bye Bye to Love* (*Bye Bye L'Ahava*, 2006), challenging the Israeli cinematic tradition that viewed women's bodies as men's property. The latter film also offers a model of feminist film aesthetics seeking to redress the model in which filmmaking is already and intently dominated by a male apparatus of cinematic conventions and expectations.

The third part of the book addresses specific feminist issues that have emerged in recent filmmaking, demonstrating a political and activist feminist militancy that overlaps with other agendas, including rape culture, political disenfranchisement, and social issues surrounding the conflict. The concern with rape and sexual abuse, a central feminist site of engagement, is the focus of Chapter 7. Rape in Israeli film is widespread and pervasive. It reflects masculine anxiety not only about women (as Kaplan has observed is prevalent in a Hollywood context) but also about the existential threat to the country's existence.[56] The potential rape of female soldiers serves as a metaphor for the vulnerability of the nation to foreign invaders, an ideology that Susan Sered claims leads to a socialization that necessitates the controlling of women's bodies. Moreover, the rape of women, and their potential rescue by men, marks out rape as a territory in which men can compete with one another for dominance. This motif is evident in the rape of Mizrahi women, including Pnina in *Sh'chur* and the female soldiers who are potential (or actual) rape victims in *Banot* and *Zero Motivation*, and in the rape (and often gang rape) of prostitutes. It also is evident in the rape of women by religious men. Feminist responses to rape and sexual abuse disrupt the convention of graphic and uncritical representation, instead examining sexual violence in light of activist agendas in the documentary *Brave Miss World* (Cecilia Peck, 2013) and the feature films *Invisible* (*Lo Roim Aleich*, 2011), *S#x Acts* (*Shesh Peamim*, 2012), and *Out of Sight* (*Lemarit Ain*, 2006).

Chapter 8 examines the displacement of the Israeli woman from the margins, and her move to the center, where she becomes a symbol of the hegemony in contrast to female foreign workers, who have come to replace most women as the female underclass. Unable to acquire citizenship, dissuaded from marrying or giving birth, the foreign worker is isolated and vulnerable. *Jellyfish* (*Meduzot*, 2007), *Noodle* (*Noodel*, 2007), and *Salsa Tel Aviv* (2011) consider the dichotomy that exists for women in Israel, whose own advancement depends on the subordination of other female labor.

The final chapter is an afterword that draws together an examination of a feminist filmmaking agenda with an overview of its explicit pursuit by activists who are transforming the industry from within. It considers the ways women's involvement historically is being recovered as well as the influence of the Forum for Women Filmmakers and Television Artists and the Rehovot Women's Film Festival on funding, filmmaking, and critical reception of films. These activities have encouraged greater female participation in Israeli cinema, directly challenged discrimination, and fostered a new generation of female filmmakers whose first films have debuted this decade.

Despite the discrete divisions offered by the different sections and chapters, the works under consideration reflect broader trends, including the internalizing of feminism and feminist film criticism, the expression of feminist politics and activism, and the influence of feminism on the Israeli filmmaking landscape. Ultimately, *Warriors, Witches, Whores: Women in Israeli Cinema* addresses the ongoing and continued peripherization of women, revealing paradoxes and ambiguities that remain entrenched within Israeli society regarding female empowerment. The chapters that follow consider films by both male and female directors whose focus on women, usually through the creation of central female characters, attempts to establish a female subjectivity. The book traces modes of feminist filmmaking that engage with national paradigms and subvert them in an effort to reclaim a feminist space within this previously male-dominated industry and explores the ways in which women's activism, both on-screen and offscreen, has played a role in shaping the stories that are told, the ways women are represented, and the creation of feminized filmmaking. Whether or not these efforts have succeeded is the central question this book explores.

1

Women on the Front Lines

Reconceptualizing War, Militarism, the Conflict, and the Female Soldier

1

A Woman's War
The Gulf War and the Israeli Chick Flick

In 1994, the film *The Song of the Siren* sold more tickets in Israel than all of the other Israeli films made that year combined. The screenwriter, Irit Linor, was also the author of the best-selling novel on which the film was based. Despite the film's commercial success, it received no mention at the year's Ophir film awards and was disliked by critics, who regarded it as "a pale imitation of the novel."[1] Likewise, the 1999 film *Yana's Friends* was a commercial success at home and abroad and the recipient of two Ophir Awards, yet it, too, was a failure as far as the critics were concerned. Though both films upheld the Hollywood conventions of heterosexual coupling that positioned women within the traditional spheres of wife and mother, both films also confronted the expected erasure of female subjectivity by presenting powerful female leads who dominated the plot and the screen. Their affiliation with the rise of "chick lit" and "chick flicks" in Israel may have accounted for the films' tepid critical reception, but as romantic comedies set during the Gulf War they marked the introduction of a new genre in Israeli cinema.

Scholars of women's literature identify structural differences in chick lit and the traditional romance genre that reflect the inherent difference between the passive romantic heroine and her more cynical chick lit (and chick flick) counterpart.

> One key differentiator between a romance novel and a chick-lit novel with romantic elements is that in a chick-lit novel the identity of the romantic hero isn't always immediately apparent. In a romance novel, if the heroine meets a handsome man in the first chapter, it's a good bet that he's the hero. If a chick-lit heroine meets a handsome man in the first chapter, he could be the hero. He could also turn out to be a jerk who breaks her heart, or he could become her gay best friend. On the other hand, Mr. Wrong can look like a viable option at least for a time.[2]

In the eighteenth century, the Medieval courtly romance gave way to the Gothic romance, which sought to balance the fanciful imaginary of the former with the realism of the modern novel. Despite initial rejection by the public, the *modern* romance novel evolved in both high and low culture, and by the end of the twentieth century (250 years after its initial creation) it had developed a clearly defined set of tropes. At times satirical, ironic, and even burlesque, romantic women's fiction paradoxically critiqued the position of women in society while simultaneously upholding it. The centrality of the female protagonist and her turbulent path toward true love remain the mainstays of the genre, and usually the text concludes in a symbolic submission of her independence, often represented by a ceremonial unification such as marriage, exchange of property, or a kiss.

The romantic film dominated women's films from the silent era onward in Hollywood and Europe, but Israeli cinema never made romance films, and what romance existed was folded into masculine heroic genres or ethnic melodramas with Romeo and Juliet themes of forbidden love. In the 1990s, the arrival of films made expressly with a female audience in mind signaled a new trend that identified women's lives independently of the male-centric themes that had previously dictated every aspect of Israeli filmmaking. Readily adopting the conventions of the Anglo-American romance and its most popular form at the time—the chick-flick—Israel still filtered these narratives through the regional particularity of militarism and the recent Gulf War.

As the war was taking place, satiric newspaper columns and comedy shows were quick to frame the experience, lampooning the Iraqi military establishment, commenting on the ways inhabitants of the country's traditionally safe center in Tel Aviv had become refugees piling into the country's agricultural and peripheral hinterlands, or criticizing the exile of those who managed to flee overseas. With the war's end, the subject ceased to be topical and was cast into the historical remainder bin. Its later resurrection in novels and films with strong female leads reflected the tendency to attribute a thematically feminized nature to the war, a practice that left men emasculated by the trauma while celebrating female pragmatism in the face of danger. Male characters were marginalized, making them contingent props for a plot that focused on multiple female-led story lines. These films were part of the first wave of feminist filmmaking in Israel. Nevertheless, with the exception of Einat Bikel, who was one of four producers credited on *Yana's Friends*, and Irit Linor, the directors, producers, and writers of these films were all male. Feminist themes had clearly infiltrated the Israeli cinematic consciousness, but their execution reveals an ongoing tendency to regard women's experience from a male perspective.

Linor, at the time a satirical columnist writing for Israel's leading newspapers, had established a writing persona as a militant feminist. Celebrating the rise of the supposed feminist revolution taking place in Tel Aviv at the start of the 1990s, she personified the new woman: opinionated, aggressive, and independent. Talila Katz, the thirty-two-year-old advertising executive heroine of her debut novel, *The Song of the Siren*, was in many respects an extension of this characterization—if not of the author herself—and served as a role model for women who did not live in a fictional Tel Aviv, with its rarefied egalitarian ideal, but continued to experience the daily insults of misogyny and patriarchy. Thus the book served as a kind of manifesto for women in their twenties and thirties and made Linor a feminist icon.

In his analysis of the film adaptation, Nir Cohen addresses the tension between Linor, who adapted her novel for the screenplay, and the film's director, Eytan Fox.[3] Fox, who is openly gay and whose films and television dramas frequently contain gay characters and themes, requested that Linor include a gay character in the film, a request that she refused. This conflict exposed the difference between Linor's and Fox's conceptions of the project. As Cohen shows, Fox wanted to make an "apolitical, nonartistic, genre film" whose Hollywood veneer would set it apart from the oppressive political dramas of the day.[4] In his effort to make a light and superficial rom-com, he was moving against the dominant filmmaking discourse, while the inclusion of a gay agenda reflected Fox's own identity politics. It was Fox's breakthrough film and his first feature in a career spent normalizing gay characters within mixed casts that addressed other social topics. At a time when gay filmmaking was imagined through Amos Guttman's dark imaginary of lost souls, violence, and despair, Fox was using *The Song of the Siren* as a vehicle for engaging with gay politics in a way that was light and entertaining—and offered a positive and normalized view of gay life. Just as Linor had meant for the novel's easy style to cloak feminist politics, Fox wanted the film to do the same for gay politics. In his reading of Fox's film, Cohen appropriates Talila, the strong female protagonist, claiming that she is modeled on a post-Stonewall gay man, explaining: "It is interesting to explore the dissonance in the film between the ostensibly heterosexual story and the hints at a different, gay meaning."[5] Despite Cohen's claims, Talila's transition from book to film remains relatively smooth, and she retains a forthright, feminist character. But the battle between Fox's and Linor's conceptions of the story ultimately resulted in a weakening of the novel's feminist statements in the film's adaptation, which marginalized Linor's most aggressive critiques of patriarchy. Instead, as Cohen notes, Fox, using his auteur status, encoded symbols and oblique character references that would have been easily decoded by gay viewers at the time. Simultaneously, he undermined the novel's feminist framing. Decades later many of the gay allusions are clearly visible, as heterosexual audiences have become more literate in representations of gay sensibility and now recognize the coded gay characters, social interactions, and cultural references, while the absence of the additional feminist material that had shaped the book and its positive reception by female audiences has disappeared, leaving no perceptible imprint. The perceived stagnation of the feminist revolution, particularly when compared with the success of GLBT advocacy in Israel, as well as Linor's move from liberal feminist public intellectual to increasingly conservative commentator on the radio talk show "The Final Word," undermined her status in the feminist movement. The film's failed legacy exposes the fragility of strident feminist messaging, while Linor's own fall from grace highlights the social expectation that gender and identity politics advocates will align with other progressive causes, such as (in the Israeli case) left-wing positions on the occupation of Palestinian territories. That Linor wished to spotlight feminist concerns over those of gay rights activists (in the making of the film), and later Israeli women's concerns over those of other oppressed groups in Israeli society (in her radio show) set her at odds with the progressive tribal activism and political litmus tests of third-wave feminism.

Despite the thematic differences between the book and the film, Talila's plot in both remains almost identical and revolves around her romance with Noah Ne'eman, a soy food engineer. Competing for her affection is Ofer, a copywriter and the son of the head of the last agency at which she worked. After leaving their two-year relationship and the agency, she joined a new company for a fresh start, but Ofer, who is quickly engaged to a new woman, then rejects this girlfriend and attempts to resurrect his former relationship with Talila. The novel was the first of its kind in Israel, and Yaron Peleg has argued that it "legitimized the trashy or pulp romance in Hebrew letters for the first time." It was commended for depicting "real sex," while other critics celebrated the lack of "The usual Jewish-Israeli existential anxieties like the Holocaust, the Arab-Israeli conflict, or religious or ethnic tensions. [. . .] a welcome rejection of the over politicization of life and art in Israel."[6] The romance genre that developed in the 1990s offered a new frivolous vehicle for Israeli women writers and was better received than the depressing novels about women's tragedies published during the previous decade.[7] Regarded as superficial and poorly written, with their use of slang and simple prose, these novels were particularly characterized by the sexual liberation and romantic relations of their female protagonists. They generally focused on female dramas, domestic landscapes, and matriarchies, as with Shifra Horn's *Four Mothers* (1996) and Dorit Rabinyan's *Persian Brides* (1999), which were, like *The Song of the Siren*, hugely popular, such that for the first few years of the 1990s, the best-seller list in Israel was almost entirely dominated by women's fiction. For the first time since the 1950s, a divide was noticeable in literature written by women between the popular "low" fiction of writers such as Linor, Horn, Emuna Elon, Yochi Brandeis, and Batya Gur and the more respectable "high" fiction of Yehudit Hendel, Ronit Matalon, Yehudit Katzir, Savyon Leibrecht, and Orly Castel-Bloom.

In *The Song of the Siren* the protagonist's focus on romantic entanglements and her career, along with the representation of upper-middle-class, yuppie Tel Aviv lifestyles, has led Peleg to suggest that, apart from "the Scud missiles that rain on Tel Aviv nightly, the Middle Eastern environment barely rears its inconvenient head."[8] Cohen sees the characters as "rootless Israelis; alienated from Israeli reality and culture, and reluctant to contribute to the national cause. Instead, they are part of a new global civil religion, the religion of consumerism and accumulation of goods."[9] For Peleg, Talila's "most admired trait is her stubborn and oblivious pursuit of True Love, irrespective of the primitive and anachronistic conflict that rages around her, for which she has little patience and even less regard. Part of the novel's charm at the time was its refusal to acknowledge or deal with the complex Middle East situation and its insistence on having fun like the rest of the civilized world."[10] The "low" romance genre of *The Song of the Siren* may depart from a conventional view of Middle Eastern politics and present the war through hyperfeminine imagery, but Peleg's claim that it exists without acknowledging the "anachronistic conflict" or that it disconnects from a Zionist cultural tradition, as Cohen has argued, misses the ways in which the film reimagines militarism through a feminist lens. Rather, the experience of the war and the paradigm of Israel's national survival become central and shape every aspect of the imagery, costume, plot, emotional motivations, and setting of the novel. Linor is addressing the masculinity of militarism, which excludes women, and reframing it from a feminist perspective that includes women within the national trauma. But the move from recognizing the ways in which militarism saturates Israeli culture, which serves as Linor's feminist critique, to a situation in which militarism is all but erased is part of the process by which Fox undermines Linor's feminist agenda. In part, this difference reflects Fox's internalization of his own acceptance within the hegemony as a male, even as he might claim that he is singled out within it for being gay. It is this paradox that exposes the problematics for feminism in Fox's adaptation.

Whereas in Linor's novel Talila frequently appropriates militaristic imagery in describing herself, such as on the occasion where she appears at Noah's house wearing red lipstick and a black backless dress and calls herself "a nuclear submarine, an Iraqi cannon," in Fox's rendition this scene becomes an expression of hyperfemininity in which she describes herself as sexy without the political satire. Thus the novel's subversion of masculine tropes through their appropriation by Talila disappears in the film. Instead, Fox negates Talila's direct challenge to patriarchy and inserts his own agenda by creating "a new, hybrid masculinity that blurs the boundaries of fixed definitions of gender, allowing, for instance, heterosexual men to dress and act as if they were gay men, borrowing their unique 'sensibility.'"[11] This can be seen in his depiction of heterosexual male characters as if they were gay, focusing on their clean, neat houses, their culinary skills, and their tendency to wash dishes. All of the men cook, including Talila's father, her brother-in-law (Amos), both boyfriends (Ofer and Noah), and other sundry male characters from the advertising agency, such as Yaron. Noah works as a food engineer, so that even professionally he operates in what might be regarded as a female sphere by spending his life in a kitchen, particularly as he makes soy and meat-alternative products. Ronen Marco, Talila's boss, is particular about his wardrobe and his expensive shoes. Ofer comments continually on the furniture in Talila's home and is himself an extremely organized housekeeper, even taking charge of the traditionally female role of wedding planner, suggesting glasses for the wedding list, the style of invitations, and the wedding venue, and even proposing to choose Talila's dress. In her novel, Linor presents these characteristics and interests as indicative of an egalitarian society in line with a feminist revolution, but Fox subverts them by feminizing the male characters and redefining masculinity into a parody of emasculation.

At the same time, Talila is more formidable than her American and British peers in the films of the late 1980s and 1990s that Fox sought to emulate. The chick-flick genre, which would reach its apogee during the first decade of the twenty-first century and almost die out by its end, established a set of recognizable conventions. Predicated on the central guiding principle that the female lead had to overcome social disadvantages (financial, emotional, and physical) as well as a major adversity in order to successfully unite with the romantic male lead, the genre soon became formulaic. By contrast, the Israeli version never addressed a transformation in the woman's social position, even when she was depicted living in poverty, and the local films lacked the transformative experience characteristic among their Western counterparts. Furthermore, the major site of adversity was always the Israeli political and military situation rather than any personal challenge. This difference represents two issues central to the discussion of Israeli feminist filmmaking: the pervasive influence of militarism (and politics) on life in Israel and its concomitant representation in film and the medium's historic tendency to depict unquestionably heroic males such that when women became the films' lead characters these conventions were simply mapped onto the new protagonist.

Despite the limitations of Fox's adaptation, the conceptualization of Talila Katz, her role as the story's unabashed heroine, and the very act of making a film with female (and gay) audiences in mind served as a feminist statement. Beautiful, competent, professionally successful, independent, financially secure, and responsible, Talila was a far cry from the war widow or psychologically fragile victim characteristic of the few female leads in the history of Israeli cinema. The book makes much of her professional and domestic abilities, and contrasts her successes with the failings of her less gifted sister Alona, who doesn't cook, and her friends who are financially incompetent. Although the film strips away many of these female parallels, thereby diluting the novel's feminist effects, it upholds Talila as a successful business executive (winning the lucrative Tival account) and domestically competent (she is repeatedly shown serving food that she has prepared). Her social and financial independence are marked by the luxurious apartment she owns, a notable acquisition in a country where most singles continue to live with roommates until marriage. Symbolic gestures throughout the film, such as the sunflowers she purchases in the opening title sequence, a recurrent motif of her independence (since she does not need a man to buy her flowers) reinforce this depiction. Though the book focuses extensively on her strong financial situation, the film reserves any discussion of this topic to the film's denouement. At the announcement of her engagement to Ofer, her father expresses his delight that his new son-in-law is wealthy, thereby saving him from having to help the couple purchase an apartment, but Talila quietly reminds the room that she is independently wealthy and does not require Ofer's money.

Talila Katz, with her sexual freedom, financial independence, romantic quests, and about-town lifestyle, bears a remarkable resemblance to the fictional female hero who gained prominence in Anglo-American culture during the 1990s. Comparisons have been drawn between Talila and Bridget Jones, and in turn between Bridget Jones and Ally McBeal, and later Carrie Bradshaw, though these characters appeared somewhat later in the decade.[12] The re-presentation of the central female protagonist during the 1990s and the first decade of the twenty-first century was taken seriously in feminist cultural discourse; take, for example, the *Time* magazine cover that placed the images of three pioneering feminists, Susan B. Anthony, Betty Friedan, and Gloria Steinem, alongside Ally McBeal with the title "Is Feminism Dead?"[13] Israeli feminism, however, has always had its own twist: if the near-constant state of war cannot be entirely ignored, it needs to be assimilated in a way that will allow the female protagonist in film and fiction to live the lifestyle of her American and European peers by developing a number of coping mechanisms. Both *The Song of the Siren* and *Yana's Friends* reflect Israeli cinema's tendency to depict a postmodern universal urban city disconnected from the particularity of Israeli politics and war. These films express the growing "fatigue with war, fatigue with politics, fatigue with national slogans, disinterest in Israeli history, and lack of confidence in the Israeli leadership."[14] Predicated on these very feelings of political fatigue, both works examine not only the immediate responses to the threat of Iraqi missile attacks within the larger context of the female protagonists' romantic lives but also the mechanisms of distancing oneself from the actual military conflict and of mediating the experience of war through the visual aid of a television screen or a panoramic window.

The title *The Song of the Siren* plays on both the sound of the alarm sirens that are a part of Israeli life and wartime and the sirens of Greek mythology. In the guise of the fabled creature, Talila lures men, yet she also refuses the call of the siren, the voice that commands her actions or locations. During the war she insists on driving after dark, will not seal a room, refuses to wear a mask, and drives around late at night standing in an open-top car and singing her heart out while smashing beer bottles in the street. Her rejection of others' self-imposed curfew symbolizes independence and is contrasted with the general lack of self-determination evident among her peers. Furthermore, she uses the predictability of other people's conformity to engage in acts of emotional rebellion. On meeting Noah's girlfriend in Jerusalem, moments before the girl intends to drive to see Noah, Talila surreptitiously slashes the tires of her car—knowing that she will not set out later if it means driving after dark. Her actions prevent the weekend the couple would otherwise have spent together, though in the film Talila ultimately leaves Noah, opening the door for Dana's temporary return.

The very setting of Tel Aviv constructs a recognizable vernacular of single, wealthy, carefree independence—as *Tel Aviv Stories* had two years earlier. Indeed, "the city" has been described as an essential character of the romantic comedy, serving not simply as landscape and background but as an integral aspect of representing the glamourous upscale lifestyle of its inhabitants. The material culture of Tel Aviv, like that of London (*Bridget Jones*), Boston (*Ally McBeal*), and New York (*Sex and the City*), establishes a space for female sexual freedom and economic independence, using symbols of high-priced fashion, nightclubs, and gay friends to reinforce this contemporary understanding of female emancipation. This landscape is contrasted with the rural idyll of Mazkeret Batya, the small town in which Noah's house lies within a large garden surrounded by orange groves. As the first settlement of *Hovevei Zion*, built in 1883 and approximately twenty-five kilometers from Tel Aviv, the evocation of this landscape inserts the historical Zionist narrative into the contemporary, anti-ideological symbolism of Tel Aviv as a world city. This accenting is further enhanced in the nostalgic scenes of Talila and Noah's developing romance, which include cutting wood, collecting laundry, and playing among the trees while retreating into fairly traditional gender roles as the soundtrack plays hits from the 1970s that evoke the halcyon innocence of a bygone era.

Talila offered an alternative cultural model in the 1990s, not only compared with the cultural history of Israel's representation and perception of women but also compared to women in other Western representations of the modern urban heroine. Linor drew on Shakespeare's Kate, from *The Taming of the Shrew*, with her feisty financial and emotional independence, rather than the more popular and commonly recycled Elizabeth Bennet, who depended upon marriage to benefit her own and her family's situation.[15] The erasure of this secondary text in *The Song of the Siren*'s filmic adaptation reflects Fox's tendency to mark the heroine as a distinct figure, rather than framing her within an already established discourse of strong female characters. Over the succeeding decades, as chick flicks such as *Bridget Jones* and television series such as *Ally Mcbeal* and *Sex and the City* became staples of the new feminist trend and were screened widely in Israel, they established the boundaries of the female protagonists: professionally successful women with disastrous personal lives, whose ultimate goal was happy endings with men who could be forgiven for whatever sins they had committed over the course of the narrative. But Israeli cinema had already evolved its own direction, situating strong female characters within the repertory of Zionist conventions that resulted in romantic encounters but rarely in happy endings. Thus we can view *The Band's Visit* (*Bikur HaTizmoret*), *Jaffa* (*Kalat HaYam*), *A Late Marriage*, and *Turn Left at the End of the World*, with their complicated romances set against the background of national politics and interethnic conflict, as the legacy of *The Song of the Siren* and *Yana's Friends*.

Screening the Gulf War

Jean Baudrillard's article "The Gulf War Did Not Happen" argues that the remote and virtual nature of the Gulf War, the heightened period of expectation, and its distance from previously established military norms led the Gulf War to be a war unlike any other: a war that appeared not to have happened. Though speaking to a European audience, distant from where the war took place, this conception is equally true for Israel. Discouraged by America from retaliating against Iraqi attacks and, in the main, removed in a traditional sense from the theatre of war, for Israel there are many ways in which the Gulf War did not occur. It was the first war in which soldiers and tanks were not deployed, no supplies were sent, and the Israeli government did not provide military support or engage in other public manifestations of combat. "It was the first war in which the Israelis did not face a real enemy who could be fought face-to-face or tank-to-tank."[16] Despite rhetorical attempts by the Israeli leadership to "glorify the war and Israel's role in it" by drawing on "all the old narratives of previous wars," these attempts were "doomed to failure," given the gap between "the resolute bravery and heroism they praise[d] and the absence of any bravery and heroism in this war."[17] Israel did, however, for two months in the winter of 1991, experience violence through the shelling of Tel Aviv and its vicinity by inaccurate scud missiles. "The targets perceived by Western television viewers as imaginary were described in Israeli culture as poltergeists, whose invisible hands fired missiles."[18] Though these shells were launched, they were not fired on battlefields but on urban locations—and unlike depictions of Beirut, whose images of urban war are part of the public consciousness today, most of the time Tel Aviv appeared relatively quiet, and its citizens maintained an appearance of social normality.[19] Thus the Gulf War was not like other military experiences in Israel's turbulent history, and this may explain the paucity of fictional material written about it.

In contrast to the other wars in Israel, whose rich and profuse depictions in literature and cinema reveal the abiding interest in exploring the impact of militarism, the Gulf War has been almost entirely neglected. That is, it has been neglected within a canon (usually produced by men and about men) that described the masculinity of war or offered a counter-narrative of women in combat who also experienced this war by depicting women either as hypermasculine or as victims trapped in the futility of men's wars, remote from the action and lacking meaningful agency.[20] The unusual nature of the Gulf War makes it different from all other military incursions or activities, and perhaps, in turn, this has also led to its sparse treatment in Israeli cinema. In the 1990s, the suitable topics of Israeli cinema, or at least those conventionally represented, were militarism, the Arab-Israeli conflict, the religious-secular divide, and Ashkenazi-Mizrahi cleavages within Israeli society. With no soldiers with which to represent either the internal national conflicts or the extranational conflict with the Palestinians, there was no material for male-centered narratives. Thus the Gulf War could not serve as a vehicle for depicting heroism and masculinity or as a way to critique the impact of war on the Israeli psyche, and could not be tied to the issues of the government's ongoing occupation. Indeed, the cinematic language of masculinity was absent.[21]

Israeli war films have developed a stable of visual and metaphorical tropes that include sand, rocks, bunkers, uniformed soldiers, jeeps, barbed wire, tanks, food parcels from home, reserve call-up notices (*tzav shmoneh*), guns, bases, dry land, and burning trees. The language and the imagery of the Gulf War are dramatically different and particular to this war alone. Baudrillard comments on this specificity:

> Two intense images, two or perhaps three scenes which all concern disfigured forms or costumes which correspond to the masquerade of this war: the CNN journalists with their gas masks in the Jerusalem studios; the drugged and beaten prisoners repenting on the screen of Iraqi TV; and

perhaps that sea-bird covered in oil and pointing its blind eyes towards the Gulf Sky. [...] No images of the field of battle, but images of masks, of blind or defeated faces, images of falsification. It is not war taking place over there but the disfiguration of the world.[22]

For Israelis, the Gulf War took place in people's homes, and, instead of traditional preparation and participation in battle, the activities associated with the war were domestic. They included preparing a specific room in the home, stocking up on groceries, and taking care of children in the face of bombing. It was precisely the very nature of preparing the domestic realm for war that highlighted the extent to which the private sphere, which had always served as the safe haven, was now threatened, and more importantly the fact that it was impossible for Israeli men to defend it.

Dominant images of the Gulf War included the safe room with its household furnishings (beds, sofas, lamps, and tables); carrying a gas mask at all times, and wearing it during times of high alert; providing special incubator boxes for babies and domestic animals; and stocking up on supplies such as water, canned food, and other emergency items. *Yana's Friends* structures its plotline along the air raids so that the audience can follow the development of the relationships between two main characters from one state of emergency air raid to the next. While the sirens and the accompanying panic create a visceral sense of urgency, the domestic environment and the evolving love affair provide the comic relief uncharacteristic of other war films, since it is precisely at the moment of conflict (as missiles rain down) that the sexual romance takes place.

The urban landscape associated with the Gulf War was dominated by windows with large x's in tape—so that glass that broke would be less likely to shatter, thereby reducing potential injuries from shrapnel—and by windows that were covered with plastic sheeting and masking tape. Pronounced were images of Tel Aviv's empty roads and readily available parking in a city notorious for its traffic congestion. Though similar images appeared in the representation of other wars in movies such as *Every Bastard a King* (*Kol Mamzer Meleh*, 1968) and *Kippur* (2000), for these films the empty streets signified the male public sphere, while women were assumed to be behind closed doors. *The Song of the Siren*, on the contrary, focuses on the abandonment of the city's apartments.

In cinema of the Gulf War, the trope of emptiness and desertion signified the stay-or-flee discourse. Options included staying in the region but moving out of areas thought to be targets (while often continuing to work in Tel Aviv during the day); fleeing to other parts of the country, particularly to hotels in Jerusalem and Eilat, which added a sense of vacation to the experience; or staying in kibbutzim in the Galilee region (particularly the Jezreel Valley), which suggested homecoming and protection by the land (part of Israel's historic narrative of existence). This fed into the pre-state (and early state) narrative of the kibbutzim protecting the country by being erected along the country's borderlands, a myth that constitutes the opening monologue of the Zionist promotional documentary *The Edge of Danger* (1955). Alternatively, leaving the country and going abroad, particularly to family in Europe and the United States, symbolized a flight mentality that made Israel and the persecution of Jews part of a longer Jewish history of annihilation and immigration while simultaneously undermining the unique role of Israel as the safe haven for Jews. More broadly it challenged the mythical ideology of the Israeli heroic discourse of fighting to the last man in order to defend the land. It was this last belief that had been central to the heroic-nationalist genre in films such as *Hill 24 Doesn't Answer*, and its erosion signified a breakdown of the nationalistic ethos of sacrifice and survival.

While Talila lives with Noah in Mazkeret Batya during the worst of the war, and her sister Alona stays with her family at her father's house in Petah Tikvah (another early settlement) and later at a hotel in Jerusalem, in *Yana's Friends* the heroine has nowhere else to go. The film subverts the Gulf War's local narrative of escape by focusing on a new Russian immigrant, a young woman who chose to come to Israel despite its political and economic instability. The film thereby evokes the conventional historical narrative of pioneering devotion and simultaneously critiques its abandonment. Without an alternative home or money to afford hotels elsewhere, Yana is obliged to transform the domestic environment of her shared rented Tel Aviv apartment into a safe haven—safe from the missiles, from her ex-husband, and from her Soviet past. Her perceptions of the Gulf War are contrasted with those of her sabra roommate Eli, who went through basic Israeli military training and is portrayed in the film as an embodiment of Israeli masculinity. Handsome and sexy, Eli works as a videographer and on the side turns Yana into his personal voyeuristic project as his camera and his gaze follow her along the streets of Tel Aviv and around their apartment. Eli starts out as a classical male lead—his gaze controls our vision of Yana and, functioning as a knight in shining armor, he rescues Yana from the financial troubles caused by her ex-husband. The sense of his protective power is heightened during the early missile attacks when he runs into her room to ensure her safety, discovers she has no sealed space, and takes her to his own sealed bedroom; this then leads to their first sexual liaison. The next morning, Yana refuses Eli's proffered romantic entanglement, but the following missile attack leads to a repetition of the previous encounter. Eli comes to look forward to the shelling of Tel Aviv as it becomes entwined with his sexual contact with Yana. Consequently, the sealed room becomes a physical and metaphorical space for Eli and Yana's nascent relationship.

The sealed rooms dominate the Gulf War cinematic imagery and discourse for multiple reasons. The intense fear of biological and chemical weapons was marked at the beginning of the conflict, and individuals stayed in their apartments rather than use the unsealed communal bomb shelters, which were often unprepared to function in their designated role and instead generally served as the building's communal storage area. Staying in sealed rooms within private apartments heightened the sense of isolation and decreased the impression of communal participation, collective memory, and shared experience that had characterized previous Israeli wars. Families secluded together, but, wearing gas masks, also experienced the seclusion as a social dislocation, since the masks restricted interaction, heightened tension, and added to the overall sense of claustrophobia. The psychologically stressful environment left frightened families trapped together for long periods of time. Furthermore, tension was aggravated by sleep deprivation resulting from nightly attacks. Sportswear became an iconic image of the conflict, as people slept fully clothed in case of late-night emergencies. With work often slowing down and children without school, casual wear or "sweats" in bright colors, suggesting comfort, became the clothing associated with the war, rather than the (khaki) battle fatigues and military boots evocative of other conflicts.[23]

Precisely because of these domestic landscapes, removed from the expected imagery of conflict, the Gulf War appeared increasingly feminized.[24] But even more than the absence of weaponry, Baudrillard muses over the digitalization of the war. He argues that its presentation on television and in the media increased the sense of the war's comportment as if it were a computer game or a movie. The firing was remote and nonspecific, and the war was viewed, in his mind, through television screens. In Israel this voyeuristic portrayal can be expanded to consider citizens who stood on roofs to watch the rockets being fired at night or observed the action from large apartment windows that offered a view of Tel Aviv, scenes that contrasted with the customary representations of soldiers in combat that constituted war in the mass media. Danny Kaplan noted that the radio, which often responded to external events in its programming, particularly the "management of mood in emergency situations," created an unofficial anthem out of the recently released "On the Rooftops of Tel Aviv."[25] Aiming to "provide companionship and comfort during the many nights of tension," the song evoked the isolation, confined rooms, and rooftop spectacles of watching the missiles fall.[26] Comparative to other urban war zones, Tel Aviv did not appear to be under siege in the images of the day. The absence of half-shelled buildings with personal possessions dangling in the wreckage while bulldozers searched the rubble for bodies, which had become staples of news reportage for citizens affected by urban conflict in other situations, also confused the notion of a battle on the home front. Instead, the Gulf War's impact on Tel Aviv was seen as rather minor and mediated through the safety of television screens. Eli's lens in *Yana's Friends* echoes the audience's voyeuristic experience of engaging with war from a safe and comfortable distance.

In her study of the recent portrayals of Russian immigrant women within the politics of Israeli cinematic representations of gender and ethnicity, Olga Gershenson claims that films such as *Yana's Friends* exemplify the postpolitical trend in contemporary Israeli cinema where the traditional focus on the collective experience shifts toward the private individual.[27] In both *The Song of the Siren* and *Yana's Friends*, the Gulf War is experienced as a private affair and not as a collective, ideologically motivated effort. Furthermore, *Yana's Friends* actualizes the distancing and detachment from the military action not only through its focus on the feminine and the domestic but also through the engagement of such postmodern techniques as quotation and pastiche to enhance the genre ambiguity. As we observe the interactions between Yana and Eli in their apartment, we are also treated to the sounds and visuals of the English-language news Gulf War–related footage on Eli's TV monitors. Supplemented by the authentic shots of Tel Aviv landscape produced by Eli's camera in a cinéma-vérité mode, the news pastiche creates a quasi-documentary ambience in the film, reminiscent of "reality TV" that gradually emerges as a spectacle within a spectacle.

The camera's focus on the interior spaces of Yana and Eli's mandate-era Tel Aviv apartment separates them from the urban hustle and bustle of the streets below as well as from the threat of Iraqi missiles. Within this limited space, two women—the new immigrant Yana and the old immigrant landlady Rosa—gain more and more agency as the story unfolds. At the time when Yana and Eli discover a cache of papers in the attic that reveal Rosa's only son was killed in the Six-Day War, Rosa herself discovers that Yitzhak, her long lost lover from the time they both fought in the Second World War in Europe, is presently also a new immigrant in Israel. The memories of the Second World War and the Six-Day War—with their attendant imagery and ideological baggage—intrude on Yana and Eli's romance in the sealed room. While the Gulf War might be the war that didn't really happen, the other two wars mentioned in the film left a lasting impact on the Jewish psyche.

In relation to the depictions of domestic environments during the Gulf War, it is useful to consider Begley's and Gershenson's insights into the theory behind gendered construction of spaces in this film. They point out:

> Like discourse, space is always political. Space can discipline by restricting access, and empower by giving presence. Spatial organization is a historical and cultural product of meshing and clashing discourses of the body, sexuality, and morality. Instead of being "neutral," our notions of space are informed by a set of gender, class, and race terms. Therefore, the everyday spaces of our homes, offices, streets, and cities not only reflect existing social relations and identities but also actively produce and re-produce them.[28]

In both *The Song of the Siren* and *Yana's Friends*, gendered space frames our perceptions of the Gulf War and negotiates the changing roles of male and female characters. Men's lack of specific role within this war, and their lack of opportunities to be heroic and masculine, is pronounced. Similarly, the lack of weapons as the universal phallic symbol highlights the visual focus on nonmilitary objects as well as nonmilitary subjects. Men are cast in the role of lovers and not warriors. Though confined to their urban living quarters, they work with women to build a safe environment. Within this context, the choice of romantic comedy is not accidental. Following Laura Mulvey, Gershenson states that romantic comedy is "a genre that often treats repressed social issues with aspects of melodrama, a genre that conventionally serves as a safety-valve for ideological contradictions."[29] Indeed, the traditional Israeli war narrative comes into conflict with the genre of chick flick, redirecting the paramount preoccupation with national survival toward the more generalized pursuit of happiness.

In *Yana's Friends*, the female protagonist is "absorbed" or assimilated into Israeli society through the strategy of a romantic relationship with the quintessential sabra. However, Gershenson points out,

> Intimacy between Yana and Eli takes place in the moments not only of Yana's personal fears and insecurities, but of highest national fears and insecurities—during the first Gulf War, underscoring . . . the ever-present possibility of national annihilation. Significantly, their intimacy takes place in a sealed room, during the missile attacks, accompanied by the sounds of sirens, as both she and Eli wear gas masks. The threat of war facilitates unity among the everyday disunity of Yana and Eli. Later, the gas masks become necessary equipment—prosthetics—on which their physical connection depends. The gas mask standardizes everyone's face (metaphorically united in the face of danger) and additionally renders everyone mute, eliminating linguistic gaps and muffling accents. Once the threat of war has passed, Eli's seduction of Yana succeeds only when missile attacks are simulated through his use of recorded sounds and images of past missile attacks.[30]

The Gulf War thus exists in the film on several different levels simultaneously: it is the actual historic-political context of the plot, it is the quasi-documentary reality TV quoted throughout the film, and it is also the simulacrum of the war, an integrated representation that overlays the characters' memories of the war experience.

The creative interplay between the collective Zionist mythology of the state and the individualism celebrated by the inner life of romantic chick flicks collapses in the Israeli context when the former becomes integrated into the medium of the latter. By choosing to build narratives according to the chick-flick conventions of romantic comedy, the films perpetuate the virtual quality of this military conflict. The hyper-imagined Gulf War emerges from these two films as yet another incarnation of the simulacrum. As the distinction between what is real and what is imaginary (also what is authentic and what is derivative) becomes more blurred, the hyper-imagined, televised political landscape of the Middle East can be conceptualized as a fictional terrain several times removed from anything even remotely conceived as "an original." Thus the films that deal with the transformation of gender roles within this domesticated military conflict contribute to the ways in which hyper-reality can be viewed as a form of reality by proxy.

Song of the Siren: Talila Katz (Dalit Kahan) and Noah Ne'eman (Boaz Gur-Lavi), the soy food engineer, sit in her bedroom when the sirens begin. She doesn't have a gas mask, and the room isn't sealed.

Both *The Song of the Siren* and *Yana's Friends* use the background of the virtual Gulf War to foreground the stories of women, their love lives, and their place in Israeli society. Particularly noticeable is the depiction of male responses to the Gulf War. Eli uses the war as an opportunity not only for seduction but also heroism, as he repeatedly rescues Yana, thereby assuring his masculinity in *Yana's Friends*. Noah, in *The Song of the Siren*, serves in the reserves after his first date with Talila, even though he claims he is only working as a supplies officer, and Amos (Alona's husband and Talila's brother-in-law) is described in the novel as a parachutist and an officer (though this disappears from the film), thus their heroic masculine identity is preserved in its traditional form. Nevertheless, in the face of the Gulf War there is a sense of panic, fear, and often hysteria, even among male characters, and the public manifestations of these emotions are often preceded by a period of impotence or a lack of sexual desire. Ronen flees to Amsterdam on the pretext of a conference, Amos has an affair, and minor male characters at the office openly display fear of the attacks, and their nervousness is constrasted with the black humor exhibited by the women in the office who are gambling on the timing of the next round of missiles. Ofer and Noah are responsible about wearing their gas masks, while Talila noticeably refuses to wear hers. She repeatedly refuses to take the threat of chemical warfare seriously and will not carry or wear her mask, though when alone she does recognize the danger of the shells and, after breaking up with Noah, finally uses the building's bomb shelter when she is afraid (at this time she is the only one to do so). It is here where Ofer finds her, precipitating their short-lived reunion. Thus the men are also associated with protectiveness, their behavior corresponding to the traditional male role of the "white knight." But these individual positions are not static. At the close of the novel Noah also begins to experience ambivalence about this fear of war and finally stays in bed rather than bother with his mask or with sealing the room.

While the novel drew frequent parallels between love or romance and war, the film generally sets the main romance in a fantastical alternate space in which war does not exist. At the same time, the television's constant intrusion with news of attacks, information, and updates disrupts this fantasy. Talila's mother also reflects the ambivalence of the war experience. Though she invests a great deal of time preparing for war, and moves in with her ex-husband when the missiles begin to fall, she also criticizes his girlfriend Hana for leaving.

The relentless rhythm of the war is examined each day, and the reactions to the missile attacks each night evoke a sense of the Gulf War experience for Tel Avivans. The anticipation in early January is replaced by the daily ennui of those who remain in Tel Aviv once the war starts and the nightly fears when the missiles rain down. Talila, in her observations of the city and its inhabitants, has the quality of a flâneur evoking the particularity of Gulf War imagery. She observes the absence of cars within the city, her ability to park by the door of her apartment, the rapid adoption of casual clothing that marks out the inhabitants, and even her own dramatic changes in appearance from the highly coiffed advertising executive to the prototypical housewife in Noah's borrowed casual sweats and faded t-shirt who engages in domestic tasks or plays board games at the office. Her abandonment of makeup and particularly lipstick reveals that even she is not entirely immune to war's impact on Tel Aviv. Yet, her femininity is not compromised. Instead, she is transformed from the vamp seductress to the domesticated maid, while at the same time she has also assumed the traditionally masculine role of flâneur. Her constant commentary on the landscape and the reactions of others adds a further dimension of surveillance to the already hyper-observed experience of the Gulf War.

This vigilance is echoed in references to Talila's windows that become a refrain and reflect the voyeuristic aspects of the war articulated by Baudrillard. But the film also represents the progression of people's responses, so that by its end all of the neighbors that had abandoned Talila's building have returned and sit together in the bomb shelter. It is particularly this last response that returns the war to some modicum of the normality established by other military experiences in Israel. As the war's end nears and less attention is given to fear and expectation, the routinization of response is depicted, seen in Talila's willingness to marry Ofer. But in the final moments, as the loose ends of the narratives are tied up, returning to the conventions of the chick-flick genre, Noah leaves the Boston girlfriend, Talila's sister Alona and her husband Amos reunite, Talila's mother moves out of her ex-husband's home and tolerates his impending marriage to the returning fiancée, and Talila breaks off her engagement.

Similarly, in *Yana's Friends*, Yana's Russian husband returns, only to be finally rejected by Yana. This act of empowerment is the culmination of a journey of self-realization that had begun with her abortion, finding work, and ceasing to wear the gas mask when in the sealed room with Eli. The characters in the many subplots find happiness, and justice is dispensed. Finally the war and narratives of it are concluded at a public celebration of Purim. The already carnivalesque occasion serves as a public celebration of the end of war. The streets are bedecked with bunting and flags reminiscent of Israel's Independence Day. The use of Purim in the romantic narratives evokes the medieval romantic ending of a public ceremony (traditionally a wedding) without succumbing to the *kitsch* of an actual wedding. In *Yana's Friends* all of the characters stroll among the celebrations while the central protagonists Yana and Eli walk hand in hand. In *The Song of the Siren* Talila returns home through the celebratory crowds and finds Noah sitting on the steps by her apartment, waiting for her. The couples, having overcome all personal, social, and military obstacles, and realizing their true love for one another, come together at this celebration.

Using the traditional structure of a contemporary romance, *Yana's Friends* and *The Song of the Siren* use the heightened domestic tensions of the Gulf War as a plot device for these highly feminized stories. They also reveal a new genre through which the Gulf War empowered women—who became the caretakers and held centralized positions during the war without neutralizing their femininity. In turn, despite men losing their traditional position of military commander and hero, they, too, are offered a multiplicity of roles, which complicate the notion of gender. Though subsequent literature of the intifadas and wars in Gaza return to the established modes of war representation, the peculiar case of the Gulf War offered a unique opportunity to consider alternative roles of women in wartime. By examining the treatment of the Gulf War in *The Song of the Siren* and *Yana's Friends*, it is possible to shed some new light on the feminization of the war in contemporary Israeli culture, the tropes and discursive patterns associated with the war, the treatment of female empowerment through the act of war, and the marshalling of this event within a romantic narrative tradition. At the same time, as men continued to control the cinematic apparatus, women continued to be dependent on male largesse in their representation and to find themselves in competition with other kinds of identity politics. Ultimately, as the Israeli permutations of chick flicks come into conflict with the established literary and cinematic responses to wars, we witness the emergence of a new, more feminine and rather playful, attitude toward war and peace that may be indicative of directions that Israeli culture could take in response to the new kinds of warfare anticipated by Baudrillard. We also witness a new kind of female protagonist, one who can partner with a man but retain her independence, who does not require a man for protection, and who is capable of carrying a narrative film that speaks to a female audience.

2

Women in Conflict

The Impact of Militarism and Male Hegemony on Women's Lives

At the end of *Free Zone*, Amos Gitai's 2005 film, three women, a Palestinian played by Hiam Abbas, an Israeli played by Hannah Lazslo, and an American played by Natalie Portman, sit in a car as it drives through the barren Jordanian landscape while they listen to a catchy Israeli tune with a strong Middle Eastern vibe playing on the radio. The three women begin to dance in their seats and share a moment of complete tranquility. As they approach the border, the news interrupts the song and announces heightened security due to increasing terrorist activity. The magic of the musical moment is broken. The Palestinian and the Israeli woman take up the argument that they have been having for the length of the film while the American runs out of the car and flees toward the border, escaping the confines of these two women with whom she has shared much over the past two days. As the women in the car continue to fight, they do so in different languages, one yelling in Hebrew, one in Arabic—though they both understand the other's meaning. The Israeli physically shoves the Palestinian woman, and the Palestinian woman pushes back. They stop hitting each other. Trapped at the border in a liminal space that represents neither woman's home, unable to move forward because they cannot resolve their argument in the car and unable to return to the burned-out settlement that was the Palestinian woman's abode, they are powerless. Darkness descends outside; the closing credits roll over the two women, who continue to sit in the car shouting at each other; and the film ends.

This powerful scene illustrates a pattern that has emerged in recent Israeli cinema of representing the Israeli-Palestinian conflict through the experience of women. Along with Gitai's *Free Zone* (2005), Eran Rikli's films *Lemon Tree* (2008) and *The Syrian Bride* (2004) explore women's identity as it is impacted by the Arab-Israeli conflict. These films engage with feminist modes of filmmaking, not just in character representation but also in their treatment of the women's physicality, gaze, territoriality, and agency. Though the women are represented in conflict with one another, forced onto opposite sides, they are revealed to have more in common with one another than they have with the social group within which they dwell. Despite this strong sense of identification with the plight of the other, they are forced to maintain distance. Trapped within their own social milieu, these women are powerless to effect change. Despite their ambivalence over this expectation, they consent to become tools for the male struggles in which they are forced, by circumstance, to participate.

Free Zone: The three women (Hannah Laslo, Natalie Portman, Hiam Abbas) sit side by side in the car listening to music and dancing in their seats until the news announces a terrorist threat and the positive mood is broken

By contrast, each film also contains an external observer—represented by the American woman Rebecca (Natalie Portman) in *Free Zone*, the UN mediator in *The Syrian Bride*, and the international press in *Lemon Tree*. These figures chronicle the situation, reflecting back upon the Arab and Jewish women trapped within the conflict. These observers, also portrayed by women, are impotent in the face of administrative hurdles and the persistent hostilities, and in despair they leave the subjects to their own self-imposed fate. Rebecca runs away, the UN mediator leaves not only the situation but the country, and the press—in the guise of a female friend and prestigious reporter—moves on to find another story, further heightening the sense that in this conflict only the Arabs and Jews continue to participate, while the world looking on can do little to change this stalemate.

This chapter explores these three films both in relation to one another and in the ways in which they have changed the representation of Arab and Israeli women in contemporary cinema, suggesting a feminist form of filmmaking irrespective of the fact that the directors are male. These films depict an evolution for women within the traditional genre of war films, in which, historically, women were depicted as home and femininity or contradictorily as dangerous corrupting forces. In these roles women serve as a counterpoint to the battlefield, and though they might provide a symbolic base away from the turbulent war zone, their domesticity and heteronormative lifestyles are also contrasted with the male, often homoerotic, camaraderie the military unit provides.[1] Only as war widows do women exist outside of this binary contrast to the male battle, and yet there, too, the ever-present man exists even as he is absent, through the war widow's role as a living memorial to her dead husband.[2] These positions have, in the main, characterized the part women are afforded within narratives of the conflict. Directed by internationally successful male filmmakers, these three films advocate for recognition of the impact of the ongoing conflict, indicating a new kind of mainstream. This chapter demonstrates, through a close reading of these three films, a feminist counternarrative in which women not only reclaim identity and space within the hegemonic militaristic narrative but also challenge the masculine authority that they encounter.

Liminal Spaces

The movie *Free Zone* takes its name from one of two industrial areas in Jordan that allow free trade and where goods and foreign services are exempt from taxation and import/export and excise duties. These spaces are designed to encourage foreign trade and investment in the restricted area. This "Free Zone" has a liminal quality as an area outside the normal restrictions of space. It is only at this no-man's-land that the women can come together.

This film, which is the first Israeli production filmed in Jordan since part of *Blazing Sands* was filmed there in 1960, is at the center of Gitai's border trilogy, a series that explores the experience of women within Israel in marginal and marginalized positions.[3] As Anat Zanger has argued, borders and checkpoints represent the "intermediate space that is neither on one side nor on the other." In her description, "the checkpoint creates the effect of a meeting between specific identities that it seeks to simultaneously define and conceal."[4] In *Free Zone*, the frontier theme is reemphasized in the final scene of the film as the two women sit at the Jordanian border with Israel. This ending accords with the film's beginning, where the very passage of Hannah from Israel through the Israeli checkpoints symbolizes her embarkation on a dramatic adventure outside her normal life patterns. Having left her domestic responsibilities, including her husband, her children, and her work on the farm, she abandons her feminine duties and takes on a masculine role, such that in this new liminal space even the normal boundaries of her identity can dissolve. Hannah envelopes herself in her husband's identity—driving his cab, taking on his fare, and pointedly identifying herself by his name, Moshe Ben Moshe, when she calls the number for the American to plan their meeting.

This border leitmotif is also evident in *The Syrian Bride*, a story about a Druze woman on her wedding day who must leave her family on the Golan Heights to meet her groom in Syria, never to return. The last third of the film sees the Druze family trapped at the border between Israel and Syria. Having had her passport stamped with an exit permit from Israel, Mona the bride may not return, but neither can she enter Syria with this document. In this space the previous rules of society that had dominated break down. The Israeli policeman who is determined to arrest Hameed the father for breaking his curfew is shooed away; Hameed and his son Hateem, who have been separated by Hateem's choice of a foreign wife, are finally reconciled because Hameed is no longer required to engage with the wrath of the village elders who dominate in the village but are absent and at abeyance in this border space; and even Amal, the bride's sister, who has spent the entire film engaged in conflict, makes peace with her husband.

The borderland is disrupted in *Lemon Tree*. This film deals with a Palestinian woman's battle in the Supreme Court with the Israeli authorities after the state fences off the lemon grove with which she meagerly supports herself, when it becomes the boundary between her home and the new house for the minister of defense. In this film, the border is the security wall that opens the film in a long driving sequence and closes the film as the looming concrete blocks separate the mutual suffering of the two characters in the final scene: Salma Zidane (Hiam Abbas), who has lost many of her trees, which have been cut down and symbolically castrated by the rule of the courts, and Israel Navon, the minister of defense, whose wife Mira finally leaves him.

The lemon grove that could have functioned as the liminal space is railed off, inaccessible to both women, and deemed a symbol of the contested property and theft by the Israeli government from the Palestinian people in the name of security. Itamar (Zerisi), the young soldier stationed on a platform in the grove, adds a further layer of complexity to the picture. Though the other men (security services, body guards, Salma's father's friend Abu Hussam, and Abu Kamal in the representative role of the Palestinian authority figure) all uphold the traditional status quo, Itamar's ineffectual guarding offers another reading of the situation. The sound track accompanying his guard duty is the recorded program that helps him prepare for his "psychometric" exams, the qualifying tests for university. When he is first stationed we hear the beginning of the course, and at the end of the film we hear the final assignment for the program to which he is listening. His youth, his desire to protect Salma by warning her away from the grove (and by coming down from his high perch), his attempts to negotiate with her in the Hebrew that she does not understand, and his compassion for both women and friendly interactions with Mira all suggest that the hostilities have to be learned. In his innocence, we are offered another liminal model of understanding and tolerance. Furthermore, he himself is in a liminal state, between childhood and adulthood, between school and university, between being a subject of the state and being the authority that represents it.

Despite the symbolic space of the lemon grove serving as the boundary, the women have no real liminal space in their engagement with one another or the conflict. Yet, both women have children living in Washington, DC, which is itself a liminal space, at once foreign and outside of the regional conflict and, at the same time, a nonspace in which three states meet but none has sovereignty. Their children come to represent a nihilistic solution for the conflict, one in which the younger generation abandons any rights to or responsibility for the land and rejects the historical claims, the family identity, and the land itself. Nevertheless, the women stay in the contested space and do not leave, despite invitations to go to America, choosing instead to remain in a constant state of tension. At the end of the film this metaphor breaks down when Mira leaves her husband, the minister "Israel," in both the literal and the symbolic sense. The heavy-handed allusion of Israel's name suggests the imposed masculinity of the state and the impossibility of space for a woman within this dialogue. He is juxtaposed with the Arab authority figure Abu Hassam, who tells Salma that she may neither accept the state's money nor abandon her role as sacred widow by choosing an affair with the attentive lawyer, even though she has been forsaken by the Palestinian male authorities who have responsibility for protecting her, including her own son, who will not return.

Throughout both *The Syrian Bride* and *Lemon Tree* Riklis repeatedly places the woman at the center of the dialogue. In an interview he stated that using women highlights the complexity of the conflict:

> I felt that in the Middle East the women are the underdogs, the under-privileged, and I thought, in both cases, that they should be the center of the story to show support [for] women in the region and perhaps worldwide. But beyond that I also thought the women will bring more complexity and emotion to a story where men tend to hide behind pre-conceptions.[5]

In many ways, women become a vehicle through which a more complex narrative about the situation can be conveyed, and these three films illustrate his argument that the domestic narratives (as they touch on the home lives of women such as marriage, children, cooking, houses, etc.) set within the framework of the conflict not only offer a more nuanced representation but highlight the disparity between the impact of the conflict and its rhetoric.

> I believe the people want peace and quiet but it does not always show in reality. The film community is of course more outspoken about it and I think we all feel a responsibility to tell these stories. And yet I don't think enough films about the reality of the Middle East are made.[6]

Even the reception of the films in Israel and abroad reflects the issues that Riklis raises. *The Syrian Bride* was a hit within Israel, dealing as it does with a population that exists outside of the Jewish-Zionist narrative but still within the framework of the state. The Druze are seen as part of Israeli society, though often at the margins, and the conflict represented in the film illustrates the complexity of the tensions over the Golan Heights without fundamentally questioning Israel's right to defend itself. By contrast, *Lemon Tree*, which gained international acclaim, was less well received in Israel, where the tensions over security questions and acts by the state in the name of security were brought into question. The strains between Palestinians and Israelis within the narrative of the conflict are still fraught, and, according to Riklis, this film unsettled Israeli audiences, who are less willing to engage in dialogue where they feel their own security continues to be threatened directly.

Lemon Tree: Mira (Rona Lipaz-Michael) sits in darkness deciding whether to leave her husband.

Riklis is subtle in foregrounding the conflict in *The Syrian Bride* in a way that is simply less possible within his representation of Palestinians in *Lemon Tree*. The Druze population that he presents offers a meeting point between the traditional Palestinian other who is inherently the enemy and the Israeli Arab who is more accepted as a member of Israeli society—even as a minority that is discriminated against. The Druze are a distinct monotheistic religious group in Israel, where they number around 125,000 and live mostly in the north of the country. The majority are citizens of the State of Israel, though of the 20,000 Druze who fell under Israeli rule with the conquest of the Golan Heights in 1967, most are residents rather than full citizens. Like other Israelis, the Druze have mandatory conscription in the Israeli army, vote in elections, have attained top positions in the military and public service, and serve in government. Among the Druze are writers, poets, and artists, and in general this group is considered loyal to Israel. Ethnically the Druze are considered Arab, though more correctly their history within the Levant suggests a greater diversity, including Aramaic and Persian tribes. As Arab citizens of Israel, the Druze are represented by Riklis as a "Trojan horse" for depicting the Palestinian situation to an Israeli audience that would otherwise be resistant to such narratives. Riklis highlights the similarity of the Druze situation to that of the Palestinians by portraying a family who participate in protests and march against their occupation, instead identifying with Syria. Later the father will be barred from the border because he was imprisoned by Israel for political dissidence. Thus, after all, the Druze of the film are not Israeli nationalists but instead are paralleled with Palestinians. Therefore, the sympathy evoked by their negative treatment by a capricious administration is metaphorically extended to Palestinians. Nevertheless, the oppression by a patriarchal Arab society enables Jewish Israel to abdicate responsibility for women's limited rights and opportunities, and offers a critique of the regressive social structures from which Israel can symbolically emancipate them—evident in Amal's (Hiam Abbas's) acceptance of the educational opportunities provided by the social work program at Haifa University.

The Power of a Female Gaze

Without the liminal space that the other films provide, the two women in *Lemon Tree* can never meet. Though Mira, the minister's wife, tries to knock on Salma's door, she is driven away by her Israeli bodyguard before a meeting can ever take place, again trapped in a hegemonic patriarchate in which women have no agency. Only the looks that the two women share suggest their meeting—first surreptitiously from behind curtains and blinds, later brazenly in the garden when Mira's caterers break into the grove to steal lemons, and at the trial where Mira goes to hear the case against her husband (and the state) and the two women look at each other in the foyer of the courthouse.

While feminist theory has traditionally argued that the male gaze of the camera lens renders the women passive within the narrative and reflects woman's objectification, Riklis's and Gitai's films seek to find a new kind of understanding for this gaze.[7] The cinematic gaze in their films is not one of a traditional power relationship: neither one in which the audience takes on a masculine gaze in which the woman is objectified nor one in which the masculine gaze exists in the power relationship on-screen, whereby the audience becomes complicit by supporting one woman's power over the other. Rather, the audience, like the women on-screen, is encouraged to look back. Mira's gaze and Salma's returning of it empower the Palestinian woman, reflecting a shared camaraderie. Riklis fights the objectification of women within his film through camera work in which the women's subjectivity is highlighted repeatedly as they fill the entire screen. Furthermore, his delicate treatment of camera shot, editing, and scene situates women within contexts in which objectification is questioned. On the afternoon before Mira's extravagant housewarming party, her caterers, realizing they have forgotten lemons, try to steal them from the protected grove. Salma attempts to protect her property, though she has been barred access. She confronts the men, accusing them of theft, and as a result is thrown around by the security forces. When Mira intervenes, Salma is looking physically tousled and emotionally upset. Through their exchange of stares and Mira's brief words of apology, Salma regains not only her composure but also her dignity, enacted through her untying of the cloth serving as an apron around her waist and her donning of it as a head scarf, whereby she recovers her poise.

Dorit Naaman, the Israeli scholar and documentary filmmaker, argues that the feminine gaze implies power, agency, and subjectivity, and, according to her, "[e]ven today, few films feature women as the main characters, and their gaze is often troubling and not empowering or enjoyable."[8] Not only do these three films place women at the center of the narratives but the gaze is not uncomfortable; rather, the women hold the attention of the audience, which is willed to support the women's plight in the face of the external authorities with whom

Lemon Tree: Salma (Hiam Abbas) and Mira (Rona Lipaz-Michael) see each other at the courthouse.

the women engage, even at times staring down the audience, if it dares to challenge female authority. This is as true for *Lemon Tree* as for *The Syrian Bride*, in which Hiam Abbas, playing the bride's sister, looks into the wedding videographer's lens and commands the groom to take care of his new wife; and in which Mona stares at Syria, where her intended waits, finally following her own gaze by walking through the open border gate into her future.

Women's agency is a major part of this new kind of filmmaking and is evident in the broader social discourse about the Arab-Israeli conflict. Dorit Naaman has been collecting footage at Israeli checkpoints along with several other filmmakers who have recently addressed the topic of human rights abuses by Israelis against Palestinians trying to cross. Her work has been specifically connected with Machsom Watch, an organization through which women, mostly elderly and Ashkenazi, go to checkpoints in small groups to monitor Israeli soldiers. Taken from the organization's mission statement, their objectives can be seen engaging with the primary tension Naaman sees in women participating in these kinds of activities, which is a combination of reflecting the empowerment that is otherwise denied through the traditional military and political structures in Israel and offering an alternative, "softer" view of the conflict that respects human rights and shies away from violence.

> Machsom Watch is open exclusively to women. Our quiet but assertive presence at checkpoints is a direct challenge to the dominant militaristic discourse that prevails in Israeli society. It demands accountability on the part of the security forces towards the civilian estate [*sic*] something hitherto almost unheard of (Machsom Watch d.n. [*sic*]).[9]

Naaman argues that historically women have been repeatedly sidelined, since they do not participate in military combat and as a result they do not share in the defense of Israel—and therefore, she claims, "Israeli women are victims of militarism and the occupation as well."[10] Certainly this accords with Esther Fuchs's contention that since only 50 percent of draftable women join the armed forces, and since of those who do the majority serve in auxiliary jobs (secretaries, clerks, teachers, drivers, wireless operators, and parachute folders), it would be correct to claim that Israeli women are not able to participate in the military and therefore have less power within the Israeli establishment.[11]

What Naaman sees as an ever-present power configuration at checkpoints has lessened the violence and resulted in fewer abuses because of the women's presence. For her, women in Israel remain in a double bind: "as Israelis they fight the system from within, but as women they do so from the outside."[12] Furthermore, they are perceived by Palestinians as part of the hegemonic elite. Yet, Dorit Naaman's article falls into the very traps that she is seeking to question. These women, in the main belonging to the social class of the elite (white, Ashkenazi, older), are using precisely this power to curtail the power of the male establishment. Though they continue to be marginalized in many ways, mocked, and even ignored, they are also personally respected and at times treated kindly by the soldiers. Moreover, if, as they report, the numbers of abuses are reduced in their presence, then they certainly have power. Nevertheless, these women are viewed by Palestinian men more complexly as both saviors and misplaced women; sexual objects and part of the male establishment. Despite these dynamics, and her analysis of these multiplicities of interaction between the Israeli woman and both the Israeli and the Palestinian man, the Palestinian woman remains entirely absent from her inquiry. If the Palestinian male is emasculated by the experience of passing through a checkpoint, how is a Palestinian woman treated and how does she respond both to these abuses and to the presence of the Israeli woman of Machsom Watch?

The three films considered here all take a more sophisticated and more evenhanded look at the multiple forces at work in considering the conflict from the perspective of women. These films move away from the "sexual and romantic bridge" that has been considered a way to represent the conflict (and women within it). Loshitzky, quoting Ilan Pappe, claims that "[m]ost of the films that courageously deal with Arab-Jewish relationships choose the medium of a love story, which is usually tragic (for example, in *Eastern Wind*, *The Lover*, and *On a Narrow Bridge*)"[13] because they provide the frisson of "forbidden love" and displace the conflict into a romantic sphere that

> makes it easier for the Israeli audience . . . to encounter the conflict whose roots are complex and painful. Furthermore, the transfer of the conflict to the intimacy of the private space "loosens" and sometimes even disarms, the defense mechanism erected by many Israelis when confronted with "*the*

conflict." It is easier to face the "big" conflict when it is broken down into "small" conflicts that aim to negotiate its meaning on the microlevel.¹⁴

Evoking the tragedy of star-crossed lovers also serves to romanticize the conflict, thereby softening rebuke or political critique. Riklis and Gitai reject this mode by choosing women as the subject of their dramas and not providing an interracial romance. In doing so, they fight the stereotypes associated with sexual representations, which have rightly been open to feminist critique for their often Orientalist constructions, and demand that the audience deal with central rather than symbolic issues of the conflict.¹⁵

These directors reconfigure traditional paradigms. By offering Arab and Israeli women equal standing, they avoid re-creating the discourse of postcolonial hierarchy often evident in Israeli filmmaking, whereby the white male patriarch must protect the white female from the nonwhite male (and even from herself), while the nonwhite female is absent or hidden. They also circumvent the tendency to depict the need to control the nonwhite subaltern male both for his own benefit and to safeguard the white female. Thus they avoid the orientalist-gendered hierarchy of white man, white woman, native man, and the ever-silent native woman who is at once an object and invisible. The three films recognize the historical roles that these dynamics have had by creating patterns that mirror traditional power relationships (male-female, Jew-Arab) but immediately disrupt this dynamic by presenting a strong Palestinian (or Druze) character without romanticizing or idealizing her. All the films represent her struggle against the internal system (often of the local patriarchy) and of her personal conflict, paralleling her situation with that of the Israeli female counterpart with whom ultimately she can never find resolution.¹⁶ Indeed, these films provide a sophisticated representation, not only of the conflict but of the position of women vis-à-vis Israeli society and the patriarchal military system represented by the state. By comparison with the Israeli women, the Palestinian/Druze women within the narratives may live in different physical surroundings and have less material wealth, but they are both imprisoned within the political and patriarchal systems. Mira is trapped by her husband in a home in which she is constantly under surveillance, unable to move freely without her bodyguard's permission. The *mise-en-scène* repeatedly returns to her imprisonment. In one of her final scenes, the windows' shutters descend, casting shadows that look like bars on the walls, until finally she is seated in darkness.

Hannah in *Free Zone* is harassed by the Israeli border guards, who wish to restrict her movements; by the Israeli government, which has relocated her family from Yamit to the Negev (which she despises); and by the government policies and the conflict that repeatedly destroy her livelihood. No strong Israeli female lead characters exist in *The Syrian Bride*, but the Druze women are juxtaposed with an Israeli woman who appears in the minor role of visa control officer at the airport who is trapped within a large glass box, and with Evelyna, Hatteem's Russian wife, who is a successful doctor in Russia but is reduced to silence and do-

Lemon Tree: Salma (Hiam Abbas) protecting her lemons, stares out at Mira (Rona Lipaz-Michael).

mesticity (chopping tomatoes) in an effort to appease Hatteem's family. Mona has never met her future husband, and is contrasted with the two female UN officers complaining of love's failures and their own mistreatment by men. These women, too, are shown to be restricted in their freedom, particularly characterized by the UN officiant Jeanne's inability to affect either the Israeli or the Syrian clerks responsible for Mona's migration from Israel to Syria.

Women and Their Place within Israeli (and Palestinian) Filmmaking on the Conflict

These films do not sit comfortably in any metanarrative of Israeli cinema. In the main, Israeli films about the conflict are war films, set on battlefields, in which women are inherently absent as a characteristic of the genre. Ralph Donald and Karen MacDonald have argued that Hollywood's war films "clearly show combat to be a man's job, unsuitable for women, due to the female's nurturing and nonbelligerent nature."[17] Where they are present, they serve as "either an auxiliary or a provocative presence,"[18] contingent roles also common in Israeli filmmaking. As with the war widow, women may be shown to be affected by conflict, but in these roles they lack agency and are presented as passive victims of the situation. Palestinian women, if they appear, are silent or have a momentary presence as a symbol of danger, a role that the Israeli woman may at times also share. Esther Fuchs has classified this as the Eros/Thanatos divide, whereby men represent war (and death), while women symbolize love and sex. While this is not particular to Israeli cinema, Fuchs claims that Israel has inherited this vocabulary of concepts and images and used it in unique ways. Israel's wars and political instability create "a strong need for security within the private sphere, a need that is often translated into a nostalgic and regressive move back to traditional—namely patriarchal—patterns of intersexual and martial relations."[19] At its most positive (and even this is open to feminist critique), woman becomes the symbol of the land to be protected; at its worst, this becomes a frame in which women who defy this traditional order become a source of danger. "The hostility toward military women corresponds to a masculinist insecurity rooted in the identification of virility with military prowess," in which masculine women (or those occupying male positions) "compromise the self-image of men as fighters and defenders of the civilian population, namely helpless women and children."[20] Fuchs also sees the presence of women within the military as a threat to male bonding. "Finally, symbolically identified with sex, gentleness, pleasure, and sensuality, woman embodies all the values that threaten the military ethos, which thrives on coarseness, vulgarity, toughness, and the suppression of Eros."[21] Woman, within this dialectic, can destabilize the status quo and become the "castrating bitch"; thus she represents a threat to man, who must protect himself not only from war but also from the distraction and destruction that woman can bring. Zanger points to a shift in "feminine representations" in the post-Lebanon Israeli war films that corresponds to a general change in attitude within Israel toward masculinity, whereby women acquire a more "central and active role than that of the classic 'Homefront' woman," but even within these progressive films by the end the female is returned to her traditional space outside the battlefield of the conflict.[22]

Palestinian films have offered reflections on the conflict that enter domestic spheres, particularly in the work of Michel Khleifi, but these have been dominated by masculine power struggles and often use gender as part of the process of exploring nationalism and the nation.[23] Women have played a role in Palestinian cinema, as producers and directors as well as on-screen, "However, their films, even when focusing on female protagonists, were not explicitly feminist in the sense of a declared political project to empower women in the context of both patriarchy and (neo) colonialism."[24] Within Palestinian filmmaking, Palestinian women are focused upon as the carrier of the national struggle. Maternal figures, "depicted as strong, sometimes physically big," fight for the land through familial activities, unite the family, cling to the soil, and maintain and preserve Palestinian identity through the domestic sphere and particularly cooking. "*Lemon Tree* reduces Palestinian cuisine, with its wide variety of dishes, to the single act of pickling lemons, which symbolically expresses the preservation of Palestinian tradition in jars."[25] "In Palestinian cinema the woman, the home, and the homeland are three intertwined symbols." Despite Ben-Zvi-Morad's attempt to see Salmah as an extension of this cinematic tradition, I would argue that to do so is to ignore the subversion that Riklis and his Palestinian co–screenplay writer Suha Arraf employ in this characterization. Salmah cannot hold the land together. Even though she battles for the lemon grove and gains a small symbolic victory, in many ways she loses her land and livelihood. Her son is absent (and will not return) and her daughter does not visit. She may preserve Palestinian identity in a historic sense, but she does not do so in a material sense, for she has no heirs who will inherit the traditions she offers. This lack of a future generation for which the Palestinian woman serves as *matriarch* is also evident in *Free Zone*, in which Leilah is barren. Not only does she have no children of her own but her relationship with her stepson lacks the nurturing symbolism that characterized the role of Palestinian women in the past.

Arraf would go on to direct and produce two political films, the documentary *Women of Hamas* (2010) and the feature *Villa Touma* (2014), that considered Palestinian women's experience of conflict. Though Arraf was embedded within the Israeli film industry, there were still very few Palestinian female directors making features. Annemarie Jacir's *Salt of this Sea* (2008) had been the first. Her 2012 film, *When I Saw You* (*Lamma Shoftak*), was the Palestinian entry for the foreign language category at the Eighty-Fifth Academy Awards. In 2015 The Chicago Palestine Film Festival included *Eyes of a Thief* (*Ayoun al-Haramiya*, 2014) by Najwa Najjar, her second feature; *May in the Summer* by Cherten Dabis; and *Villa Touma*. This extraordinary rise in output by Palestinian women (including Hiam Abbas's own feature *Inheritance* [2012]) marks a dramatic shift in Palestinian women's ability to represent themselves. In the process, many are upending the convention of presenting Palestinian women as a substitute for the (lost) land and the symbol of homecoming, by offering nuanced and feminist explorations of women's experiences.

Whereas Palestinian and Israeli cinematic traditions had tended to depict the Palestinian woman in the role of possession, to be protected and in whose name (though not agency) the struggle is fought (while sidelining women's actual encounter with the conflict), these cinemas have evolved since 2004, creating more complex female roles even before Palestinian women began making their own films. *Free Zone*, *The Syrian Bride*, and *Lemon Tree* disrupt stereotypical depictions of Palestinian women, reflecting a growing consciousness of feminist values in representation that include diversity and shy away from the exoticization and sexualization (the traditional orientalization) of Arab women. The involvement of Palestinian women in the production and in the cast may in part be responsible for these artistic transformations.

These powerful images of female experience have ultimately resulted in narratives that also go beyond representations of Palestinian women in traditionally domestic roles. *Women of Hamas*, in particular, presents women who are military activists, thereby equating the Palestinian female image with that of the Israeli female soldier, which had become ubiquitous, often deployed in wildly contradictory circumstances that both celebrated female equality and objectified women as sexual fodder. Despite the many ways in which Gitai's and Riklis's films shatter previous representational paradigms, they still return to a demilitarized female character who is presented as a pawn in a male-driven conflict.

Notwithstanding their differences, Gitai's and Riklis's films are exemplars of the turn in Israeli filmmaking toward a rising political consciousness that first emerged in response to the 1967 war. The siege mentality that characterized the Six-Day War films and informed the heroic genres also inspired the rise of a new left-wing style of cinema.[26] Judd Ne'eman, who is often cited as a leading member of this generation of filmmakers, is described, "like many of his fellow travelers," as intensively politicizing Israeli culture on-screen and giving "exalting expression to the resentment at measures taken by the Right, primarily in respect to the Israeli-Palestinian conflict."[27] Nitzan Ben-Shaul places Judd Ne'eman within a context in which, from 1967 onward, "this social awareness was due to the military rule imposed by the State of Israel over the million or more Palestinian inhabitants of these territories and the slowly expanding Jewish settlement within these areas."[28] Ne'eman, in an interview with Janet Burstein, claimed that the seeds for this reaction were laid during his childhood when he saw the desertion of a Palestinian village with which he was intimately familiar, and in serving in the Golan Heights during the 1967 war, where he saw the expulsion of Syrian peasants from the hills: "I had been aware of the plight of the Palestinians before 1967. I was aware of the catastrophe of 1948. But I had repressed its emotional resonance. When I saw the emptied villages in the Golan Heights and re-experienced what I had seen in '48, I could no longer turn my eyes away from the Palestinians and from what we had done.... A new feeling developed in me: of having been deceived by all those who believed, and still believe, that we could thrive in a land where the homes of 'others' are erased and so many have been displaced."[29]

Ben-Shaul sees Ne'eman alongside "fellow travelers." Though he never names the group explicitly, he contends that, like Ne'eman, who reached the "apparent limits of his group's potential consciousness through his filmmaking, other group members reached this limit when faced with the outbreak of the first Palestinian *Intifada*, evidenced in their turn away from cinematic dealings with the Israeli-Palestinian conflict altogether."[30] Ben-Shaul suggests that "the reason for this is connected with the fact that the Palestinian uprising necessitated this group's resolving their conflict between ethnocentrism and altruism by way of choosing one side over the other. Such a choice went beyond the limits of what had constituted them as a group. Hence the group effectively dissolved."[31] Thus there was a period in which the conflict was relatively marginalized, and filmmakers changed their focus away from films about militarism and toward the social fabric of Israeli society, and, with the exceptions of *Fictitious Marriage* (Bouzaglo, 1988) and *Beyond the Walls* (Barbash, 1984), the films became personal introspections. Where the filmmakers represented the military, the enemy was absent and the emphasis lay in exploring the distance between national ideology and the individual's emotional experience of combat.

The changes in Israeli war films and films that deal with the conflict in militarized ways parallel the transformation in American Vietnam-era war films.[32] Anat Zanger has called these new kinds of war films "progressive." She argues that whereas previous war films from the heroic era had strictly delineated the conflict into binary oppositions, progressive war films have an actual homology created between two entities, and "these films dissolve the separately excluded categories into each other, at least in part."[33] Several films in the 1980s and early 1990s sought to reframe the dialogue, including *Fellow Travelers* (*Magash Hakesef*, Judd Ne'eman, 1983), *Cup Final* (*G'mar Gaviya* Eran Riklis, 1991), *Ricochets* (*Shetei Etzbaot Mi'Tzidon* Cohen, 1986), and *A Time for Cherries* (literally *Cherry Season, Onat HaDuvdevanim*, Bouzaglo, 1990).[34] Many of these Israeli films starred Mohammed Bakri, a Palestinian actor, director, and activist, who went on to direct Palestinian films that explored localized impacts of the conflict, such as *Jenin, Jenin* (2002). These films, on multiple levels, including the narrative, the characters as representative symbols of Palestinians within Israeli society, and even the larger production contexts of the films whereby Bakri was increasingly able to negotiate with directors over the Palestinian character's behavior,[35] revealed a new focus on confronting the Arab enemy. Not only was he no longer dehumanized but, by offering a sympathetic character played by a handsome lead, the film redirected the focus from an "othered" Palestinian toward the internal attitudes, politics, and ideology of Israel, thereby questioning national myths.

This new Israeli filmmaking had finally begun to engage with the Arab, rather than simply representing him as the enemy other. During the 1980s, "[t]he major films of the decade addressed Palestinians suffering from the occupation, depicted Palestinian activists as freedom fighters, gave voice to the Arabic language and Arab worldview, and evoked positive feelings toward those who were perceived by the general public as threatening."[36] Nevertheless, these films have been criticized by Ella Shohat and Nurith Gertz for reflecting the Left's construction of a binary Israeli response, one in which they are not complicit but are instead subject to the authoritative control of the state, and more specifically the Israeli military, thereby obfuscating responsibility.[37] These films were highly masculine, thereby reinforcing the already masculine discourse with its traditional power structures.[38] Ben-Zvi-Morad contends that *Lemon Tree*, like Israeli cinema of the 1980s, depicts "the wall that Israeli leftists erect between themselves and Palestinians."[39] Yet it is precisely in using women at the center of the film that Riklis and Gitai move beyond the "leftist" tradition and out of the discourse that once prevailed into new territory that confuses responsibility and authority, thereby undermining the hegemony of both the Arabs' and the Jews' political and patriarchal systems. These choices followed from the feminine exploration of the progressive war films.

In *A Time for Cherries*, Joanna, the documentary director, chooses her subject, appears in Lebanon, and displays a more powerful female role than was traditionally evident in war films, but, as Zanger contends, by the end of such films the woman's new role disappears: "as the narrative unfolds, this active promise is neutralized and the women are returned to their traditional narrative statuses."[40] The dramatic change in representation, where women are in every way the focus of *Free Zone*, *Lemon Tree*, and *The Syrian Bride*, suggests a transformation in women's roles within the conflict. Mira leaves her husband, Israel, at the end of *Lemon Tree*, and as he is the minister of defense this act further represents an abandonment of the state. Suggesting vestiges of the traditional discourse in which the personal is sacrificed for the collective (which demands total loyalty to the nation), by leaving she commits treason. However, a feminist reading considers her departure not an act of betrayal but a further emphasis of the profound disconnection women have with the militarization of Israeli society that is so prevalent in the male cinematic canon. There is no further dialogue after Mira's departure, a fact that creates a symbolic vacuum, suggesting that what exists afterward has no narrative. The film's feminist poetics imply that without engaging with women's roles in Israeli society, instead creating a world of hypermasculinity in which women are silenced and excluded, there can be no mediation of the Arab-Israeli conflict.

Riklis's film *Cup Final* situates him among a generation of filmmakers increasingly concerned with complicating the Israeli political narrative. Similarly, Gitai's film *Day after Day* (*Yom Yom*, 1998) worked to confront the use of political stereotypes that functioned as shorthand for commenting on the conflict. His story of forbidden love rejects the conventions of the Romeo and Juliet narrative in which one or both will die by offering the mature relationship of two elderly people who have been together for fifty years (the age of the State of Israel at the time of this film's release). Furthermore, they have "produced" a son, a living testimony of their love and a material demonstration that it is possible for relations between Arabs and Jews to be fruitful. Simultaneously, Gitai's film marginalizes the love story, thus avoiding a simplistic rendition of the viability of Palestinian-Jewish coexistence. While the couple's relationship is genuine, reflecting Gitai's own pragmatic attitude toward the present binational character of Israel that assumes the two sides are in dialogue, the couple's son, Mussa/Mosh, is sterile, undermining the possibility that the current status quo is sustainable.[41]

Though evidence of this nihilistic ending remains within *Free Zone,* where the women seated in the car represent conflict's futility, in other respects the film does convey woman's empowerment. This motif is central to all three films. In *The Syrian Bride*, Mona chooses to walk through the border gate toward her groom despite the bureaucratic impediments that had closed it to her, while Amal rejects her husband's authority and chooses to study social work despite his injunctions against her desire to study and later work outside the home. In *Lemon Tree*, apart from Salma's story, in which she confronts the authorities through legal measures, we are given Mira's transformation from passive victim to a woman in control of her own destiny. This is demonstrated through the gesture in which she leaves her husband, who, the film suggests, is having an affair with his assistant. Other commanding women appear in the guise of the female journalist, the political wives who visit Mira, the singer who takes over the microphone at the housewarming party, and even the judges on the Supreme Court. For a Hebrew-speaking audience, the judges' presence is particularly jarring when the court's verdict is read out in female-gendered language, highlighting women's reclamation of power within the framework of the institutions of the state.

3

Women Waving Guns
Does Feminism Meet the IDF on the Israeli Screen?

In the summer of 2014, *Zero Motivation* was lauded by critics, winning Best Narrative Feature and the Nora Ephron Prize (given to a female writer or director with a distinctive voice) at the Tribeca Film Festival in New York. This zany dark comedy about female soldiers in the human resources office on a remote army base in the middle of the Negev desert, disillusioned, bored, and resistant to the obligations of their military service, captured the critics' imagination. Yoffi Tirosh has argued that the film draws a link between sexism and militarism, highlighting the ways in which women are trapped within a patriarchy that fundamentally disenfranchises them of the right to equal treatment despite changes in the law that mean women are entitled to it and should be able to serve in almost all the same roles and positions as men.[1] But, in many ways, its pretension to offer a feminist position on military service and a new way of viewing Israeli militarism failed to offer anything other than an office full of incompetent, mostly unattractive, lazy women.

Even before the State of Israel existed, a culture grew up around military service and defense that lauded the heroes willing to confront those who threatened the newly established communities in pre-state Palestine and attacked Jews throughout the Diaspora. Hebrew artistic responses to the pogroms in Europe and the First World War established the dual images of victims and heroes, and suggested that if Diaspora Jews were victims then it was beholden on the New Jew to be a hero.[2] The image of the pioneer plowing the Promised Land by day and protecting it by night served as an iconic rallying cry for the nascent national movement. Early documentary films, often made to raise funds for the settlement in Palestine, repeatedly drew on this image to highlight both the success of the laborers and the imminent danger from marauding bandits that threatened to wipe out every victory over the newly hewn land. The first feature films shared this focus, and after the hiatus of Hebrew filmmaking during the Second World War the few films of 1947 and 1948 returned to this image even before the victory of the 1948 War of Independence was to prove a watershed moment in the establishment of the State of Israel.

Drawing on the epic history of battle and victory, the soldier became a key figure throughout the history of Israeli culture and dominated Israeli cinema. For a highly militarized culture with national conscription for both men and women, depicting military service captures a rite of passage shared by 50 percent of the population. The films characteristically depict basic training, the development of camaraderie, learning the skills of warfare, managing the emotional burdens of family and homeland, and operating within the hierarchy of an army unit. In other cultures, coming-of-age films set in high schools or on college campuses serve the same role as military films often do in Israeli society.

At eighteen, in their final year of high school, most students receive their call-up papers, apply to particular units, undertake physical and mental examinations, and find out where and when they will be serving. Regular military service in Israel is three years for males and two years for females, though non-Druze Arab citizens are exempt. Married women do not serve, and exceptions are also made on religious, physical, and psychological grounds. Historically, Ultra-Orthodox males studying in yeshiva are exempt from service, a law currently under review, while Ultra-Orthodox women do not serve at all. Some Arab males, such as in the Bedouin community, volunteer to serve in the army. For Jewish women and the Jewish Orthodox community there is also the option of choosing national service instead of military service. The compulsory nature of military service for Jews marks it as a specific rite of passage within Jewish-Israeli society, and the absence of the religious communities further accentuates the nature of military service as an activity of the mostly secular population. However, national-religious Jews, in contrast to the Ultra-Orthodox (*Haredi*) community, have developed an alternative model to the three years of service, and instead many complete five years, interweaving time spent studying in a yeshiva (religious seminary) and serving on active duty, a process known as *Hesder*. These soldiers have become members of elite corps and as such have changed the historically secular nature of the army. *Time of Favor* (*HaHesder*, Joseph Cedar, 2000) offers a glimpse into these religious military units. But despite the presence of women within the military from the earliest period, their representation on-screen has taken a backseat to that of men. While women have served as romantic opportunities, victims in need of protection, and (as Yael Zerubavel has shown) the living memorial of the war widow,[3] they have rarely been ascribed a role on-screen comparable to that of men in military service.

The landmark film *Hill 24 Doesn't Answer* is emblematic of the model of the heroic male offering up his life for the salvation of the Jewish people, while the shadowy presence of Esther Hadassi, the only female soldier in the unit, is never fully explored. Her presence nods at social equality, a value whose importance was publicly lauded in Israel, if rarely attained, and yet her ultimate marginalization within the film highlights women's symbolic presence and actual absence. Though they were encouraged to be helpmates to the male heroes, they could not be represented as equal to them. This established pattern of nationalist and military war narratives was given new life after 1967, following the Six-Day War. The triumphalism that swept up Israeli society in the wake of Israel's powerful victory was reflected in a cinema in which soldiers rediscovered their purpose on the eve of battle, abandoning the decadent ways of Israeli society in the face of national dedication. Yehoram Gaon's performance in *Every Bastard a King* (Uri Zohar, 1968) characterized this period of masculinity and heroism. The pretty blonde soldier waiting for him at the safety of the base camp would serve as the prize for the victorious hero, embodying her role as the accommodating helpmate, secretary, and fetcher of coffee, a portrayal that showcased the place assigned to women within cinematic representations of the military long after the triumphalism of war films had faded.

Avi Nesher's *The Troupe* (*HaLahaka*, 1978) would extend the image of the pretty soldier to that of the singing, dancing, attractive, and sexually available female—whose uniform merely served to heighten her sexual appeal. While most of the women in the unit would spend their time fighting over men and solos, Miki (Liron Nirgad) would also establish another convention, the female soldier as peace lover, and through her guitar playing and rendition of well-known songs of the American peace movement of the 1970s suggested an escapism beyond the boundaries not only of the Israeli military but of Israel itself. This infiltration into the very heart of Israeli society suggested the female soldier had the power to destabilize the normative order, and resulted in her casting as a marginal figure for fear of her capacity to corrupt the very essence of Israeli society.

Hamesh Hamesh (*5 and 5*, Shmuel Imberman, 1980), a cult hit that fell into obscurity, shared much of *The Troupe*'s cast. A metastatement on the American teen film, it juxtaposed the conventions of the genre with Israeli teens' reality of military service. Paralleled with the American high school experience, the musical comedy drew heavily on *Grease* for its inspiration. The simplistic plot of *Hamesh Hamesh* is built around men's service on an army base and the agricultural labor they provide for the women of the kibbutz next door (while the kibbutz's own men are away on military service) thereby offering opportunities for romantic trysts. The connection to *Grease* is transparent, and the film intertext is invoked with direct references to John Travolta and Olivia Newton-John in the lyrics and with the parallel of boys and girls courting. But the film reveals the indelible print that Zionist ideals have left on Israeli cinema. The boys are not greasers with motorbikes but instead conscripted soldiers; and the girls, though dizzy and giggly, are hardworking farmhands who take their duties and responsibilities toward the collective agricultural project seriously. The coming together of the two groups—the army and the kibbutz—represents the enduring love affair that Israeli cinema has with the dual image of the soldier protecting the borders and working the land, returning to the earliest cinematic representations of the Yishuv.

During the 1980s, bombastic and comic films such as *Hamesh Hamesh* disappeared as Israeli cinema looked inward and began questioning the impact of war on soldiers and the horrors of military service, including the brutality of serving in an army unit. Disrupting the idyllic representations of camaraderie that had saturated the depictions in the past, these new films also reconceptualized the enemy and offered the experience of the Palestinian as an increasingly complex character. Following the Yom Kippur War, which Israel won, a devastating crisis occurred in Israel and in its faith in the military. The recent introduction of television meant that this was the first war in Israel broadcast in people's homes. Images of weak and captured Israeli soldiers undermined the heroic images that had previously triumphed on the screen. Moreover, the war in Lebanon, and particularly the massacres at the Sabra and Shatila refugee camps that followed soon after, would strike a powerful blow against Israel's military triumphalism. A cynical and critical note crept into the cinema through directors such as Ram Loevy, in his landmark TV film adaptation by the same name of the novel *Khirbet Khizeh* (1978), and Judd Ne'eman, in his films *The Paratroopers* (*Masa Alunkot*, 1977) and *Fellow Travelers*, and through films such as *Ricochets* (Eli Cohen, 1986), *A Time for Cherries* (Haim Bouzaglo, 1990), and *One of Us* (*Ahad MiShelanu*, Uri Barbash, 1989). While these films began to question the myths of military heroism, they did little to change the representation of women, who, if they appeared at all, were seldom more than decoration, serving to undermine the soldier's real purpose.

Like *The Troupe* and *Hamesh Hamesh*, *Late Summer Blues* (*Blues Lahofesh Hagadol*, Renen Schorr, 1987) would also employ the musical form in its presentation of army service, but unlike its predecessors it had come to embrace the critical distance that was now a key aspect of military representations. A film exploring the rite of passage from high school to military service, it follows a group of friends and their conflicted attitudes toward conscription. Set during the War of Attrition (1969–70) between Egypt and Israel, a period of ongoing violence lacking the dramatic cachet of previous military campaigns, but before the terrors of Yom Kippur, this film couples the danger of military service with a critical view of the prime minister's position and the encoding of a heroic war culture instilled in the nation's youth. Viewed at times through the cinéma vérité footage filmed by one of the group, and offered with his later commentary about the fate of all concerned, the film's tragic outcomes are not sentimentalized but instead act as a form of political protest.

The plot revolves around the end-of-year school production and the students' appropriation of this event to commemorate a friend conscripted weeks before the end of the school year and killed in a training accident on his base. The intended performance, with its critique of the government and war culture, is derailed by the head teacher when she learns of their plans in a rehearsal, and instead the students substitute their planned program for a simple memorial ceremony. Much of the film is built around songs and skits (such as the song "*Lo Rotzim*," "*We Don't Want*," with its powerful lyrics rejecting war, widowhood, and orphans) that will never come to be performed before the other students—but of course are seen by the film's audience. The film's cult status signifies a change in youth attitudes toward military service, reflecting disenchantment with Israel's military authority and the shadow it casts on Israeli society. Yet despite its political dissent, the film continues to perpetuate female stereotypes and women's marginalized place within a society dominated by militarism. In a series of social encounters, minor female characters serve as sexual fodder, encouraging the men to enroll in prestigious combat units and perpetuating the usual conventions of the Israeli war film genre. Later the sacrificial goat is not mourned by these females, undermining an aspect of the women's role as war widow. Indeed, their faithlessness further accentuates their roles as chattel, whores, and auxiliaries and paints them at the very margins of all that is important in Israeli society. The only central female character, Shosh, marries one of the male leads and is therefore excused from service, returning her to the traditional role of wife and monument to her husband's later sacrifice. The secondary female character, Naomi, is a love interest that serves to disrupt two male characters' friendship and whose military service will be completed in a musical troupe. She signifies the disruptive female presence to male camaraderie, and her unit reinscribes the marginal role women serve in war.

These films would prove a gateway to a new kind of military cinema that reconceptualized masculinity. By the later part of the first decade of the twenty-first century, *Beaufort* (2007), *Waltz with Bashir* (*Valtz im Bashir*, 2008), and *Lebanon* (*Levanon*, 2009) offered a military space that, like Amos Gitai's *Kippur* (2000) and *Yossi and Jagger* (*Yossi VeJagger*, Eytan Fox, 2002), depicted a war zone far from home that excluded women from the battlefield. They might appear as disembodied voices on radios (such as with *Every Bastard a King* and *Yossi and Jagger*) or as symbols of home (such as Shosh's role in *Late Summer Blues*), but they were not present in the action. As a result, women were constructed as symbols of the homeland, and their presence often served as a metonym for the nation. Their voices or photographic images situated females as projections of the male imagination that served to reference women, rather than to establish them as a material presence. The only physical women who appear in these films are enemy figures: either old women who are depicted lamenting hysterically and thus without language, or young sexual hazards, since they may be a honey trap. These stock characters may also be used to show the Israeli soldier's humanity when he risks his life to save the enemy female. The women serve as yet another symbol of the inhospitable and treacherous landscape in which the men are trapped. As in the later *Rock the Casbah* (*Rock BaCasba*, Yariv Horowitz, 2012), set during the Intifada, men are alone in battle, trapped in an alien environment in which the rules of war are unclear, the mission and its purpose confused, and the film's introspection focuses on the long-term consequences of war on Israeli masculinity.

The representation of war in every form of Israeli culture is central, widely recognized, and canonical. Conventions include cinematic shots of a barren landscape; representation of the diversity of Israeli society, including Mizrahi, Russian, kibbutz, and Tel Aviv recruits as they are transformed into an image of the "Israeli," manifesting the Zionist philosophy of the country as a melting pot; and flirtation between men and women on the base, and depiction of women as support staff, often fetching coffee and working as secretaries while the male soldiers are combatants and officers. These cinematic images suggest an entrenched repertoire that has come to serve as shorthand for the Israeli military experience of basic training. *Zero Motivation*'s use of these devices operates within an accepted cultural repertoire, while its substitution of women for men at the center of the film is a subversive attack on the dominance of war, the military, and the culture of masculinity.[4]

Ultimately, however, *Zero Motivation* provided no critical engagement with these patterns and failed to challenge the sexist underpinnings of female representations within the Israeli army, either in reality or on the Israeli cinematic screen. It offered little that the 1985 film *Banot* (*Girls*), written by Assi Dayan and directed by Nadav Levitan, had not already proposed: that women's experience of conscription and military service was different from that of men, tempered by their own social interactions and limited by the glass ceilings imposed by a male hegemony. But unlike Dayan's film, in which the women's fervent attempts to be recognized ultimately resulted in their professional advancement, in *Zero Motivation*, the juvenilia of office politics, computer games, and the desire to rebel against any authority figure undermined the women's own credibility, suggesting that, unlike the more successful men in the film, they did not deserve and could not be trusted with anything more serious than the paper-pushing jobs they had been assigned.

The symbolic roles women occupied during wartime reinforced their duties as emotional support, "birthing the nation" and fighting the ideological war on the home front by providing resources, nurturing care, and protective home environments for the soldiers.[5] In embodying fecundity, women offer up their womb to the state, furthering their objectification. When not supportive of war, women are perceptually associated (or actually involved) with peace movements.[6] These dual associations of women with the domestic space and with an anti-war position further devalue women's military service.

Though historically women's role in the Palmach and later the IDF meant that Israeli women could be associated with militarism, in time, their association with "CHEN" (the women's corps), whose acronym spells "charming," further institutionalized the perception of Israeli women soldiers as attractive objects, "comprised of two overlapping components.... Neatness and sexuality—women serve a sexual need for the army."[7] In this vein, women are taught to use the army as a place to find husbands, and the hypersexual atmosphere, whereby women are encouraged to be sexually available and are placed in subservient positions to male commanders, models institutionalized sexual harassment. They continue to be viewed as "decoration," and, as Susan Sered claims, the representation of the model "CHEN" soldier situates her on the correct path to motherhood within the collective.[8] Thus the "obsessive fear that women soldiers will be raped by the enemy is an expression of the deepest possible threat to patriarchy: that women's motherhood will slip out of the control of the men to whom it 'rightfully' belongs."[9] Constructing women as male property embeds them further in a patriarchal hierarchy in which men, as long as they are the 'right' men, may do with women whatever they see fit. This control undermines female agency at every level, not only fostering a culture of discrimination and harassment but also leading to the characterization of a woman's sexual assault by nonmilitary personnel as an assault on the male hegemony for whom woman serves as a possession, a violation of the home, and an attack against the national womb. A woman's violation and the ramifications to her person are not part of the issues under consideration in this kind of military culture.

Orna Sasson-Levy's sociological research on women in the IDF has shown that women are increasingly attempting to articulate their own experience of military service, which not only confronts the accepted male narratives but also highlights women's previous silence.[10] Employing the language of men's experience of war, recently women have begun to narrate their own counterexperience of engaging in violence, being heroic, and *serving*. It has become clear, however, that in contrast to the hyperfeminization of most IDF women, those who do serve in elite units, important jobs, and higher ranked positions are prone to increased masculinity, thereby complicating the feminization of this discourse. Sasson-Levy notes that "women soldiers in masculine roles adopt various discursive and bodily identity practices characteristic of male combat soldiers, which signify both resistance and compliance with the military gender order.... At the same time, women's adoption of masculine identity practices can be interpreted not as subversion but as collaboration with the military androcentric norms thereby strengthening rather than challenging the military gender order."[11] Furthermore, "on some bases women soldiers are ordered to 'conceal their femininity' and are forbidden to wear perfume, makeup, or jewelry. These orders reflect the military perception that women cannot command as women."[12] This creates a dichotomy for military women, who can either conform to the expectations of women's roles as wives and traditional homemakers, which manifest as army domestics, or can engage in *masculine* roles in masculine ways. Thus there is a conflict between the apparent empowerment of women as soldiers and their actual experience of military service that is carried out in their representation in popular culture and Israeli cinema as sexual subjects—simply serving for the benefit of male soldiers. As an iconic phrase from the 1960s put it, "the best (men) become pilots, the best (women) are for the pilots."

Reluctance to deploy women to serve in combat has further resulted in few women having illustrious service records, serving in positions of leadership, and receiving the status and respect that men acquire for fulfilling these tasks. Fuchs has observed, in reference to fiction about the War of Independence, that there is a distrust of the "active army woman" that threatens the traditional Judeo-Christian endorsement of "woman's place in the home."[13] Her sexuality becomes a weapon, she is described with "sadomasochistic proclivities," and there is "not only contempt for military women in power, but a vision of woman as an outsider who is incapable of comprehending even the most basic facts about the army."[14] In fact, "successful military women may compromise the traditional image of male fighters and defenders of women and children and may also undermine the ethos of male bonding."[15] As Fuchs explains in the context of Israeli war fiction:

> In a military context, woman is reduced to a sex object and sex to a mechanical activity intended to relieve physiological tensions rather than to gratify emotional needs. Because one must not give in to normal human needs for love and intimacy, women and sex become objects of derision.[16]

Women are excluded from the experiences and narratives of war, while their traditional roles as "nurturing and protective" in the position of "wives and mothers outside the army or as nurses and auxiliary soldiers within the army"[17] are highlighted. "On the other hand, the constant threat of war and the continuous political instability create a strong need for security within the private sphere, a need which is often translated into a nostalgic vision of the patriarchal tradition."[18] In turn, the "military mobilization of men depends upon women playing the 'proper' roles of being feminine; that is, prone to capture and worth defending."[19] The depiction of violent women, as soldiers, spies, or policewomen or in rape-revenge fantasies, disrupts the associations between violence and masculinity and undermines women's feminine position. "Yet, at each moment when the violent woman emerges on a wide scale in film history, the films in which she appears go to great lengths to frame her violence within the very symbolic system that her violence threatens to undo."[20] This cinematic relationship between women's violence and a need to maintain the status quo of a society that has motivated it provides a tension that destabilizes the possibility of a single message of women's social empowerment through her physical empowerment.

Zero motivation appeared during a change in representation of Israeli militarism that since the first decade of the twenty-first century has begun to depict women as authority figures within a military frame and to represent women's military service. Portraying women as capable of wielding a gun and the equal of men, these depictions offer a radical change from previous films, which viewed war in masculine terms. Most notably in films like *Close to Home* (2005) and *Room 514* (2012), women soldiers' experience of serving in the military situates women at the forefront of everyday conflicts and in positions of power over men. But in the final account, the films were unable to overcome the suspicion that women should not be carrying guns after all, and perhaps they were not quite cut out for men's work. As Hilary Neroni observes: "in films starring violent women, the mise-en-scène that surrounds the violent woman is almost as important as the actual violence in shaping our ideas about the woman and subsequently about her violence."[21] *Room 514*, which pitted a female military investigator against the culture of male brutality that represents service within the occupied territories, and *Close to Home,* about the military service of women during the suicide bombings of Jerusalem in the first part of the initial decade of the twenty-first century, encountered similar issues, raising the question of whether representing women in roles previously the exclusive purview of men is in itself a feminist act or whether in Israeli society, which is a culture dominated by militarism, the possibility of making feminist films lies at odds with the very notion of representing women within traditionally male spheres. That is to say, do women in male roles change the status quo, or do they merely become a poor representation of men who would have traditionally been in their place? Defining these films as feminist merely because they represent women in roles traditionally occupied by men is problematic. Feminist attempts to challenge conventions may lie in the act of presenting female characters only if these characters indeed attack the hegemony, defying the center, often by exposing it from the periphery. Alternatively, undermining the status quo by reading the text against the grain offers another opportunity for reading an otherwise hegemonic text as feminist and subversive.

Banot offered an attempt to radically transform the notion of militarism and the role of women within the IDF. The film, which takes place at a women's training base, follows the first four weeks of a group of conscripts. This small band of women symbolically serves as a metonym for women's military training and for military training more generally. Adopting many of the patterns and archetypes of military films (such as the vicious commander turning the ragtag recruits into accomplished soldiers, the issues with discipline, and the building of camaraderie), along with the characteristics particular to the Israeli male genre (such as including the melting-pot ideal of the IDF, which brought together Jews from different strands of society in a process of education and coalescence from the disparate individuals who represent various sectors of Israeli society to the coherent group standing together that they become at the end of the film), in many ways this film takes the well-worn formula of films set on training bases and simply substitutes women in the lead roles. For a cinema with a history of representing female soldiers, this act alone is not by its nature feminist; however, the film's attempt to showcase women and women's networks independently of a male patriarchy, even as the army itself is the embodiment of masculinity and male values, offers a curious study on the ways in which feminist filmmaking can open up traditional male spaces to female subjectivity and women's representation.

The remainder of this chapter considers the ways in which Israeli films depicting women in the military have constructed their diegesis, focusing particularly on the image of the "mefakedet" (the senior female officer) and on the image of rape, in order to consider modes of feminist resistance on-screen. The role of the senior female officer, first represented in *Banot*, would become one of the most repeated tropes of these kinds of films, creating a tension between the advances of women professionally in the service of their country (rejecting the expectations of motherhood that had previously dominated) and the threat to a male hegemony in which the male's power is symbolically castrated by the dominant and domineering female presence. The Israeli army has had a history of sexual discrimination "that results in the most senior ranks being closed to women, including the head of the women's corps."[22] Yet, unlike the American *The General's Daughter* and *G.I. Jane*, even at their least feminine these women do not become physically superior specimens with rippling muscles who can beat the men at their own game until they are physically forced into a position of subservience, usually through a violent sexual attack. Instead, these women are assigned to head female units with female recruits.

In the IDF, women frequently serve as the training officers for men on basic training, as exemplified in the reality television program *Ken Hamefakedet!* (*Yes Ma'am!*), and yet in feature films they are only ever represented as the head of female units with male superiors to whom they report. At some level, presenting the women's isolated world, which embodies a feminist discourse of women's experience, imagines women as isolated and marginalized from the true business of the army, which is war. Even on a base, the women continue to be depicted as support staff, in the entertainment corps, in the military police, working in agriculture, and serving as medics. Ultimately, though the women may taste combat, they are rarely configured as combat soldiers, and thus within the heroic codes of the Israeli military they remain "jobnicks" (desk jockeys), whose social advances continue to take place within a safe and noncontested space. At the same time, the move to present women as professional soldiers who experience training, are able to develop camaraderie and professional military skills, and prove excellent at the jobs they are assigned, significantly advances women from their earlier presentations as eye candy and "sexual rewards" for the heroic male soldiers. In many cases, the very act of placing women at the center of the action, driving the plot and engaging in relationships that do not require the presence (or symbolic presence) of a male to fulfil them, can indeed be read as a powerful feminist gesture.

The mefakedet is drawn from an Israeli historic model of the modestly dressed, defeminized, and unadorned labor pioneer, an image that dates back to the dawn of the twentieth century. In a culture that rejected the bourgeois luxuries associated with decadence and laziness, the socialist sabras eschewed formal dress, choosing instead rough workman clothes, boots, and simple peasant shirts. The perfection of the body was a result of a cult of work and not of grooming, and men were clean shaven only as a symbol of their rejection of the bearded Diasporic Jew, while they were otherwise relatively unkempt, wearing no ties, leaving shirt buttons undone, and wearing their hair longer than was characteristic of city folk, among whom pomade and a sharp cut were in greater evidence. Women shared these values. Hair was arranged in simple braids rather than elaborate hairstyles, and women often dressed in workman pants or simple skirts and other than a simple locket were unlikely to wear either jewelry or makeup: "the simplicity of women's hairstyling projected the simplicity or asceticism of the pioneer, socialist, frontier society, even as the modest, unstylish, uniform hairdos of both boys and girls reflected the Israeli culture of togetherness, comradeship, and devotion to the social group. Gathering the hair into a ponytail or a braid, or cutting it to shoulder length, proved functional for women who spent much of their time outdoors and who had no easy access to hairstyling or cosmetic services. At the same time, however, these feminine hairstyles also encoded value systems."[23] This image of the plain, simple—if at times mannish—wardrobe translates repeatedly into the image of the Israeli mefakedet. Often more buttoned up than her male counterparts, whose dress and body language reveal a more casual approach, this woman nevertheless operates within a culturally defined spectrum that differs markedly from the models of American culture where women were expected to maintain their femininity even in uniform, or at the other extreme, the hypermasculine muscled Rambo figure embodied in *G.I. Jane*.

Drawing on the Zionist ideals of the sabras and the country's early militarism, in *Banot* the mefakedet presents many of the physical and symbolic ideals of the Zionist woman. She is free of makeup, her hair is held back in a braid or ponytail, and she wears pants. By contrast, the more junior officer, whose hair is curly and less severely restrained, wears a skirt with little ankle socks, portraying a more feminine version of the soldier. The new recruits first appear with large earrings, lipstick, and civilian dress that denote difference (from the army and from one another), coding social, economic, and ethnic divisions. As they abandon these "bourgeois" ideals and displays of individualism by donning military uniform, they conform not only to the rules of the military space and the ideology of the melting pot but to the larger values of Israeli society as exemplified in the images of the sabra-soldier—one willing to work and sacrifice for the collective.

The mefakedet is first shown with her hair unrestrained while off duty, kissing her boyfriend—an image that undermines her hierarchical position and returns us to the femininity and subjection of the female space. Yet even in this scene, her boyfriend's lack of masculinity, his simpering behavior, and his easy seduction by the misbehaving recruit Shuli reassert the mefakedet's authority, which culminates in her dismissal of the boyfriend and restrained reaction to her charge. By the end of the film, the mefakedet is beloved by her unit for supporting them in the face of Shuli's kidnap and attempted rape, and the women gather outside the head of the base's office to show their support in a small demonstration, where they chant that she is the "queen of the CHEN." These repeated motifs create a feminization of the military without undermining its myths of heroism and camaraderie. In this sense it retains and promotes a feminist agenda.

The symbolic characterizations and the stereotypical behaviors associated with the recruits, including the privileged Tel Aviv yuppie, Niva, the economically disadvantaged Mizrahi, Shuli, the nonconforming Russian immigrant, Anna, the giggly girls—two indistinguishable friends who are always together—and the drug addict, Shirley, serve as a vehicle for representing the diversity of Israeli society. This metaphor is extended to include the "Jewish people" in its broadest construction through the presence of the Canadian, Karen, who refuses to leave the base despite her father's vigorous protests, declaring that "this is my home." Even the unit outcast, Shirley, who spends much of the film in the sanatorium, is ultimately brought back to the fold through her willingness to help when Shuli is in danger. The film destabilizes conventional notions of Israeli heroism as masculine. It presents women's courage, women's issues, and women's lives whereby the army can serve as an opportunity to reach beyond the patriarchal systems of home and family by allowing women independence through a military career. However, the film's feminist agenda is sidelined in scholarship that has addressed the film, which instead focuses on the ways in which the Ashkenazi shifts blame for patriarchal behavior onto the Mizrahi male, whereby "[t]he victimization of the Sephardi woman by Sephardi men and her implicit salvation by the Western world, and particularly by a Western man" displaces responsibility for women's treatment onto traditionalism, rather than recognizing the endemic subjugation of women throughout Israeli society.[24]

Despairing that she has failed her audition for the prestigious military troop, Shuli returns home to her Mizrahi town, where she is rebuffed by her boyfriend, Moshe, whom she had treated poorly. In response and in order to taunt him, she turns to the wild, drunk, and ill-mannered Mizrahi males for some fun, but her agency is soon compromised, and she becomes a victim of their physical strength. As they drag her with them to an abandoned house and then attempt to force her to take drugs, they model the uncivilized patriarchy of the Mizrahi world. Ella Shohat has argued that their attempts to rape her play into stereotypes of the Mizrahi male as a danger to the white hegemony that the army represents.[25] Lubin highlights the axis of ethnicity and gender that serves as a dominant mode to project the patriarchy on Mizrahi men, thereby affirming the Ashkenazi establishment's clean hands.[26] Yaron Shemer points to an intersectionality of gender and race in these films, interested in determining "whether their position is primarily gender- or ethnicity-based," with the aim of discerning "whether the emphatic markers of Mizrahi women's identity in Israeli cinema differentiate them largely from Mizrahi men or from non-Mizrahi women."[27] The intersection of gender and race in Israeli cinema sets up power structures that allow the Ashkenazi hegemony to abdicate responsibility for the suppression and marginalization of women by suggesting that the responsibility for patriarchy lies with the Mizrahi. By off-loading this responsibility upon the Oriental, the Ashkenazi abdicates responsibility for challenging this position. Thus women are oppressed, and yet this oppression is denied because it is always attributed to uncivilized and uncontainable forces.

The film challenges this simplistic reading of women caught between two male poles, by staging the rescue as a military exercise that the women undertake. The attack is stopped only when the women from Shuli's unit, armed for combat and alerted by Moshe, appear in a heroic simulacrum of a battle scene, including an attempt to batter down the door. Though Moshe mocks the appearance of the women, wondering why paratroopers were not sent instead, the female soldiers surprise him while he stands by passively. The women slash the tires of the men's truck, thereby displaying the tactics they have learned; use tear gas to disable the perpetrators in order to rescue Shuli, thus showing their mastery of military skills; and heroically confront the men, demonstrating their bravery. Finally, in an act of female empowerment they force the men to strip naked, thereby emasculating them. Through the women's execution of violence, strategy, military superiority, heroism, and the men's disrobing, they establish the Mizrahi male as an object of mockery and ridicule. Laughing, the women drive away with Shuli, throwing the men's clothes from the back of the truck. While the film plays with female vulnerability and sexuality, this scene is part of the film's concerted effort to rethink the imagery typically used to represent women on the Israeli screen. *Banot* steers clear of the lingering shots over women's naked bodies and exposed breasts that were common and widespread in Israeli cinema, particularly during the 1980s, and takes pains to mitigate the effects of the male gaze, in order to avoid the exposing tendencies of the Israeli camera lens. Portraying the men's nakedness and their embarrassment not only upends the convention of women's nudity, it makes the very idea of exposing anyone to undress ridiculous. The image also addresses the humiliation of marking out an undressed body on-screen and the imbalance of power between the person who can remove clothes and the person whose clothes are removed. As the women take away the men's symbolic protection, they not only show their military prowess, they restructure the male-female power relationship and disrupt expectations about female roles. At the same time, the men are Mizrahi and criminal drug addicts, who, as Shemer, Shohat, and others argue, are already marginalized, thereby tempering the gendered critique and limiting the extent to which the gender order may be overturned.

The film's conclusion also weakens the feminist backlash. As each soldier is assigned her future unit at the course's completion, the assignments provide a saccharine happy ending that does depict women's success (and plays on the film's comic elements) and their future relationship with the army. Shuli is recruited to a military musical troupe, and Niva will serve at the prestigious radio station "Galei Tzahal" (IDF Waves), demonstrating that they have both succeeded in their musical careers. Shirley, who has spent most of the film in the sick bay, is assigned to a medics course; Anna, the Russian who never stopped eating, is being sent to teach sports; Karen, the Canadian who refused to return home, is being sent to a Nahal outpost where she will engage in agricultural work (in a symbol of Zionist spirit); and Galia is sent to an officer training course where we assume she will learn to train her own troop of female recruits. While the conclusion suggests the group's success, the postings reveal the deep-seated issues that remain even in a film that so clearly attempts a feminist agenda. The assignments are prestigious, but none of the women are assigned to combat units. This delimitation of women's roles within the army repeats the patterns established previously, where women serve in symbolically domestic roles in the army, and the patterns established by the musical *The Troupe* and that would again be invoked in *Late Summer Blues*, where ultimately women are shown singing and dancing through war. Nevertheless, despite falling back on the conventions of women's military representation, in many ways the film does offer a feminist reading. It reveals a concerted effort to represent women as empowered subjects in control of their own destinies. Operating in women's worlds, they are able to advance socially and professionally and choose their romantic relationships, which are modeled as socially affirming and empowering. Even the mefakedet ultimately becomes an inspiration and an ally, recruited to the communal cause of female liberation.

By contrast, *Zero Motivation*, which is more openly branded as a feminist film and unlike *Banot* was directed by a woman, subtly and repeatedly undermines women's power and authority. The women, who work in the human resources office on a remote base in the desert, share the patterns seen elsewhere. They are a group of women who despise each other in the main, coming from a wide range of social backgrounds, and include a woman from the kibbutz, Mizrahi women from development towns, and a Russian immigrant. The women's duties include making coffee and serving it at the morning briefings, where they are ogled by the male senior staffers. Their jobs are framed as fetching, ordering, and providing paperwork for the male soldiers. This parodies the expectation that women's military duty is to serve the male soldiers, reenacting the expectations of women as helpmates and sexual fodder. Their inefficiency and unreliability and their supervisor's own failure to act with dignity and authority undermine the notion that there is a glass ceiling for women's professional roles in the army and instead suggest that these women cannot be trusted to serve in more senior or important roles.

The mefakedet is an angry, pushy supervisor who lacks the respect both of her unit and of the other unit supervisors, who are all male. She is inefficient, ineffective, and represented as highly masculine and ultimately as extremely unattractive. This effect is emphasized by her physical bulk and stature as she towers over the diminutive conscripts, who seem infantilized by the tasks they perform and the task master who instructs them. The lethargy, laziness, and inefficiency that dominate her office, the constant computer games that the women play in order to avoid working, the squalid kitchen with its dirty dishes, and the lack of discipline undermine not only the mefakedet's credibility but also that of the women themselves. Ultimately the mefakedet fails to receive her long-awaited promotion and is instead discharged from the army, which she had anticipated would be a lifelong career. Yet when she protests that this decision is because she is a woman, the commanding officer points out that it was a woman who received the promotion she was refused, thereby emphasizing that sex is not a barrier to advancement, merely inefficiency and incompetence. The images of powerful female leaders, including Golda Meir and Margaret Thatcher, that line the walls of the mefakedet's office seem less aspirational than parody. Her leaving speech ultimately embodies this mockery and her own lack of intelligence. She quotes Kafka on bureaucracy, and while his words are a satire on the futility and ignominy of bureaucratic offices, she reads Kafka as a celebration of the importance of her work, but in the middle she is cut short by an urgent call, and the male officers file out of the room to return to the more important business of war.

The power politics of the film repeatedly reinforce the concept of women's failure, and Daffi—the only conscript to advance professionally and to become an officer—does so in order

Zero Motivation: Rama (Shani Klein) the *"mefakedet"* stands with Daffi (Nelly Tagar) as they appeal to Boaz, the base commander.

to escape the desert hole to which she has been assigned, yet upon receiving her orders she is sent back to replace the mefakedet on the base she had tried so hard to escape. It is only after a crisis in which her friend Zohar is ultimately imprisoned that she is demoted and sent to work as a secretary in the country's center, where she had long sought to be based. Even there she continues to complain, and the film ends on her ridiculous and ultimately futile appeals to the authorities for alternative conditions, including an office that is free of the afternoon sun.

The representation of women's experience of the military is shown in two pivotal story lines that might offer a feminist reading of the film. In the first, a woman comes to the base masquerading as a soldier in order to reach the man who had been her lover when on leave, had promised his undying devotion, and then had gone suddenly silent and disappeared. When confronted (while another woman is hidden under his sheets), he claims that their relationship is over and apologizes for not answering her texts but sees no meaning in her protestations of love. She returns to the dorms and commits suicide. The other women find her in the morning, lying in the bed, having cut herself and bled to death, enacting a prevalent convention of the unit suicide, as seen in *Infiltration* (*Hitganvut Yehidim*, 2010).[28] The representation of the callous, conquering male soldier is a familiar trope in Israeli cinema, and the woman's hysterical and extreme reactions do little other than to imply he was lucky to escape her pathological clutches. Moreover, his new girlfriend is the base psychologist, suggesting that he has no trouble with strong, assertive, or educated women whom he might consider his equal.

In another scene, the film repeats the trope of an attempted rape, a theme that appears not only in *Banot* but also in *The Day We Met* (*Neshika BaMetzah*, 1990), an awkward rape comedy in which senior men on military reserve are paired with young female soldiers in order to catch a rapist. While a successful rape is often linked to prostitutes and women of Mizrahi origins, the attempted but failed rape of Israeli female soldiers serves as a reminder that these women are ultimately soldiers and that the rape of a soldier would be tantamount to an attack on the state. Therefore, the men who attempt to rape the female soldiers are outside of the establishment and particularly the military. In this symbolic role, though the female soldiers remain "vulnerable" women, they are ultimately protected emblematically by the institutions of the state. Hence any attempted rape of a female soldier is represented as unprovoked and ultimately wrong. In *Banot* this role is played by the Mizrahi men, who seem to reject the military and by extension their national obligations, thereby making them social pariahs, while in *The Day We Met* the rapist is a mentally unstable murderer. In both these cases the marginalization of the rapist further emphasizes the female soldier's place within the nation.

In *Zero Motivation*, however, this pattern is challenged. The female soldier standing on guard, rather than in her usual bureaucratic position, propositions and seduces a male soldier visiting the base from the field. She does so as part of her mission to lose her virginity, and thus the aims are clearly stated from the outset for the audience, though not for the soldier, who reads the situation as a sexual proposition, without the context of her innocence. He behaves with gentlemanly kindness and patience, Chopin plays in the background, and they romantically hold hands. It is only when they begin to have sex that he becomes rough, tearing at her clothes and hastily undressing her. Though she calls for him to slow down, she does not explain that she is a virgin. As he moves from lover to attacker the audience's affection for the soldier weakens. Her lack of consent and his aggressive drive establish the problematics of contemporary rape scenes. While she is clearly attacked and therefore appears the victim in the scenario, the context the audience is given, and her apparent teasing behavior previously, leave the audience not entirely unsympathetic to the soldier. His frustration, which is played out in his accusation that if she wanted gentle sex she should have picked a "jobnick" (an office worker) rather than a hungry man just returned from the battlefield, serves to further denigrate her role on the base and aggrandize the notion that he has somehow been mistreated. The ambivalence toward sexual violence here, in feminist terms, can be said to expose the way rape culture in Israel protects soldiers. The attack is stopped when the Russian, possessed by the ghost of the girl who committed suicide, appears waving a gun and threatens the soldier. She forces him to undress and to stand naked and then to simulate sex with a trash can while the women leave. Again the act of emasculation that had characterized the rescue in *Banot* is repeated. However, here the audience rejects the victorious celebration that characterizes the viewing of the rescue in *Banot* and instead feels sympathy for the confused and ultimately sweet male soldier, a sympathy heightened by his comically ridiculous underwear, in bright-patterned silky fabric, his vomiting in the trash can out of fear of the women, and the terror he expresses about not having his gun returned which will lead to his imprisonment. In arming the female soldier when she is on guard duty in the first place, it appears that the normative order of the army itself has been disrupted, and ultimately the film portrays women as a trap for men, thereby undermining their professional credibility and suggesting that they disrupt the very operational frame of army life. At the same time there is an implied feminist rebuke. The man is afraid of being imprisoned for losing his weapon, but is not concerned that he might be imprisoned for attempted rape.

If this film ultimately represents women as lazy and inefficient, with no place within the army, while simultaneously representing a world of women for whom men are marginal and incidental characters, can it be considered a feminist film? While a surface reading of the film and the women within it would certainly push against this possibility, a resistant reading of the film might offer an alternative perspective. If the army may be considered a dominant male rite of passage, in repeating the presence of women in a military context who are neither heroic nor masculine, is the very form of the film questioning a representation of masculinity and the militarization of Israeli culture in its broadest sense? By having female recruits who are so incompetent that one has to have a job invented for her as the office shredder, since operating the shredding machine is about the only skill she can manage at the start of the film, and by highlighting the lack of cleanliness everywhere, the discipline of the army is undermined, while the domestic housewife—a role traditionally ascribed to women—is not substituted in its place. In this reading, each rejection of military orders, each

Zero Motivation: Daffi (Nelly Tagar) imagines her military service in Tel Aviv.

attempt to exert personal wills and desires over the professional environment, and each act of disobedience becomes a form of resistance to the pervasive dominance of Israeli military hegemony and by extension the masculinity of Israeli society.

As Daffi imagines herself walking through Tel Aviv in her army uniform and black stiletto heels, waving her handbag in the air, carefree and happy, the conventions of the military film are radically undermined. She is not wearing the correct uniform, her bag replaces the gun she should be carrying, the landscape is a modern urban scene instead of the military base (in the desert wilderness) or the barrack's office space, and her walk is that of a joyful young woman rather than the military march of the Israeli soldier.

Daffi's hopes for her military service, which boil down to a desire to live away from home and have her own place, and the friendship between Daffi and Zohar, echo the partnering of the two new recruits in *Close to Home*. This film follows two women as they serve in Jerusalem and its environs, collecting the ID cards (and numbers) of Arab-Israeli citizens in Jerusalem or searching and questioning Arab women at border crossings during the suicide bombings of the Second Intifada. Mirit longs to be free of her overprotective parents, who live in the area and to whom she returns every evening. A diligent and earnest soldier, she obeys the rules, and her desire to do her duties actually excludes her from the group camaraderie, which celebrates a continuous misbehavior and a desire to evade the watchful eyes of the mefakedet. By contrast, Smadar lives alone while her mother is overseas, and is an aggressive, disruptive, and rebellious soldier who seeks every opportunity to defy the military orders. She quickly befriends other members of the unit, particularly the seasoned Russian veteran, Julia, who longs to return to Russia to see her boyfriend and uses her duties as time to knit the sweaters she sells to raise money for the trip. As in the other films of this genre, the two ultimately become friends, and Mirit learns to be a sloppy soldier, which lands her in the brig but garners her the acceptance of her peers. The attempt to maintain a feminine quality for the soldiers, even in the face of their homogenizing green uniforms, is shown in the efforts to get haircuts during their break times, the desire for a hat in a store window, the knitting, and the celebratory party on the Russian's discharge.

As with the conventions of the mefakedet, the senior officer responsible for these women is strict and orderly. As in *Banot*, she, too, is seen kissing a man in an alleyway. However, on this occasion the mefakedet is not off duty but supposedly responsible for checking (and supervising) the women patrolling. The incident remains a secret between her and the girls who catch her, and they assume that this complicity will protect them. Instead, she will later send Mirit to prison for a short time for abandoning her post at a hotel security station to dance with a handsome foreign stranger. Yet, at Julia's leaving party the departing soldier says warm words about the mefakedet and gives her a sweater she knitted as a gift, suggesting that the other women also will be reconciled with her by the end of their tour of duty, just as the women in *Banot* were reconciled with Talia, their commanding officer.

Close to Home's conclusion undermines the notion of women's necessary participation in military service. The majority of the women's duties have been to request ID cards of Arab citizens as they pass in the street. The women's frequent refusal to ask for them and their failure to identify Arab citizens are in part a comment on the injustice of profiling Arab citizens. However, the suicide bomb (and the bomber) that the women fail to identify undermine the critique of the stop-and-search police and instead emphasizes the women's incompetence and their failure to carry out orders that are necessary for Israel's protection. Moreover, in the final scene a man refuses to give the women his card and exposes the female soldiers' lack of authority They are unable to compel him, and when the crowd joins in to berate the man for failing to respond to the soldiers' request, the young women are unable to control the crowd or to stop them from invading the space of their investigation. The yelling that ensues cannot be contained, and it continues after the women are on a moped, driving away, with the audience left without a resolution to the encounter. The female soldiers' lack of agency in the situation, and the final scene that suggests they have fled, undermines the heroic elements of standing in battle combating the enemy and highlights their essential powerlessness. Their situation is paralleled with that of the Arab women whom they have repeatedly searched and strip-searched, suggesting that despite the illusion of control the Israeli women have no more power and little agency.

Room 514 plays on many of these same issues of military service. Anna, a Russian-Israeli in the military police charged with investigating military crimes, stumbles upon a unit whose brutality in the West Bank operates against the rules of combat. The film is staged minimally, in muted tones, set almost entirely within room 514, where the investigations take place and where she manages an affair with her soon-to-be-married superior officer, Erez. As with the earlier representations of the mefakedet, she is dressed in a mannish style, her hair is worn in a simple ponytail or braid, she has little sign of makeup, and she wears only stud earrings and a simple chain around her neck. A grey hair at the side of her head suggests that she is a little older and is the only disruption to her otherwise militaristic order. Each time a man walks into the room to be interrogated by her, she disarms him, taking away his weapons and firing magazines, an act of emasculation that the men resent. They habitually question her role, her status, and her right to interrogate them, even assuming that she is the secretary rather than the lead investigator. She repeats a ritual of looking through the files, as if for the first time, and her silence invariably triggers insults from the soldiers. Yet at the moment where they are insulting her role as an investigator serving in the military police rather than in a prestigious combat unit, and accusing her of being unfamiliar with the field of battle, they also refer to her in the masculine plural, evoking her status as a representative of the military institution and denying that she can possess authority as a female. In their eyes her power defeminizes her, since she cannot be both a woman and in command. Despite their attempts to leave, she maintains control in the investigation, eventually solving the case. Her investigative technique includes invading their physical space, offering a sexual element to the proceedings by serving as a temptress, or offering a comforting ear, masquerading as the trustworthy mother figure, thereby creating a false intimacy. These manipulations that depend upon her gender ultimately serve her ends, as the soldiers confess. By playing into the gender stereotypes she is able to achieve professional success and yet undermine the larger project of feminism that combats female stereotypes and forces women to adopt masculine traits in order for their authority to be respected. Simultaneously, she proves that a woman can be in authority.

Outside of the investigations Anna is also represented as powerful in her sexual encounter with her supervisor. She sits astride him, controlling the situation sexually, and later controlling the situation emotionally when she rejects his suggestion that they might be more than just lovers. In a powerfully symbolic gesture that inverts decades of representation (and reality), he fetches her coffee. She even suggests that while she has the courage to do her duty and investigate the case, his cautiousness and fear over the political implications of doing so make him weak and vulnerable. Moreover, she emphasizes that he doesn't have her back and that he has betrayed the rules of military camaraderie by abandoning her in the field. Each of these acts (and charges) serves to undermine traditional symbols of masculinity and at the same time switches the gender roles, with her becoming the aggressive "male" lead to his "vulnerable" female.

Yet, despite all of these different manifestations of her power and authority, which gesture at feminism, her position and status are constantly undermined by the mise-en-scène. The film's opening shot has her crying after she reaches for an informally written letter on paper torn from a notebook. It is only in the final scene that we learn that this moment was her discovery that the soldier she had caught and arrested had committed suicide. However, the imagery preceding the film as a whole sets her up as vulnerable and female. As we will see at the end, the commanding male officer does not cry when he charges her. Similarly, when the first soldier suspects she is the secretary, the audience also is led to assume that this is her role, since she has not displayed any authority up to this point.

During the investigations, her authority is continuously and repeatedly undermined by phone calls from her mother that serve as a repeated motif infantilizing her as she discusses the rent and the gas company bills. These conversations, which frequently take place in Russian, also undermine her role within the Israeli sabra collective. Though all four of the films considered in detail here (*Banot*, *Zero Motivation*, *Close to Home*, and *Room 514*) have a Russian female protagonist, unlike the other characters within the films the Russian women rarely achieve the level of integration and socialization that the military represents. By maintaining a distinct and separate identity, including the reading of Russian literature in *Zero Motivation*, Julia's desire to return to Russia in *Close to Home*, and Anna Sokolova's Russian boyfriend and her refusal to conform to the body stereotypes in *Banot*, their depiction suggests that Russian women remain foreign, and therefore, an unassimilated element. They cannot conform to the expectations of Israeli society, even when they profess loyalty to it by their very act of military service.

In *Room 514*, Anna's Russian identity plays an important role in undermining the audience's confidence in and sympathy for her. Even when she speaks Hebrew to her mother, she does so with a pronounced Russian accent that disappears when she turns back to the suspect in the room. Her hangover also emphasizes a hard-drinking Russian characteristic, playing into stereotypes that are accentuated by her sexual abandon in a contemporary society that often views Russian women as sexually promiscuous and frequently as prostitutes. The Russian language anomaly and cultural behavior simultaneously imply that a Russian woman can be "hard" and serve as a contrast with the absent sabra female, who could never take on such a defeminizing role. This absent Israeli woman is embodied by the commanding officer's fiancée, who is depicted as soft, feminine, and struggling to keep her man. Unlike the hard Russian, she is unable to engage in the level of interrogation required to discover the secrets of her partner's sexual activities.

Anna's dreams about her absent father further compound this image of the abandoned, isolated, and ultimately "un-Israeli" female. Though her dream suggests that she is replacing the father figure with her commanding officer, a symbolic substitution of her personal life with her place within the state, his rejection of this association and ultimately his abandonment of her to the authorities emphasizes the impossibility of such a replacement. Images of her washing her face or sitting alone on a bus also punctuate the investigations, emphasizing her vulnerability and further undermining her credibility. At the end of the investigation, moments before she will receive her final discharge, she finds that she, too, will now be investigated for the officer's suicide. Erez disarms her, and unlike the soldiers at her investigations, she quickly breaks down in tears, returning to the position of the weak and defenseless woman. The general who comes to conduct the investigation himself reminds her she has not served in the field and she cannot know what goes on there, further undermining her status. As he claims at the end, "I know my soldiers. Who are you?"

While the film clearly challenges the very attempts at feminist filmmaking that it in many ways seeks to proffer, it raises an issue seen in *Close to Home* and also in *Invisible* (Michal Aviad, 2011), where a parallel is drawn between women in Israeli society and the Arab-Israeli conflict, specifically the occupation and the subordinate position of Palestinians. As Anna notes, there seem to be two rule books for the army, the code of the unit and the legal code of the army, and these two seem in conflict. While the army stands against the abuse of human rights, in the code of the unit it is acceptable to humiliate Palestinians through violence and bullying, reflecting a lack of honor in the army's behavior. In *Invisible* this is played out through the documentary that Nira (Evgenya Dodina) is editing and the political activism of Lily (Ronit Elkabetz), who is attempting to protect Palestinian olive trees from violent settlers while the police and army stand by, failing to do their duty. This axis of nationalism and gender returns us to the earliest representations of women within the frame of the conflict, in which Jewish women were symbolic of the land and therefore shown to have connections with female Arab peasants, and they were to be protected from the potential miscegenation, probably by rape, of the violent male Arab infiltrator. These feminist films reverse the camera, showing the oppression of women and paralleling it with the oppression of Palestinians. While I reject the simplistic nature of this comparison, I do think that the employment of this trope is part of a broader pattern in feminist filmmaking that challenges the militarization of Israeli society, indicting the occupation for its proliferation into everyday life, affecting the behavior of its men and, by extension, serving to not only disenfranchise women of their rights—by enforcing the dominance of patriarchy—but create a society in which brutality is an acceptable watchword. It is this violence (physical, mental, and verbal) that spills out into women's daily experiences.

While *Banot, Close to Home,* and *Zero Motivation* offer a view of women's worlds, *Room 514* offers an isolated female in a man's world, a woman who can barely survive since she lacks the privileged codes of the masculine military environment. Like films of female assassins (*The Assassin Next Door, The Debt*), *Room 514* is troubled with the role of a woman in such a film. Can she maintain her femininity, serve as a military and national hero, and still stay alive at the close of the film? The challenge of creating a feminist film within this context remains, and avoiding the transectional hierarchies of nationalism and ethnicity offers an alternative route for feminist filmmaking to develop in the future.

These different films all offer women wielding guns, and while the first half of the plot represents the women's heroism, overcoming adversity and their exposure to the brutality of the male military world, in the final calculation these women are unable to assimilate into these societies and to possess the qualities required to succeed beyond the most conventional of support roles. In *Close to Home*, the women abandon their post and flee, and in *Room 514*, Anna's assertion that "I had a mission, and I fulfilled it. I fulfilled it, Sir!" seems little more than a hopeful plea, as she is ultimately stripped of her own weapon, humiliated, and left crying. Rachel Brenner, the female protagonist of *The Debt*, one of three Mossad agents who cross into East Germany in 1965 hunting a Nazi, repeats these trends of female weakness and failure.[29] Ultimately, she is unable to kill the Nazi or bring him to trial in Israel. Her attempts to catch him again decades later will lead to her own death.

The paradigms established by Miki and Shosh, the first a soldier with a clear peace agenda in *The Troupe*, the second a woman who does not serve though her friends do in *Late Summer Blues*, suggest that women are not capable of the military heroism of their male peers and, by extension, can only remain marginal in the national project of creating and defending the State of Israel. Even in the films of the first two decades of the twenty-first century, it seems that though women might carry guns and pretend to occupy the same military roles as men, the endings of the films undermine their capacity to fulfil the role of hero so easily embodied by men. But reading against the grain, one might also argue that a feminist agenda exists in the inactivity of women within the army, an idea that *Zero Motivation* seeks to explore. Can we claim that passivity is a mode of resistance that serves to undermine the dominant male narratives of action, war, and destruction, or do the representations of women in *Banot*, *Zero Motivation*, *Close to Home*, *The Debt*, and *Room 514*, films that present female soldiers with guns, offer a feminist agenda by rewriting the presence of male soldiers on-screen by offering female figures and female experiences of war? Can we say that women in uniform, carrying guns, and in positions of power are ultimately feminist figures, or do these films serve as a smokescreen for female empowerment and instead reinforce the stereotypes of women's failure and the centrality of masculinity with the IDF, ultimately suggesting that men must remain in authority in order to protect women in society, by showing that there is no place in the military for women?

At their best these films display a limited degree of female empowerment, suggesting, as *Banot* does, that women can master the tasks set before them within the limited repertoire of positions afforded to them. But it is more usual to see depictions that show women have no place in the military, since they are not part of (and do not understand) military culture, they have no real authority, and they are incompetent. This circular argument is one in which women are excluded from serving in the kinds of combat units that would give them authority and experience of military culture (in the hegemonic masculine sense in which they are usually denied knowledge of it) and would prove the kind of competence that would give women status. One might imagine a film that could rewrite this circularity by showing women being successful in combat units (which does reflect an avenue of feminist activism in Israel, in which women are fighting for the right to serve as pilots and in other prestigious frontline positions), but there is little likelihood of such a film appearing, since cinema in Israeli society operates within a more generally leftist discourse. Feminist filmmakers are not reinventing the heroic genre of the country's bombastic early years for women but instead operating at a time when film generally takes a liberal position that ultimately critiques the army's enactment of government policies on the occupation of Palestinian territories and discrimination against Arab citizens in Israel. Thus films aspiring to feminist credentials are usually directed at critiquing the treatment of Palestinians and the military hegemony, highlighting the institutionalization of male violence and demonstrating women's social marginalization from spheres of influence in which the army becomes a metaphor for Israeli society more broadly. As a result, there is no space in which an Israeli film can successfully make a claim for women's equal participation within these male-dominated spheres. If, as these films show, women can have no real political or military influence and only peripheral roles within the army, then these films will continue to reaffirm women's marginalized place within the conflict.

2

Women in the Home Guard

Religion, Ethnicity, and Sexuality

4

"A Woman of Worth"
Who Sees the Religious Woman?

The move to represent women in traditionally female-gendered spaces nodded at feminist engagement in Israeli film. Concerned by the patriarchal treatment of women within the religious community, Amos Gitai atempted to showcase the female voice in his film *Kadosh*, which would be the first of several Israeli films that sought to penetrate into this private world. Made by secular male directors, these films used the representation of religious women to challenge the androcentrism they perceived as an inherent part of the Ultra-Orthodox (*Haredi*) community. Deeming the treatment of women intolerant and abusive, the directors sought to expose the mistreatment they considered a by-product of religious limitations on women's education, dress, and comportment. These films share two major themes: the repression of sexuality, which informs the control of women while manifesting as deviance or perversion among men; and the separation of women through a process Dan Chyutin has referred to as *mehitzah*.[1] For filmmakers who seek to penetrate women's domains, these segregated female spaces have proved captivating, particularly those that remain traditionally exclusive to the religious community and are usually concealed from the male gaze.

In turn, the religious community, which had been making films for its own viewing and adhering to strict social codes to do so, has begun to make mainstream films that hit back against what they deem prejudicial representations of the religious world. Instead, they showcase the strengths of the community model, and through affirmative depictions of prayer and religious observance strike at the secularism driving the mainstream cinematic community. By contrast to the *Haredim*, whose monochrome uniform and black skullcaps mark them as other in the public space, the modern Orthodox Jewish community, delineated by its modern but conservative garb, married women's more liberal interpretations of head coverings, and men's knitted or leather skullcaps, are generally more integrated into Israeli society. Independently, this community has also become the subject of films and television series; however, these focus on the normalization of religious life within Israeli society and often address political issues. Thus the othering of the *Haredi* community stands in contrast to the ways in which the Orthodox community is treated on-screen.

Despite the filmmakers' often publicly articulated intentions to liberate and empower women and to offer feminist agendas, Lubin's contention that a film may reinforce negative representations of women or subvert such representations through the manner in which the film constructs the diegesis and mise-en-scène that was integral in considering the representation of women in the military in the previous chapter also serves as a frame for viewing the representation of women within films about and by the religious community.[2] Thus this chapter considers the limitations of avowedly feminist mainstream filmmaking in representing the Ultra-Orthodox and Orthodox communities in Israeli cinema.

Controlling a Woman: Religious Rules

One of the most powerful axes of social division within Israel, the differences between the secular and religious communities often overshadow domestic politics, and the religious parties have played significant roles in the right-wing government coalitions that have dominated the Israeli government since the 1990s. Regularly, they head several ministries, including religious affairs, social-welfare, housing, and education. In a society with no civil marriage or divorce, the religious establishment also maintains control over these institutions. Many of the most personal areas of people's day-to-day lives are controlled by those with a vested interest in maintaining a Jewish (and religious) system.[3] Though the Ultra-Orthodox may live separately, they cannot be viewed as marginal, and their influence on the lives of secular Jews is significant. Because they refuse military service, reject Hebrew culture, and are a significant drain on the welfare state (leading many in the secular community to deem them wastrels), and because they disavow Israel (many groups within the Ultra-Orthodox community in Israel are anti-Zionist), secular society resents the religious community. This hostility is evident in cinematic explorations that frequently depict *Haredi* religious observance as fanatical, oppressive, misogynistic, and at odds with modernization. A number of critical films, including *Eyes Wide Open* (*'Eynaim Petukhot*, Haim Tabakman, 2009), *The Wanderer, My Father My Lord* (*Hofshat Kaitz*, David Volach, 2007), and *The Secrets*, have attacked *Haredi* insularity and traditionalism.

In an effort to overcome the prejudice of secular filmmakers such as Gitai and rehabilitate the religious establishment on the screen, there have been several different responses within the filmmaking industry in Israel. The Avi Chai Foundation encouraged the "Jewish" content of filmmaking by offering funding opportunities that ultimately resulted in more positive representations of the *Haredi* community. Galeet Dardashti, who researched the organization's influence on television, noted that "In line with Avi Chai's self-proclaimed goals of encouraging those of the Jewish faith toward greater commitment to Jewish practice, observance, and lifestyle, and encouraging mutual understanding and sensitivity among Jews of different religious backgrounds, the foundation has invested millions of dollars in 'informal Jewish study'" in Israel.[4] These efforts took place in two primary ways within the television and film industry: through long-standing seminars that were specifically for writers and directors, which often led to workshopping cultural products that would appear later; and by providing funding (which came with editorial input in the early stages). The Avi Chai Foundation provided 20 percent of the television budget for approved programming, a significant input in an industry that receives almost no government funding (unlike film), and partnered with the Gesher Film Fund, whose own agenda was to increase the representation of diversity in Israeli productions. The combination of "education" and funds created a climate change in the representation of religious-secular relations and the diversity of religious characters on the screen, establishing previously unseen complexity and disavowing the kind of stereotypes upon which *Kadosh* had drawn. As Dardashti showed, the foundation's influence can be seen in the high viewer ratings its sponsored television shows achieved and the numerous coveted awards they received from the Israeli Academy of Film and Television.[5]

The Avi Chai Foundation generated a paradigm shift that opened up the kinds of representations of Orthodox Jews that were possible. The creation of *Srugim*, the hugely popular television series about twentysomething Orthodox Jews living in Jerusalem, which received no funding from Avi Chai, which at the time was still focused on religious-secular interactions, came about in an environment that was not only tolerant but actively interested in considering religious and political diversity within a community once viewed by the secular television establishment as monolithic, impenetrable, oppressive, and dull.

Moreover, the religious community no longer relied on the secular world for its depiction. *Haredi* filmmaking broke out into the mainstream from its previous cultural insularity, changing views of the society through positive, if at times fairy-tale-like, narratives. While there has been a rich *Haredi* film industry since the early 1980s, the films remain exclusively available and screened within the community. The targeted audiences for screenings are split by gender. Consequently, what is deemed appropriate for male and female audiences is different, resulting in two distinct categories. Men's films are more risqué, dealing with action and adventure (that crosses into political territory). These historically have been purchased on video and now are purchased through DVD and streaming options.[6] In a culture in which owning a television is frequently frowned upon, the viewing of these films within the home space is regarded as illicit, but evidently it is viewed as less problematic than allowing *Haredim* access to non-*Haredi*-sanctioned films. Though these films were imagined for a male audience, their screening within the privacy of a home space suggests that other members of the family may also view them. By contrast, films that are expressly made for female audiences are generally more conservative, and their screening takes place in public venues, usually rented for the occasion during the intermediate days of festivals such as Passover and Succot. They avoid male and female characters on-screen together, usually feature exclusively female casts, and are screened to an exclusively female audience. Sanctioned by the rabbis (censorship takes place at every stage), these films are permitted only if they obey strict *Haredi* rules. They may not show characters in immodest dress, "men and women may never be shown together on screen; plotlines considered subversive or counter to *Haredi* beliefs are forbidden; and when the credits roll, the audience must have a lesson or moral to take home."[7] The recent creation of the mainstream films *Ushpizin* and *Fill the Void* by newly religious *Haredim* who had previously trained in the secular film industry utilized the language of secular cinema (in imagery, cinematography, story lines, and character relationships) to create positive depictions of the faithful. Made under rabbinical supervision, like the more commercial films made intracommunity, these intercommunity films are careful not to transgress many of the social and religious codes, so as to ensure that the filmmakers retain approval, while they simultaneously serve a religious agenda that presents the Ultra-Orthodox way of life as attractive, warm, and rewarding.

Shuli Rand *Ushpizin*'s scriptwriter, and Rama Burshtein, who wrote and directed *Fill the Void*, both trained at secular institutions before they became religious. However, the newly created Ma'aleh school for religious filmmaking is educating a generation of writers, actors, directors, producers, and technicians interested in making films about the religious community within its own cultural language and strictures. "With a mostly religious student base, the school teaches students to shoot films that explore their Jewish heritage, challenging the secular media monopoly. Ma'aleh's graduates, in particular, seek to produce media content that addresses Jewish issues in complex ways."[8] The teachers and curriculum observe the rules of the religious community and do not show scenes of graphic sex or improper behavior in class; however, the school's library does maintain an extensive collection of uncensored films, and students who wish to avail themselves may do so. While the school is mainly directed at the Orthodox community, it is having an effect on both the *Haredi* and the secular film industries through public screenings at festivals, through screenings on television stations, and by virtue of the awards they are winning, particularly in short and documentary categories. Nor do the films exclusively tackle religious subject matter or persons. Recent graduates include Nurith Cohn and Emanuel Cohn, Shira Gabay, Tehila Raanan, Anat Zuria, Hava Deevon (Srugim), Lihi Sabag, and Hadar Freidlich.[9] Their works include television productions, student films, and feature films, including comedy, documentaries, and shorts, and have been nominated for awards at several international film festivals.

By contrast to the Ultra-Orthodox, who live apart, the Orthodox community is more assimilated into modern secular society, and its members are viewed as strongly Zionist. Through the *Hesder* program Orthodox men combine religious study and military service, and many Orthodox women do national service. Orthodox Jews are integrated into all aspects of civil society and participate in the larger political parties, as well as special-interest parties that have been included in government coalitions. Frequently viewed as politically right wing, particularly for their involvement with the settler movement, religious Zionists are subject to criticism from the secular Left but in general have had more control over their depiction in television and cinema. The television series *Srugim* and the film *Campfire* were made by members of the Orthodox community and offered complex characterizations that crossed ethnic and social lines and critically explored social and political issues. Over the course of its three seasons (2008–2010), *Srugim* was notable for its consideration of topics previously considered taboo subjects within this community, such as homosexuality and the pressures to conform to a heteronormative society, the settler movement, the challenge feminism poses to the Orthodox community's traditionalism, and the lure of the secular world. It also considered the social trappings of the religious world, which remains attractive even for those who have ignored its praxis, demonstrated in portrayals of the *datlash* (an acronym for the formerly religious: dati le-she-avar) who continue to be involved in the social orbits of the community even when their religious practice no longer adheres to the community's standards.[10]

Underpinning any discussion of films about and by the religious community in Israel are the values that preserve the religious way of life, which depends on the separation between holy and profane, sacred and material. Though both men and women have religious obligations, in the language of cinema this metonymy has been reduced to the male obligations to fulfill two commandments: to have children and to study religious law. In order to facilitate these obligations, women are expected to bear children and in the *Haredi* community to liberate men of responsibility for providing an income or maintaining a home. While in other cultures women's employment outside the home is a sign of female empowerment and, conversely, "in the context of religion and tradition . . . the inclusion of a woman in the male working environment"[11] denotes social disorder and disruption, within Israeli cinema the requirement to work outside the home is conceived as yet another burden upon the religious woman, particularly as these women are depicted in low-paid employment within the community.

The separation between men and women serves as an extension of the need to preserve order within the religious world and acts as a form of control that perpetuates the system. The separate education of men and women exemplifies the culture's strictures. Men study in a yeshiva using primary religious texts and are encouraged to engage in analytical discussions through the *chavruta* system (a traditional form of learning that pairs two students to work through a text together), while women studying in a *midrasha* (woman's seminary) are generally given parsed religious sources or secondary texts that provide instruction rather than encouraging independent critical engagement with the texts.[12] Before marriage, religious women are expected to preserve their modesty (through dress, speech, hairstyles, and behavior) to heighten their eligibility for marriage.[13] With their marriages arranged by matchmakers, women may have the opportunity to reject a proposal, but the compliance advocated by the society and the negative reputation she will incur for refusing too many suitors suggests that women have few choices in choosing their spouse. After marriage, women are expected to continue to preserve their modesty publicly in the ways they had previously and also to cover their hair (either with an approved head covering or with a wig, depending on sectarian rules) and to observe the laws of family purity that include rituals of washing and purification following bloody vaginal emissions. These rules govern the contact between husbands and wives, obliging women to attend the *mikveh* (ritual bath) after menstruation before they may be touched by their husbands. This places the burden of fertility upon women, who publicly reveal their failure to be pregnant each month that they appear at the baths. Secular filmmakers demonstrate the subtle codes that maintain the social order by representing women's limited access to traditional texts and sources of knowledge—the source of power within these communities; by demonstrating women's limited agency in such areas as having a husband chosen for them, often without their explicit consent; by portraying the objectification of women through the monitoring of modesty and *mikveh*; and by demonstrating the blame attributed to women (even when unfounded) for unions that fail to produce issue. Commonly, these films show even more extreme forms of social control by representing sexual, physical, and emotional violence.

Generally these films share aesthetic sensibilities, depicting the religious world in monochromatic tones or limited palates, often representing it as a dark place of shadows and silence. Soundtracks are sparse and rarely use music. This oppressive environment is frequently depicted in bare, minimalistic, and impoverished interiors. Exteriors are usually derelict and desolate urban spaces, also shown in muted light. The cinematic language of the films focuses on the ways in which the community is constantly watched and constantly watches others in order to maintain its rigorous rules, shown in static scenes and tightly cropped shots. Male and female interactions are limited, even within marriage, and dialogue is sparse and purposeful, while lacunae in communication convey alienation and isolation. This solitary world with its oppressive and repressive rules breeds a culture that is aberrant, turning its rage into violence against women. *Kadosh* and *The Wanderer* exemplify these cinematic conventions and the secular filmmakers' view of the religious community as an oppressive and patriarchal culture that disenfranchises women of basic rights, is woefully behind the times, exists in poverty (often at the expense of the taxpayer), and is hostile to other Jews outside of the *Haredi* community.

Kadosh and *the Wanderer*: Male Violence, Female Subjugation

As Shai Ginsburg has argued in reference to *Kadosh*, among secular filmmakers, "Jewish religious life . . . is perceived as nothing but oppressive and repressive, and the only possibility open to characters who wish to be true to themselves and realize their aspirations is to shed its yoke altogether."[14] *Kadosh* offers a marriage destroyed by the community's zeal for reproduction within a limited range of options. Meir and Rivka are forced to divorce after ten years of marriage because they have not had a child. Mocked by his compatriots at the yeshiva for his ongoing barrenness and believing he has sinned in not fulfilling the commandment to have children, Meir feels compelled to leave his wife and take a new woman in the hope of rectifying this situation. The *mikveh* attendant offers the religious view that the cause of barrenness lies with the wife, whose infertility is a punishment for sinning by failing to observe the laws of family purity correctly. Hence, according to this reasoning, it is Rivka's fault that the marriage fails. Meir's father clarifies the religious view of women's roles and responsibilities: "You know that the only task of a daughter of Israel is to bring children into the world. To give birth to Jews and enable her husband to study." In this rhetorical frame, fertility is a woman's responsibility, along with liberating her husband for the religious study that, in turn, will hasten the coming of the Messiah. At the yeshiva, increased political agitation toward overthrowing the secular government and eradicating the nonobservant Jews in Israel in order to hasten a messianic age links the community's social and political needs with the importance of bearing children. With the community engaged in this political war that is fueled by growing demographic power, in failing to give birth Rivka not only prevents Meir from fulfilling the biblical commandment but also thwarts the entire community.

The motif of her sterility symbolizes her social and personal erasure, as exemplified by the letter she receives that warns her, "A women without a child is no better than dead," citing traditional religious sources.[15] This link between barrenness and death has a long history within Jewish liturgy and signifies women's failure to fulfil their purpose. Rivka's humiliating interrogation at the hands of the *mikveh* attendant, who is also her mother, and later from the gynecologist she visits, establishes barrenness as her responsibility, constructing the social conventions within religious discourse. These social conventions are then inverted to reveal their hypocrisy when it emerges that it is not she who is the cause of the couple's failure to have children. Gitai implies through the doctor that Meir is unable and unwilling to be examined and to undergo fertility treatment with his wife. Thus Rivka's rejection and abandonment by her loving husband for the sake of the firstborn male child that his own father demands, and that he will never have with his second wife, demonstrates both the hypocrisy of the community and the ignorance behind allowing this to be a cause of women's subjugation.

Abandoned and banished, Rivka, lying on her bed, begins, after a long period of silence, to recite the prayer for childbirth. This descent into madness signifies her destruction by the community. Through her increasing silence, insanity, and finally death Gitai's attack supposedly argues for the women's rights he sees as destroyed by the religious world. Yet, at the same time, his representation of Rivka reveals that at a deeper level she becomes a sexually illicit fantasy for a secular male gaze interested in the exposure of the previously concealed woman. Reading the film through Laura Mulvey's contention in "Visual Pleasure and Narrative Cinema" that women are gazed upon in voyeuristic fascination by a male audience (or one trained to think in male ways about women's bodies) establishes Rivka's availability as potential sexual gratification. At the same time she symbolizes male castration, as her empowered sexual liberation destabilizes the strictures of the religious community. The symbolic role that Rivka plays as a woman within a patriarchal culture positions her as "signifier for the male other, bound by a symbolic order in which man can live out his phantasies and obsessions through linguistic command by imposing them on the silent image of woman still tied to her place as bearer of meaning, not maker of meaning."[16] Gitai ritualizes this annihilation of woman's identity in his repeated offering of Rivka as an erotic thrill, not only when she engages in sexual acts with her husband but also in her nakedness at the *mikveh* (though she is somewhat concealed by the water) and later as she begins to undress alone, slowly and sensuously feeling her own body and touching her breast. Though her exposure is shot from side angles, the increasing tension, heightened by her husband's rejection, situates the audience as the voyeur in these scenes of her nudity. Rivka, with her back to the camera, slowly begins to strip as the audience watches her in the mirror, even as she watches herself. The scene offers a voyeuristic and scopophilic gaze that fetishizes the religious woman's body, which is otherwise hidden from view.[17] Jyoti Sarah Daniels has addressed the film's treatment of the female body as a "source for impurity (represented in the mikveh ritual), the sexualized female body as seen through hair and clothing conventions and a woman's only worth located in motherhood, in which the themes of motherhood, impurity, and sexuality coalesce."[18] She further argues that "through Gitai's portrayals of Hasidic life, the viewer is being shown and told that the female and feminine are conceptualized as impure, profane and sexual in Hasidism," thereby emphasizing the role of women as subordinate beings.[19] Gitai's claim that by looking Rivka is empowered, since this is one of the few times when Rivka ever looks directly at herself or others, owes more to an artistic history of audiences leering at women undressed at the toilette than it does to an empowering female conceptualization of womanhood.[20] For a woman whose gaze is generally directed down and away from her husband, this suggestion of her secret and hidden sexuality becomes a fantasy for the (male gazing) audience, which is offered the religious woman's otherwise masked sexual desires.

Rivka's exposed leg is the catalyst in enticing her husband to their marriage bed. After undressing her, Meir removes her hair from its covering, further suggesting not only her disrobing but symbolically the very "temptation" that must be hidden in the traditional Jewish world and that seems to the secular world a further degree of oppression. In the scene's final shot she sits up, alone and isolated. As the film progresses, Rivka's attempts to lure her husband into a further repetition of this act are rejected. Though there is no religious prohibition on sex in marriage, Meir's anxiety over their lack of children engenders the act as a sin. Cast out by her husband, Rivka stops speaking and becomes entirely isolated, living alone in a single room. Despite being remarried, Meir comes to Rivka in a drunken stupor, kneeling on the floor by her bed. The implication that even in divorce she remains available to him is implied by his appearance in her room, though she is clearly shocked by his presence. Finally she goes to him, again exposing herself and hidden parts of her body, such as her thigh, and lies with him. In the morning when he awakes, she is dead. These associative connections with her white nightgown, *mikveh* immersion, and madness evoke a Western tradition of depicting female suicides after women have been driven to madness for unrequited love. Characterized by innocence and virginity, these allusions suggest a male violence against a chaste woman through psychological means. The Victorian visual representation of this female state is captured in the pre-Raphaelite's romanticized imagery in works such as Sir John Everett Millais's painting of Shakespeare's Ophelia and John William Waterhouse's painting of Alfred Lord Tennyson's poem about the Lady of Shallot.

Rivka's sister Malka, by comparison, does not wish to be married at all. She is in love with Yaacov, who has been cast out by the community. Adopting a more politically liberal position, Yaacov wishes to exist as a religious Jew within the secular world symbolized by his military service—a flash point in *Haredi*-secular relations in Israel. This participation in the state and the implied desire to support Israel's existence is contrasted with the sect's secret plans to overthrow the government. The gendered experiences of members of the Ultra-Orthodox community can be seen in the difference between Yaacov's and Malka's reactions to the community's strictures. Though Yaacov has some agency even as it comes at a great price, Malka is always a victim. At the wedding ceremony for her arranged marriage to Yossef, she looks pained under the chuppah, and her groom never looks in her direction, and afterward they celebrate separately, he with the men and she with the women. Immediately after the ceremony she cuts off her own hair in the mirror while crying, symbolically surrendering her feminine identity in an act of self-castration. Dressed in a Victorian nightgown with the blanket pulled up to her neck, Malka appears terrified as she awaits her wedding night.

Kadosh: At her wedding Malka (Meital Barda) is ignored by her groom.

Kadosh: Malka (Meital Barda) at the mirror on her wedding night.

Yossef, with a few short, formulaic sentences, begins his sexual conquest. He launches himself on her without affection or tenderness, bucking repeatedly while she cries out in pain. Her suffering in marriage is juxtaposed with that of Rivka as the scene cuts away to the bedroom she shares with Meir, where the couple, in separate beds, is not talking. Gitai suggests that women are disempowered and suffer alone within marriage.

The constantly suppressed emotional violence that increasingly characterizes Rivka and Meir's relationship, shown in repeated bed scenes in which they are isolated and at meals where they barely communicate, is aggravated in Malka and Yossef's relationship. Malka's declaration that "I can't stay here anymore, I'm suffocating, I'm suffocating" leads her to hunt for Yaacov in a bar late at night where she removes her head covering publicly and then engages in the first sexually positive and fulfilling act within the film. Though Yossef is ignorant of what has happened, Malka's defiance by leaving the marital home without his permission leads him to violence. He removes his belt and begins to strike her, pushing her nightdress into her face aggressively and forcing her onto the bed. Though she is beaten offscreen, the audience can hear the sounds of the belt whipping her and his cries of "slut!" Gitai's attempt to empower the women on the screen by highlighting their oppression falls short. Instead, it exposes both Rivka's nakedness and Malka's beating as a voyeuristic pleasure for a male audience, whose members can both consume the women's bodies and celebrate their own imagined sexual gratification while reveling in the religious males' impotence.

The Wanderer (Avishai Sivan, 2010), a coming-of-age story about Isaac, an Ultra-Orthodox youth who lives in a world of isolation and silence in which he is unable to form meaningful connections with others, becomes a meditation on the religious man's reproductive obligations and his suppressed sexual urges. His diagnosis with kidney stones leads to the discovery of a potential issue with sterility. This, in turn, signals his sexual awakening as he realizes both the possibility of not fulfilling his reproductive obligation and, in time, the physicality of women. The gendered hierarchy in this film is played out through the relationship between Isaac's parents, and is one he later comes to repeat. In an early scene in which his mother comes to his bedside while he writhes in pain, the appearance of his father causes his mother to look down and away, a position in which she sits frozen for several minutes. As with *Kadosh*, the religious woman makes no eye contact and has little agency, and though it appears that in a former time the couple were not religious and the mother was a police officer, as a religious woman she has become subservient. The emotional and sexual disconnection between the parents is repeatedly portrayed: they nap in separate rooms (he on the bed, she on the sofa); they do not speak to one another; and when they engage in sexual relations, Isaac, standing outside, hears the violent, brutal, animalistic noises, and then, moments later, his mother appears fully dressed and walks out of the bedroom door. The only on-screen engagement between mother and father occurs when Isaac's mother speaks out to her husband in order to defend her son. The father immediately leaves the table, demonstrating his displeasure. Her outspoken act is a disruption of the normative order.

Isaac's growing sexuality is first triggered by his illness, and he is asked to give a sperm sample, after which the film becomes increasingly occupied with his emerging sexual identity and future marriage. At first, unable to give the sample, he is given a "magazine aid." At the bus stop moments later he begins to see immodestly dressed women everywhere as they rapidly fill the screen. On his wandering he sees a religious girl who is smoking with some other religious boys, and later he takes her for ice cream. The girl's social engagement with the boys is outside the bounds of usual social behavior (both for smoking and for doing so alone with the opposite sex) and thus marks her as improper and therefore potentially sexually available. Though at first Isaac seems innocent, the increasing information about sex strips him of his innocence and feeds his increasingly aggressive libido. When Eliezer, one of the boys smoking, asks Isaac to buy them condoms, it opens up the possibility that others are also having sexual relations. Moments later, having bought the condoms, Isaac meets Eliezer's sister. The sexual implications are part of the material symbol of the condom. Later, they meet again by chance at the hospital, where she is a nurse, and she becomes the object and focus of his lustful desire. Finding her alone, he violently grabs her and forces her to kiss him until she can escape from his grip. Visibly shaken, he runs home and showers, vigorously scrubbing himself, only to go out again hunting for new prey. As with *Kadosh*, women come to represent dangerous seduction, impurity, and contamination. By washing Isaac can free himself of the sin of sexual desire, but until this lust is satiated he will continue to be tempted because, in the film's language, women provoke uncontrollable passion in men and are therefore guilty, while men have no responsibility for controlling their wants.

The film's sexual tension builds through a series of scenes, such as Isaac's attack of Eliezer's sister. He repeatedly imagines and desires immodestly clad women, and Eliezer's sister's modest dress cannot protect her from what has become his lascivious gaze toward all women. Moreover, her modesty is contrasted with his consuming nakedness, exemplified in his operation, during which he is laid out naked except for a small white sheet, with his arms stretched out in a Christ-like pose. This scene not only becomes suggestive of Isaac's role as martyr to *Haredi* sexual attitudes but also foreshadows his encounter with a prostitute, whom he propositions for sex without a condom, evoking the image of Christ's salvation by Mary Magdalene. The old whore refuses and begins to scream at him, and her pimp chases him with a knife. He walks away, only to encounter a drunk woman who gets out of a cab and vomits. Barely able to stand, she accepts Isaac's help to her apartment. But rather than using this as an opportunity for his own redemption, instead, when she passes out on the bed, he strips her and then rapes her. She wakes up and fights him, but he violently holds her down and covers her mouth. The camera, positioned above the rape, places the audience at a vantage point by which they become complicit in the woman's violent attack. As her pants and underpants are stripped off, Isaac moves out of shot, leaving the viewer positioned over her in the role of attacker. Later, as she is held down while he bucks violently, holding her hands and later her mouth, we are given a voyeuristic position in which to watch the scene take place.

The Wanderer accentuates many of the cinematic conventions used in *Kadosh*, offering tunnels, shadowy spaces, and a desolate and impoverished world, accentuated by a soundtrack that is made up almost entirely of traffic noises with minimal dialogue to disrupt this oppressive isolation. The overall impression of imprisonment and sexual degradation address an alienated *Haredi* world, creating a constant atmosphere of negativity and sadness. As in *Kadosh*, there is no redemption within the religious world, a place that fosters a deviant attitude toward male-female relations and toward sexual relations. Woman's reproductive inadequacy becomes the source of anger and angst for the religious male and his society more broadly. In turn, measures must be employed to control a woman's behavior, firstly to ensure she fulfils her duty to her husband—that is, bearing children and working to enable him to study—and secondly to prevent the wantonness that exists beneath her modest exterior, which will erupt at any moment where it is allowed to be uncontained. If the first reflects the social structures that exist to perpetuate the religious model, then the second reveals the ideological underpinnings that operate to sustain the need for these structures. Moreover, since the obligation ultimately lies with the women, who must protect themselves and their good name, these films establish the religious male as their direct enemy—one with absolute power. Yet he, too, is constrained by the repressive regime of the Orthodox world and, exasperated, sexually and emotionally frustrated, and suffering under a threat of ostracism from the community, is unable to contain the sexual impulses that are otherwise denied him. Thus these films depict religious men exploding violently, beating the religious woman into submission or raping the nonreligious woman. Chyutin considers these films as a genre whose "texts imagine observant women to be not only the principal victims of Israeli-Judaic reality, but also its primary challengers. Their challenge is seen as originating from a desire for sexual exploration—a desire that is deemed natural and thus inherently in conflict with Judaism's artificial laws of sexual management. Accordingly, these works place their characters on a collision course with Judaism's power structures, a process that ultimately necessitates they abandon their religiosity or live in painful tension with it."[21] Echoing the problematics of Turkish cinema by which attempts at feminist filmmaking remain trapped within hegemonic patriarchal structures that ultimately offer women only death or an alternative male presence to that of the oppressive religious regime, these films reveal patriarchy's entrenchment within Israeli society. While the secular filmmakers attempt to strike at this oppression, they are no less free of the bias in secular society that they view within the religious world. The deviance these films offer is ultimately realized in acts of unremitting violence from which women can escape only through death.

Ushpizin, Fill the Void: Reclaiming the Jewish Woman

If *Kadosh* and *The Wanderer* typify secular ideas about *Haredim*, then *Ushpizin* and *Fill the Void* offer a contrasting vision from within the religious community. They offer a celebration of religious life that is exemplified in the rich, warm palette of colors in which the scenes are shot and the richly decorated interiors and vibrant fabrics that embrace the viewer. While *Ushpizin* plays into a folkist narrative reminiscent of a Chagall painting and characteristic of the modes of Yiddish fables, celebrating the traditionalism (and conventionalism) that is part and parcel of the ways secular audiences view the religious community through Hassidic fairy tales, *Fill the Void* rejects this pastoral image and creates a film that challenges many of the stereotypes in representations of the religious community, focusing particularly on the kindness present in social interactions and the diversity that exists between individuals.

These films appeared on the back of several television series that sought to reshape the representations of religious women while operating within a religious context. These included the eight-episode 2006 miniseries *Merhak Negiah*, which attempted to penetrate the mysteries of the religious world and offer up positive representations that explicated the allure of religious life. The female characters in *Merhak Negiah* are presented as inspirational figures within the Ultra-Orthodox community, showing independent spirit, intelligent thought, and freedom of movement and holding the respect of the male characters on-screen, while at the same time obeying the rules regarding modesty and women's roles within the family, serving their domestic and marital duties, showing faith in God, and obeying Jewish laws. Rejecting the assumed toleration of domestic violence within the religious community, one story line explicitly condemns an abusive new husband. The serial's portrayal of religious and secular Jews interacting and sharing language (Yiddish), interests (plum brandy), and friendship attempted to break down many of the stereotypes that represented *Haredi* Jews as isolationist. Moreover, the affectionate interactions between the Ultra-Orthodox husband and wife would become staples in representing the religious community positively. The films that would follow, made by the religious establishment, did not transgress the taboos of religious society by questioning women's equality, for example; however, they worked hard to challenge the representation of negative characteristics of the society, both those that were real and those represented cinematically, such as physical and sexual abuse, as well as social violence more broadly.

Like *Kadosh*, *Ushpizin* portrays a principal couple, Moshe and Mali, struggling with infertility. The first breakthrough film from the religious community, Rand's *Ushpizin* bridges the divisions between the secular and religious worlds and represents the latter in a positive light. Addressing many of the prejudices the religious community faces, through the prop of the husband's former friends, ex-convicts who appeal for help and shelter during the festival of Succot—known for its injunction to welcome guests—the film demonstrates the secular world's ignorance about religious tradition, and the exploitative nature that underpins secular values. The religious world is offered as a place of hope, kindness, and charity. Despite the couple's poverty, their personal difficulties in having a child, and the threat that they must part if they are unable to produce issue soon, the couple open their home to the convicts and also display numerous instances of pleasure and happiness, both alone and when with one another. The demonstration of great affection and tenderness is revealed in shots and reverse shots. Men and women look directly at one another and talk to each other, and the husband brings his wife earrings as a gift. The narrative frame of the film posits the strength of their communication as the source of their marital happiness, which ultimately allows them to transcend their many difficulties. Maintaining their faith and working together, by the happy ending of the film they have overcome their poverty and are anticipating the birth of their first child.

Using religious actors (Shuli and Michal Rand, who were themselves a married couple at the time), *Ushpizin* benefited from insight into the community that was marketed as verisimilitude. The film thereby appeared to offer an authentic portrayal of the religious world. That it did so by evoking a Jewish repertoire of nostalgia made it palatable for a secular audience trained to enjoy the warmth and idealism of the religious world only when removed from a realist tradition. By remaining within the social codes of the religious community, the film passed the censorship of the religious authorities while reaching a wider nonreligious audience, ultimately playing in the international arena to much acclaim.[22]

Kadosh and *Ushpizin* both depict the Orthodox world, and both focus on a central childless couple, where the men are forced to choose between their wives (whom they love) and a religious edict that calls on them to divorce their wives in order to fulfil the commandment to "be fruitful and multiply." Yet, as Ginsburg argues, while *Ushpizin* reveals the presence of God in everyday life, and the love the couple shares brings them closer to God (and to a love of God), enabling them to "overcome the obstacles life puts in their way," *Kadosh* depicts a cold world, "without grace, a world in which the edicts of the Halakha, Jewish Law, are a synonym for paternalistic chauvinism used to control and subordinate women."[23] Gitai's treatment of scopophilic fetishization in *Kadosh* did little to empower women; instead, it presented religious women as consumable, sexually available to a devouring cinematic gaze. In *Ushpizin* the shots that follow Mali position the camera at eye line, placing her in a position of equality, neither subservient to the viewer nor reified in an oedipal act of mother love. Employing Mary Anne Doane's notion that a woman's body is always written and encoded but can only be reclaimed by feminist filmmaking through an act of demystification that rewrites the representation of woman on-screen, *Ushpizin* can be seen to deconstruct many of the conventions that had become established in negative portrayals of the religious community, and particularly the stripping gaze of the male spectator.[24] Yet, *Ushpizin* never seeks to challenge the domestic placement of Mali, and ultimately reinscribes the religious woman within the traditional strictures of a patriarchal community. Similarly, *Fill the Void* positions religious women within the domestic fold, even as it challenges stereotypes of coldness and isolation within the *Haredi* community. Though the film carefully adheres to the many religious strictures of filmmaking that are characteristic of the religious community's industry, it seeks to open a view of this world to an international audience, with many of the lead characters played by secular actors. Moreover, the film was directed by Rama Burshtein, a religious woman who had previously made several woman's films for the religious community and used this as a vehicle with which to create "art" rather than simply "entertainment." The agenda of religious feminism may be different from the classical articulations of second-wave feminism, though religious feminists may still be concerned with these issues. However, "there is a trend in Orthodoxy that seeks to change the way their communities think about and 'do' gender."[25] The participation in cinematic culture reflects an expression of this activism. The content of the films offers another, by providing a space in which to consider the issues that specifically face women within the Orthodox community.

In *Fill the Void*, though eighteen-year-old Shira is preparing for her arranged betrothal, plans are halted when Esti, her elder sister, dies in childbirth, leaving her parents bereft. Yochai, Esti's widower, considers remarrying and taking his son to Belgium, but Shira's mother works to arrange a match between him and her younger daughter in order to keep the child close. The film traces the growing passion between the two, while never crossing the boundaries of propriety or aggressively challenging the religious social codes. The warmth, love, and

Fill the Void: Shira (Hadas Yaron) plays the accordion.

affection between all the members of the family and the extended family, as shown in the visit by Yochai's mother to Shira's mother and even in the visit for approval with the rabbi of the community, offer a positive portrait of the community. In this world rich in a full range of emotions, including joy, sadness, frustration, indecision, excitement, and disappointment, we see complexity and multidimensional characters. Shira is offered at least some part in the decision-making process, and ultimately it is her visit to the rabbi and the note that she gives him that leads to permission for the betrothal. Despite many constraints, it is her agency that drives the plot to its romantic conclusion. Thus the story's universalism works to normalize the Ultra-Orthodox community.

As with *A Touch Away* (*Merhak Negiah*, 2006), Shira's female friends reflect a variety of personalities and experiences, a fact that allows her to shine as an individual without having to serve as the sole representative of the community. In addition, her accordion playing, which is used to entertain the children, comfort the baby, and allow the expression of her emotional turmoil through her music, facilitates her depiction as a multifaceted character. The presence of the baby, around which elements of the story revolve, also challenges the preoccupation with barrenness that has frequently framed the religious woman's identity.

Religious Jewish feminism has carved out a space that "reinterprets religious strictures in a positive feminism such as regarding modesty-regulated spaces as an opportunity for women to 'express and strengthen a self-conscious identity,'[26] or by expanding the purview of modesty to all members of the community."[27] Shira serves as a paradigmatic example of Ultra-Orthodox feminism, since she models correct behavior while simultaneously demonstrating independent will. The perception of *Haredi* feminism outside the framework of the *Haredi* community is problematic. The Ultra-Orthodox community predicates its defense of the treatment of women in its community with an equal-but-different logic. This way of thinking is characterized in a *Forward* op-ed titled "How Orthodoxy Is Most Feminist Faith," in which the director of public affairs for Agudath Israel states, "There are, to be sure, clear roles for the sexes in traditional Jewish life. Men study Torah and are expected to attend services (and be caring husbands); women best express their femininity as mothers and caregivers (and caring wives). But the average Haredi husband loves and values his wife. And, increasingly, it seems, is dependent on her income." Secular feminists consider these kinds of arguments apologetics. They assume a gendered inequality that plays out in ways that directly affect women, such as denying women positions on religious courts that govern marriage and divorce law and therefore favor men. In addition, arguing that women working demonstrates the society's feminist bent ignores a reality in which many men do not work, thereby obligating women to take on these responsibilities for fear of destitution. Nor do women breadwinners have increased capital within the community's institutions. Nevertheless, as with other feminisms, it is appropriate to consider the ways in which *Haredi* feminism operates within the internal mechanisms of its own society.[28]

The formation of B'Zhutan (IN THEIR OWN MERIT) in 2015, the first Ultra-Orthodox female political party, occurred in response to the refusal of the two Ultra Orthodox parties, Shas and United Torah Judaism, to allow women candidates.[29] In a community that has forbidden women to hold public office, the party is considered radical, and its founders have faced threats (including excommunication) by religious authorities. *Fill The Void*, and more generally the creation of strong female leads by the *Haredi* community, even trapped within a traditional world, reflects a transformation within the society and demonstrates the infiltration of feminist values retranslated into an Orthodox culture.

Even the storyline might be seen as a religious feminist gesture to recover a form of equality within a religious discourse through an allusion recognizable to religious viewers. Yibbum (Levirate marriage) is a biblical law according to which a man must marry his brother's widow if she has no issue. *Fill the Void* inverts this plot by having Shira marry her sister's widower. In this way the plot recovers a female reading of religious law. Despite the film's feminist intentions, the very realism that drives the scenic representations and seeks to positively portray the religious world also depicts the *mehitzah* that enforces women's silence and marginalization within the phallocentric culture in which women remain a disruptive and sexually problematic force. Women sit at meals silently while the men sing (as women are not permitted to raise their voices in song), they inhabit the balcony in the synagogue while the men occupy the main floor, and all the positions of authority in the film are held by men. Though women can ultimately use soft power in order to manipulate situations and demonstrate some control over their lives, they do so within the constraints of a well-established and fixed androcentric society. As much as these films work to represent women positively within this society, they do not, and cannot—due to the influence of rabbis on the making of these films (in order to gain approval within their society)—challenge this normative order. Though they can find ways to show women's subjectivity, they ultimately cannot stop women from being objects within the limitations of the society itself. The religious community, which fails to deal with women's negative social experiences and lack of power within religious areas, even over their own bodies, nevertheless protects the woman from exposure to the gaze to which she has been otherwise subject in her portrayal by secular male directors. But in their eagerness to convey women's position within the religious community from their respective ideological positions, these films remain constrained and are unable to offer a challenge to the dominant patriarchal order.

Campfire and Sexual Violence

The assassination of Prime Minister Yitzhak Rabin by Yigal Amir, a religious fanatic who opposed the Israeli-Palestinian peace process as a betrayal of religious Zionist values, coming on the heels of Baruch Goldstein's murder of Muslims in prayer in Hebron, revealed the growing Jewish domestic terrorism in Israel and the West Bank.[30] The preaching of hate toward other Jews and the messianic fervor associated with aspects of the settlers' movement among the Orthodox have radicalized youth, who see a greater Israel as part of a biblical prophecy, settling the West Bank areas of Judea and Samaria (acronym Yesha) by virtue of religious-historical claim to these territories. The Yesha rabbis, "the most important ideological forum, to which the political leadership have become increasingly subservient . . . have issued public statements that governmental decisions which negate the Greater Land of Israel ideology are in contradiction to Torah law and are therefore 'immoral' and not to be observed. As the national religious population has become increasingly fundamentalist in matters of religious observance and ritual in the past two decades, so too the Rabbis have greater influence over the political activities and decisions of the settlers themselves."[31] This extremist element of Jewish Orthodoxy in Israel, characterized by racism, anti-Arab sentiment, and the refusal to obey civil law—claiming religious interpretations that supersede it—differs from the *Haredi* community in its fixation with extreme forms of nationalism.

Joseph Cedar, on the political left of Orthodox Judaism, began to make films that critiqued the social and ideological values of the community that had shaped and galvanized the violent activists. His first film, *Time of Favor*, which follows *Hesder* soldiers who combine military service with yeshiva study, was based on real incidents in which some of the leading rabbis within Yesha, including Meir Kahane, pitted themselves against the government and through vitriolic language incited their followers to violence. The first examples of this Jewish terrorism occurred with a group called the Jewish Underground (*Makhteret*). led by several influential rabbis, which operated between 1979 and 1984. They conducted a series of attacks against Palestinian figures within the West Bank and had plans to bomb the Dome of the Rock that were eventually foiled by the Israeli authorities. Many members of the group were eventually imprisoned, but only for a relatively short period, and then most returned to their previous communities, where they continued to preach for a Greater Israel. They were among those who would later escalate the incitement by religious Zionists and groups of alienated Mizrahi Jews who were against the government's efforts in the peace process of the early 1990s, whose goals included the establishment of an independent Palestinian State and the assigning of Yesha territory to it. This fanaticism has been attributed as the root cause of Yigal Amir's assassination of Prime Minister Yitzhak Rabin.

Cedar's film considered the ways in which the venomous rhetoric that underpins rabbinic teachings in the settler movement serves to inspire Jewish religious fundamentalism. A desire to impress the rabbi's daughter motivates a small group of radicals to plan an attack against the Muslim holy sites built on top of the Temple Mount by planting a bomb in underground tunnels. Cedar reinterprets secular Israeli masculinity and its cinematic tropes of military service, leadership, and *kibbush* (conquering and subduing the land) through a religious lens, revealing the internalization of Israeli expectations, even as they come to challenge the secularity that originally underpinned them. The daughter, around whom most of the film's story lines revolve, symbolizes the men's commitment to religion (as the daughter of the rabbi), to the settlement project (where she lives in the community her father established), and to the national homeland (as the woman who must be protected and defended). Even as she forms the pivotal center of the entire film, she is a passive site for the rebels' projections. Only in her romantic relationship is she offered any agency, and as such highlights the film's repetition of secular conventions by which women serve to inspire male heroism and national projects, but in which women qua women are ultimately marginalized in the larger issues of national destiny.

Cedar's second film, *Campfire* (2004), explores the creation of a new settlement from the perspective of a widow and her two daughters. Rachel Gerlick is ideologically committed to the settlement project and longs to be included in the pilot group (*garin*) founding the new community in Samaria (West Bank). With her two daughters, Tami and Esti, she hopes to begin afresh, unconstrained by the social limitations facing a household with no men in a society that devalues women's economic and social independence. Her early attempts to conform to the social expectations of the new collective fail, as her family encounters increasing isolation, marginalization, and silencing by the Orthodox community that ultimately alienates them from the settlement project. Cedar's film uses the Gerlick women as a vessel by which to critique the patriarchal hegemony within the Zionist religious community and the settlement project, and offers them as a catalyst for exposing the racism and prejudice of the movement toward other Jews and toward Palestinians. The shameful treatment of women in the film is paralleled and equated with the settlers' dishonorable conduct more broadly, and the women serve as a symbol that can be substituted for other symbols, such as Mizrahi or Arab, in order to highlight the inequities of religious Zionist culture and the settlement project. Yet, despite its apparent critique of the religious Zionist community, the film's frame and mise-en-scène reinforce a patriarchal discourse that supposes women's conformity to the social norms, and their marginalization and exclusion if they deviate from such expectations.

Campfire: Rachel Gerlick (Michaela Eshet) and her daughters Tami (Hani Furstenberg) and Esti (Maya Maron) sit discussing the deception required to sell the family car.

The opening shot establishes the film's feminist agenda and simultaneously undermines it. The camera follows Esti's movements in the kitchen to the table where her mother and sister are seated, taking a position outside of the kitchen, framing the family scene with the ceiling, walls, and windows, reflecting the subjectivity of the women on the screen and controlling the audience's gaze, thereby offering them as objects within the film. As the women discuss plans to sell the father's car, devising a ruse about his well-being and whereabouts for potential clients who refuse to deal with women, the film complicates a feminist reading. Though there are three women present, it is the absent male who remains the dominant force able to negotiate economically for the family, while the women's presence is established as marginal and powerless (as will be later confirmed when the buyers refuse to do business with the women). Both the camera's positioning and the opening scene's narrative establish a pattern that at once seeks to empower women and ultimately undermines them.

Rachel's story follows her attempts to persuade Motke and Shula, the husband and wife who head up the new settlement, to accept her application to join. A highly conformist group, the religious Zionists are parodied in a montage of almost identical interviews held by Motke. The couples dress similarly, with the women in high-necked clothing and long sleeves, representing their modesty and religious obedience, and the men appearing to wear *kippot*, showing their religious devotion. Slight differences, such as one woman's American accent, are erased in the uniformity of their behavior, signified in the auditioning couples' recurring response to the question "Who do you think should be included in the group?" with the repetition of the refrain "People like us." By contrast to this Noah's ark pairing, Rachel is interviewed alone, and she disrupts the homogeny of the group with her answer "People like you." Without a man by her side, she is considered a waste of the settlement's limited resources because she cannot serve in a religious quorum (minyan) and cannot (according to Motke) do guard duty. This twist on the Zionist pioneering rhetoric of working the land and defending it reimagines the national mission in a religious light.[32] Motke's patriarchal attitude is evident in his dismissive "keep up the good work" at the end of Rachel's interview, and Esti, who hates the entire enterprise, argues that "they treated us as though we were lepers or something."

Without the presence of a man, the Gerlick family is isolated and unprotected within the social conventions established in the diegesis. Despite her relatively recent bereavement, Shula will attempt to return Rachel to the fold by offering her Yossi, the virginal bus driver, and later the aggrandizing cantor Moshe Weinstock, as potential husbands. Cedar highlights the community's hypocrisy in Shula's enthusiasm for Moshe, despite his unsuitability for the settlement enterprise, shown in his sneering distaste for the projected site: "No one told me there would be cows here." Moshe, just by virtue of the fact that he is male, is more desirable as a pioneer in the community's eyes than Rachel, who is passionate about the landscape and the rural enterprise and committed to the work it will take to build the new settlement. Shula and Motke's devotion to finding Rachel a husband in order to reestablish the normality of a nuclear family and the presence of male authority within the home demonstrates social normativity. Yet, it becomes rapidly clear that Rachel never loved her first husband, a fact indicated by the daughters' conversation and later in her confession to Yossi, and thus the illusion of the successful marriage unit is undermined, further highlighting its social role, rather than its romantic or domestic one.

The highly sexualized treatment of the three women of the Gerlick family implies that a woman unmarried is wild and unregulated; she must be returned to the stability of the norm by whatever means are necessary. Rachel's sexuality is subtle and develops over the course of the film, awakened in her growing affection for Yossi. By contrast, her daughter Esti's unseemly sexuality pushes at Rachel's own views of acceptable behavior—demonstrating her underlying tendency toward conformity. Esti uses sexual suggestion to attack her mother in an act of teenage rebellion. Declaring that she will not join the settlement, she tells her mother that instead she will become a prostitute and live on the streets. Playing into the paradigm of virgin or whore, Cedar exposes the community's greatest fear: the violated virginity of its women. At the same time, the lack of a male authority figure within the women's domestic arrangements suggests that Esti's behavior is a result of the unregulated family space, which can only be modified through the presence of a man.

Esti's implied sexual liberation plays into the religious community's notion of *marat ayin*, the idea that one must guard against seeming impropriety lest one raise suspicion that one has actually transgressed the religious laws. By declaring her willingness to become a prostitute, even though the statement is made in jest, she opens up the possibility that she is sexually promiscuous. Thus, when she invites a boy into her bedroom and locks the door, the audience, like her mother, is encouraged to assume that she is involved in a sexual relationship. This effect is further exaggerated by his suspicious behavior in sneaking out of the room in the middle of the night. In response, as part of her attempt to regain control of the family reputation and limit her daughter's disreputable behavior, Rachel smashes the glass window in Esti's bedroom door, thereby preventing any illusion of privacy, of course with the intention of preventing her daughter repeating the act. In response, Esti refuses to talk to her mother and continues meeting with her young soldier in the building's basement. This story line foreshadows later incidents within the film in which the women's reputations are quickly compromised with scant evidence, and is a ploy that Cedar uses to reveal the ways in which reputation can be easily compromised within the religious community. He also draws on the cinematic conventions by which women live under constant scrutiny in a society obsessed with watching one another to prevent religious infringements and maintain obedience. It is only much later in the film that the audience, through the mother's voyeurism, sees that Esti's teenage groping is relatively innocent.

Tamar appears at first more innocent than her sister and mother, but the constant taunts of Tamar by her peer group are also highly sexualized. Dancing alone in the living room, she performs a wild and seductive routine that involves her gazing at herself in the mirror and striking sexually exaggerated poses. Later, at the bonfire, the boys are being sexually vulgar and in order to fit in she participates by telling a joke of a sexual nature. Though the scene is cut away and we never see the joke's final punch line, we imagine that she tells it.

The opening of the film, which offered the family's attempt to sell the car and be accepted into the settlement project, and Esti's sexual rebuke cut away to a confessional voiceover with accompanying music (which has not appeared previously) that reframes the film and is repeated at the end. In this voiceover Tamar declares, "this year I decided no matter what the price that I was going to be happy," a statement that places her experiences at the center of the film, and it is her sexual abuse by her male peers, a group of teenage boys at a Bnei Akiva (religious youth movement) bonfire celebration for Lag Ba'Omer that serves as the film's climax. Tamar is pushed to the ground and smothered by the older boy, who forces his kisses on her. When she stands up in shock and tries to turn away, he grabs her and starts to squeeze her breast. As he holds his hand over her mouth so she cannot scream or escape, she looks violently shocked and somewhat bewildered by the experience. Rather than letting her go, the older boy forces her to touch his penis, and then those of the other boys. The scene is cut away, and the next shot presents her coming home early in the morning. The incompleteness of the joke, like the semi-observation of the sexual act, implies not uncertainty but confirmation that it took place.

Motke and Shula's son spies the girl's attack, but rather than either trying to help her or rushing to call others he walks away. Later, he uses her assumed "complicity" to stage his own attack in caves at the settlement. This crisis will provide the watershed between the first half of the film, which establishes the women's lives, their broken relationships with one another, and the battle to be accepted within the community, and the second half, in which the women are isolated by the community but draw closer to one another, creating a sisterhood of female friendship and trust. The women's isolated status, shown in Rachel's marginalization, in the taunts Tami experiences from boys in the street, and in the expectation that the family will be able to fulfill Rachel's ideological dream only if she remarries, sets the film's themes.

While Tamar's sexual attack, which remains an abyss at the heart of the film, establishes the hypocrisy, violence, and male-controlled social codes that regulate the religious Zionist community, ultimately the treatment of the attack within the film offers a problematic representation for a feminist discourse. Tamar is deeply shaken by the experience. Despite the display of sexual violence, which the audience experiences viscerally in the scene's cinematic tension, within Tamar's community the reaction is different. Not only do the children (and to some degree Motke) imply that Tamar was complicit in the act but she is increasingly accused of culpability for it. Represented as a prostitute, signified by the elder boys shoving money in her pocket and later the graffiti that appears on the walls of the town claiming that "Tamar Gerlick is a whore," she is represented as the cause of the sin and portrayed as the destructive temptation that corrupts the boys' innocence. Even as the original incident comes to light, the boys are never admonished, and the event is passed off by Motke in a racist slur as the work of Mizrahi boys. His bigoted response fails to recognize or acknowledge his own son's complicity in the initial attack and his responsibility for a subsequent attempt to repeat the assault.

The positioning of women as sexual objects, reflected in the act of abuse and the responses to it, is also explored in the film's camera work. The issues of privacy and exposure, which form a repeated motif in the film, are reflected through the gaze of the camera's lens and reflect the characters' own gazing. The women are framed in the opening shots, the community watches the women (an ongoing fear of Rachel's is that she or her daughters will be seen to transgress), Rachel breaks her daughter's window to make sure that she can watch her, later she watches her daughter's fondling through the broken window of the basement door, Esti watches Tamar dancing, and the boys watch the women passing. Thus Cedar suggests that in the religious community no space is private and no area is too intimate to brook involvement or interference. Lubin has shown that in Israeli cinema, "Whether under the penetrating gaze of the man in the film, the male viewer in the audience, or the male camera/director on the set, the woman becomes a thing, a displayed object to be used. This is the dominant mechanism through which the cinema marginalizes women as the Other."[33] Despite Cedar's apparent critical stance, the suppression of the abuse and Tamar's silence undermine his attempts to denounce the religious community. Rather than suggesting her liberation, Tamar's silence presents a masculine fantasy whereby the act of rape goes unpunished. In Tamar's confrontation with Rafi that led to the initial attack, her offer of friendship and not rebuke not only situates her as a victim but further establishes her as expendable within the male-controlled religious community. Notwithstanding a weak attempt to represent agency in offering her proud gaze as she walks along the path (which forces the other boys to turn their heads in shame), twisting the conventions of gaze that have recurred throughout the film, the audience is left unsatisfied, believing justice has not been served.

Tamar's empowered gaze is linked to her repetition of the confessional statement that "This year no matter what I had decided to be happy," which brackets the film's narrative. Historically, the role of confession, which has played a prominent position in the Christian world, offered the confessor the opportunity to expose his or her sins in order to receive absolution. A trope common in nineteenth-century literature, confession came to represent an exposure of feeling and experience in a secular sphere through an emotional and psychological study of human drives. *Confessions of an English Opium Eater* by Thomas De Quincy and *The Private Memoirs and Confessions of a Justified Sinner* by James Hogg, which explores religious fanaticism, are examples of this style. The Jewish form of confession, the *viddui*, is a formulaic recitation of sins, recited in private or as part of the prayer service on the high holy days (*ashamnu bagadnu*). Bearing witness to sins has come to be viewed as a way to give testimony in the Christian tradition, which is associated with a process of coming to know God and functions as a form of proselytization whereby through the transformation that the individual has experienced he or she bears witness to God's (and Jesus's) work on earth. By contrast, testimony in Jewish tradition means bearing witness in a court of law to legal matters. More recently, in secular Jewish culture the term has become associated with victims of the Holocaust and their witnessing of the horrors for a public audience. Captured on film through projects like Claude Lanzmann's *Shoah* and Steven Spielberg's Holocaust Archives, these testimonies frame the emotional experience of bearing witness as a Jewish obligation to past and future generations. This form of confession articulates a human responsibility toward mankind rather than the *viddui*, which articulates a personal connection between man and God. Consequently, confession is then associated with trauma and abuse and the narrativization of these experiences on-screen. Tamar's abuse in the frame of the confessional statement becomes a comment on society's complicity in women's abuse. And Motke's son, who as the son of the *garin* leader represents the group's patriarchal authority, not only witnesses Tamar's abuse but does not stop it. In addition, when alone with Tamar at the site of the future settlement, he attempts to repeat Tamar's sexual trauma and physically attacks her.

Cedar's use of Tamar's voice can be seen in the philosophical frame of Rousseau's idea of confession that people should be tested on the strength of their feeling. Taking this to the extreme, the film posits the possibility that events should not be judged by an external moralistic observer but only according to the framing given through the feelings of the confessor. When Tamar claims that she intended to be happy no matter what, and she is not traumatized by her experiences, we, the audience, are expected to accept her silence as an indication that she has moved past the events. This is a highly misogynistic reading of the film's text—in which if the woman doesn't mind being raped then there should be no consequences for the perpetrator(s). A resistant reading of the film, framed within feminist discourse that offers the possibility of alternative understandings, could suggest the audience's enraged response to the conspiracy of silence and to the suppression of the girl's horror (which means that the boys are never brought to account or punishment) and the community's collusion in the act of abuse by association and enforced silencing of the Gerlick family, means that the audience is also enraged about the entire community's behavior. Cedar is calling on the audience to become incensed at the religious Zionist's patriarchal utopianism. Moreover, as Cedar has coupled the women's experience with that of the settlement plans, the audience's anger is directed beyond the conspiracy of abuse over one young girl to the West Bank settlements and the absent yet implied abuse of the Palestinian population (again echoing the implied but offstage rape). As Philip Hollander has argued in his analysis of this film, "in *Campfire* [Cedar] again employs gender to comment on conformist pressures within religious Zionism that have bound it too tightly to settlement rather than efforts to transform Israeli society from within the sixty-seven borders."[34] Such a reading of Cedar's efforts would suggest that we, the audience, in not speaking out against the abuse, both of the girl and of the community's settlement expansion, in turn become complicit. In this reading, the director implicates the audience, calling it out for its passivity by not taking action against settlements and against sexual violence. However, the film's idyllic conclusion undermines any such political or feminist statement.

According to Hollander, Rachel chooses Yossi over Moshe, rejecting the pressure to conform, thereby serving "as a role model for her daughters."[35] But as the film fails to resolve the tension of Tamar's silence over her abuse and marginalization, and Rachel's removal of the family from the religious community's settlement project does nothing to destabilize or even disrupt it, such a reading sanctions Cedar's failure to hold the religious Zionist community to account for its discriminatory character. Rachel is marginalized within the group even before she chooses Yossi. Like a sacrificial goat sent out into the wilderness, the process by which the Cohen Hagadol absolved the community's sins following the communal act of confession, the women are offered up as the ultimate and permanent victim of religious Zionism, and in the final scenes when the Gerlicks reject the settlement and are seen driving off in the father's car with Yossi, Rachel exemplifies the extent to which she has been completely excluded and ultimately erased.

Portrayals of women in the religious community in films made and directed by nonreligious male directors reveal a trend. These films use the opportunity of representing religious women as a way of critiquing the patriarchy inherent to religious communities, and frequently explore this subject through the emotional, physical, and sexual abuse of women as part of a larger criticism of the religious community. Cedar, coming from the religious world, attempts to nuance his analysis of this environment, yet I have demonstrated that, despite his attempts, he fails to create a feminist work. Though he successfully compromises the religious Zionist community and attacks the politics of Zionist settlement, particularly the symbolic erasure of Palestinians, he reinforces gender stereotypes about the sexual deviance of women, suggests that women ultimately need a male presence, and inadvertently sanctions the importance of constantly scrutinizing behavior as a way to safeguard women—even if this observation ultimately results in women experiencing greater discrimination rather than community protection.

The Secrets and Bruriah: Knowledge, Sexuality, and the Feminine Mystique

In Cedar's previous film, *Time of Favor*, Michal the rabbi's daughter leaves the settlement in order to explore the possibility of studying in a seminary. The recent interest in representing women's religious education offers a concrete way of representing a feminist standpoint, since so much of religious life is dominated by the study and knowledge of religious law, an area that remains a sphere of male influence and control. *The Secrets* (2007), set in the contemporary period, depicts the inner workings of a women's seminary in Safed through the vehicle of Naomi and her three roommates. The title gestures at the secret world of women and the mysticism of Safed, where the secrets of Kabbalah flourished during the sixteenth century. The highly educated female lead, Naomi, whose knowledge extends beyond that of her peers, has a close relationship with her father, who favors her (by contrast with her sister) by educating her in Jewish law. Her impressive knowledge of Halakha, and the religious scriptures more generally, is roundly acknowledged by her peer group when she joins the seminary after choosing to delay her marriage. In contrast to films like *Kadosh* and *Ushpizin*, which assume women's exclusion from the sources of Jewish education and hence exclusion from the sources of power within the religious community, *The Secrets* adopts a feminist position that posits an equality between men's and women's intellectual ability to engage in Torah study, modeling Naomi as an intellectual, religiously observant woman.

The female "rosh" yeshiva argues that in her youth the *midrasha* (seminary) and its kinds of learning were inconceivable for her generation, and even predicts a future in which women may also be ordained as experts in religious law.[36] Far from establishing educational equality as the norm, through Naomi's boorish fiancé the director presents the conventional religious position, which disapproves of women's education. Played by a well-known comic actor, his preposterous manner and patronizing demeanor make him ridiculous as a grotesque figure, thereby alienating him from the audience and undermining his intellectual views, serving to emphasize his role as a straw man for the Orthodox establishment—at least in the secular imagination. While the film appears to establish positive representations of women's education and to deride those who would stand in its way, the obsession with the female body and purity undermines the more critical intellectual vision of this film.

Anouk (Fanny Ardent), an ailing French woman, is searching for absolution. Believing she has committed grave sins and that she is being punished by God, she reaches out to a rabbi for a way to atone but is rebuffed. After coming across Michelle, the French-speaking and spoiled ingénue of the group, she requests the girls attend her and provide domestic duties (part of their charitable work at the seminary) as a ruse to have them hear her conundrum and provide an answer. The brilliant Naomi studies the religious sources in search of a solution. However, because she is cast as "Baba Naomi," a pseudosaint and spiritual leader, using a title found among those practicing a mystical form of Jewish folk religion, the scholarly nature of her search is undermined by her association with superstition and primitivism. Moreover, as her hunt moves her away from traditional scholarship and into the kabbalistic (mystical), a pursuit that is emphasized by the *midrasha*'s setting in Safed, Naomi's solutions increasingly resemble folk religion, mysticism, and witchcraft. The use of fires, a special *mikveh*, incantations, and sackcloth and the constant and determined need to purge and clean hark back to the imagery in *Kadosh* and Jyoti Daniels's determination that Gitai's film is preoccupied with women's bodies as "defilement, impurity, and profanity."[37] The female body as a source of impurity that is represented in the *mikveh* ritual, the sexualization of the female body "as seen through hair and clothing conventions," and the obsessive association between a woman's worth and her ability to produce issue means that "the themes of motherhood, impurity, and sexuality coalesce."[38] Anouk's abandonment of her two children, her elopement with her artist lover, and her nude artistic modeling in poses of sexual ecstasy establish her as immoral by disrupting each one of these conventions. That her deprivation eventually leads to the artist's death (whether the accidental result of a passionate argument, as Anouk claims, or the murder she is convicted of by the courts) is simply an extension of her already-established wickedness. Her failure as a wife and mother haunts her at the end of her life as she becomes fixated on seeing her children. By contrast with her domestic failures, Naomi and Michelle perform the roles of dutiful women in the care and affection they show her. Determined to see Anouk on her deathbed, despite being forbidden to do so, the two motherless young women adopt the role of daughters, thereby signifying Anouk's forgiveness as she symbolically receives absolution through the guise of the returning children she had once abandoned.

The transformative process that Anouk undergoes is composed of a series of rites that Naomi devises using traditional and mystical sources. But even as these serve to heal Anouk through exorcism, atonement, and purification, Naomi serves as a proxy and ultimately absorbs Anouk's sins. Her dabbling in the mystical leads to Naomi's own awakening—a transformation that will ultimately distance her from the religious society to which she belongs. In a ceremony at which the paintings are burned and the women chant, Anouk will vomit out her defilement (alone and on the sidelines), while Naomi will collapse center stage, supported by the other women attendants. In the *mikveh*, Naomi, in a symbolic act of baptism, will awaken to her own passions, which will increasingly lead to deviant behavior. She dons the sackcloth garment she has made for Anouk to wear, and in a voyeuristic scene in which, lying in her bed, she appears to be in a state of orgasmic ecstasy, she scratches at her own skin until Michelle stops her and proceeds to strip her. Finally, during an incantation ceremony, Sigi, the *ba'alat tshuva* (born-again) member of the dorm, breaks down, leading to Naomi's exposure to the religious authorities. Naomi will later be punished and expelled from the seminary for her defilement of the traditional sources and her corruption of the normative order in which men, and not women, have the capacity to lead penitents to absolution. Unlike the frequent depictions of witchcraft in Israeli cinema that are commonly used to represent marginal ethnic women (Arab, Mizrahi, Russian, and Berber) whereby women draw on folk wisdom for power over the supernatural, examined in the next chapter, Naomi is unusual because she operates from a place of male knowledge, held in the traditional religious sources, a place that she ultimately corrupts.

Naomi's relationship to text and religion is problematic. Her husband-to-be will be a rosh yeshiva like her father, but as she notes, as a child it was she who wanted to be the rosh yeshiva and walked around stroking her chin in emulation of her father's gesture of stroking his beard. Naomi's absent beard, like her misuse of religion, implies that she cannot really be trusted with the learning that she has acquired. Finally, Naomi's ultimate rejection of the normative order comes in her lesbian encounter with Michelle. Writhing in pleasure, they appear to transgress the boundaries of heterosexual Jewish society, only for Michelle to learn that there is nothing forbidden in their love. Here, too, Naomi is able to call on the texts to permit this behavior, with its implied perversity since it fails to fulfill the injunctions of marriage—to produce issue, and thus she undermines the traditional world of her father's scholarship. Their kiss in the night on the rooftop of the seminary is accompanied by the sounds of a jackal howling, suggesting a supernatural deviance and further reinforcing the unnatural element of their union. In the final scene of the film, Naomi attends Michelle's wedding to the unconventional but kind pharmacist-come-klezmer clarinetist, who plays while the two women dance. Harking back to Bat-Adam's *Moments*, in which the union between two women was facilitated through the man's presence, and to Avi Nesher's *Dizengoff 99*, in which the two women's affection is facilitated through a ménage à trois with the male lead, who refuses to commit to a relationship with either woman, the clarinet serves as the phallus that enables the two women to symbolically consummate their forbidden love during their wedding dance. The fulfillment of their love is enabled through the male presence, which simultaneously disrupts the female bond and facilitates it.

Michelle has returned to the fold, and her transgressions remain minimal at best. Her good *shidduch* and conformity to tradition (and desire for that conformity) surprises not only

The Secrets: Michelle (Michal Shtamler) and Naomi (Ania Bukstein) dance ecstatically at Michelle's wedding.

the viewer but Michelle herself. But Naomi, whose intellectual capacity may be seen to lie at the root of the path that they have taken and that ultimately led to their exile from the yeshiva, from her community, and from her family, remains alone. Though she may dance with Michelle, she may not live with her, and though she may study, she has ultimately undermined the feminist project and is excluded from the canon that the radical matriarch is attempting to create within the *midrasha*. Naomi has no place but her own apartment, and her future is uncertain.

The film's effort to create a liberated female space instead fetishizes the naked young female. The preoccupation with sexual explicitness in the film, shown in the full frontal nudity during scenes of the ritual bath, and the lesbian sex between Naomi and Michelle in the dorms expose the women to the male gaze, serving them up as erotica. The representations of deviance undermine many of the film's attempts to represent the women's empowerment, suggesting that those who achieve religious knowledge, demonstrate power, and take on the roles of men will exile themselves from the communities in which they most hope to succeed. At best they may look on from the sidelines, observing the society of which they are no longer a part.

Bruriah similarly tackles women's education and sexual betrayal, yet takes a more consciously intellectual and feminist position. A symbol of the educated and sharp-tongued woman, Bruriah appears several times in the Talmudic cannon as an important and knowledgeable sage. The wife of Tanna Rabbi Meir and the daughter of Rabbi Hananiah ben Teradion, who was burned as a martyr, Bruriah is commended for her wisdom, even being praised for her contributions to halakhic discussions. There have been several meanings ascribed by later commentators to explain Ma'aseh Bruriah, an unexplicated reference in the Talmud, among the most well known of which is the interpretation given by Rashi. He writes that Bruriah mocked the Talmudic injunction that women are light-minded, and as a result Rabbi Meir attempted to entrap her by sending a student to seduce her. Though she resisted at first, she finally succumbed, but when she discovered what had happened, she committed suicide (or possibly became deathly ill), and her husband, out of shame and despair, fled to Babylonia. Other rabbinic sources take issue with Rashi's interpretation, and there is a custom among Orthodox rabbis to name their daughters Bruriah, for her wisdom and righteousness.

The Bruriah of Avraham Kushnir's film is an intelligent and virtuous wife, mother, and daughter. She works in a bookstore, cares for her aging father, and helps her secular hairdresser secure a divorce at the rabbinical courts by trading clothes. The modesty that is a sign of her religious observance is contextualized as a symbol of her goodness, rather than offered as religious hypocrisy or suggestive of her religious ghettoization, and thus she is willing to give up her modest attire in order to protect a woman from a greater religious injustice at the Beit Din, and later dresses as a prostitute to seduce her husband in an effort to remind him that she is faithful. Her clothes deny the oppression implied in other representations of female modesty within films about the religious community. Nor does she have to remove them in order to liberate her sexuality, as with *Kadosh* and *The Secrets*. Bruriah flirts with her husband when dressed modestly at home, when lying together on a blanket at the Jerusalem zoo while their children are playing, and in other appropriate venues.

Her independent thoughts and action, and even her transgressions, manifest as actions for the greater good. Moreover, her intelligence is recognized not only by her husband—for example, he finds her working through a tractate of Talmud in her bedroom—but also by his friends, who welcome her contributions to their study sessions. The film purposefully disrupts the traditional gender conventions of films about the religious community. The husband, Rabbi Yaacov, teaches in a school within the community, while it is the wife who works outside of the religious world. Rabbi Yaacov also takes on domestic tasks: he is seen wearing an apron, sweeps up a plate that he drops, cooks on several occasions, and helps to clear the table, suggesting an equal division of the domestic tasks traditionally ascribed solely to women. The film also complicates the Orthodox/Ultra-Orthodox divisions. While the daughter's school is single sex, the audience that watches the end-of-year performance is mixed, and Rabbi Yaacov defends the presence of men to a concerned colleague. Though Bruriah wears a *sheitel* (wig), and her clothes are modest, she does not appear to fit into the conventional religious world of the Ultra-Orthodox and occasionally her neckline would not meet the additional strictures of that community. Rabbi Yaacov's clothes are not *Haredi*, and though he wears a black *kippah* he teaches in a modern Orthodox high school. It appears that he comes from a *Haredi* background, as indicated by his fluency in Yiddish when he returns to his childhood synagogue to speak to his estranged father. The diegesis suggests Yaacov and Bruriah were born into the *Haredi* world, but their limited acceptance within it since the excommunication of Rabbi Shmuel Halevi and his daughter, Bruriah, and the symbolic exile that Yaakov takes on when he is banished from his father's court for marrying an excommunicated woman, have led them to a more inclusive form of religious observance with greater social tolerance. Thus they are religiously but not socially *Haredi* and have therefore found a place within the modern Orthodox community. This comes with a price. Yaacov and Bruriah's eldest daughter assumes the values of education and egalitarianism of the modern Orthodox community, which increasingly encourages attendance at the kind of *midrasha* that may ultimately lead to a form of female ordination. This social change in modern Orthodox society (reflected in the film) is making it possible for women, within very specific areas, to offer religious rulings (*posek*), thereby displacing the totality of male religious authority over women. While her daughter is looking forward to a new kind of religious future, Bruriah looks to the past, searching for the book her father wrote that was burned by the community for heresy and was the cause of her father's excommunication.

The intertext of "Ma'aseh Bruriah" resonates in the narrative, creating one of the major areas of tension within the film. The attractive new teacher that joins Rabbi Meir's school and becomes a family friend takes on the role of mentee, echoing the student the Talmudic Rabbi Meir sent to tempt his wife into adultery. But the film undermines the audience's anticipation of the classical event, and instead of retelling the story of Bruriah's seduction, the film becomes the story of Meir's redemption. This inversion of the traditional texts reflects the film's outlook, which seeks to confront the stereotypes about women (and men) within the Orthodox world and offer a more complex view of female experience. In turn, it also preserves Bruriah's traditional role as subject rather than object. Ultimately, the story comes to retell the Bruriah narrative, arguing that it is not women who are light-headed and may be seduced but men who are light-headed, since, as his wife, a woman knows exactly how to seduce her husband. Consciously disrupting the gender segregation of the *mikveh* and addressing the sexualized imagery of the naked body descending into water that had become a staple of the religious film, seen not only with *Kadosh* and *The Secrets* but also in male-male relationships in *Eyes Wide Open*, the *mikveh* in *Bruriah* connects the married couple. The *mikveh*'s situation in nature removes many of the stigmatizing elements that depict it as a depressing and imprisoning space in other films. Lying in the water in a wooded area, Yaacov is surprised by his wife, who is dressed seductively and, without being revealed by the camera's gaze, slides into the water to be with him. The shared dip erases the tensions that had existed between them and culminates in the film's climactic explication of the past, in which, unbeknownst to Bruriah, her father was exiled by Yaacov's father.

Ultimately, films about the religious community end up telling simplistic narratives with limited perspective. While the secular filmmaker is removed from the intricacies of the religious community and its own nuanced feminist forms, the religious community is

Bruriah: Yaakov (Baruch Brener) and his wife Bruriah (Hadar Galron) embrace in the *mikveh.*

constrained by the rabbinical oversight that controls the extent to which they can push against the society's boundaries. The popularity of these films within the context of high art may lie in their ability to offer a limited vantage point on a society that is otherwise invisible, but they do so with an agenda that shapes not only the film but the viewer's expectations, often working to reinforce the viewers' own internalized views of this society—negatively (because they have too much control in Israeli society) or positively (because of its charming, folksy lost world of nostalgia). The television serials are more successful in offering a rich and varied take on the religious community because they have multiple characters and multiple story lines across seasons, therefore allowing for differences and making the products less single-issue-based. This has allowed for the representation of diversity and women's subjectivity within the religious community. Ultimately, it is perhaps in this venue that attempts to consider women will make the greatest strides, though, as *Bruriah* shows, it is possible to present a complex depiction of a female character in a multidimensional and sophisticated way that both respects the position of women within the religious world and provides a sensitive and nuanced reading of the feminist issues that face Orthodoxy, and through which women can articulate a dynamic feminist position.

5

Witches and Wailers
Mizrahi Women's Power

Reclaiming a female-centered narrative, particularly associated with domestic spaces, has been a key characteristic of a feminist turn in filmmaking about the Mizrahi community. The coalescence between gender and identity politics in films usually but not exclusively by women filmmakers is fighting against previous representations on multiple fronts. The films attempt to overcome the stereotyping and marginalization of the Mizrahi community and to create an empowered narrative about female experience. This has often taken place through the evocation of nostalgia that displaces the Mizrahi woman from a specific time and an identifiable place. In so doing it has created a new kind of exoticization that depends upon the association of Mizrahi women with primitivism, folk customs, and the passing of ancient knowledge through matriarchal lineage. The Israeli film *My Lovely Sister* (2011), written and directed by Marco Carmel, presents the breakdown of two sisters' relationship as a result of the younger sister's marriage to an Arab. Magical realism becomes the vehicle through which the marginalized position of these women of Moroccan-Jewish origins are able to overcome their differences and resolve their alienation from one another. Breaking down the boundaries of the real world through fantasy is effective precisely because it engages with a population (female and Mizrahi) who fall outside of the hegemonic Israeli framework. Simultaneously, the magical elements feed an orientalist narrative about *Mizrahiut* (Mizrahiness) that places the folktale in a romanticized space, further marginalizing the very population it seeks to bring to the center.

In many ways, *My Lovely Sister* may be considered Israel's first magical realist film. This stylistic tradition, most associated with Latin America (though it has appeared in other literatures) was late to develop in Israeli culture. It first appeared in the mid-1980s in David Grossman's novel *See Under Love*, but, as Robert Alter reminds us, "it is important to keep in mind that any manifestation of fantasy in Hebrew fiction has to be made against the heavy weight of a dominant tradition of intent realism that goes all the way back to Hebrew writing in nineteenth-century Russia."[1] Within Hebrew literature, magical realism has appeared in novels that engage with significant historical moments of the Jewish experience, throwing into sharp relief the extremes of the situation and humanity's capacity to grasp the inconceivable. Grossman's novel layers multiple experiences of the Holocaust. Each of the four sections explores a different manner of engaging with the terror and absurdity of the events of Nazi atrocity, as well as the impact of trauma on the survivors and the generations that followed them. The imaginary Bruno Schultz, who is unassailable and cannot be killed by the bullets fired at him, appears to live in a world of fantasy as wild as his own literary creations. Thus the actual murder of the real Bruno Schultz during the Holocaust disarms the reader while heightening the sense of loss, both of this seemingly gentle, charming, and brilliant man constructed in his parallel fictional form and of the literary genius in the figure of the author who was killed. Similarly, Meir Shalev's novel *Roman Russi* (*The Blue Mountain*, 1988) explores the ways in which the historical narratives of Zionism offer an ordered, rational, and logical framing of the past. This imagined representation of history is at variance with real life in Palestine among the pioneers and serves to challenge the illusionary constructions of the past that have fed the national narrative. Using magical realism offers a way to disrupt constructions of Israel's sense of self.

As with Shalev's novel, the rural idyll serves as the landscape of *My Lovely Sister*, though, unlike the former, which is situated in the lush green valleys of Israel's farming and agricultural landscapes, *the film* is set in an undetermined southern and somewhat barren, desert-like environment. Whereas Shalev's novel presents the early moshavim (farming collectives), the Middle Eastern town evoked in *My Lovely Sister* lies outside of the Zionist national discourse, offering not an ideological landscape but one empty of the nationalist fervor generally associated with Israel's geography. Frederic Jameson's argument that "magical realism now comes to be understood as a kind of narrative raw material derived essentially from peasant society, and drawn in sophisticated ways on the world of village or even tribal myth"[2] certainly pertains to the Israeli form of magical realism, applying to both the green pastures of Shalev's world and that of *My Lovely Sister*. Yet, there is a vast difference between these two Israeli geographical and anthropological landscapes. While Shalev engages with a "white" narrative of Zionist settlement, in *My Lovely Sister,* as with the magical realism of South American literature, in which, as Jean Franco has discussed,[3] race is an inherent part of the origins, this genre's "blackness" is the underlying narrative. The Arab-Jewish element, encapsulated by the desert, the town, and more broadly the film's treatment of race, may be seen as the key to reading this text, as it writes against previously dominant Zionist hierarchies in which Mizrahim were subordinated in the country's political power structures. *My Lovely Sister*'s treatment of color functions within Israeli cinema's already well established handling of the socioeconomic positioning of Mizrahi Jews, who were generally resettled after immigration around the country's periphery in development towns that often lacked agricultural or professional opportunities. This geographical marginalization is part of the larger critique of the way Mizrahim have been treated by the Ashkenazi (white) hegemony.

The film is part of a larger movement of Mizrahi cinema that has engaged in roots journeys, exploring subject matter such as the large waves of Mizrahi immigration to Israel and the first years within the state in order to identify the systematic discrimination and through its fictionalization offer imaginative directions for reclaiming Mizrahis' previously silenced voices.

The arrival of around a million Jews from Arab lands in the first four years after the establishment of the State of Israel (1948) and the subsequent smaller waves over the next decade constituted the Mizrahi population as a physical majority but a social and political minority. The fledgling state attempted to absorb these new immigrants by creating transit camps, known as *ma'abarot*, whose housing consisted of tents and then basic huts with corrugated metal roofs that were ill equipped, often without plumbing. A building frenzy took place, and new towns sprang up, which provided housing (though this was often created with Ashkenazi families with two to three children in mind, rather than the large domestic groups that included many children and extended family members that were characteristic of Mizrahi domestic arrangements). These dwellings were characterized as idyllic and were situated around the periphery of the country, usually near a local factory that would provide work mostly for the male immigrants. This paradigm forms the basic landscape of many films depicting the Mizrahi community and has become a metonym of social, political, and racial inequity.

Social injustice was first represented through the *bourekas* comedies' surreptitious critique of Israeli society's racism in biting satires that exposed the prejudice, discrimination, and conflict between different segments of Jewish Israeli society at a time when literature entirely neglected the Mizrahi figure. The presence of the marginalized Mizrahi in these films, captured in poverty, with limited education, religiously traditionalist, and operating in a patriarchal (and hence highly gendered) society, created two key tropes around the Mizrahi in development towns: isolation and deprivation. The final scene from *Sallah* (1964), as the immigrants are resettled in the new dwellings, typifies the perception the establishment had of the edenic environment, but this view would quickly turn sour when it emerged that these communities were actually isolated and economically dependent on factories that were not locally owned and that therefore held the employees for ransom. These factors had fostered a culture of impoverishment, lack of education or opportunity, and social and geographic marginalization.

Satire served up a double-edged sword of entertainment and criticism that was not always acknowledged either by audiences or by scholars. Since comedic films, particularly in Israel's cinematic heyday of the 1960s and 1970s, were targeted at the lower classes, who often belonged to the ethnically marginalized sectors of Israeli society (Mizrahim) and had generally been housed in Israel's periphery outside its social and political centers, cinema's commentary on Israel's racism was generally directed at an audience personally experiencing this discrimination. "While directed mostly at Mizrahim, the *bourekas* were mainly produced and directed by Ashkenazi filmmakers and often used Ashkenazi actors to play both the roles of Mizrahim and Ashkenazim."[4] Ella Shohat, in *Israeli Cinema: East/West and the Politics of Representation*, has claimed that the Ashkenazi film industry recycled stereotypes about the Mizrahi community, and in so doing diffused and hence marginalized any critique of the establishment.[5]

Nevertheless, filmmakers such as the inordinately successful Ephraim Kishon did create powerful moments within their films in which race, color, and prejudice in Israel were challenged. His most famous film, *Sallah*, won him a Golden Globe and an Oscar nomination despite receiving no funding from the ministry, who deemed his comedy frivolous in contrast to the "serious" films that were funded in this period: films that dealt with "the myth of the war of independence and with personal Ashkenazi dramas (the effects of wars on soldiers and widows, the personal versus the collective in postsocialist Israel)."[6] Through monologues Kishon challenged the racial status quo, though they were discreetly hidden within comedic moments. In *Sallah*, the Mizrahi buffoon title character, of no clearly defined national origin though suggesting something North African, appears lazy, irresponsible, a clown, and a drunk. Yet, as with a Shakespearian fool, his comic utterances conceal his wisdom. Like a naïve child, Sallah Shabbati holds up a mirror to the Israeli establishment, critiquing housing plans, the corruption behind charitable solicitations abroad, the kibbutz movement, and institutionalized racism.

Though *bourekas* films exposed the rifts in Jewish Israeli society, in the final account the reconciliation between disparate groups, often through the medium of a wedding, undermined the harshest of criticisms. Shohat's overly monolithic construction of the *bourekas* genre and the Ashkenazi comedies of Kishon, Zielberg, and Davidson ignores the presence of indigenous filmmaking within the *bourekas* genre inspired by Turkish and Iranian melodramas, such as those of George Ovadiah, which explored the Mizrahi experience of migration, representing the changing fortunes of the Arab-Jew on his journey from exile to Israel. These films focused on the Mizrahi's experiences and the cycles of his fortune without depending on the need to merge with an Ashkenazi world. But while comedies offered positive endings and were considerably more popular than their melodrama counterpoints, it was not until the 1980s that the representation of Mizrahi experience took a more critical look at the long-term results of Zionism for Arab Jews. Nissim Dayan's work, particularly *Light Out of Nowhere* (*Or Min HaHefker*, 1973) and his television series *Michelle Ezra Safra and his Sons* (1983) paved the way, but it was Ram Loevy's television drama *Bread* (*Lehem*, 1986) that evoked the poverty and lack of opportunity for the isolated development town, where crime and violence had become the social currency of those unable to escape. When the only factory in town, and the area's sole employer, closes rather than pay workers a living wage, the town starves to death.

In *Bread*, the once idyllic architecture rises from the barren landscape as a colorless, inorganic blight that as much imprisons the community as houses it. During the 1980s, women in films about these Mizrahi development towns remained marginalized characters, and the plots continued to be driven by male concerns: the factory, political organization, radicalism, crime and punishment, and the need to support a family. Mothers served as ancient domestics, traditional homemakers who rarely spoke. Their daughters, however, in a contradictory

Turn Left at the End of the World: The bus leaves the development town with Nicole (Netta Jarti) while Sarah (Liraz Charhi) looks on while her hope of leaving goes with it.

gesture that implied feminism but really served to critique Mizrahi patriarchy, were offered alternative opportunities through military service or education that would free them of the development town, and by extension the patriarchal traditionalism that bound them. However, these possibilities quickly evaporated when the factory closed or the matriarch died, forcing the young women to return to the domestic fold. Frequently the image of a woman watching the bus leave symbolized her inability to escape and the pitilessly blocked future that awaited her.

The rise of the Israeli Black Panther movement, which first developed in Jerusalem in the 1970s and grew out of contact with the American Black Panthers, indicated ways Mizrahim began to identify their experience of exclusion and racism in terms of the American Black power movements of the 1960s onward. These comparable protest activities gave Mizrahim language and an ideological frame within which to challenge the status quo. Like earlier *bourekas* films, these new films by Israeli directors were responding to this political wave and called attention to the long-term impact of racially motivated urban planning solutions. Films such as *Turn Left at the End of the World* (Avi Nesher, 2004) and *The Band's Visit* (Eran Kolirin, 2007) would repeat this trope of the stagnating Mizrahi existing in an undisclosed barren location, limited economically and socially.

Ashkenazi filmmakers, while critiquing much of the treatment of Mizrahi society by the white establishment, continue to view women as oppressed within Mizrahi patriarchy as previously discussed in reference to Banot. The boom in women's filmmaking during the 1990s, in which films were increasingly made for women (though not necessarily by women), echoed a trend that had been happening in British cinema during the 1980s, with films such as *Educating Rita*, *Shirley Valentine*, and *Truly Madly Deeply*.[7] Israeli filmmakers, like British filmmakers before them, now confronted the conflicts and vicissitudes of contemporary gender relations, foregrounded charismatic and transgressive female protagonists, and offered what were, within the context of mainstream cinema at least, refreshingly radical resolutions to the conflicts they portrayed.[8] Most significantly, as with British cinema, Israeli filmmakers allowed "their respective female protagonists to resist the generically conventional drive towards a reinscriptive and punitive ideological and narrative closure."[9] Instead, they offered the women opportunity for escape, which Justine Ashby has described as:

> a movement through a liminal space, a realm of possibility. Once this threshold has been crossed, once she enters this realm of possibility, the female protagonist is able to remove herself from her initial narrative (and cultural) situation, distance herself from the demands and entrapment of everyday life, and undergo a redefining and re-empowering transformation of identity or rite of passage.[10]

While leaving, and particularly education, offered the Mizrahi woman an alternative and hopeful future, not all endings to these films offered a positive fate. In *The Band's Visit* the departure of the Egyptian Police Band who had accidentally appeared and stayed for the night demonstrates the final impossibility of liberation for the Mizrahim who remain and are imprisoned within a powerful socioeconomic trap.

By the 1990s, a trend had developed in which the Mizrahi family and particularly its women, located in an impoverished and peripheral landscape, served to depict the Oriental experience. "[A]ll of them take place in a vague unidentifiable and nameless geographic space that serves as a background for the deconstruction of the Israeli subject as well as the investigation of the origins of his existential malaise."[11] Shohat's analysis of films of the 1960s and 1970s focused on male protagonists, reflecting the male-driven history of Israeli cinema, but the shift in Israeli filmmaking during the 1990s opened up cinema to a feminist discourse. These films continue to re-create the development town as a place of patriarchy and religious Jewish traditionalism, maintaining many of the political aspects of Israeli cinema in the 1980s such as the television film *Bread*, which had represented these spaces as hopeless, dead-end communities whose poverty, crime, and misery represented Mizrahi marginalization. But they redirected the center of the film from a patriarchal male-driven plot to a matriarchy where the man retained absolute power, but in absentia, while the films focused on the inner lives of women.

These films also depended on the intergenerational split, whereby the immigrant parents belonged to a world of traditionalism while the immigrant children were often divided between the men, who were frequently thuggish and likely to turn to crime, and the women, who were trying to assimilate into the "New Hebrew" culture represented as Ashkenazification (*Lehitashknez*, the Hebrew term for "passing") as a result of education, by leaving the settlements and by abandoning their families. A better life faced those women who succeeded, but women who failed were likely to be portrayed as prostitutes, who were often raped, who were linked to a criminal underworld, who used drugs, and who usually died under tragic circumstances. Both the Mizrahi prostitute and the assimilated woman would continue evolving during filmmaking in the 1990s and the first decade of the twenty-first century, but a new figure of the witch emerged, representing a powerful female subculture of folk religion and mystical power over life, love, sex, and death. At the same time, these films also re-created the intergenerational split present in the 1980s regarding the opportunities available to women. However, they carefully framed this mystical witchcraft in historical films set decades earlier (usually during the 1950s and 1960s) in the heyday of separated Mizrahi culture, which was represented as still impermeable to the threat of Ashkenazification, thereby reframing the Mizrahi as a once-empowered figure whose culture had since been eroded by a process of cultural assimilation.

The nostalgic iconography of these films counters the portrayal of the older generation of women as domestic drudges and instead offers them as powerful matriarchs dominating the home front and possessing powerful secrets that allow them to protect their families in a society in which they are fundamentally powerless. Shemer has claimed that where Mizrahi women face a crisis of intersectionality, they can be empowered as women, whereby "gender considerations overwhelm ethnic ones," or they can exist in "the elaborate context of the ethnic," which negates a feminist positioning.[12] In his formulation, gender and ethnicity override one another rather than intersecting. Moreover, Shemer sees Vivianne's aborted love affair in *To Take a Wife* (*Lakahat Isha*, Ronit and Shlomi Elkabetz, 2004) as the tragedy of star-crossed lovers, disconnecting the scenes of romance with her lover from her violent pleas with her husband, Eliyahu, to divorce her. This first film in the Viviane Amsalem trilogy pits the unhappy Moroccan wife against her religiously observant Moroccan husband within an ethnic community in which unhappy marriages are typical. Albert, the lover, offers Vivianne the prospect of personal fulfillment in their potential elopement, but her happiness comes at a price that includes the loss of her children and a betrayal of religious law. Abandoning her children would betray her identity as mother, a female role whose duties she continues to observe across all three films, thereby refusing to disavow her gendered identity. While Shemer focuses on critical reception of the film that failed to see its ethnic discourse, he fails to address the oppressive religious element (in her husband's refusal to travel on the Sabbath, to eat out, or to get a divorce) at which gender and religion intersect. All three films in the trilogy accentuate a gap between traditionalism, which brings family together, and religious observance, which is a male sphere from which women are fundamentally excluded, remaining powerless and at the whim of male authorities enacting the letter of the law. Vivianne's French-accented name evokes the exoticism of the Orient; her passionate and impassioned behavior treads the line between emotionality with its sexual connotations and hysteria with its risk of madness, and thus she is the embodiment of the sexual, mystical, Oriental object of lust. By contrast, Eliyahu, with his Hebrew name and its religious reference, his tight manner, and his closed outlook, embodies the stilted and unyielding force of an oppressive religious subject, casting formal Judaism as an exclusively male sphere. The film plays out Vivianne's intersectionality in masculine religion's ethnic counterforce—folk wisdom—a female space of knowledge and practice. This trope enacted in grief rituals and witchcraft serves as the paradigmatic exemplar of the Mizrahi female's intersectionality. Rather than selecting a single identity from the options available to a Mizrahi woman, as Shemer suggests, by allying with Mizrahim against Ashkenazim or with women against men, Mizrahi women exist in a space of permanent hybridity. This means not only that the experience of being an ethnic female is inseparable from that of being female and that of being ethnic but that their shared meaning and interpretation produce a specific signification for the Mizrahi woman. These overlapping aspects of gender, ethnicity, and folk religion manifest in the Mizrahi woman's supposed place at the center of major life-cycle events in these films about the Mizrahi community in which her power over life and death, love, sex, and health coalesce into the often overlapping archetypal images of the Mizrahi matriarch as a witch and a funeral wailer. This chapter explores the construction of these two roles and the ways in which the Mizrahi woman is constrained in an imaginary that perpetuates her marginalization.

The Wailer

Shiva (2008), cowritten and directed by Ronit Elkabetz, is the second episode in the Vivianne Amsalem trilogy. While the film continues to track the breakdown of Vivianne and Eliyahu's marriage against the background of traditional Mizrahi patriarchy, its major focus follows the seven days of mourning of seven siblings whose different conflicts are explored during this liminal period in which the normal rules of life are suspended as the mourners (parents, spouses, and siblings) engage in the religious rites. The first three days of this period in the wailing cultures of the Middle East are known as the days of tears, during which time wailers come and offer support to the mourners through rituals of grief that combine the chanting of words and the exposition of grief in ritualistic forms that commemorate the deceased, comfort those grieving, and enable a cathartic release of emotion.

In their countries of origin, male and female mourners did not grieve together, and women's wailing took place in a circle, in which each person participated in the ritual. Often led by an older, postmenopausal woman familiar with the local tune and experienced in crafting poetic and emotional language and encouraging others to do so, wailing served a specific function, not only in commemorating the dead or facilitating the expression of grief but in creating a sense of community. Tova Gamliel, analyzing the mourning culture of Yemen and its transposition into Israel, explains that wailing today takes place in a mixed group and is usually done by a single person known for her expertise in wailing. The drama of formalized mourning through wailing is culturally specific: "The local audience in each wailing culture finds itself immersed in the tension that the emotional imperative of commiseration creates. This is the rule of all wailing and the goal of every performance; it places the wailer at the center of attention. If the wailer does not follow the rules of emotional expression, wailing would presumably lose some of its potential emotional impact and social-political relations would suffer."[13] Wailing is not simply an expression of grief by concerned members of the family but a profession at which certain women excel and are called to a house of mourning to perform in order to create the necessary mood. While "the official purpose of women's funerary lamentations is to honor the dead,"[14] wailing also serves to construct hierarchies of grief and suffering and to signal women's roles within the process. As a tradition it is dying out due to its conflict with contemporary commemoration practices whereby the younger generation views the wailer instrumentally as someone who can facilitate their own personal grief, often finding the wailing, led by a stranger, to be false and insincere. In the Yemenite tradition the words play a central role in the formulation of a lament, while the gestures are small, symbolic, and usually involve covering the face with a handkerchief. Gamliel noted in her fieldwork that Yemenite Jews view other cultures' mourning practices, including the Moroccan practice of wailing, as hysterical due to the wild gesticulations, screeching, and tearing of clothes and hair.[15]

Many Jewish communities have traditions of wailing, but in films the image is almost always restricted to Moroccan Jews. Moreover, in cinema, this mode of commemoration is depicted as particular to female culture and is contrasted with male commemoration rites. As with *To Take a Wife*, in which Shemer sees only gender and not ethnicity, in *Shiva* he sees ethnicity and not the gendered experience of women within the grief culture.[16] Wailing lamentations are performed in Arabic (or the local form of Judeo-Arabic), which denotes them as part of female discourse and thereby demarcates the occasions and locations of wailing as female space. By contrast, men use Judeo-Arabic or French when speaking with women, particularly as women of the older generation rarely use other languages (while the younger generation of women born in Israel almost always prefer modern Hebrew). However, men use religious Hebrew (accented according to the particular nusach [rite] of the origin community) in prayer and ritual, including for mourning customs. Thus, language is used to denote belonging within the wailing culture, showing the older generation's mastery and the younger generation's neglect of this traditional area of women's lives. But it also denotes a gendered hierarchy, as men relegate women's mourning culture to a subsidary position while their own mourning practices takes place within the parameters of Jewish religious law and therefore hold an elevated status within the community structure.

In cinema, the wailing culture is depicted through metonymic tropes that include women with their heads covered, wearing black, waving aggressively, and flapping like crows. In *Shiva* the older women and the daughters flock to the matriarch who has lost her son, wailing

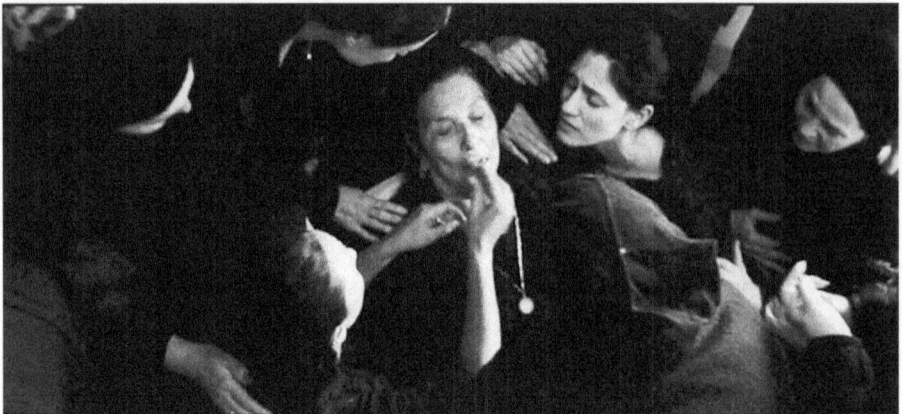

Shiva: Daughters attend their grieving mother.

in the traditional modes used to signify women's mourning.[17] These actions establish the family's traditionalism and Moroccan origins and signal to the audience the adherence to patriarchal culture.

The respect afforded to the older generation situates the Mizrahi matriarch in a position of authority that allows her to hold the family together despite the external pressures of modern Israeli society, which include the siblings' battles and the threats imposed by the Gulf War. Coming together in the face of a common enemy, the final gathering expands to include men as the family huddles together, wearing gas masks. In a reconfiguration of the earlier scene in which the matriarch performed her weakness so that the appropriate mourning rituals could take place, in this penultimate scene she now serves as a Madonna figure in a pietistic mode, rising up from the family she protects.

"Shiva" is the seven days of religiously prescribed mourning following the funeral for immediate relatives or for a spouse. Though this religious practice is common to all Jews, ethnic dramas share the mourning ritual of prostration and loud wailing characteristic of Arab-Jewish societies. A custom common to Moroccan Jews of the Atlas Mountains, it was not widespread among other Moroccan Jews, and despite a decline in this practice within Israeli society generally, it continues to serve as a symbol of Mizrahi mourning within literature and cinema. In *Turn Left at the End of the World*, Nicole's mother, dying of cancer, parodies this by summoning the wailers so that she can inspect their performance and supervise the comments that will be made upon her death. The film gestures at the conventions of this ritual in order to emphasize Moroccan-Jewish primitivism. The wild prostration, digging in the sand, and staged hysteria, for an audience not moved by this ritual, stresses the exoticism of the women engaged in its practice and conflates the position of wailer and witch-crone.[18]

Witches as a Vehicle of Political Satire

A new element of fantasy developed within the realist film tradition depicting Mizrahi women as witches. In performing black magic (*sh'chur*), they were enacting power within a

Shiva: The mother shelters her children as the siren announces incoming rocket fire during the war.

community in which they were powerless as women and as Mizrahim. In *The Witch Sima Vaknin* (*Sima Vaknin Machshefa*, Dror Shaul, 2003), the widowed Sima is searching for love but is a stern and angry woman whose children are leaving the unidentifiable development town to start a new life in Tel Aviv. This symbolic move from the periphery to the geographical center represents the image of escape that serves as a repeated trope. Determined to keep her grandchild close and fighting her son's relocation, which suggests a breakdown in the traditional family values of the Mizrahi community, Sima asks her son to build an extension to her apartment. To the chagrin of the upstairs and symbolically Ashkenazi neighbor, the son uproots the building's only tree and begins to lay a foundation for the new room. When the neighbor takes every measure to stop them, and Sima is at risk of losing her family, her anger boils over and she curses the neighbor, his wife, and his father, who is the local mayor. When events start to take place that suggest her curses have been fulfilled, she is designated "a witch." Her son commercializes this arrangement, and his increasingly gratuitous behavior, including yelling, rudeness, laziness, and stupidity, evoke the Sallah character of an earlier generation. But without the wisdom and sympathy that Haim Topol created with his ethnically marginalized hero, the parody becomes a racist farce. Sima increasingly rebels against the vulgarities of her society, though it is unclear whether she is naïve or is aware of her community's bigoted attitudes.

Shohat evokes the Bakhtinian model of the grotesque to explain the *bourekas* films' subversive power, yet seems to flinch in the end, fearing that celebrating the *bourekas* as purely subversive would lead to the celebration of Mizrahi stereotypes. But what if we take this model to its expected end and do not conceive of the characters' stupidity as fundamentally espousing conservative ideals? Sima and her son Avi represent the two poles of Bakhtin's notion of the grotesque body. Sima is mostly interested in participating in the entire enterprise as a way to facilitate her quest for love, which she has failed to find by other means. Though the reasons for Sima's actions are innocent, the situation ultimately results in corruption and humiliation. Avi's vulgarity suggests the degradation of humanity, further evinced in

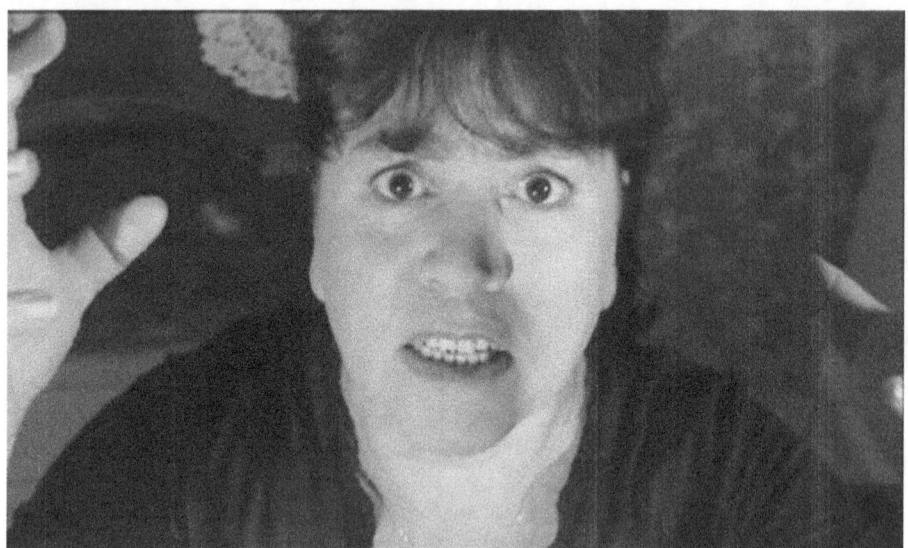

The Witch Sima Vaknin: Sima (Tikva Dayan) the witch curses her neighbors.

the political vitriol and racist remarks made by the figures who visit Sima. These include the Russian doctor's call to evacuate all Israeli and Palestinians, sending them across the border into Arab countries, as a solution to the Arab-Israeli conflict, and his Russian friend's racism toward Thai foreign workers; the policeman's misogyny and sexism; the Ethiopian woman's anti-Russian sentiment; the contractor's racism toward Ethiopians; the religious settler's fanaticism; and the displays of homophobia. When Sima's grandson Bibi finally begins to chant all of the political rhetoric of racism, intolerance, and corruption mentioned by each of the customers who have visited the witch, while the audience of local inhabitants chants "Bibi," the film becomes a satire of the current Israeli political climate and its slogans. Its mockery of Benjamin (Bibi) Netanyahu, the Israeli prime minister, serves as a critique of the ways in which he has courted right-wing voters, also serving as a condemnation of these segments of the Israeli population. Sima's decision to walk away and escape to a Mediterranean island with the town's mayor pretends to a romantic ending of the film. This also symbolically suggests the sea as an escape from the oppression of the Middle East, and particularly its sandy Arab environs and its bigotry. The witches are neither good nor evil in the traditional Hollywood fairy-tale mode, but practitioners of a traditional folk sphere in which their temperaments as women have the greatest impact on the kind of magic they perform. As in the *bourekas* comedies of an earlier generation, misadventures, disasters, and family dynamics serve to satirize the Mizrahi world.

Sh'chur (Shmuel Hasfari, 1994) is a darker film exploring violence, rape, and abuse within a Moroccan family. While Sima's magic is predominantly of the cursing kind, in *Sh'chur* magic can be evoked through amulets, incantations, spells, and potions. With power over love and death (the Thanatos/Eros bind), the mother and her mentally disabled daughter, Pnina,

Sh'Chur: The mother (Gila Almagor) casts a spell of protection in the family living room while daughter Pnina (Ronit Elkabetz) assists her.

control the secrets to the unknown. In addition, Pnina has telekinetic power, which later her sister Cheli's own disabled daughter also seems to share. In the modern world this familiarity with the supernatural is preserved by those who do not conform to traditional mainstream behavior, and therefore their inner lives are set apart from those of other characters.

Anthropological research on witchcraft and "healers" in contemporary Israel reveals an abiding belief in the power of the supernatural among socioeconomically low and ethnically Arab populations, both Jews and Palestinians. The magic is composed of a triumvirate of powers, including the evil eye (*ayin hara*), witchcraft (*sh'chur*), and demon possession (*jinn*). It is rare that all three methods appear together in Israeli films; instead, the representation of any one form functions as a metonym of Arab-Jewish attitudes to magic and as a way of indicating social backwardness. While in reality male healers are a feature of this discourse in Israel, within cinema set in a Mizrahi context only females are represented as engaging in mystical practices.

Sh'Chur tells the story of Cheli's return home from her modern, Ashkenazi Tel Aviv life to her traditional Mizrahi family, living in the country's periphery, following the death of her father. The journey becomes a historic return to her childhood, with its magic and mystical practices. As she drives into the barren landscape, she recalls her childhood with its primitive rituals and discrimination against women. When her sister, played by Esti Yerushalmi, gets a job in the local factory, the family casts a spell to protect her chastity. This scene sets up the conflict that exists between traditionalism and the ever-encroaching modernity that becomes Cheli's future aspiration. Yet here, at her point of origin, we see the double standards that exist for men and women. The older brother, Shlomo, is not subject to the strictures imposed on the women, but it is he who will impregnate his girlfriend. While he freely adopts the patriarchal attitudes that situate him as the future head of the family, unlike his father he, too, is compromised by the desire for a different life and longs to study at the Sorbonne in Paris. Appearing to reject the responsibilities of establishing his own family, he takes his girlfriend for an illegal backstreet (medical) abortion rather than recreating his father's life of marriage and children, but he will be drawn back into the traditional circle, ultimately unable to escape from the desert wasteland.

This theme of fecundity, which ultimately serves to mark Shlomo as a patriarchal figure, is undesirable for the unmarried women. Just as the family hopes to prevent the factory worker from becoming pregnant, they must also manage the rape and subsequent pregnancy of Pnina, the older, mentally handicapped sister. Pnina's sexual abuse is an act of revenge that marks her out as family property that can be damaged as an attack against Shlomo by the people he slighted. Pnina is defended through the mechanism of female power, and her mother performs a magic ritual to cause her miscarriage. This structuring of female forms of power through witchcraft is also identified with Shlomo's girlfriend, who, it emerges, has cast a spell over him preventing the emotional escape that would allow him to travel to France to study. Having previously mocked the women's traditions, he then begs his mother for a ritual to free him. This fails when it emerges that both he and his girlfriend engaged in black magic (*sh'chur*)—thus witchcraft comes to represent a domestic sphere of interpersonal strife, fertility, sexual relations, and love. Anthropologically, "[M]ost witchcraft is considered to be 'love magic' that aims to increase the man's lust or to preserve the wife's loyalty,"[19] a tradition that is played out in the films. In *Sh'chur*, these witchcraft practices ultimately frame women's magic as a reclamation of power within the framework of their domestic powerlessness. The magical ritual that leads to Pnina's miscarriage demonstrates women's power in the face of male power—if men can take women, can impregnate them, and can abandon them, then women can, in turn, control the future of male seed. Thus control of the female body passes from a male hegemonic space into a female, mystical one. We also see that folk wisdom becomes a counterpoint to the rational models offered by Israel as a modern and Western society, from which, through their physical marginalization, Mizrahim remain excluded. Thus the non-Cartesian mode of *Sh'chur* operates as a model through which to empower traditional life and reject that considered the norm.

Through extranormal power that subverts the women's marginalization because it literally empowers them, we see an antirational discourse that by extension becomes an enactment of women's political power. Brought to a modern society that is built on the technological and legal norms of the West, magic is a revolt against the breakdown of family that the migration to Israel has produced on the one hand, and the ongoing patriarchal hegemony within their traditional communities on the other. The films offer a paradoxical representation of women that is characteristic of an occidental gaze at the Orient. The women often provide color, evoke traditionalism through religious customs, and are shown to be sexually available, while at the same time they are inaccessible: physically because these films allude to the patriarchy in traditional societies that discourages women's presence in public spaces, and spiritually because of the women's mystical powers. These tropes establish a repertoire of images and allusions that connect the Mizrahi women to the Middle East in a way that distances them from the Western ideology of Israeli hegemony. They serve to suggest that because women are hidden away, oppressed by their society, and ultimately primitive, they are therefore in need of Israeli society's protection (that is, the dominant Western aspects of it). These films allude to the disruptive anticommunity nature of Western society but ultimately direct a preference for this way of life. But while modernity will ultimately save these women, the films' nostalgic gaze suggests that these women historically were able to enact power within their own communities through their mystical powers and knowledge of witchcraft. Thus sorcery subvert the images of Mizrahi women's powerlessness in the past, but reaffirms a prejudicial view of Mizrahi women in relation to the present. While the former exemplifies the occidental imaginary of Mizrahi women by feeding the allusions to Middle Eastern stereotypes, the latter position is achieved by allusions that demystify the supernatural, as we see in the construction of *sh'chur* as the local variant of psychology, or acts of rescue that remove the Mizrahi woman from Mizrahi society. By resituating the women and their acts within the realism that is the dominant medium of Israeli cinema, the films negate efforts to imagine a Mizrahi historical reality from within the society, rather than as a projection of fetish by an Ashkenazi filmmaking establishment. While Yaron Shemer points to New Mizrahi Cinema's efforts to overcome this Israeli cultural bias, the price of this self-introspection by Mizrahi filmmaking has often been the disappearance of female characters and women's story lines. With the exception of *My Lovely Sister*, the image of the witch is almost entirely eliminated, and it is the adaptation of this mystical image in the frame of the film's magical realist style that overcomes both New Mizrahi Cinema's efforts to circumvent the prejudicial nature of the image and Ashkenazi cinema's realist style that positions all mystical representation as primitive and antinational.

For those films that do employ the imagery of witchcraft, their representation of the younger generation's abandonment of Mizrahi traditionalism situates the orientalized past as a stage of migration that moves from a pre-Israeli reality, through the process of immigration-absorption-acculturation, to a Westernized future in a contemporary Israeli reality. In *Sh'chur* Rahel moves to a boarding school, thereby leaving her family and ultimately adopting the "more Israeli-sounding—less Oriental and diasporic—nickname Cheli ... and eventually ... [becoming] a successful television personality," and her older sister Miriam, who attends an Orthodox yeshiva returns home but rejects the religious customs and traditions of her family, instead choosing to dress, pray, and eat according to the laws of Ashkenazi Judaism. Only Cheli's mentally handicapped daughter can access the historic Mizrahi past through her aunt Pnina, and therefore inherit what is left of her family's matrilineal legacy.

Yosefa Loshitzky has described *Sh'chur* as "a form of ethnic document through its unusual juxtaposition of fantastic realism with a simulacrum of anthropological-like observation of ethnic rituals and daily activities,"[20] in which Cheli has become the model of "whiteness" until she is forced back into a world that she has entirely rejected by the death of her father and his upcoming funeral. This can be read in light of Carol Bardenstein's claim that passing in an Israeli context happens along a scale of identity from Palestinian Arab to Israeli Arab to Mizrahi to Ashkenazi. Among the reasons for engaging in passing is that such acts may "substantially or even radically challenge or subvert hegemonic configurations of social identity—or blur fixed categories and hierarchies."[21] The acts of impersonation, mimicry, and passing in Israeli and Palestinian cinema create a layered and multidimensional notion of the act of integration, demonstrating not only slippery, indeterminate, and malleable social boundaries but also internal fluidity of identity that "can be pointedly effective in exposing essentialized or reified social identities as constructed performative fantasies."[22] Therefore, cinema is particularly adept at highlighting the ways in which "passing" identity is constructed and performed, while simultaneously stressing that success at passing threatens the stability of these defined boundaries.[23] Sometimes both the essentialized, socially sanctioned identity and the new one created in the response to it are fluid performative fantasies that fluctuate with the ebb and flow of political and social changes.

Turn Left at the End of the World

Turn Left at the End of the World opens with many of the conventional patterns employed in representations of the Mizrahi community literally "at the end of the world": the isolated landscape, the factory that closes and signals the death and decay of the area, and the isolation of women trapped within this landscape. Shemer has termed these films "post-*Bourekas*" because they use the stable of clichés and stereotypes of the *bourekas* genre but repackage this imagery in a postmodernist critique of color and race in Israeli society, evident in other films such as *Sh'chur*, *Desperado Square* (*Kikar HaHalomot*, Benny Toraty, 2000), *The Witch Sima Vaknin*, *The Ballad of the Weeping Spring* (*Balada LeAviv HaBohe*, Benny Toraty, 2012), *Shiva*, and *The Band's Visit*.

Complicating the issues of race and color and challenging the language of ethnic hierarchy, *Turn Left at the End of the World* brings together the Moroccan immigrants with a French colonialist history and the Indian Jews with a British colonial history. The film extends the metaphor of "nonwhiteness" to Indian Jews, who were treated like Arab, Turkish, and Iranian Jews within Israeli society more generally, thereby undermining the binary convention of Mizrahi or Ashkenazi and ignoring the multiple differences between groups. Not only did Indian and Moroccan Jews have different religious and cultural traditions, languages, patterns of dress, and social dynamics, the film highlights the gap between the different colonial experiences of each group. While the Moroccans were raised within a francophone society, demonstrated through their love of music, perfumed soap, and an ever-present eroticism, a stereotype that further suggests the sexualized romanticism of Oriental Jews, the Indians, by contrast, speak English, drink tea, and play cricket. Though there is an apparent dislocation of the Mizrahi-Ashkenazi division onto the Moroccan-Indian division of this film, suggesting, in the spirit of colonialism, that the Indians are portrayed as more Westernized (the "civilized" native), nevertheless the Indian is then also corrupted by contact with the "Arab native" through their association with the Moroccan and Berber neighbors. The Indian man is seduced by the Moroccan woman, while the Indian woman is forced to turn to the local Moroccan-Berber witch-healer for a magical potion to win her husband back. As this film suggests, the only solution for the individual who wishes to advance socially and rid him- or herself of this backward, rural, and primitive society is to flee.

The men are generally seen in public spaces, in the café, playing football outside (and later cricket), and wandering in the empty landscape. Women are signifiers of the domestic space, so that even when outdoors they are usually shown in the yards between the houses, hanging laundry or engaging in social exchanges with their neighbors. The young women's wandering alone outside the town's perimeter signifies their transgression, emphasized by being found naked at the pool of water. As the story unfolds, the young women will be returned to their traditional place within the home. Their mothers' domestic dramas (illness, cheating husbands, boredom) serve as a counterpoint to the men's political issues (the closure of the factory, the hope that sports will bring attention to their plight). But while the men come together and form a collective, particularly in the communal involvement in the cricket game, the women's engagement generally happens in smaller social interactions between two individuals. The Indian woman is helped by the Moroccan woman when she discovers that her husband is cheating on her with the Moroccan widow across the courtyard, with the Moroccan woman sending her to the Berber crone. This imagery sustains female marginalization, in its representation of the Berber woman's primitivism and the powerless Indian woman's need to turn to the mystical sources of female power in a situation in which she is doubly powerless, unable either to affect her husband or to know the secrets that the Moroccans possess.

Ariela Popper-Giveon and Jonathan J. Ventura have shown, in their anthropological research on magic and witchcraft among Palestinian women in Israel, that "women healers are afforded a marginalized position by the religious establishment. Their training is informal and, while some inherit their practice from their mothers, others claim to be recruited by the supernatural. Women healers are less identified with the use of holy writings, and most of their treatment practices have an oral and magical nature. They are viewed as representatives of the feminine, popular, and oral traditions, deviating from the official written ideologies and thus considered inferior and marginal."[24] In the morphology of folk religion, "witchcraft's main ingredients include body parts and excretions: items such as blood and substances, which may be found on the margins of the body or are excreted by it (nails, hair, urine, etc.)."[25] The corporeal reality of these bodily fluids, read through Julia Kristeva's notion of the abject, forms the basis of the witchcraft that women can perform against men. Thus the threat witchcraft poses to male hegemony is precisely that which men fear—the use of the female body (and its waste) as a way of disrupting the social order. *A Late Marriage* takes this manifestation of female control through witchcraft even further, since the necessary ingredient for the successful spell is the man's stolen semen. In a film that pits a Mizrahi divorcee against a Georgian patriarch who controls not only his wives and daughters but also his son, the witchcraft used by all of the women, Georgian and Mizrahi alike, serves as an attempt to display power in a society in which women are otherwise powerless.

In his doctoral thesis, Shemer argued that when competing claims of identity (sex, race, social class) interact in Israeli film, Mizrahi women can be seen to share the experience of Ashkenazi women, choosing gender over race in their hierarchical identity construction. "[T]ime and again women are pitted against men—spouses, partners, or fathers—and often, these films' central conflicts revolve around the war between the sexes."[26] But when Mizrahi women are viewed as possessing an intersectional identity that is always both female and Mizrahi, they can be seen independently of (and in conflict with) the Mizrahi male and the Ashkenazi female. It is this latter category which is often in particular evidence in plots that focus on female spaces. The films set in Mizrahi communities and removed from Ashkenazi social spaces create a stand in for the Ashkenazi woman in the guise of a female who has been made Ashkenazi, and who serves as a symbolic foil to the Mizrahi female. As with *Turn Left at the End of the World*, in which Mizrahim from Morocco are pitted against the anglicized Indians who symbolize the Ashkenazi, Nicole departs to join the army, where she will be socialized as an Ashkenazi, and in *Sh'chur* the daughters abandon the family traditions after being educated elsewhere in Ashkenazi religious or social practices. Thus, ultimately, the portrayal of witchcraft exists in a nostalgic space of the past, contrasted with the assimilation and modernization of the present. Though representations of witchcraft appear to destabilize the gendered order and empower women, thereby serving as both a social and a political critique, ultimately the erasure of this female power in a path to westernization serves to depict the Mizrahi woman as primitive, with her only salvation lying in her Ashkenazification.

My Lovely Sister and the Reworking of Mizrahi Womanhood

My Lovely Sister recycles many of the tropes commonly found in Israeli films representing magic and witchcraft: the Mizrahi woman with a low socioeconomic status, usually part of a large and ever-present family, appears to have control over the supernatural world. Following the conventions, whereby a moment of emotional trial precipitates the engagement with the spirit world, Rahma's fight with her husband (and her sister) at her grandson's *brit* (circumcision) becomes the trigger for her supernatural episode. She talks to the wall. Though the audience hears a voice calling her, and sees her engagement in a conversation, it is only after a few moments that we realize her conversational partner is the wall and that she hears the wall talking back to her, demanding baked goods, which she quickly sets out before it. This act is an externalization of processing, memory, and experience, evoking the British film *Shirley Valentine*'s household wall, and through this encounter the audience sees a lonely woman, rejected in her marital relations, who feels deeply unloved. The wall serves as an emotional and spiritual sounding board, providing the psychological support, through folk means, that marks out Rahma's traditional way of life. However, by contrast with *Shirley Valentine*, for whom the wall serves as a vehicle by which to depict a psychological portrait of the protagonist, the wall's response to Rahma elevates *My Lovely Sister* to the magical realist form. Furthermore, the wall in *Shirley Valentine* is also a pun on the notion of the theatre's invisible "fourth wall," since she repeatedly breaks this imaginary boundary, which is a mark of cinema's intended realism, both by addressing the wall and, in an act of metacinema, addressing the audience directly. The breakdown of realism in the film, through its heightened connection with magic, nevertheless maintains the illusion of a closed environment in which such activities (the wall responding) are logical, given the rules of this world. Thus *My Lovely Sister* remains magical realist, though not hyperconscious metafiction. Moreover, Rahma's daughter's response to her mother's relationship with the wall is to advise her mother to see a therapist, as she has done, both representing the normalization of Rahma's conversation with the wall by mocking modern therapy practices and also denoting that the change between generations has led to the end of an authentic Mizrahi culture in which the magical exists. The wall's response to Rahma answers Alter's contention that "a recurrent principle of much magic realism is that the physical universe of the fiction is in part governed by psychological rather than physical laws."[27] As with *Shirley Valentine*, before the film's close the husband will also talk to the wall, and in a local variant will offer it an uncooked chicken soaked in Arak.

In a Jewish context, Rahma's pleas that the wall protect her husband and keep him safe also speak to the symbolic relationship between the Jewish people and the Kotel (Wailing Wall) in Jerusalem. This last remaining wall of the ancient temple serves as a site of pilgrimage and religious prayer in Israel, and it is customary for supplicants to write wishes on pieces of paper and put them in the cracks between the stones. *My Lovely Sister* therefore translates other cinematic experiences (magical realism, ghosts, women's drama) through a Jewish cultural lens. In the morning, when Robert returns from his night shift, the cakes are gone and instead he picks up an amulet left on the plate, which we presume the wall has left him for protection. As with most of the witchcraft in these kinds of films, it is often enacted over matters of romance and health and can frequently be connected to cursing, the evil eye, and other superstitions; nevertheless, it is rarely used to garner wealth for the family. When used for matters other than sex and health, it is often used for the betterment of the family or extended social group. In *My Lovely Sister*, Robert is protected by his wife's magical relationship with the wall. When he offers up the amulet for a night of passion in a brothel, his protection is removed and he is struck by a skin rash that is the wall's punishment.

The image of passing is pronounced in this film. The modern daughter who rejects her mother's traditional world and way of life is called *Levana* (white). Rahma's daughter offers a contrast to the traditional way of life. She drives a 4x4, the only car seen driven in the film, and she talks of psychologists and important work projects, thereby dismissing the economics of her family. She lives in Tel Aviv, wears sunglasses, and sports a tattoo on her leg, suggesting symbols of the modern world, and she wears tailored, fashionable, contemporary clothes. By contrast, the wardrobe of the other characters has a pronouncedly vintage feel, constructing an aesthetic landscape outside of particular time. Like Ben Lulu's bicycle, the characters' names (Robert, Marie, Rahma), Marie's desire to do "the 60s dance," Robert's suits, and the women's dresses all suggest an Arab-Jewish world that has been forgotten by time. This immutability adds to the overall impression of a world disconnected from the modernity that Levana offers. Moreover, her way of life is mocked and dismissed by the two sisters, who laugh at her seriousness when she visits the grave in a formal act of commemoration that is radically different from that of both her parents. Its sterile formula (lighting a candle) is contrasted with the passion (both love and anger) that Robert and Rahma express toward Marie. Levana's pattern of mourning may also be reminiscent of Holocaust memorialization, and by evoking the Ashkenazi, and therefore "correct," form of commemoration, serves to distinguish Mizrahi from Ashkenazi and engage with the formal expectations for a "proper" Israeli citizen.

Even the film's title, "Ahoti" (sister) evokes connotations between the Mizrahi community and its family dynamic. Like the Hebrew "Ahi" (my brother), drawn from military slang and influenced by Arabic (and American slang: bro), the film's title evokes the informality and tribalism that stand in contrast to the Zionist ideals of modernization and Westernization. "Ahoti" is also the name of a Mizrahi-feminist organization and woman's charity in Israel,

> devoted to raising feminist awareness of women from non-European backgrounds living in the peripheries and disadvantaged neighborhoods, who are deprived of their labor rights, and whose voices go unheard. Ahoti is dedicated to closing the economic, social and cultural gaps, managing projects, workshops and conferences, empowering them personally, informing them of their rights, and developing alternative economic solutions.[28]

Despite the proactive and politically resonant title of the film, its modifying adjective "Yafa" (lovely) reconnects the film to the legacy of the sexualized Oriental Jewess. The filmmakers' consciousness of the language and position of Mizrahi women, their customary depiction in Israeli cinema, and the overt (or covert) tone of racism generally used to address them highlights their subjugation within Israeli society for being Mizrahi, and within the patriarchal Mizrahi community for being female.

Like *My Lovely Sister* and *Sh'chur*, *Shiva* similarly brings together the Mizrahi family through the death of a family member. Though *Shiva* steers away from the magic seen in other films conveying witchcraft, the family dynamics, and the constant threats of curses and evil eyes, evoke a similar atmosphere. *My Lovely Sister* opens with a funeral, setting the surreal tone of the entire film. A man addressed as Bouskila stands at a bus stop when Ben Lulu pulls up riding a tricycle and pulling a makeshift tilbury carriage. Bouskila gets in and asks if he is dead. Ben Lulu replies in the affirmative and advises him that they are off to his funeral. As they watch the procession of mourners, the dead man is honored by the good showing, commenting on his wife's melodramatic wailing and the appearance of an old friend with whom he has not been on speaking terms. In death they have resolved their previous dispute, which will later serve as a foreshadowing for Rahma's relationship with her sister Marie. Thus, the opening scene, through the woman's wailing, the sandy landscape, and the domestic familiarity, establishes the poverty and North African–Jewish ethnicity of the Israeli town. By capturing the impression of a rural community, steeped in tradition, the film constructs the expectations of superstition, folk ways, and ignorance. But by virtue of Bouskila and Ben Lulu's conversation, the film also creates an imaginative world in which reality and fantasy live together.

The relationship to the dead who are absent, though recalled through memory and conversation, which is the process of the shiva in *Sh'chur* and *Shiva*, does not happen in this film. Instead, the dead are awake and present. As in the British *Truly Madly Deeply* (Anthony Minghella, 1990), or the American *Ghost* (Jerry Zucker, 1990), the specter is connected to the living participant through love. This cinematic trend that was popular in the 1930s and 1940s (in British and American cinema), in which a ghostly apparition would help the living, often as his final mission on earth before being able to move on (such as in *Here Comes Mr. Jordan* [Alexander Hall, 1941] and *Stairway to Heaven* [Michael Powell and Emeric Pressburger, 1946]), had not been previously used in Israeli cinema, and is a unique feature of *My Lovely Sister*.[29] Helped by Ben Lulu's carriage, which serves as a motif of this link between life and death, the audience, who sees his rejection of a passenger as an indication that the person will live, understands that Robert is saved from the wall's wrath at the end of the film when Ben Lulu will not give him a ride. Similarly, the exhausted and dying Marie rests at the bus stop, and Ben Lulu's arrival offers her a gentle journey to the end.

Unlike Bouskila in the opening scene, the dead Marie does not rest in peace, since her sister will not allow her to be buried in a Jewish ceremony or, more particularly, next to her mother. In lingering within the living world, Marie's role is to help the bereaved move through the stages of grief, to understand the mistakes of both Robert and Rahma's pasts, and to find peace in the present in order to move into a future in which the ghost will be laid to rest and the connection between the living and the dead will be severed. It is only following Marie's death that the two sisters finally begin to speak again after twenty years, during which time Rahma rejected her younger sister, following Marie's marriage to Ali, because he was Arab. Though she accuses her sister of shaming her parents, through the course of the film it becomes increasingly clear that Rahma's racism and prejudice were a pretext to rid her of the sister whom she felt threatened her own marriage—but her jealousy and suspicion ultimately result in her creating barriers with her own husband, and it is she who is the obstacle to her own joy. Only by liberating herself of these feelings can she find a positive resolution with her husband.

At the same time, Robert must also resolve his feelings toward Marie. He develops a skin ailment following Marie's death, though he is told by a doctor that his red blotches are psychosomatic, or as his son Kobi explains to his father, "It's like when someone can't get it up, and it is not because of what's in his pants but because of what is in his head." This explanation, which effects a psychological account for Robert's affliction, circumvents the apparent cause, which is the sexual relationship with an apparition of Marie—who may or may not be a figment of his imagination, and may or may not be a ghost, during which time he surrendered his amulet. Recalling *Sh'chur*'s reading of black magic as Middle Eastern psychology, Robert's lesions in *My Lovely Sister* become a physical manifestation of his psychological trauma—but also serve as a mark, a symbolic scarlet letter, of his sexual betrayal. Chasing his vision of Marie night after night, he becomes increasingly cruel toward Rahma until she finally walks out on him. Drunk, pacing the streets looking for her, he yet again sees Marie, but he finally rejects her, choosing to run after Rahma instead. This moment of crisis transforms their marital relationship. In the morning, finding his wife prostrated over her sister's grave, he sends her home and proceeds to dig up Marie's body for reburial, with the help of her husband Ali.

The previous days of visits to the grave and sitting in mourning, during which Marie tears Rahma's dress and Rahma rolls in the mud and wails over her sister's temporary grave, evoke the same grief rituals enacted in other films depicting the Mizrahi women. But now the sisters have reconciled, and Rahma finally consents to have her sister buried alongside her mother within the boundaries of the cemetery; Robert has understood that he must change how he behaves toward his wife; and finally all of the characters' dramas are resolved. It is at this stage that the fantastical mourning at the graveside transforms into the ordered rituals of the realist world, and the shiva practices take on their formal Jewish religious frame in the last scene of the film. Robert and Rahma are reconciled, Rahma's severe personality, represented in her makeup and dress in the opening scenes, is now relaxed, and the estranged brother-in-law Ali is invited into the house to sit with the family and mourn for his wife.

The appearance of *My Lovely Sister* occurs within a cinematic tradition of representing the semirural and domestic life of Mizrahi Jews, within which family quarrels are resolved

My Lovely Sister: The reconciled sisters Mary (Reymond Amsallem) and Rahma (Evelin Hagoel) hold hands, facing the sea.

following the death of a loved one. Moreover, we expect to see a community that is superstitious, is engaged in at least one form of witchcraft, and is itself racist. Though *My Lovely Sister* has all of these elements, by using the medium of magical realism it is able to disrupt audience expectations of the grotesque evidenced in *Sh'chur*, *Turn Left at the End of the World*, and *The Witch Sima Vaknin* and move beyond the time worn conventions of Israeli cinema. In recasting the landscape from the barren desert of *Turn Left at the End of the World*, *The Band's Visit*, and *The Witch Sima Vaknin*, to a community on the edge of the sea, the notion of a backward, isolated, and peripheral town is abolished. As with Sima's final embracing of the Mediterranean, the portrayal of the sea in *My Lovely Sister*, which is connected to Ali and his life as a fisherman and is seen from the cemetery, is an unusual addition to the landscape of the Mizrahi town. The beauty of the scenery transforms the geographical experience, and it also evokes the North African port town communities from which Robert and the sisters originally came, engaging with a Mizrahi tradition beyond their current marginalization in Israel. In addition, this link to life in an Arab world, further supported by the presence of an Arab with his own home and profession, disrupts the present boundaries between Arab and Jew, recalling a time of collaboration. In an open landscape with a horizon reaching beyond the town's limits, the possibilities remain positive and infinite, in contrast to the habit of representing trapped Mizrahi communities.

Arabic is painted on the wall of Ali's home by the sea, and the characters move frequently between Arabic, Judeo-Arabic, French, and Hebrew, as they do in *Sh'chur*, *Shiva*, and other films depicting Moroccan Jews. However, in *My Lovely Sister* these languages are generally not subtitled for Hebrew audiences, so only the English subtitles offer a translation of all the conversations taking place, and, for the untrained ear, these linguistic nuances are then made invisible. For the members of the Hebrew audience, who recognize the changes but may not speak or understand the other languages, the use of Arabic and particularly Judeo-Arabic exoticizes the characters, making their world inaccessible. This both heightens the magical elements of the film and speaks of the impossibility of Ashkenazi Jews penetrating the life of the Mizrahi Jew they have long sought to control and assimilate into Israeli (meaning Ashkenazi) culture. As with the Latin American tradition of magical realism, this film ultimately seeks to comment on the silenced voice of the colonized. Whereas the previous tradition of representing Mizrahi women (and the family more broadly) focused on traditional Arab-Jewish practices as archaic, presenting a people in need of civilizing and modernizing, *My Lovely Sister* departs from this stance. It offers a Moroccan Jewish perspective that resonates not with the Ashkenazi fantasy of comedy and satire but with the melodrama of the *bourekas*'s early years that attempted to present the Arab Jews' own experience of migration. However, in contrast to that genre, which played well for a Mizrahi audience but was critically rejected among an Ashkenazi cultural elite who found its violence, crassness, and vulgarity alienating, this experiment in magical realism offers a warm but gentle world. Though it recycles many of the traditional tropes common among films about Mizrahim (poverty, witchcraft, lack of education), it deviates from these conventions through its charming exploration of a town filled with kindness and affection. Though the people love and hate to extremes, their behavior inverts traditional stereotypes of the community in myriad ways. Kobi's pornography business functions as a symbol of this nontraditional mode of representation. When he offers a wheelchair-bound man sexually explicit DVDs, the audience is surprised to learn that this is an enhancement for his active sexual relationship with his wife. Rather than presenting pornography as deviance, conveying the criminality of Mizrahi youth, the film presents Kobi as a generous and thoughtful boy. The Ashkenazi's perception of the Mizrahi's immorality with his dissolute behavior is internalized by Robert, who assumes his son has come to tell him that he has gotten a girl pregnant, rather than that he is in love. The audience expectation that she will then reject him when she discovers his sideline is defied by Carmel's sensitive rendering of Kobi's ideals. Instead, he takes her to hear the town at night and to listen to the sexual joy that can be heard from the windows, and in response they drive through the town on his moped, throwing sexual paraphernalia into the street for the residents to enjoy. Finally, watching the sun set in the sea, they kiss. Like Pedro Almodovar, Carmel challenges our notions of sexual love and engages with a landscape and a people who appear hyper-real in their passion.

Throughout this film, Carmel uses the real and the fantastical as a way to confront the hierarchies of culture within the Israeli cinematic tradition. In this film, Ashkenazi experience, often depicted within films that depict Mizrahim negatively, stands as the social pinnacle, offering an escape from the magical world—a place of barbarism—to a place of civilization. However, this dominant and "civilizing" force is also shown to eradicate the traditional culture of North African Jews, replacing it with empty values and a breakdown in community networks. In a "white" culture of modernization, it remains the political fantasy of the "black" Moroccan to reclaim her own narrative within that of Israeli society and to tell the stories that have not yet been told.

6

Hot and Fertile
Sex, Sexuality, and Prostitution

Among the most radical developments in feminist filmmaking of the last two decades in Israel has been the exploration of female sexuality and the reclaiming of this image from a tradition in which women were co-opted by a male discourse and parsed into a regional variation of the virgin/whore dialectic. This chapter considers the cult of the female body within Zionist discourse, its evolution during the hedonistic decades of the 1960s and 1970s, the exploitation of Mizrahi and later Russian women through images of prostitution, and the ways in which contemporary feminist filmmaking has sought to reframe women's subjectivity in films such as *The Slut*, *She's Coming Home*, *Or, My Treasure*, and *Bye Bye to Love*.

The contradictory origins of Zionism lay between the European idealism of Theodor Herzl, who imagined a Jewish national homeland in Palestine, and the Russian socialist pioneers who did much of the early work of agricultural and industrial settlement, which gave the nascent Yishuv its identity. Herzl's vision of a Jewish Viennese-café-society, and the pioneers' vision of a hearty labor force, shared an anxiety over masculinity. In Europe the experiences of anti-Semitism, the inability to own land or work in agriculture, and the stereotypical representations of most Jews as weak, sickly, luftmenschen inveigled the development of Zionism and the determination to produce a new kind of Jew. This New Jew would be able to defend himself from attack, be of superior strength and fitness, and stand tall and independent of the coercive authorities under whose yoke Jews had lived for centuries. For Herzl, women were subservient, relegated to *kinder* and *küche* (hearth and home), and their importance was limited "to their role in reproducing and sustaining the Jewish nation."[1] Though socialist ideology imagined women as equals, in reality women often found themselves in less prestigious positions, assigned to domestic tasks, discriminated against, and marginalized from the corridors of power. "Women did not feel in the early days of Jewish nationalism that they occupied secondary roles. They rather believed that Zionism offered them a new kind of equality: the right to vote and to be elected to office. But once they actually emigrated to Palestine to create the new society, women came to realize that their dream of equality between the sexes was not likely to be achieved; that in fact their position in the new society and in the new land of Israel was not much different from what it had been in Europe."[2] Michal Aviad's documentary *The Women Pioneers* (*Nashim Halutzot*, 2013), using diaries and letters from the period, shows the revolutionary ideas that the female pioneers brought with them that were supposed to liberate women from "the shackles of tradition and religion" and grant "full partnership in duties and rights" rarely offered the independence the women craved. However, in eschewing the legal forms of a monogamous relationship and rejecting the institution of marriage, women unexpectedly gave up a protection they did not imagine they needed. The old conventions that had forced men to take responsibility for a wife, a home, and children no longer applied, and men were liberated from domestic fidelity. In this new utopia, only single, unfettered women could maintain the illusion of freedom. For, once saddled with children, women were often abandoned and left to raise progeny alone, while their mates searched out new romantic and sexual opportunities, sometimes concurrently and sometimes sequentially.

In the new settlements, the children's house, laundry, and dining room were meant to create a collective that liberated women, but instead most women were assigned work in these institutions, and thus the kibbutz merely expanded the traditional domestic role from the individual unit to domestic responsibility for the collective in its entirety. Occasionally women worked in the chicken house, dairy, or gardens, but a clear division in gender roles could be observed in most cases, and women were frequently subordinate while men held most positions of authority. The secular social experiment had succeeded for men, and it was they who drove the Zionist project forward, and women, who had had such high hopes for their emancipation, now faced a life of isolated domestic drudgery.

The erotic revolution that socialism promised may have materialized for a small segment of the male population living within the kibbutz structure, but for most, traditional middle-class social and familial structures were the norm, and particularly returned women to a sociosexual structure in which virginal women were considered marriageable, and sexual women were viewed as whores. If "only pure and modest women [were] supposed to reproduce the next healthy generation,"[3] women tainted by promiscuity not only risked their position they jeopardized their children's inclusion within the national pantheon. The socialist pioneers had appropriated childbirth in the name of nationalism and simultaneously denied women parity within Zionist structures. The gendered experience of pioneering further weakened women's place within nationalist ideology and positioned them in secondary roles—as women to be protected and defended.

For woman qua woman, the only space available in these narratives was as a metaphor for the land's fecundity and male prowess. Individual women's wants and desires were considered bourgeois and had no place in the creation of the nation. Instead, women were expected to shed the perceived trappings that constructed femaleness and adopt an androgynous identity. The successful pioneer woman could either become an earth mother, caring for an entire collective, or a man. Shohat explains, the price of women's equality was "conformity to Zionist pioneering ideals: the hard-working pioneer is portrayed as a Madonna, the hedonistic bourgeois as a whore."[4] In the socialist-Zionist mind, the trappings of bourgeois femininity constituted weakness, false consciousness, and decadence. Only later would sexual

A Hole in the Moon: The parody of the pioneer contrasts the previous expectation of women's association with the land and the beauty queen society of the 1960s.

promiscuity and criminality become part of this imagery. Thus in the Zionist context the virgin/whore dialectic had a particular inflection more reminiscent of Soviet attitudes than its classic formulation within Western European and American contexts.[5] Women were expected to sacrifice comfort and luxuries, along with their beauty, for a hard frontier life on the new settlements. But, in the main, this pioneering ethos was characterized in cinematic culture through a male fraternity that celebrated male heroism and male exploits as men mastered the land, defeated their enemies, and protected their womenfolk. The land was female; an unchartered territory to be conquered and subdued, the ultimate symbol of womanhood writ large, and it was men's duty to hoe and fertilize it, to water and weed, to lead it to bloom. The feminization of the land, and men's ability to make it fruitful, offered a solution for the expression of homoerotic love. Only through the symbolic transference onto the land of their otherwise repressed sexuality could men solve the problem of child bearing.[6] This, in fact, robbed women of the symbolic sanctioning of their roles as sexual beings and as mothers and made real and symbolic fecundity a communal act, such that children came forth from a collective womb. *Womankind* may have been idealized and venerated, but the individual woman was a distraction and liable to destroy the group's cohesive identity and threaten the more fundamental male relationships.

Sexuality was not absent from the Israeli screen, but its expression was contained within the language of Zionist ideology. It could be seen in the representation of heterosexual desire between heroic characters, in the homoerotic camaraderie between brothers-in-arms, and in the erotic association between women's bodies, fecundity, soil, and water. The life-giving sources (food, water, and woman) were paralleled, and sexual seduction (always heterosexual) frequently took place outdoors within nature, creating a triangular sexual economy between the female body, the heroic male-pioneer-soldier, and the land. These images, which redirected sexual desire into militarism and agricultural pioneering, became so ubiquitous that Uri Zohar would parody this motif in *Hole in the Moon* (*Hor B'Levana*, 1964) with his satire of the bikini-clad woman carrying a rifle and driving a hand plow across a barren landscape.

The Beauty Queen and the Rise of a Zionist Bourgeois Femininity

By contrast to the pioneering ideal, the rise of the Israeli beauty queen in the 1950s corresponded with a return to "a bourgeois model of womanhood" that "reinforced the idea that woman's main obligation in society [was] being a housewife and mother"[7] and discouraged female sexual expression. Simultaneously, the turn toward popular culture opened a door to worshipping the female body, seen in the beauty pageants the magazine *Laisha* (For the Woman) established, that would ultimately lead to Miss Israel and her participation in the international competitions Miss World and Miss Universe. A tension existed between the image of the *Halutzah (female pioneer)* and the new breed of female role models who exemplified the modern ideals of "the national body"[8] who may have compromised past ideals, but took Israel to an international stage—not only appearing in pageants but starring in Hollywood films and European art cinema.[9] Thus the image of the Israeli woman had evolved to become the alluring exemplary of Zionist dictates. The magazine increasingly focused on fashion and cosmetics, often promoted by these stars, and also offered women entertainment in "love stories," features about the life of Miss Israel, and lifestyle spreads for Israeli actresses and models, recipes, and advice on housewifery. As Oz Almog observes, in the development of the beauty parlor culture during the 1950s and 1960s, "femininity was not merely a matter of gender identity but also a profession to be learned, internalized, and practiced."[10] For most women the attraction of this new Israeli woman lay in her glamour rather than the domestic expectations that accompanied this turn toward the bourgeois: "Thus emerged the new stereotype of modern womanhood as a cross between housewife and model, princess and passionate lover," which marked an ideological change of attitude toward women's visual representation and served as a radical break with the pioneering past.[11]

In Israel, the beauty queen phenomenon created an image of the ideal female that drew on the specific cultural markers of Zionism. Julie Grimmeisen has shown that women were expected to be athletic, reflecting the prevailing militaristic ethos, and female soldiers were particularly encouraged to compete in the pageants. Moreover, several of the pageant's winners were encouraged to hebraize their names, an action that "pronounced their Hebrew identity."[12] This interest in the female body inspired a period of Israeli pinups and local actresses who were celebrated for having "the right athletic, well-formed body but with round curves. These ideals stood for elegance, cleanliness, and 'keeping up appearances.'"[13] The competitions and the magazine culture associated with them continued to link a healthy body to Zionism, as pioneering culture had previously: "The young patriot's beauty proclaimed the young nation's beauty, and his or her health was a reflection of the health of the nation as a whole."[14] In time, the cult of the body that emerged would frame the local variant of the sexual liberation movement and the increasing Westernization of Israeli culture—at least within the center of Israeli hedonistic liberalism—Tel Aviv.[15] As cinema began to move away from its puritanical roots and the determination to represent heroic pioneering tales, it, too, directed attention toward women's bodies as sexual rather than simply sacrificial. If the pioneer represented a "heroic past," then the beauty queen promised a dazzling future, and both positions were co-opted into the national enterprise, ultimately to serve patriarchal narratives about women's roles in society. As Doane has shown, women are assigned "*a position, a place* in patriarchal culture," which is then enacted on-screen; Israeli cinema denoted women's status and their choice of roles (pioneer, glamour queen, and dutiful housewife) clearly.[16]

This change in attitude toward the female body became evident in the pervasive display of women's nakedness in Israeli cinema. Women's voyeuristic exhibition was consciously employed by filmmakers, who provided characters peeping at naked women as the camera enjoyed spying on these explicit scenes for the enjoyment of the male filmmakers and "male" audiences looking on. In an industry dominated by men both on-screen and behind it, a cinema that served male fantasies, by the 1960s women were increasingly offered up in lurid sexual display, which served both to gratify male lust and to signify women's servility to male needs. Frequently women were also presented as domestic and functionally compliant, thereby reinforcing gender positions and maintaining patriarchal authority. Lubin has condemned Israeli cinema's tendency to parade women's bodies: "The device of the penetrating gaze is employed in almost every Israeli film in which there is a female character. In almost all such films, women's sexuality is displayed—not as a central theme or a plot catalyst, but as a contingent prop. However, careful analysis reveals that despite the recurring use of this mechanism to position women as inferior, it is not the dominant one. In Israeli films, the dominant mechanism is not the penetrating gaze but rather social positioning—women's professional standing, their place in the community, and their role in the family."[17] The films' social positioning of women did indeed inform their potential roles, but their sexual display was no less a part of establishing gender power structures. Parading women in sexually explicit situations, revealing their breasts and sexual organs, did more than simply offer woman as spectacle. These representations also framed women's sexual duties within the Israeli collective: as a wife, girlfriend, fetish, or prostitute, a woman's sexual gratification was irrelevant—rather, her purpose was to serve male needs, in male plots, for a male spectatorship.

Woman as Tombstone

Aviad's documentary that examined the establishment of *Ein Harod,* one of the first kibbutzim, revealed cracks in the idealism of the socialist endeavor and uncovered the ideological role that emerged for women—as the national womb. Under David Ben-Gurion, Israel's first prime minister, this role was codified as women's contribution to the national project. Responsible for producing sons to serve in the army, for replacing Jewish lives lost during the Holocaust, and for providing fodder in the demographic battle by which maintaining a Jewish majority within Israel would be the only way of maintaining Israel as a Jewish state, procreation was clearly articulated as women's primary duty.[18] Time has not softened this attitude toward women, and during periods of heightened militarism and increased demographic threat, the expectation that women procreate continues to enslave women within cultural expectations.

Women's purpose has always been clear: they are wives of soldiers, mothers of soldiers, widows of soldiers, and their identity is defined by the Zionist project. Though their role was different from that of men, it was no less contained by the mythic stature of national ideology. As symbols of home and the reasons for men's sacrifice, women had no space to have separate independent identities, and their sexuality was contained within their gendered domestic roles. Nathan Alterman's iconic poem "The Woman" encompasses the entirety of women's duty in its short four lines:

> The woman said: My God,
> You have appointed me since days of old
> to fall at the feet of the living,
> And to stand at the head of the dead.
>
> Translated by T. Carmi

Written as a woman's prayer, the poem recalls the traditionalism and religiosity of a Jewish past, at odds with the secularity of the socialist pioneers. Furthermore, it is a reminder that women devote themselves to men and serve as a living memorial to the fallen. In this poem, as with the pioneer films, woman is constructed as a symbolic signifier and defined in relation to men. Elizabeth Cowie, in her examination of women's sexuality in film, offers the claim that women are made absent:

> The image of the woman refers not to the referent woman, existing in the real world outside of representation, but to a meaning produced by and for men. Patriarchy controls the image of woman, assigning it a function and value determined by and for men, and in the service of the construction of definitions of the male and more especially of masculine desire. Patriarchy and the interests of men become a unified field which is able to determine meanings outside of the process of signification.[19]

Though she may serve as a central character, the woman who loses her husband in his service for the nation comes to stand in for the man who is remembered through her.

Yael Zerubavel's analysis of war widows in Israeli films explains that the war widow is "a symbolic extension of the fallen soldier."[20] This national role obligates the widow into a complex and conflicting ideological position—while she is expected to overcome her grief, social expectations dictate that she must remain chaste, staying "loyal to her social role as living memorial."[21] Moreover, as the carrier of the husband's memory, she "embodies the connection between a personal and a national sacrifice."[22] Mihal Friedman has described the role of living memorial as a "pernicious projection" that appears to position women at the center, while actually marginalizing them in favor of the men for whom they serve as a lieux de mémoire.[23] The rupture to the social fabric that Pierre Nora imagined in his coining of this idea is created in the husband's death. The repetition of his memory in national ceremonies serves to imbue the sacrifice with national meaning—a purpose that is facilitated through the presence of the war widow, whose own loss moves from that of the personal to that of the collective as it is co-opted in the service of national memory. Through this memorialization the woman's body is symbolically embalmed as the locus of the man's memory, her sexual body is destroyed, and her femininity is slowly erased, in a process by which she ultimately adopts the androgeneity of the national body. In many of the films that depict the war widow, the woman's body becomes a contested space. Her own desires conflict with the role thrust on her, and ultimately her metamorphosis into the role of "the war widow" is such that the signified woman is present while the *actual woman* becomes absent. Michal Friedman has argued that she is "deprived of her body."[24] These elements are exemplified in *Siege*, a film made in the new sensibility style that examines the social isolation of Tamar (Gila Almagor), a young widow with a small child bereaved by the death of her husband. Filmed in black and white, its atmospheric stylized shots, minimalist sets, and montage sequences with overlaid voices gossiping on the widow's future highlight her public role and therefore the public's claim to the national memory the widow represents.

At thirty, Tamar is expected to remain in mourning for her husband and serve as a living memorial to his sacrifice. She is visited by his close friend Eli (Yehoram Gaon), who maintains the link to her dead husband by constantly talking about him and taking Tamar to visit his wounded friends and thus enacts the social structures that maintain her position as a national widow. This duty, and her relationship with Eli, serve to construct her social imprisonment. Her husband's death and her concomitant sentence as chaste war widow signify both a personal claustrophobic psychological trauma from which she cannot heal, and as a metaphor of the country's own experience of besiegement and military trauma. Despite Eli's hints that he may be attracted to her, he cannot act, as he, like her, must conform to the social expectation that she remain the wife of his friend, even after his death. When an unnamed interloper (Dan Ben Amotz) threatens to disrupt her implacable petrification by reawakening her as a sexual and passionate woman, Eli feels deceived and believes she has betrayed her husband's memory. But ultimately the role of war widow is an eternal and a universal one for the Israeli woman, and when her new lover goes to the front with his unit, the ambiguous ending of the film suggests that she will again be widowed. Eli returns to her side in the hunt for the potentially deceased new lover, regaining his identity as loyal friend and as a symbol of societal expectations for the bereaved widow. While the film is reflexive about the condition of the war widow, despite her appearance in almost every shot of the film and notwithstanding the story's presentation through her, the widow ultimately remains a spectre. Even as the film critiques the eternal widow role, it continues to offer up the women as a symbolic paean to a male ideal that his sacrifice will be forever commemorated and that he will continue to live on through her.

The figurative immolation of the war widow that had sanctified female martyrdom (if only in the service of men) would begin to give way to an anxiety whereby women refused this role. Cast as sexually liberated without a restraining male presence, the war widow was increasingly viewed as a threat to the national project, as evident in two kibbutz films, *Atalia* and *Sweet Mud* (*Adama Meshuga'at*, Dror Shaul, 2006), in which the oppressive role of national bereaved (and its accompanying social isolation) becomes a trigger for madness. In both films, the woman is widowed at a young age. Isolated and socially ostracized, she becomes alienated and yet is expected to serve as a memorial to the dead husband she knew for only a brief period many years earlier. As "a lonely and malfunctioning woman who becomes increasingly alienated from her immediate social environment,"[25] the war widow becomes transgressive, driven to madness, violence, and sexual abandon. Zerubavel points to Dan Wolman's made-for-television film *Sex, Lies and Dinner* (Sex, Shkarim VaArukhat Erev, 1996), in which three war widows reveal their loneliness, loss, and social marginalization. The expectation that they remain faithful as a symbol of everything that has been sacrificed, and, at the same time, their abandonment by female friends who view the war widow as a potential threat to their own marriages, exacerbates their isolation. The young war widow exists in a paradox in which she is viewed both as asexual, preserved in a living tomb as a symbolic extension of her dead husband, and as hypersexual, having the potential to threaten the social order by undermining her national duty in favor of personal desire if she acts on her sexual subjectivity.

Besieged Sexuality

These interwoven themes of female madness and the threat to the nation are exemplified in *My Michael*, a film adaptation of Amos Oz's novel, which offers a psychological melodrama about the troubled relationship of a young couple, Michael and Hannah Gonen, set against the background of 1950s Jerusalem. The partitioned city, divided between the State of Israel in the West and Jordan in the East, is split by fifteen-foot walls, barbed wire, and land mines. The sense of besiegement that conveys Hannah's troubled mind is echoed in the cityscape, and, like Almagor in *Siege*, she is physically and mentally restricted, triggering her sexual exploration and an erotic awakening. Her recollections of the Arab boys of her youth develop into violent sexual fantasies whose intensity increases as her marriage breaks down. For Shohat the twins "serve little narrative function beyond mirroring and metaphorizing the repressed Dionysian inner self of the protagonist and her romantic frustration with her humdrum and unimaginative existence. In this sense, the Arab presence penetrates the hallucinatory space of Jewish-Israeli subjectivity, but is silent as a national, political voice."[26] Loshitzky, reading through a postcolonial discourse, thinks the twins "can be read as the revenge of oppressed and repressed." The ambiguity with which Hannah views them may be read as subversive, since her attitude transgresses taboos "regarding interracial (Jewish/Arab) sexual relationships."[27] But it is through contact with an exotic and forbidden "East" that her sexuality is liberated. Loshitzky addresses this economy of desire through which "fetishization" of the "low class" emerges.[28] As with Hollywood's colonialist films in the first decades of the twentieth century, the film's portrayal of a white woman's lust for "men of color" acknowledges "a specific form of (white) woman's sexual desire while simultaneously depending on categories of race and nation to represent that sexual desire as dangerous for women."[29] In the Israeli context, Hannah's transgressive libidinousness threatens to undermine the hegemony of white Jewish nationalism, particularly through her fantasy of the Arab twins' return as men, whereby they appear as armed Palestinian terrorists. Her sadomasochistic fantasies and her pedophilic longings for Yoram, a young boy whom she tutors, destabilize the normative order whereby the patriarchy must defend its women from attack by the enemy.

Wolman's adaptation of Oz's novel privileges Hannah's gaze, using it for erotic ends. "Here, female desire is expressed unequivocally and emphatically," and it is she "who activates the gaze" in many of the erotic encounters of the film.[30] Using her sexuality to *other* the child and the Arab men, Hannah displaces her *otherness*. Ultimately, however, Hannah is a destructive force whose fantasies serve to reward male anxiety and its orientalist position in which the Jewish female (and her womb) can be occupied, thereby displacing Jewish male authority. In addition, her depiction in the novel offers her as a "self-hating woman who rejects her femininity and especially her maternal role. She is portrayed as a 'bad mother' who is completely indifferent to her son."[31] This dereliction of her biological and national purpose casts her out of the body politic and thereby emphasizes the corruption that female sexual subjectivity produces.

The anxiety over the potential female threat to the social structure, and the flouting of sexual taboos, is a central theme in *Eastern Wind* (*Hamsin*, Daniel Wachsmann, 1982), a drama about a Jewish family in an old farming village in the Galilee and the tension with their Palestinian neighbors who once owned the lands, which were appropriated. Gedalia and Khaled's friendship is limited by their difference as Jew and Arab. But their shared passion for the land, offered up in their exhausting labor, facilitates a male economy of politics and homoerotic love. Gedalia's sister, through her sexual relationship with Khaled, forms a triangle that connects them. Rather than serving as an expression of female sexuality, the female becomes a vehicle (much like the cows waiting to be inseminated) that enables the expression of the Palestinian's nationalist and sexual awakening. As a woman, she serves as "mother earth," symbolized in her name, *Hava* (Eve), but she is androgynous, like Hannah Gonen before her, and avowedly nonpioneer, leaving farming to her brother and willfully disconnecting from the land until Khaled returns her to it as they care for the house where they create a love nest. Her relationship with Khaled exposes the power dynamics at play: "Hava is the white lady/master while Khaled is the dark slave who relinquishes his own desires to hers."[32] The bull that Gedalia releases in angry response to Khaled's growing love for Hava kills Khaled and exposes the libidinal desires that rest in Gedalia. As the dominant male, he will maintain ultimate control over the land and the womenfolk, but at the price of his own isolation.

The ethnic transgressions that liberate women's sexuality are neutralized through a process by which female identity is annihilated. Hannah Gonen in *My Michael* and Hava in *Eastern Wind* cut their hair short and are shown in cinematic shots morphing into male figures, which both establishes additional layers of (female) transgression and facilitates the homoerotic connection between the Arab and Jewish males, thereby marginalizing women and returning the central male conflict to the screen. Moreover, the women exist in positions of privileged "whiteness," and the sexual fantasy, and sexual control over the Arab *other*, remains within their control. This is a male fantasy, as Loshitzky argues, in which the white female remains protected.

The inverse is also true, as the white male, in a position of social and economic power, may fetishize the low-class ethnic woman. As facilitators of male pleasure, in the service of male hegemony, Mizrahi women, who are read multiply as "women of color" and as "low class," are offered up for sexual exploitation, while they experience even greater limits on their agency than those experienced by white women or the ethnic men in a cinema that pits Arab against Jew. The Mizrahi woman's potential salvation is a major feature of the prostitute film, in which she exists as a creature of the male imagination and as a projection for Ashkenazi male fantasies of sexual exploration and heroism.

Mizrahi Prostitutes and the Ashkenazi Hero Complex

The Westernization signified by the beauty queen image opened the door to male spectators' desire for the sexual gratification denied in the representation of virginity and the chaste domesticity of the pioneering woman. Israeli cinema responded with a seductive temptress outside the traditional representations of the national project: either as a male plaything depicted in the secular, hedonistic, and symbolically antiestablishment Tel Aviv of the 1960s, 1970s, and 1980s or as a prostitute connected to a criminal underworld, living on the margins of society and polluting the purity of the national body. By comparison with cinema's early years in Israel, when women's sexuality was generally contained within the prescribed ideological roles of the earth-mother-pioneer-soldier (or exposed in depictions of the ideological vision's failure), a new convention emerged in which "a woman's incorrect sexual behavior posed a threat to the national community. In particular, women who sold their body for money were associated with dishonor, disease, decay, and treason, and accused of endangering the nation's unity, health, and future. The negative image of prostitutes was used to control the boundary between 'good' and 'bad,' national inclusion and exclusion."[33] The representation of prostitution and sexual promiscuity served as a warning of women's failure, thereby reinforcing and reinscribing the importance of women's need to remain inside a patriarchal order in which life as a wife and mother offered social protection, a process Mary Ann Doane has referred to as "a recuperative strategy."[34] But the division between the prostitute and the sexually liberated modern Tel Aviv woman was framed not only as a socioeconomic difference but also one of color and ethnicity: the liberated woman was Ashkenazi (white), while the prostitute was Mizrahi (of color).[35] This ethnic coding achieved two results: firstly it discouraged women from escaping life within the patriarchal rules of the traditional Mizrahi community by warning them that they were simply trading the benevolent protection of a father or brother for the exploitative "protection" of a pimp, and secondly it served to educate and socialize Ashkenazi women to their superior position in the social hierarchy and to warn them that deviance would lead to a Mizrahi woman's fate.

Images of prostitution served as a reminder to all women that marriage, with its domestic ideal, was the preferred goal, and rejecting a patriarchal hegemony that discouraged female economic and sexual independence would only result in disaster. In addition, as Russell Campbell shows in his study of prostitution, "The married woman, under the sign of Western individualism and at the cost of rigidly curtailing her sexual activity, has been able to claim something approaching legal equality with her husband; the prostitute battles away against discrimination, against laws that hedge and confine her."[36] Ilana Szobel argues that the preoccupation with the prostitute in early Hebrew writing aroused "fear and revulsion in the protagonist, to the point that he negates her womanhood ('they scarcely belonged to the female sex') and, no less important, his own manhood ('his attitude seemed to him unmanly, morbid, and childish')."[37] Thus the rejection of the prostitute from Israeli society, in which the female body is revered and sanctified, upholds the normative order, while the flirtatious and sexually promiscuous Tel Aviv woman may be viewed as a tease who can be returned to the traditional sexual structure without serious damage to her or to the body politic. Few women attained the ideal of either the pioneer or the beauty queen that popular culture venerated, but neither were many Israeli women sexually liberated or working as prostitutes, despite the proliferation of these images in the cinema; rather, most lived within a conservative society that condemned decadence and excess, even as Western cinematic influences would lead to avant-garde and sexually explicit films that appeared to contravene Israel's social mores.

The depiction of Mizrahi women as prostitutes is used to encode the Ashkenazi critique of Mizrahi patriarchy (as previously considered in chapter 3) while absolving white men of responsibility for their exploitation of Mizrahi women. Ironically, Ashkenazi female actresses would play the roles of the Mizrahi prostitutes, offering a twist in the chauvinistic misogyny that viewed Ashkenazi women as protected and unassailable, in contrast to viewing the Mizrahi woman as sexually available and degenerate. The patriarchal colonialist logic that considered the white woman virginal offered up the "black" woman as a site of colonization, exploitation, and sexual permissiveness as part of an orientalist fantasy whereby the woman of color is available and desirous. Simultaneously, the flirtation with the oriental space, with its sexual promise, also connoted an element of danger that expanded the allure but also delimited the bounds of the experience, exemplified in the prostitutes' criminal associations, violent pimps, and drug culture. The Mizrahi label enabled Ashkenazi actresses' sexual expression while shielding them from any consequences for this demonstration. Playing a prostitute provided a subversive space that permitted expressions of female sexuality, but the story lines' morality reined in any possibility for powerful opposition to the patriarchal hegemony by enacting punishment (rape, violence, or the loss of a child) that stressed the negative consequences of sexual behavior, fortifying Israeli society's repudiation of prostitutes (and, to a degree, Mizrahi women as well). Furthermore, the failure to offer Mizrahi leading roles to Mizrahi actresses reveals the deep-seated prejudice that existed within the cinematic industry in Israel. Because the prostitutes were represented as ethnic "others," female spectators (even Mizrahi women) could distance themselves from the female oppression on-screen through an identification with the Ashkenazi male hero and the Zionist ideology that rejected multiple presentations of pathology, including ethnicity, drugs, rape, and criminality, that stood as the antithesis of the pure healthy body and the cult of labor central to the national ethos.

Eldorado, Queen of the Road, Dead End Street, A Place by the Sea (*Makom L'yad Hayam*, Rafael Revivo, 1988), *Or, My Treasure*, and even the grotesque satire *An Electric Blanket Named Moshe* (*Smicha Hashmalit U'Shema Moshe*, Assi Dayan, 1994) are among the films that repeat this convention of the Mizrahi prostitute, living on the edge of a seedy underworld.[38] Ilana Szobel, adopting Thomas Heise's analysis of literary depictions of lawless subcultures for a Hebrew literary context, shows that these associations between criminality and prostitution "give us a glimpse of the milieu of others who share our world, but those representations are also what enable us to misrecognize such others and not have to deal with their subjectivity."[39] As with representations of prostitution in Hebrew literature of the revival period, the woman's voice is absent, as these women are cast from a male perspective and viewed through a male gaze that tells "us less about prostitutes than about the desires and terrors of those who write (and read) about them."[40] While these films all address prostitution as a social problem, postulated through the interweaving of drugs, criminality, and violence, the depiction of prostitution as a quotidian part of a male-centered Israeli reality can also be seen in many Israeli films, including *Peeping Toms* (*Metzizim*, Uri Zohar, 1972), *Colombian Love* (*Ahava Colombianit*, Shay Kanot, 2004), *Sixtieth Street* (*Rehov Shishim*, George Ovadiah, 1976), *Julia Mia* (Yuval Granot, 2007), *Madame Rosa* (*La Vie devant soi*, Moshé Mizrahi, 1977), and *On the Third Day* (*Be Yom HaShlishi*, Moshe Ivgy, 2010).

Israel inherited its law code from the British Mandate, and prostitution was illegal, but in 1949, after the state was established, prostitution was decriminalized. Changes to the law in 1962 meant that "prostitutes were prohibited from 'working under a roof' (in a house, even the prostitute's residence, a vehicle or a boat). . . . Prostitution thus remained a street phenomenon, practiced in backyards, beaches and highways."[41] Until the wave of Russian immigrants from the former Soviet Union during the 1990s, it was a profession dominated by Moroccan Jews. Most recently, temporary migrant workers from Moldova and the Ukraine, and issues of human trafficking, have changed the nature of the debate and the material situation of prostitution in Israel. Massage parlors and conventional brothels have become more widespread; prostitution is increasingly controlled by the Russian mafia, who use it to launder money; and prostitution is often a cog in a larger (international) criminal network.

After the 1990s wave of immigration from the former Soviet Union, the prostitute's ethnicity changed from Mizrahi to Russian on-screen. As Gershenson and Hudson observe: "Recently, the Russian immigrant woman emerged as a new 'other' of Israeli cinema. She appears in multiple films and television dramas. As in the print media, an image of a Jewish immigrant is often conflated with an image of a non-Jewish sex worker. At this point, it is difficult to find an Israeli film that does not feature a seductive or bizarre 'Russian' woman as at least a minor character."[42] Though there had been a change in ethnic hierarchies within Israel, the image of prostitution continued to pervade. This fixation in contemporary cinema may be viewed in light of the negation of national ideology, with its philosophy of the pure body, and thus often serves as a metonym for the breakdown of moral values within Israeli society, an issue whose poignancy was again evident when Israel found itself ranked high among the list of countries responsible for human trafficking.[43] Amos Gitai's *Promised Land* (*Ha'eretz Hamuvtachat*, 2004), *What a Wonderful Place* (*Eize Makom Niflah*, Eyal Halfon, 2005), and *The Assassin Next Door* were among several films to examine the commercial sexual exploitation of Russian women, which, along with a poor ranking for tackling this issue by the US State Department's report on human trafficking, embarrassed the government and led to several measures to stop the smuggling, to prevent abuses within Israel, and to protect the victims. Even when the prostitute serves as a central character within the drama, she does so from a position of ethnic otherness, which enforces a perception that the decay of modern society lies not in its own corruption but in the presence of the deviant *other*.

Raz Yosef, reading the Mizrahi body through Kristeva's notions of the abject, addresses the ways in which the Mizrahi subject served as a site to be repudiated and rejected, lurking "at the boundaries of our existence, threatening the apparently settled unity and cleanliness of both the subject and the social body."[44] The elements of decay associated with prostitution are evoked in the cinematic landscape in the makeup, dress, behavior, and intellect of the women, thus conveying a Mizrahi body whose corruption is so absolute that it exists within and grows out of a putrefaction that threatens to overwhelm the clean, healthy body represented by the New Jew; to destroy the venerated building (and agricultural) projects of the new state; and ultimately to overwhelm the country's Westernization with a consuming and destructive Levantine pollution. Teasing out her reading of the abject female body, he reads the construction "of female sexuality and corporeality marginal, indeterminate, and viscous,"[45] whereby the Mizrahi prostitute denotes a consuming threat to the nation with her very body, its fluids, wastes, and secretions. The viewer's pleasure in her libidinous behavior lay not necessarily in the display of her sexuality but in the moral lesson indicated by her often-violent end.

Poorly educated and a symbol of the social periphery, the prostitutes' aggressive attitude, meant to ward off comment or attack, offered the veneer of a hard shell, while in intimate spaces their depiction as vain, capricious, and delusional, often trapped in emotionally abusive relationships with unsavory criminals, situated them as pitiful and loathsome, but also victims of their situation. The brutality of the prostitutes' lifestyle and behavior is tempered through a convention of representing each woman's softness, thereby creating sympathy for an otherwise unlikeable character. Usually demonstrated through acts of kindness toward animals or those less fortunate, a quality that is offered to explain the prostitutes' easy duping, the prostitutes' naïveté is constructed by the films in order to suggest that circumstance rather than character led to their situation. These films suggest prostitution as a mechanism of survival in a patriarchal society where women are already oppressed. Viewed ideologically as a cancer on the state's utopian image, in reality prostitution demonstrated the state's growing normalization. As a popular apocryphal statement attributed in turn to Theodor Herzl, Haim Nachman Bialik, and David Ben-Gurion has it, when there is a Jewish thief, a Jewish prostitute, and a Jewish murderer, then Israel will be a real country.[46] The prostitute, as Russell Campbell notes, "is created and sustained by patriarchal society to service men's desires: she is required to make her body available to men on demand, and then condemned for doing so."[47] Her abject state can be read in the contradiction of her existence. As an *object*, the prostitute facilitates men's needs, but as a *subject*, she poses a threat to society, highlighting the hypocrisy of a system that wants her but is simultaneously repelled by her.

Prostitution challenged not only Zionism's ideas of sexuality (and purity) but also its ideology of labor. It is the gendered nature of the discourse, rather than the corruption of Zionist ideals, that has framed criticism and shaped legislation, particularly with a view to protecting minors and more recently trafficked women. The discussion about prostitution that took place in the 1970s was shaped through the impact of "women within the state bureaucracy [who] constituted the driving force in raising the issue and in its framing as an administrative service issue. They also gendered the debate by insisting on its gender-specificity, based on a mixture of professional-traditional approaches—pathologizing the young women—at the same time creating for themselves an organizational and professional power base for addressing the unique needs of women."[48] The development of a feminist response to prostitution moved the conversation from the protection of the moral fiber of the country[49] to a consideration of women's welfare: "for the first time in Israel the debate about prostitution was formulated as a social, physical, mental, emotional and moral problem—both for the girls involved and for society at large—permeating all governmental levels: government, parliament, local councils, as well as women's organizations, professionals, the media and the public at large."[50] Israeli cinema would couple together these elements—pathologizing the prostitute, the proposed salvation of the woman, the criminal apparatus that surrounds prostitution—and color the film in the local reality of Moroccan (and later Russian) women, operating outdoors at landfills or on desolate building sites or surreptitiously and illegally in the prostitute's apartment or a rundown hotel. It was not until the 1990s and the first decade of the twenty-first century, in films dealing with Russian gangsters and the white slave trade, that brothels would commonly appear on-screen.

Eldorado, among the earliest of the films featuring prostitution, is an adaptation of a play by Yigal Mossinson that explored the social trappings of poverty and criminality. Benny, a small-time gangster who spends his days in pool halls in Jaffa, wants to go straight, but when he is accused of a crime his lawyer refuses to defend him, and, forced to plead guilty, he must find the real criminal in order to have his conviction overturned. The motivation for his volte-face lies in the pretty young female whose Tel Aviv address, fine clothing, and elegant manner mark her out as a symbol of the upper classes. By contrast, Margo, the prostitute who is devoted to Benny, remains trapped in a life of poverty and petty crime. As with the later *Queen of the Road*, the role of the Mizrahi prostitute was played by Gila Almagor, who more generally played in conventional heroic Ashkenazi roles as social worker, kibbutz member, or widow.

Margo, a beautiful and cheerful prostitute, works from her apartment, helped by local hoodlums who send prospective clients her way while quietly robbing them of the occasional possession. We first see her dressed only in underwear, her long legs traced by a lingering camera gaze, while she casually flips through a magazine as rhythmic popular music plays on the radio propped by her side. Trapped within the ill-fated life and situation of her profession, Margo's poverty, low-class life, and criminal associations doom her, and, unlike Benny, she has no hope of an alternative life. In this role, Almagor would develop the archetypal prostitute, faithful to her boyfriend/pimp, comic and sad, generally kind, and resigned to her future.

The convention of representing the Mizrahi prostitute as a "passive and subservient" victim of Mizrahi masculinity meant that the only possible redemption available to her came

Eldorado: Margo (Gila Almagor) as the prostitute.

from "the Western Ashkenazi world and in particular . . . the native-born Israeli man (the Sabra)."[51] But for most Mizrahi heroines, the reality was that the Ashkenazi male served as a fantasy of an alternative life that within the diegesis of the film would never materialize. Margalit, in *Queen of the Road*, becomes pregnant by the Ashkenazi man she loves. Abandoning prostitution, she plans for motherhood. On a visit to her mother in the development town that serves as a metonym for the poverty and social depravation of her Mizrahi life, she is violently gang raped and as a result gives birth to a retarded child. Yosef explains that "[t]o the 'enlightened' viewer, the prostitute's wretched fate arouses compassion and identification with the female victim, a kind of rescue fantasy of the Mizrahi woman," yet this reading fails to account for the complexity of social attitudes toward prostitution and toward Mizrahim living in Israel's periphery.[52] The contextual framing of the Mizrahi woman discourages any identification with her suffering or her social situation, and in a feminist reading of her situation it is apparent that the film's manipulative positioning of the prostitute as a victim of the male hegemony, one that repeatedly etches out her vulnerability, positions her and all women as in need of male protection.

Widely critiqued in rape-revenge fantasies, the eroticization of rape collapses the distinction between rape as violence and rape as sex. Furthermore, the eroticism of the rape not only provides pleasure for a sadistic male (and masochistic female) audience, it feeds a rape culture that rejects responsibility for violence against women and projects it onto ethnic others. As Campbell reminds us, "Commission of the act itself, however[,] may be displaced from the male protagonist onto a surrogate figure, such as a pimp or a serial killer, so that the murder [or rape] may be simultaneously enjoyed and disavowed: the existence of violence against women in society is thus acknowledged but attributed to bad elements who will themselves, very likely, be obliterated," a fact that feeds its own separate pleasure for an audience trained to identify heroes and villains.[53] The terror of the attack reminds women spectators of their own vulnerability, while at the same time Campbell contends that a prostitute's killing on-screen "may serve to assuage male fears: for a time at least the anxieties that the female as sexual being provokes can be stilled," a concept that, I would argue, can also be extended to the act of rape, through which the prostitute is symbolically punished for her transgressive nature.

The film's rape touches upon the duality of attitudes toward prostitution and sexual violence; their paralleling not only provides the realism that is characteristic of Israeli cinema, it also conflates all acts of sex by a prostitute with rape and violence, and undermines the possibility of prostitution (and the living earned from it) providing female subjectivity. In the attempt to focus on the problems women face by offering up a gang rape, the film ends up overdetermined by the terms of patriarchy, since even as it points to women's oppression it reinforces its necessary parameters by offering up female vulnerability in need of male protection. Despite the prostitute's potential redemption, her former life threatens to leave a scar that serves as a permanent stain on the collective. Instead, her annihilation provides cathartic release for the viewer, removing her threat while allowing the audience to indulge in the pleasures of sympathy and regret. Thus, because she is a victim of Mizrahi patriarchy, the Ashkenazi hegemony can disclaim responsibility for her situation while simultaneously continuing to condemn her for failing to attain the lofty heights of ideal Israeli femininity.

The very title *Queen of the Road* evokes the "Beauty Queen" ideal and the pageants that had evolved out of the traditional Queen Esther imagery of the Jewish holiday of Purim, in which Yemenite women were frequently cast in the royal role.[54] In the postbiblical tale, the beautiful Jewess saves her nation from the evils of the king's advisor Hamen when she marries the king and engages in sophisticated palace intrigue. Thus the title "Queen" in the Israeli Jewish context is associated with the elevation of a commoner to a privileged life by virtue of her attractiveness and intellect, as well as specifically identified with women from Middle Eastern origins. In the context of this film, the reference addresses Margalit's hopes for a better existence while situating her as an Oriental fantasy. The film's bitter irony lies in the vast chasm between this dream and the Israeli reality, in which the Mizrahi prostitute remains condemned to a life of debasement and violence. Israeli films that focus on prostitution (as opposed to those that include it in a peripheral way) exhibit a pattern in which gender and power transect the axis of ethnicity. The Mizrahi characterization of the criminal element and of the prostitutes caught within its net allows the viewer to regard prostitution and violence against women as ethnic issues, distancing the viewer from a feeling of responsibility for women's subjugation and creating a space that allows for feelings of both moral superiority and sympathy, reminiscent of the sociopolitical position taken by feminists, who shaped the debate on prostitution in Israel from the 1970s onward.

Based on a true story, *Dead End Street* offers a protofeminist reworking of many of the themes that appear in other films featuring Mizrahi prostitutes. Reading social and ethnic marginalization alongside the question of gender, the film explores the possibilities available to a woman who dreams of an alternative life. Alice, a seventeen-year-old prostitute trapped in a violent and abusive relationship with a dangerous pimp, is offered the chance to feature in a film about prostitutes when she captures the attention of Yoram (Yehoram Gaon), the film's director. His original plan to make a film that brings attention to the plight of "these women" and draws attention to an institute that hopes to rehabilitate them situates the film as a documentary and Yoram as a passive (if earnest) observer who wishes to help with the women's redemption, thereby reenacting the Ashkenazi-male-rescue paradigm. Moving from the symbolic gesture of rescuing all women to the particular desire to save Alice, Yoram develops a rescue fantasy through which he hopes to save her from a life of poverty, violence, and abuse. As the crew follows her around while she muses endlessly over her grand plans (to travel to America, to model, to wear fancy clothes), she represents their ideal of the woman who wants to change. Feeding this hungry audience, Alice talks constantly, outlining a history of abuse and neglect that led to her situation in order to evoke their compassion. Yoram serves as a stand-in for the audience's sympathetic position and desire to help her. Thus her aggressive stance and confident demeanor are projected as a false mask that enables her to survive in a world of unimaginable horror. The audience is led to perceive an emotional truth behind this front in which the right environment and other life circumstances would allow the kindhearted woman to have had a different life. The filmmaker's project of creating a film (within the film) that will create sympathy for prostitutes and support the organization that hopes to save them is modeled in the audience's early reaction to Alice.

As the documentary mise-en-abyme develops and Alice is threatened by her pimp, for the film crew's convenience and her own protection Alice is brought to live with Yoram in his bourgeois apartment, where his books and music symbolize a life of unimaginable luxury. This move exposes her to the reality of her own fantasy—and the encounter is jarring. While she is extremely successful at getting men to choose her, even over other prostitutes, has a wide range of clientele, and has a fun and bawdy manner, it becomes increasingly clear that this is a protection that allows her to do her job while distancing herself from the acts. She is a professional who is in control of her body and receives money for a job she does well. Thus, now that she has encountered an alternative life, Yoram's request that she perform these tasks in the different context of the mis-en-abyme, staging what she does for the benefit of the camera, disrupts the power balance, removing her previous agency. Ironically, this then produces images of an unhappy prostitute with no control over her situation who stares out blankly at the camera, thereby reinforcing the stereotypes that serve the documentary's agenda. Here what essentially is offered as Yoram's voyeuristic pleasure, the looked-at-ness by which male power over the gaze controls (and owns) the woman, robs Alice of her authority and independence.

This moment serves as a watershed between the film's first half, which creates the stock fantasy of the "tart with a heart," and the second half, which destabilizes the viewer's sense of emotional truth by destroying the image of Alice as a victim of a violent Mizrahi world. As Yoram continues to investigate, serving as the spectator's proxy, Alice's lies are increasingly exposed, revealing her self-destructive nature and ultimately alienating Yoram and the audience. The claim that her father sexually abused her, that she ran away at thirteen, and that she became pregnant by a man who abandoned her, forcing her into a life of prostitution to pay for an abortion, establishes the conventional narrative of a prostitute's unfortunate past, which is then systematically unraveled. Yoram travels to her family home to interview her parents for the film, where he encounters a kindly, religiously traditional family living in abject poverty, caring for a young baby whose presence is never explained. The father's sadness over "Aliza's" abandonment of the family when she was fifteen, and his understanding that she longed for more than they could offer her, situates Alice as materialistic and highlights her avarice, lack of compassion, and irresponsible nature, thereby undermining her credibility as a victim. The Hebrew translation of *Alice in Wonderland*, the Lewis Carroll children's story, renames the heroine "Aliza," and through this connection *Dead End Street* gestures at the childish fantastical, if not delusional, reality that Alice has spun for Yoram, for herself, and for the audience.

As Yoram becomes increasingly devoted to Alice while she takes up residence and domestic duties within his home, foreswearing her former life, the film offers the audience a conventional pattern of hope for a fairy-tale conclusion in which the prostitute's redemption and return to the fold of heterosexual normative domesticity signal her readmittance into society. This idealistic vision is threatened by Yoram's producer Miri. Her own sexual relationship with him, and her jealousy and possessiveness, paint her as an antagonist who wishes to exploit Alice as a prostitute for the film and, unlike Yoram, does not wish to save her. Played by Gila Almagor, whose roles as the prostitutes Margo in *Eldorado* and Margalit in *Queen of the Road* create a resonating intertext, whereby the original viewers of the film (who would undoubtedly have been familiar with Almagor's previous performances) destabilize the viewers' notion of victim and aggressor. Conflating the actress's previous roles with her present role, as the intertext does, Almagor's presence suggests that the prostitute may leave her life of prostitution but she will never enter the normative ideal of wife and mother (she is maintaining an affair with Yoram). The film also implies that a reformed prostitute's survival depends not on kindness but on a determined will for selfish rewards. The reformed prostitute will not use her newfound status to help save other women but will instead exploit their situation for her own professional advancement. This commercialization of human relationships, signified typically by prostitution, will be repeated in Miri's exploitation of Alice and in Yoram and Miri's relationship that advances his career—suggesting that all relationships depend upon commodification. The prostitute may exist on the lowest level of the totem but she is not the only character to barter her body.

The film attacks a simplistic reading of prostitution as the unfortunate condition of women who might otherwise be helped, highlighting the patriarchal attitude that arrives at such a conclusion. It draws attention to the commodification of women, and of sex more broadly, revealing that women can actually claim their own bodies for trade, thereby not only having a stake but also being invested in maintaining their own identity within the transaction so that it does not necessarily result in a loss of power. In turning the camera on Alice, the film showcases the issue of gaze and power, suggesting that there are other forms of exploitation and that prostitution may be just the most morally abhorred. Miri's implied ownership of Yoram, and Yoram's exploitation of their sexual relationship for his own professional advancement, are other ways that sex and power are traded.

Furthermore, the film implicates society more broadly in this commercial arrangement, and in women's oppression. In contrast to the convention of projecting the travails of Mizrahi women on a Mizrahi patriarchy, the film quickly establishes that the oppression of women is not the result of just one sector but of patriarchy more broadly. Though Alice has a violent and controlling pimp who represents every stereotype of the genre, and her previous pimp is in jail, the Mizrahi criminal element is quickly disrupted in the arrival of the pimp's brother wearing an army uniform. His threats and demands for a thousand shekels (since she belongs to his imprisoned brother and by this logic owes her money to him) suggest that the military is neither clean nor heroic, and implicate all men in the exploitation of women. Later she will be shown having sex with a man in religious garb. Religious or secular, rich or poor, soldier or civilian, all men are in a position to exploit women for their own ends. The film attempts to disrupt the previous pattern of Mizrahi prostitutes, which offered a clear binary between good and bad men and "white" and "black" Israelis. However, Alice can neither free herself of her old life nor assimilate into the world she desires. Her tragic death in the final scene plays into the model of Greek tragedy that Lubin has argued is a feature of Israeli cinema, and also returns her to the binary option of motherhood or death that was constructed as the only possible life for an Israeli woman.

In the final account, the film remains a symbol of Mizrahi dispossession and invisibility. Alice's central role certainly offers her greater representation than the prostitute in *Eldorado*, who remains a support character, or the prostitute in *Queen of the Road*, who is portrayed as a victim of Mizrahi patriarchy. Although *Dead End Street* establishes female subjectivity and offers a complex portrait of female prostitution and women's subjugation, the Mizrahi woman continues to exist in the shadows of an Ashkenazi-dominated narrative. Just as with the

Dead End Street: The prostitutes (including Hana Maron and Tikva Dayan) gather with Alice (Anat Atzmon) waiting for clients.

Ashkenazi Almagor, who passed as the Mizrahi prostitute in the earlier films, Alice is played by Anat Atzmon, the green-eyed daughter of Shmulik Atzmon, the founder of Yiddishpiel, the Yiddish Theatre in Israel, and herself an icon of Tel Aviv's artistic community and secular, Ashkenazi hegemony. As with Almagor before her, Atzmon displaces an ethnically Mizrahi actress from this central role.

In a critical deconstruction of the conventions associated with representations of Mizrahi prostitution, the 2004 film *Or, My Treasure* moves beyond *Dead End Street* to present a complex reading of prostitution and the social structure that condemns Mizrahi women trapped in a life of poverty to such a profession. Despite attempts to prevent her mother, Ruthie (Ronit Elkabetz), from continuing as a prostitute through various attempts to earn money, Or (Dana Ivgy) is ultimately pulled into her mother's world. The film's avowedly Mizrahi feminist agenda is evident in the choice of lead actresses, women of Moroccan-Israeli origin. As Yosef has explained, the film "exposes the hegemonic social gaze as a political mechanism of power and violence that terrorizes the Mizrahi female body . . . the trauma of Mizrahi women is their imprisonment by the oppressive social gaze in a gendered and racialized abjected body. The Mizrahi woman's unceasing daily encounter with class and gender oppression, which she comes to internalize, constitutes an ongoing ordeal" by virtue of which she is condemned "to repeat the trauma."[55] As Or collects empty bottles from the street and the beach she repeats the streetwalker's promenade in a conscious and disruptive gesture that reimagines the relationship between the Mizrahi female body and the public space. But Or's attempts to reclaim the streets from her mother's prostitution and send her inside to the protected space of the home fail, as Ruthie begins to take clients into their apartment.

The film's preoccupation with rituals of cleansing, and Or's attempts to find work through acts of cleaning (washing dishes, cleaning stairwells, returning empty bottles) as well as finding her mother work as a cleaner, while denoting menial and domestic work also highlight the social order's desire to whiten and therefore civilize the woman of color. Or internalizes these ideals, a fact that is evidenced by the white sweater she brings to her mother at the hospital and begs her to wear. Covering up her mother's red dress, the sign of her life as a prostitute, serves as part of Or's plan to persuade her mother to abandon her former way of life, but as Yosef reminds us, "Or fails to understand that her mother's body is not polluted and dirty; rather, the sexist and racist society that Or is trying in vain to join has constructed Ruthie's body as abject."[56] Yosef points to the film's unrelenting exposure of the male gaze used to trap the women, as they are stared at, as they are made invisible, and in the merciless camera shots that challenge the viewer (by denying the shot/reverse-shot technique that allows the viewer access to the character's field of vision, and the use of fixed camera shots that create a static landscape that "slices the bodies of the characters as they come in and out of it").[57] In the film's final scene, Or stares into the camera, an action that Yosef views as a call to the viewer to "take ethical" and "ethnical" responsibility as she assumes work as a prostitute, thereby establishing prostitution as a cycle that is doomed to repeat in each generation.

The very manner in which the mise-en-scène is constructed in these films serves to undermine the idealism of the Israeli dream. Where previously sexual intercourse in nature served as a bond between the Zionist and the land and alluded to the fecundity (both agricultural and human) that resulted from the efforts of the pioneer in the heroic-nationalist genre films, these prostitution films challenge this vision in multiple ways: by offering a dead landscape that is usually a highway or garbage dump; by providing sexual acts whose eroticism is debased and disconnected from the positive emotions and iconography previously evoked; and because these acts fail to result in natural issue or to transform the woman into the mother figure that otherwise pervades the Israeli discourse. *Or, My Treasure* will even challenge the notion that motherhood is, in itself, redemptive.

Israeli cinema's attitude toward women's sexuality in its formative phases echoed nationalist ideas about women and their bodies. Women's role was to serve the nation through personal sacrifice, domestic labor that freed men to pursue higher tasks, and the production of children. Women were not welcome to independent desire, for it threatened to disrupt male camaraderie whereby woman as property could be traded without permission, it threatened to erase the memorial duty (and thereby erase the men they were supposed to be commemorating), and it threatened the very heart of the national enterprise by allying women with the *enemy*. The existential threat posed by the Arab man who might seduce the Israeli woman lay in his capacity to appropriate her national womb and to liberate her sexuality. It also lay in the brutal cruelty of the Mizrahi pimp, women's prostitution, and an underworld fueled by drugs and crime whose urban depravity was a far cry from the self-sacrificing pioneering ideals.

Feminist Filmmaking and the Independent Woman

The breakthrough film *Tel Aviv Stories* was radical precisely because it disrupted the narratives that had become conventions of Israeli cinema. In the first of three shorts, "Sharona Honey," Sharona is expected to choose one of the three men courting her: the emotionally abusive lover/boyfriend, the married friend who wishes to impregnate her despite his wife's expectant state, and the voyeuristic neighbor who has been staring at her through his binoculars while quietly stalking her. Lubin draws attention to the men's obsession with Sharona's sexuality and the film's preoccupation with her body. Her constant changes of clothing, bathing, and wild mane of hair evoke the conventional tropes for displaying females in Israeli cinema. But the film subverts these expectations, and, "in order to constitute the female subject, the film turns to the sexual body and the relevant mechanism—the penetrating gaze."[58] Sharona smashes the binoculars that have allowed the friend to observe her, and later gazes at the parade of men who have pursued her throughout the short film. These acts draw attention to the male gaze, thereby undermining it, and, in turn, allow Sharona to constitute "herself as a sexual subject according to her own model."[59] In the final passionate sequence in which Sharona rejects the male claims to her, the camera follows her through long, unstable tracking shots, providing the viewer with a sense of the persistent and pursuant force that is the relentless objectification of a woman, and through tilt angles demonstrates the conflict that ensues when she takes control of her own image. Jump-cut editing that in another context would suggest female hysteria is used to demonstrate anger and frustration with the lack of male ignominy. In a triumphant break with the romantic expectations of the film, Sharona runs away toward a garbage truck, abandoning the parade of men. Her sudden disappearance suggests that she has committed suicide by falling under the truck, playing on the paradigmatic death of a prostitute, but she reemerges a moment later riding triumphantly on the side of the vehicle. As the film draws to a close, Sharona fills more and more of the shot as she finally exists only for herself. Her face increasingly occupies the entire screen as she looks on at the three men standing by impotently, staring at her, as they slowly recede into the distance and into darkness while she continues to be consistently (and implausibly) lit. This radical display of independence disrupts the binary expectations of conformism (marriage or death) that had served as a major feature of women's representation on-screen.

Tel Aviv Stories: Sharona (Yaël Abecassis) looks out at the men from the back of the garbage truck as they recede into the distance.

In the second film, "Operation Cat," Zofit, a reporter, must find her subjectivity. Playing on the stereotypical conventions of a fragile, passive, and helpless woman, exemplified in her obsession with rescuing a cat trapped in a drain, the film offers the viewer the female who must be rescued by the Israeli male. But when the municipal services fail to help her, she realizes, through the mentorship of an older, dying actress, that she must take charge of her own fate and that of the cat. In saving both, she constitutes "an autonomous female subject—one who is not dependent upon or subservient to the surrounding male milieu, who is able to choose her own goals and attain them by her own efforts."[60] In the third episode of the trilogy, Tikva, a policewoman and mother, spies the husband who has abandoned her but failed to grant her a divorce, thereby keeping her chained to the marriage, since she is unable to remarry or symbolically start a new life. After kidnapping several passers-by, who quickly join her cause, she must capture her husband and turn him over to the authorities for due punishment. Among her prisoners is a rabbi who is able to make the rabbinical authorities facilitate her divorce, but she rejects their offer when the conditions include letting her husband go free. While Lubin has argued that "in the final analysis, she still needs the official sanction of the establishment, which, she feels, is preferable to her own,"[61] I would argue that Tikva, by agreeing to accept the rabbinates' offer, sanctions male control of women's rights. Her rejection of the deal, and her willingness to live, unmarried, with Prospar (the romantic interest), creates a new paradigm whereby the choice is not a single life or a married life sanctioned by the nation's authority but a feminist way in which a woman decides the rules by which she will choose (and live) her own life.

Sharona rejects motherhood, at least on the terms that it is offered to her; Zofit substitutes caring for a cat; and Tikva rejects the conformity of wife and mother as authorized by the establishment.[62] Thus the practice of containing women's sexuality within the legitimate bounds of motherhood or chastity is rejected, while these women choose and reimagine the conditions under which their sexuality may be realized. The feminist elements of the three films that make up *Tel Aviv Stories* also fight back against a history of representing women in Tel Aviv as sexually promiscuous and as objects available to male needs and conditions. Standing against a tradition of Tel Aviv–based films, such as *Peeping Toms*, *Lemon Popsicle* (*Eskimo Limon*, Boaz Davidson, 1978), *Dizengoff 99*, and others, that glaringly gorged on the exposed female body, lasciviously enjoying female exploitation, these films bared the conventions of the male gaze in Israeli cinema and marked out a different female space. Rejecting the portrayal of the city as a sexually liberal (if not immoral) cityscape that served as a home for licentiousness and orgiastic behavior on male terms, these shorts reconceptualized female agency and women's control of their sexuality and their bodies.

The reemergence of the female sexual body occurred alongside the appearance of the female experience, precisely because filmmakers were responding to women's previous *othering*, and thus they forged a space in which to create female subjectivity that rejected both the male gaze and the social positioning that had framed women for men's pleasure.[63] The legacy of *Tel Aviv Stories* can be seen in efforts to reclaim women's sexual identity across the genres of Israeli cinema. Feminist filmmaking in Israel did not have a history of women's films to draw on, but it did have an artistic past framed by its engagement with national ideology with which to engage, and an international history of feminist responses to the woman's films to use as precedent. It would do so by remaking male genre films, such as the military unit, as female films, as previously discussed in chapter 3; or consider the feminization of war and the empowerment of women in Israeli chick flicks as read in light of *The Song of the Siren* and *Yana's Friends*, as discussed in chapter 1. It would also serve as a model for female-centered films that specifically explored women's sexuality, such as *The Slut*, Hagar Ben-Asher's first feature film. In a reimagined version of the kibbutz, she engages with the tradition of representing the exploitation of women that had become a staple trope in its representation by constructing an idealized version that enacts the egalitarian ideology that had been a central tenet of the kibbutz movement. Unlike in *Atalia* and *Sweet Mud*, where the war widow is shown as sexually promiscuous and therefore a disruptive force to the social order, Ben-Asher's Tamar is a female who pursues a liberated sexual lifestyle within the agricultural community without censure. With Tamar cast as a chicken farmer who sells her eggs, the metaphor of women's fecundity is overtly played, and this is seen also in the two daughters she is raising who seem to have no ostensible fathers, though hints in the film suggest different men fathered each of the daughters. Her carefree roaming of the desolate farmlands and her time in the little hut where she sells her eggs, whose purchase serves as a way for men to indicate their desire for sexual intercourse, allows her to freely arrange her life as a series of libidinous encounters. When an old friend, Shai, a veterinarian, returns to the settlement after his mother's death, they begin a relationship, and while he moves into her home and takes on the domestic roles traditionally ascribed to women (caring for the children, maintaining the house, preparing food), she returns to her sexually promiscuous lifestyle.

The film is problematic, offering an unsympathetic female lead by contrast with the kindly veterinarian, thereby undermining the audience's capacity to identify with her principled independence. Its attempt to represent the woman's free spirit and her symbolic entrapment by the emotional ties Shai creates, portrayed in clumsy metaphors as he repeatedly puts animals in cages, creates a reductive story line that suggests men enact abuse against women in their desire to have sole sexual control over them. The film exposes a cinematic immaturity in its failure to move beyond rote sex scenes, in the limitations of its exposition, and in its unresolved cryptic riddles, which taunt the audience. Yet, as a film written, directed, and starring Hagar Ben-Asher, it proudly stakes a claim at the control women can have over filmmaking. Despite the lack of other female characters (except Tamar's two young daughters), the film's uncompromising presentation of female sexuality confronts a history of Israeli filmmaking that had viewed women's bodies only in relation to male desires.[64]

In a similar vein, *She's Coming Home* explores a young woman's sexual desires and consideration of her own femininity in the claustrophobic environment of her childhood home. The film self-consciously attacks the myths of male heroism and female weakness as well as the conventions of the romance story. Ze'ev, the new replacement head at the high school, a man two decades her senior, crashes into thirty-three-year-old Michal's car as she is returning to live with her parents after a breakup with her Tel Aviv boyfriend. Though she is the victim of the accident, he takes an aggressive tone toward her, but rather than succumbing she stands up to him, rejecting his patriarchal attitude and refusing to "serve" him by fetching the details that must be exchanged. Instead she hands him the paperwork and advises him to find what he wants. When she cannot restart the car, he steps in as if to save her but cannot start it either. Her father arrives in a taxi and also cannot help, since now neither has a vehicle they can use to return home. Ze'ev finally drives them all, and while the two men in the car discuss his military service, his unit, and his position in the reserves, from which he is returning, Michal is relegated to the backseat. Thus, from the opening scene, the director establishes the conventions of masculine discourse and the expectation that men will rescue women in distress, and then denies these male assumptions by providing a strong female lead who confronts the anticipated positions of female victimhood and male heroism by rejecting either role. Her hostility and ingratitude, rather than undermining her representation (as they do in *The Slut*), repudiate the expectations of subservience and veneration that unsolicited acts of male munificence generally demand. Thus the film establishes the conventions of the hegemony and provides a mode of female resistance to it.

The film examines the contradiction that exists for a woman returning to her parents, who expect her to be both adult and child but negate both options. On one hand, they insist she eat with them and dress according to their rules, and they spy on her burgeoning romance with Ze'ev; on the other, her father shows alarm at her sexualized body while at the same time being drawn to it, and her mother constantly criticizes her aging face, warning her daughter that youth is fleeting, while also considering her to be a sexual and romantic rival. The childhood bedroom, which has been preserved with children's clothes in the closet, speaks to the stunted preservation of memory, a position in which Michal, as a child, is adored. However, as an adult she disrupts the family dynamic. Her confidence, independence, and sexuality are shown alongside her transgressive smoking, drinking, and stealing (from her mother's purse).

Uncertain about her future and dressed in gender-neutral T-shirts, jeans, and boots, Michal eschews the trappings and expectations of femininity that her mother exemplifies in her manner and dress. Her aggressiveness is contrasted with her mother's victimhood and hyperfeminization. Her mother's constant search for compliments, infantilization (she chooses not to drive), heavy makeup, insistent flirtation, and expectation that every romance leads to marriage present a grotesque alternative to her own detached and independent womanhood. The mother's commodification of her daughter as "fresh meat" and her passive aggressive attempts to get her daughter to leave the house, including the inscription on her birthday cake that reads "leave home little sparrow," represent a traditional pattern of female power that works subversively and insists upon control without appearing confrontational. Whenever Michal directs attention to this behavior, her mother responds in a childish voice, saying, "a mistake" as a way of deflecting criticism. By situating the daughter within the childhood space, the film constructs her behavior as a simulation of teenage rebellion, but she is not a child, and because she is a woman and an adult, the film's exaggeration of this theme highlights problematic ways women are compromised by patriarchal control. Female independence liberates women from social constraints and classifications, most importantly by allowing them to escape the designation of woman-as-child, which creates the dichotomy of paternalistic pleasing or rebellious tantrums, to become woman-as-adult, in which the female creates a provocative depiction of female consciousness.

Michal's exaggerated response to her parents' microaggressions through drinking, smoking, refusing to eat with them, and sexually permissive behavior addresses the disparity between the reception of such acts by a youth and, contradictorily, her right to perform these acts as an adult. The actor and director Eli Cohen, in the role of the father, offers the conventional position to women's sexuality by declaring his daughter to be a whore, and she responds by reflecting back the underlying tensions that have been present in the house since her return: her father's leering observation of her body when he walks in on her naked in the bathroom; his refusal to sell (or give) her the car that would liberate her, instead trapping her in the house, just as her mother (who does not drive) is trapped; and his accusation that "Nobody is holding you in this house." Michal responds by invading her father's space and, watched by her mother, plays at a highly sexual attack on him in which she reminds them both that she is "fresh meat" and aggressively kisses her father until he pushes her off in shock, performing her resistance by literally enacting the behavior for which they have casually (and metaphorically) castigated her.

Michal, by returning to live in her old bedroom, to her family, and to the high school where she was once a student (as part of research for a film she cannot write), enacts a reversion from which she can emerge a more successful female. The conflict with her mother inverts the Israeli tendency toward father-son dramas and the preoccupation with an oedipal compulsion to destroy the father, by addressing a female archetype in the evocation of Electra. Michal's creative impotence is part of the metaphor for her undeveloped psychosexual self in what Karl Jung has termed an Electra complex that pits her in sexual competition with her mother for her father. The Electra complex is the inability to pass through the phallic stage and form a discreet sexual identity that leads to maturity. The film therefore reenacts the process of passing through the five stages ([1] the Oral, [2] the Anal, [3] the Phallic, [4] the Latent, and [5] the Genital) and serves as a focus for director Maya Dreifuss's feminist project that depicts a woman's journey of self-discovery.

Michal's regression into childhood that is facilitated by her return to her parents' home allows her to revisit the sites of psychosexual development as she moves through the stages to womanhood. With the ball games she plays in the school yard, the time spent in the school corridors and bathrooms, the group of students she befriends, and the forbidden act of smoking in the bushes, she reenacts childhood. This symbolic reversion culminates in her attendance at the school dance. Her oral fixation is marked by smoking; the sensual devouring of food, which she holds in her hands rather than with cutlery; alcoholic intoxication; and passionate kissing. The camera focuses on her mouth as she uses it to whisper, to seduce, and to devour the attractive and sexually alluring head teacher and the handsome high school youth in the film. But Michal is not a student, and through the film she moves through the other stages of the Electra complex until she becomes a sexually mature woman.

Dressed provocatively in a short red dress, knee highs, and black heels, with red nails, red lipstick, and large amounts of the makeup she has previously rejected, Michal theatrically enacts her sexual availability in a hotel room with Ze'ev. This performance and the heavy makeup tie her hypersexualized body with her mother's constant pressures to fulfil prescribed social expectations. Previously, Michal's mother insisted her daughter wear rouge and feminine clothing, accoutrement that would make Michal into the accepted form of womanhood. Adopting these symbolic gestures would, in turn, make Michal more like her mother. But her mother is a grotesque example of a woman whose sole value comes from her sexual desirability. She is constantly engaged in a game of sexual flirtation in order to reassure herself that she is desirable and therefore valuable. Moreover, her deep anxiety at aging is attributable to her potential loss of value if she is no longer desired.

The commodification of women that occurs by demarcating a woman's value according to her sexual desirability to a man ties sexuality to prostitution. "You have made a whore of me," she accuses Ze'ev and in an overstated way acts out the role of prostitute before him. The dissociative relationship that Michal has with her body in this scene can be seen in this confused sexual mask represented by the prostitute's clothing and makeup. But Ze'ev rejects her performance and wipes away her lipstick. His efforts to make love to her serve as an attempt to make her own her sexual desires. Michal rejects the emotional truth of their relationship, which represents her ongoing sexual immaturity. Ze'ev's further attempts to awaken her sexuality through his efforts to bring her to orgasm trigger a panicked response, and in an angry attempt at a rebuff she accuses him of betraying his wife. He deflects her attack and instead claims that he has left his wife for her, advising her to look in the closet. Afraid, Michal refuses to look. In Jungian psychology the closet is associated with the story of Bluebeard, whose dead wives are inside, and thus it denotes fear, the unconscious, and marital infidelity. Dreifuss inverts the meaning of the closet because Michal is invited to look inside but chooses not to. Unable to force an emotional crisis, Michal instead pushes Ze'ev to physically attack her. Exploring the boundaries of her own sexuality with Ze'ev, Michal ends up in an erotic masochistic encounter in which he smacks her, massaging her bottom until he arouses her and she demands sex that leads to the anal stage in which her recklessness and defiance explode in a powerful orgasm. As an older man, Ze'ev stands in as a substitute for her father, and the violence foreshadows the sexual scene of attack that will later occur in the family kitchen. The scene's ambivalence is directed at the problematics of women's roles as sexual creatures in which reclaiming sexual control, through aggression, creates a masochistic relationship with the self. At the same time, passing through the anal stage is part of Michal's ongoing effort to recover from her Electra complex.

Shocked by her beating and her powerful sexual response, Michal flees from the hotel and cries until she collects herself, creating a watershed in her identity between her sexually precocious yet virginal identity (in which she dressed androgynously) and her initiation into womanhood, from which point forth she will increasingly wear dresses and arrange her hair in feminine ways. Her transformative sexual experience is followed by a scene of private masturbation in which she "discovers" her genitalia, and then by a latent stage in which the encounter with the student is unfulfilled when she lies beside him but refuses to have sex. Finally, in the genital stage her sexual interests mature as she realizes her affection for Ze'ev and desires him. But at the dance, the film's denouement, Michal and Ze'ev meet in the bath-

She's Coming Home: Michal (Tali Sharon) looks at herself in the mirror.

room and Michal realizes that their relationship has no romantic future. This becomes the film's symbolic end. Michal has acquired sexual maturity as she has moved from childhood to adulthood and now no longer requires the forbidden fantasies that were necessary during her sexual development.

Michal's experimentation is part of the process by which she comes to know herself and is a response to other people's repeated attempts to identify her in particular ways. This search is offered through a repeated refrain in which Michal stares at herself in the mirror, without makeup, testing different ways of looking and ultimately washing her face so that she is always physically and emotionally naked before the mirror.

The mirror has had a long history in imagistic arts, traditionally denoting the fragility of life and in a female context usually representing female vanity. As a woman looking back through the mirror at those who peer at her, she is frequently cast as the objectified courtesan and demonstrates the position of to-be-looked-at-ness that Mulvey has defined as an integral aspect of the male gaze in cinema, even as she watches herself being looked at. In classic odalisque paintings, the mirror is also an instrument of ambivalence. It forces and legitimizes the hiding of the naked body, but the body's potential revelation creates the allure of the striptease. At the same time, the mirror is a space of female introspective gazing, which, whether for vanity or not, permits a measure of subjectivity that is often lacking in the genre's exposure of female bodies to full view. But while women in paintings are often looking out, through the mirror's illusion, Michal does not look beyond the glass; she looks only at herself. In this way she denies the striptease, particularly since she avoids the mechanics of the gesture (looking out teasingly then at herself, or looking at herself while knowingly being watched). Whereas Gitai used the convention of the mirror in *Kadosh* to heighten the eroticism of the scene, Dreifuss uses the mirror to convey Michal's introspection. Thus staring in the mirror becomes an outward manifestation of Michal's inner search for her identity. Moreover, her body is hidden from the voyeuristic gaze of the viewer, and whether she is clothed or naked, the audience can see only her face. The subversion of this trope is part of

She's Coming Home: Michal (Tali Sharon) masturbates in her childhood bedroom.

the film's feminist agenda. Dreifuss is questioning the ways in which women are defined by others and privileging Michal's search for self-definition. The question of seeing and being seen that underpins the mirror trope is again inverted from its traditionally gendered usage when Ze'ev accuses Michal of rejecting him because she does not *see* him.

Michal's sexual awakening is offered from a position that considers it in light of patriarchal attitudes and the Israeli repression of female subjectivity. Inverting the conventions by which women are expected to behave in modest, restrained, and compliant ways, Michal becomes a rebellious and sexually liberated woman. The age gap is the same between her and each of her two lovers, such that she can be both the ingénue to the older man and the older woman with the young lover, and in this way Dreifuss disrupts the usual casting of an older man and a younger woman by directing attention to its conventionality. Though sexually explicit, the film focuses on Michal's ownership of her own sexual pleasure, particularly represented in the scene at the hotel and her masturbation at home. The scenes' staging, and the fact that Michal is dressed in both scenes, denies the striptease, even though the eroticism is maintained, thereby preventing the audience from taking a voyeuristic pleasure in the consumption of the actress's body.

Ultimately the film highlights the ways in which women are infantilized within a patriarchal environment and raised with the expectation of respectful compliance (eating when others do, getting up when others do, following orders, being directed into activities by parents) while living within the competitive sphere of a mother's jealousy (as the daughter becomes a female interloper in the house). As an adult woman who asserts her independence and agency by eating when she wants, smoking, drinking, and bringing home men, she pushes against conformity and traditional authority and so liberates herself from the baggage of an unsatisfying relationship, a stalled career, and other people's expectations. The film's powerful feminist message offers a space for female identification with the heroine, and her transgressions and the unresolved ending present an opportunity for self-realization that lies undirected by conformity to a normative truth.

While *She's Coming Home* employs staging, dress, and camera angles in ways that are sympathetic to women's representation, it is mainly through the story line that Dreifuss advances a feminist agenda. *Bye Bye to Love* raises the problematic issue of attempting to make a feminist film in light of the dominance of patriarchy in every aspect of filmmaking. In an extreme gesture that attempts to rethink the very parameters by which film has framed a masculine view of women, even by women, *Bye Bye to Love* reimagines filmmaking aesthetics by creating film as a feminist art form, disavowing the traditional narrative frame and cinematic conventions. The interplay of disrupted narrative with video art performances, the inversion of traditional story formats, the scenography, and the ways in which the cameras are situated work to reinvent filmmaking in feminist terms.

Masquerading as nonfiction, the film's premise is built around a dinner party that Sophie, a video artist, organizes at which seven divorced women discuss questions she poses by telling their own personal narratives. Sophie's own experience as a child of a mother abandoned in her seventh month of pregnancy serves as the first narrative: "I was born into a breakup. I was taught that men are shit, that relationships are always obsessive, love—there's no such thing, it's always a fantasy, whose time, like the clock on the wall, is always borrowed; that it doesn't last; that it's like a ticking time bomb. I wanted to ask or to understand how love dies." Her mother, who would periodically seek out Sophie's father by looking up through a window at him with his new family, establishes the daughter as a woman unable to grow into a conventional relationship because she has no model for it and will not or cannot buy into the traditional romantic narrative. The divorced women before her all have children of their own, and thus serve as the "mother" of whom she can ask the questions she could not ask of her own divorced mother. Thus the symbolic "daughter" is attempting to engage with a theoretical "mother" figure to understand her identity as a woman, thereby creating a dialogue that explores the conflict between consigned roles (mother, wife, daughter) and a female identity independent of the expectations of these social positions.

Visually, the film offers a powerful account of femininity. The set is entirely contained within an open loft space, and the movie was filmed in real time with a camera dolly that ran 360 degrees around the table in the center of the room, but at a distance so that the crew (and camera*men*) did not interrupt the intimacy of the shared female space. The production team, including the director, were in an adjacent room, so that the scene and the actors could interact organically. The faces are shot so that they never appear with the face fully turned toward the camera, even during monologues. Rather, the faces, and the camera angles at eye level, work to position the women in conversation at all times and to create a privacy during the women's revelations that maintains their subjectivity. While the women wear mostly black evening dress, the set and the meal served are staged in reds, blacks, and purples. These colors, which evoke a womb or women's genitalia, gender the space as female.[65] The strong hues on the table and dresses are contrasted with the white of Sophie's dress and the wedding

Bye Bye to Love: The women sit eating, drinking, and smoking, discussing the breakdown of their relationships.

dresses that appear in each of the stylized vignettes interspersed with each woman's narrative in which the primary speaker removes her dress in a dance that reflects her attitude toward the end of her marriage. For some this is a triumphant burning of the veil or ripping of the dress, while for others this disrobing is cloaked in sadness, portrayed in the reverence with which the items are preserved. This video-art thus punctuates the realist conventions of the meal, providing an emotional and imaginative personal space that expands the dimensions of the conversation.

The shared sisterhood that develops as the women reflect upon their marital experiences produces an intimacy that disrupts the isolation that the breakups produced. Many of the women note that couple-hood offered the intoxicating and ennobling power of love, but the move to "family" with the birth of children disrupted the pairing and ultimately led to the destruction of happiness. At the same time, the women appear to operate as a collective that displaces the centrality of the traditional family unit. The different narratives paint the diversity of female experience and female desires, while the individual stories highlight women's personal experience and are also symbolic of "women's experience," including rape, domestic abuse, betrayal (sexual and emotional), hysteria, and depression. Yet the stories also push at predictable stereotypes, and thus the battered woman is a doctor, the woman who was sexually abused as a child was in love with the man who took her from her family at fourteen and then married her, the woman who finds her husband cheating becomes a stripper, and so on. In every case it was the woman who asked the man to leave, even when the relationship had broken down irrevocably before that, so that ending the relationship becomes an act of empowerment whereby women regain selfhood following the period of annihilation that the relationship's disintegration engenders. This is exemplified in the woman who would faint so that her husband would come to her side, only to come to the realization that if she asked him to leave she would stop fainting.

The film's focus on divorced women and their transgressive display of drinking and smoking disrupts the traditional expectation of correct women's behavior and concomitant marriage (or death) and inverts the conventional domestic ideal in which marriage is the conclusion of the fairy tale. By starting from a place of fracture, in which many of the women have found happiness in their independence and in the act of claiming their freedom from a difficult situation, they open up the possibility of new kinds of endings. The film's focus on the contradiction that love can produce a feeling of power, worth, and invincibility, while its loss creates a feeling of despair and invisibility, raises questions about the ways in which women's identity and emotion lie externally in validation by men. The feminist premise of the film makes women visible, through their stories, by taking responsibility for their emotional well-being (the film repeatedly concludes that one is lonelier in a failed relationship than when alone), and by disrupting stereotypical expectations about motherhood. While for some their children were the most defining and worthwhile act of their lives, for others motherhood was oppressive and strangled creativity. Sex and expressions of sexuality are viewed from a female perspective and are not the sole defining aspect of a relationship; rather, the women searched for multiple qualities in a man, including friendship, partnership, sexual gratification, a willingness to share in child rearing, and domestic help. The film's agenda not only rejects essentialist labelling for women but also refuses any attempt to find universalizing descriptions of men's qualities, instead highlighting that men, too, are all different.

Bye Bye to Love's noticeable weakness can be found in the criticism directed at much of second- and even third-wave feminism in Israel—a trend that has continued since *Tel Aviv Stories*—that Israeli feminists, in their attempts to celebrate women's voices and improve women's position, operated from the viewpoint of a middle- and upper-middle-class white liberal elite. Women of color saw that their own narratives remained excluded, and they continued to be constructed as peripheral characters, living on the country's margins.[66] While Hiam Abbas would play an important role in transforming Palestinian female subjectivity, as discussed in chapter 2, Hannah Azoulay Hasfari, Keren Yedaya, and Ronit Elkabetz would play prominent roles in reimagining the Mizrahi woman's representation on-screen. The paradox of ethnic women's feminist filmmaking lies between a desire to narrate a particularity of experience previously denied space within Israeli cinema, often told through a fantastical lens that conveys the emotional beauty and nostalgia of an otherwise bitter historical existence, and the presentation of Mizrahi women in orientalist conceptions, including the role of primitive witch or ill-educated prostitute, which risks a repetition (and therefore a reinforcement) of ethnic stereotypes that relegate Mizrahi women to the social periphery as an object of male sexual fantasy.

Sex and the Body

The "New Jew" preoccupation with the healthy body meant that sex always existed within Israeli cinema. In the early years, sex and the female body were situated in service of the nation. In later years, both were offered up as titillation, particularly in the films of Avi Nesher, Boaz Davidson, and the candid camera films of Yehuda Barkan, but also in the high art of Jacques Katmor's *To Know a Woman* (*Mikra Ishe*, 1969) and the historical dramas of Moshé Mizrahi. The tropes that had delimited women's sexuality and had revealed male anxiety at women's potential corruption of the national project created a body of female stock characters that could be deployed at will in support roles for the central male characters and themes. Women's ownership of their own bodies, and a critical reflection on the ways in which ideology and Israeli institutions established control over the female body, particularly female sexuality, would not find a place on the Israeli screen until the 1990s. The push back feminist filmmaking enacted on these stereotypes by reclaiming women's bodies and sexual identities offered a plurality of female experiences and instituted a new female subjectivity that had been previously absent.

Women's impact on filmmaking is seen most directly in the changes taking place in the representation of women's sexuality, and in the more circumspect depictions of scenes of a sexual nature. Though Israeli cinema has long since moved away from a woman's body as a symbol of national ideology or a metaphor for the land, male filmmaking continues to demonstrate a tendency to feature women as property to be fought over by men, as a visual pleasure for male desire, and in roles that subordinate females in positions of fantasy. Feminist filmmakers (both male and female), by contrast, offer female characters sexual autonomy that nuances female experience and female emotions, demonstrating subjectivity otherwise denied women on-screen. At its simplest, this is shown in women's ability to choose the ways in which they display sexual interest and sexual availability; more broadly it is evident within the films' diegesis, which no longer posits women's sexuality as shorthand for suggesting kinds of judgment to the viewer.

Women directors also shoot sex scenes, but in general these tend to show women's pleasure (or displeasure), frequently show women in assertive positions, and, when women are being physically violated, take greater care to represent these acts as oppressive rather than sensual. Women filmmakers display male bodies and male genitals often in a referential gesture toward the history of women's objectification, while significantly reducing the amount of time women's bodies are naked on-screen. In addition, they frequently show a variety of women's faces and bodies—including elderly women, scarred women, and fat women, in various stages of undress and with the potentiality for erotic desire, in a move that forces the spectator to consider the reality of women, challenging the fantasy of airbrushed models, confronting the role of the media in creating beauty ideals, and ultimately, by displaying different bodies, empowering female audiences. In this regard women filmmakers demonstrably engage with feminist ideals about women's corporeality, rewrite sexual codes and conventions, and make an effort to consider larger issues about society's attitude toward and treatment of women's bodies. Ultimately, these films show that a woman's body is hers, to do with as she pleases, and coercive attempts to control, shape, or exploit a woman's body are patriarchal acts of oppression. The move toward a feminist filmmaking aesthetic has forced a consideration not only of the ways in which women's oppression is explored but also of how it is displayed. As women filmmakers take on explicitly feminist agendas, they also turn toward feminist issues, including prostitution, abuse, and rape, which they approach critically and with a fervent attempt to avoid reinscribing the extant patterns that expose and demean women in crisis.

3

Feminism, Postfeminism, and New Directions in Israeli Feminist Filmmaking

7

A Question of Rape

Feminism, Postfeminism, and Issues of Representation

Israeli cinema has always had a political agenda, whether this was displayed overtly in promotional films about Israel's establishment; was embedded in narrative films' subtext, plot, or characterization; or was part of the commentary on Israeli society represented in documentary films, the relationship between art and politics in Israel was inexorable. In turn, cinema profoundly influenced Israeli society. Since *Tel Aviv Stories* and the rise in the number of women filmmakers, this politicization has also included addressing feminist issues. Rape, which feminist film scholarship has identified as "a particularly versatile narrative element that often addresses any number of other themes and social issues," has become a focus for feminist filmmaking in Israel. Its representation as a cinematic image was always widespread and became cinematic shorthand for depicting women's abuse by patriarchy. However, while the image may often critique women's treatment, it simultaneously reinforces a gendered social order in which women are weak and must be protected by the men who save them. This can be seen in the rape of Mizrahi women, which is shown to encourage a condemnation of the primitive and paternalistic nature of Mizrahi society and is contrasted with an idealized Ashkenazi rescuer (such as in *Queen of the Road* and *Dead End Street*). It can be seen in the violent mistreatment of Russian women, often by clients or pimps, which situates rape—and therefore rapists—outside of the normative social structure (as seen in *The Assassin Next Door* and *Promised Land*). This condemnation is key to the depiction of women who are raped and abused by religious men, in order to showcase religion's deviant treatment of women, who can be rescued only by the secular community (as in *Kadosh* and *The Wanderer*). This symbolism repeats previous representations of women's rape within traditional Israeli power structures whereby the "right" kind of men can save women from the "wrong" type of men. Thus it is Ashkenazi men who save women from Mizrahi men, secular men who save women from religious men, and Jewish men who save women from Arab men. While these examples reference larger cleaveages in Israeli society, the nature of rape as an act that can serve to uphold men's status within society serves to inform the trope so that it can also be used to uphold national ideology in ways that venerate national instutions and marginalize those who are outside official and state-sanctioned bodies. Therefore, soldiers protect women from nonsoldiers, a fact that serves to symbolically demonstrate the importance of belonging to the collective, the heroism of the Israeli military, and even the state's supposedly egalitarian ideals (as in *Banot*, *The Day We Met*, and *Zero Motivation*). Thus as feminist scholarship on rape in American film culture has shown, rape may be used in order to provide a vehicle with which to offer social and political critique.[1]

In the Israeli context, rape may be used to implicate the spectator in other acts of political aggression, such as the settlement project (as in *Campfire* and *Invisible*). Rape can be used as a way to uphold patriarchal values by representing the act as a response to female behavior that, as Sarah Projansky has shown, can be contradictory, and to punish a woman either for being strong/powerful/masculine or for being weak/naïve/innocent (as in *Banot*, *Queen of the Road*, and *Dead End Street*). The visual representation of rape also "draws arresting attention to the ambivalence of spectatorship, and the question of our complicity and participation in scenes of violence."[2] Tanya Horeck identifies the ethical dilemma that screening rape creates, which arises in many of the examples provided here and is considered in previous chapters of this book. The public display that cinema offers moves rape from the private sphere into the public sphere, thereby confronting its nature as taboo. Feminists view this project as an opportunity to uncover the silence surrounding sexual violence with the aim of encouraging women to speak out. Nevertheless, the display of rape as a primal trauma may prove titillating. This eroticization in representation bolsters the allure of sexual assault and confuses the meaning of rape as a manifestation of power with rape as a sexual act.

The conceptualization of the female body as weak and vulnerable, as shown through acts of rape and sexual assault, situates women in a subordinate position and privileges a patriarchal vision of women as victims in need of protection. A woman's rape can serve as an attack by one man or a group of men on the property of another man (or group, or nation). In this exchange the men share the view that women are a possession, which is why she must be protected by her owner and can be attacked by his enemy in a gesture that insults the male owner while the selfhood of the female being attacked does not exist for the purpose of this equation. As feminist scholarship on rape in American culture reveals, rape often extends beyond the victim-perpetrator interaction and can serve additional roles, including facilitating male fraternal bonding, as a homoerotic ritual that transfers male desires onto an external female object, illustrating to a defeated group the violation of its boundaries, and dividing the attacker from the person who defends the woman from attack. In all of these scenarios, the woman's experience of rape is secondary, if not entirely immaterial, to the situation—such that rape is not a question of female experience but of male interests. Even attempts to view rape as a civic problem that considers the social and cultural context in which rape occurs and by which women are assaulted may work to reinforce the institutions and the culture that underpin rape.

The militarization of Israeli society further accentuates the disparity between the warrior male and the passive female. In Israel the veneration of masculinity translates into a culture that views women's experiences of violence as secondary, since men's experiences of violence occur in the name of protecting the country. The country's ongoing state of war "put men in this society in an advanced status as soldiers and protectors at the expense of women, who were expected to cater to and worship the macho image of the frontline soldiers—their brothers, sons, and husbands."[3] This creates a "rape culture" by which "sexual violence is a normalized phenomenon, in which male-dominant environments (such as sports, war, and the military) encourage and sometimes depend on violence against women, in which the male gaze and women as objects-to-be-looked-at contribute to a culture that accepts rape, and in which rape is one experience along a continuum of sexual violence that women confront on a daily basis."[4] Though women also serve in the military, in the main they do so in subordinate positions that further accentuate the gender hierarchy, and the "sexual harassment of women soldiers takes a variety of forms in the IDF, and is so widespread as to be all but unremarkable. It is common for male soldiers to shout sexual invitations and comments at women soldiers, and while the extent of this behavior varies from unit to unit, it is an acknowledged part of IDF culture. Moreover, it seems to be the case that sexual harassment is seen as a problem that women in the IDF need to learn to cope with, rather than as a practice that men need to learn to refrain from."[5] As a rite of passage, the military serves as a training ground for socialization into Israeli society, and behavior learned during the formative years of national service extends into postmilitary life. Thus women are taught how to receive abuse, while men are taught how to give it. Moreover, "violence against women is intimately related to other forms and practices of violence," and this is especially so in the context of the Israeli occupation of the West Bank and the Arab-Israeli conflict.[6]

Though representation and reality are distinct, Horeck claims that the fantasy is an aspect of the act of rape and is not incidental to it. "For to acknowledge that there is not a simple causal relation between watching a representation of rape and committing one, is not to say that there is not any relation at all."[7] Thus the representation of rape also creates a vision of reality, and it is this that affects the way the representation of rape continues to inform reality. Employing Lubin's reading of the phallocentric nature of Israeli cinema in the context of rape representation, we see that the tropes used in many of the rape scenes discussed previously construct "a normative world in which the woman is always perceived as inferior. Lacking any position at the center, she does not function as an autonomous, coherent self. Instead, her entire existence depends on and is marginal to that which lies at the center, that is, the normative phallocentric system that sees that which the phallus represents as perfection. Thus, the female (margin) is not a counterpart of the male (center), but an object to be used by him. She exists solely to fulfil a function for him: to be the object of his sexual voyeuristic gratification."[8] The representation of rape can, therefore, offer up the female body to be consumed by the spectator in a permanent repetition of her defilement, for the pleasure of a patriarchal audience.

Moreover, rape may be co-opted as an image for other political or civic agendas, which marginalizes female experience. Terrifyingly, the frequent and ubiquitous representation of rape can serve to normalize the act in a way that makes sexual assault permissive, feeding an already ambivalent rape culture. Given that so many of the portrayals of rape, even in avowedly feminist films, can fall into a trap whereby the film undermines the female character's agency and returns her to the position of object rather than subject, the representation of rape participates in the rape culture that it may seek to critique. Projansky contends that in postfeminist culture, "rape discourse is *part of* the fabric of what rape is in contemporary culture. Discourses of rape are both productive and determinative. They are not simply narratives marketed for consumption in an entertainment context or 'talk' about real things. They are themselves functional, generative, formative, strategic, performative, and real. Like physical actions, rape discourses have the capacity to inform, indeed embody and make way for, future actions, even physical ones."[9] Moreover, representations of rape serve as a way to determine "popular ideas about femininity, feminism and post-feminism," and they "position men and women in particular ways."[10] Drawing heavily on Projansky and Horeck's consideration of rape in the American cultural context, this chapter considers the particularity of representing rape on the Israeli screen and considers the ways in which feminist filmmaking can reclaim the discourse surrounding rape and use it to advance feminist agendas.

Israel, Rape, and the Law

Israeli society's attitude toward rape is broadly one of horror. The consciousness raising of the feminist movement in Israel during the 1970s and 1980s disabused the authorities of the notion that "no such problem existed in Israel."[11] A series of high-profile rape cases, including a serial rapist operating in Tel Aviv during the late 1970s; the *Beeri Case*, which was a gang rape at Kibbutz Shomrat in 1988; the Buhbut Case (1995), in which a woman who was serially abused and killed her attacker was sentenced to seven years' imprisonment and successfully "challenged the severity of her punishment";[12] the imprisonment of former Israeli president Moshe Katzav on two counts of rape (2010); and recently the arrest of four soldiers on Hatzerim Air Base for gang-raping a female soldier, demonstrate an understanding that rape can happen anywhere, to anyone, and, as President Shimon Peres declared in response to the Katzav verdict, "There are no two kinds of citizens here; citizens of only one kind exist in Israel—and all are equal in the eyes of the law."[13] Yet an imbalance remains, evident in the small number of cases that actually make it to court. For example, within the military, "The number of complaints in the IDF relating to sexual offenses has been rising steadily in recent years, with 777 complaints in 2012, 930 in 2013, and 1,073 in 2014."[14] Nevertheless, many of the victims are unwilling to complain to the military police. "Thus, in 2014 only ... eight cases of suspected rape were investigated."[15] As women's rights advocates in Israel note, "there is a large gap between Israel's relatively advanced laws in areas like rape and sexual harassment and their enforcement."[16]

The move toward a legal framework protecting women from sexual harassment, violence, and discrimination began with the rise of feminist activism during the 1970s. Israel's assumptions about the existence of social and gender equality, which had been part of the nation's founding myths, were disrupted following the rise of black identity politics, which highlighted the institutional prejudices toward Mizrahim and the social inequities that prevailed. Like the wave of American-led feminism that garnered increasing attention in Israel following the Yom Kippur War (1973), identity and gender politics encountered hostile responses from the establishment. Early attempts to raise feminist issues and to provide support for battered women met with opposition and "the worst kind of stereotyping."[17] Irit Umanit explains that Israel fell back on the timeworn prejudices through which women were disparaged as "whores, lesbians, or ugly man-haters" for their feminist activism.[18] It took private enterprise to establish the first women's shelters, rape crisis centers, advocacy and support groups, and rape hotlines, but by the 1990s government took over the running of these institutions, and with the new regime came additional legal, medical, and social support for abused and raped women. In 1989, the Karp Report showed that the police generally favored measures that were aimed at "keeping the peace" in domestic disputes rather than upholding the law, and had little familiarity with the sensitive handling of rape victims.[19] In response, new guidelines were drawn up and additional measures have been taken, and periodically reviewed, as part of an effort to transform police attitudes and practices. Police forces now have dedicated units with personnel specially trained to deal with violence against women, rape, and domestic abuse. Among the many changes has been one of attitude, as a "shift in the awareness of violence against women as a social and as a gender issue, rather than as a personal one" has led to new kinds of responses.[20] In Israel, legislation is progressive and the values of feminism have been internalized—even when they are not explicitly enacted in a shelter's philosophy, they do inform media coverage of rape, and it is understood that violence against women is unacceptable.

While the public discourse on rape in Israel accedes to a Western legal and social model in which sexual assault is a crime and those who commit it should be tried and punished, the reality of a culture weighted down by its militaristic patriarchy complicates the dispensing of justice. Women are symbolically positioned as the "raison d'être of going to war … a particular sort of corporeal construction in which women's bodies carry the weight of national purity and honor, yet possess neither the power nor the strength to defend or define the nation."[21] In return for this masculine protection, women are expected to play the proper role and conform to models of "femininity" that serve to gender power structures. Only by conforming to these prescribed roles are women afforded the protection to which they are entitled by law. And yet the militaristic culture in Israel has facilitated a brotherhood whose common discourse sexualizes women, employing language that regards women as sex objects evaluated in terms of physical characteristics and desirability. In a national discourse that already constructs women as service providers for men (and particularly for soldiers), serving male sexual needs and desires is viewed as an extension of women's responsibilities.

National conscription and the processes leading up to it take place during high school, and thus the sexual objectification of girls begins early as both males and females are socialized into this value system. Paradoxically, men are taught that women are available to them and must be made to submit, while women are taught that they must avoid being raped. Participating in male sexual culture may afford women limited status in hierarchies in which they are otherwise completely disempowered. Rela Mazali has argued that "Where men's ostensibly elective military mission—in the service of the state—is lauded and valorized, the rape, harassment, and sexual assault of women—in the service of male supremacy—are explained away as individual bad luck, at best, or the victim's fault, at worst."[22] According to Israel's general cultural attitude toward rape, it is not men's behavior that must be modified but women's. In order to prevent rape, women must avoid certain areas, at certain times, in certain clothes; behave in a particular way; and avoid going out without being chaperoned. Such thinking legitimates rape and assault for those who do not follow the clearly demarcated social rules that would keep women "safe" and imputes the responsibility for rape on women.[23]

Given this climate, charges of rape and sexual assault more broadly are evaluated in relation to a moral value system that assesses women's "rapeability" and translates into the kinds of legal sentencing given for sexual crimes. As with other Western societies, "[t]he reporting of rape is often biased, inaccurate, and irresponsible.... The press presents a distorted picture of the nature of the allegations, the victims, the offenders, and the conduct of rape trials. The reporting more often than not seems to be directed at discounting women's allegations of rape and justifying the masquerading of rape as seduction."[24] The tendency to present rape as a more ambiguous woman-man interaction is compounded by an alleged openness about rape evident in graphic descriptions of the sexual acts performed and a liberal use of the names of the sexual organs involved.[25] The press, like the courts, often presents issues from only the male perspective, and therefore the defendant's standpoint, which is depicted as the only objective and rational position. "The complainant's voice, her experience, and her account of what happened are constricted and curtailed from the start."[26]

Hagar Lahav's study of newspaper coverage of the Ramat Hasharon rape of a teenage girl by several of her peers over a period of time reveals seven characteristics of the coverage of rape and points to the "given social and cultural codes" by which the discourse around sexual assault is framed in Israel. She concluded that this coverage also served to reinforce rape culture. The seven patterns she identified were[27] (1) The normalization of rape, (2) the sensationalization of rape, (3) viewing rape as individual incidents rather than as a larger social pattern, (4) the eroticization of rape, (5) turning coverage of rape into entertainment, (6) examining the victim in order to consider the circumstances and hence culpability of the assault, and (7) appraising the perpetrator and thereby calculating the likelihood that he would commit an assault (and whether in doing so it was indeed his responsibility or whether other excusable circumstances might be brought to bear).

Lahav shows that by viewing sexual violence as yet another form of general social violence, and regarding sexual offenders as common, a society diminishes the gravity of the crime and ignores its gendered nature. While most rape may be regarded as routine—a single act, against a single victim, by a single perpetrator usually already known to the victim, and with no other violence (except for the rape)—these kinds of crimes are rarely reported in the press and are not deemed newsworthy. For rape to appear in the newspaper and to be discussed publicly, the event must be regarded as exceptional or unexpected, involving violence and deception, uncommon circumstances, or other unusual features. Even in these cases, the press usually characterizes attacks as isolated "private" incidents between the parties involved. This position disguises the social roots of sexual violence and ignores other forces at play. This form of "modern 'silence'" discharges communal responsibility and frees society from investigating social causes.

Reportage of the incidents often includes an inordinate amount of detail that can reach pornographic levels—and even eroticize the attack. The voyeuristic and exposing narrativization of the rape in the press is tied to the representation of violence in pornography, and particularly the ways in which man is expected to forcefully subdue the woman he desires. Following Mackinnon (1987) and Brownmiller (1975), these kinds of representations make rape about power and control, with the phallus serving as a weapon, and therefore the act is not simply about sexual satisfaction but a way of asserting male supremacy and ensuring female subjugation.[28] This language of erotica and pornography has already established a culture of theatricality around the representation of violence against women, one that the press gleefully adopts in a society in which news reporting is also regarded as a form of entertainment. This attitude is particularly evident in the use of witty nicknames for the perpetrator, such as "the polite rapist."[29] Furthermore, the casual and pervasive undermining of women's consent seen in popular culture reinscribes possessing a woman sexually as a display of masculinity, a fact that is, in turn, used to normalize men's behavior within a court of law.

The centrality of male experience is encapsulated in the Israeli popular song "When You Say 'No' What Do You Mean?" Written in 1962 and first recorded by the mainstream group "Hatarnegolim" in an upbeat and peppy tune, the song has since been covered by several leading Israeli singers, including a duet by Gidi Gov and Yehoram Gaon, and its lyrics have often been cited by defense attorneys in rape cases.[30]

When you say no

Hatarnegolim (1962)
Words Dan Almagor
Music Sasha Argov

When you say 'no' what do you mean?
What do you mean when you say "no"?
Is your "no" a real "no"
Perhaps it's just "perhaps" but "just not now"
Or is your "no" just "not quite yet"
Perhaps it's "aye" perhaps its "try"
Because you say "no" with such finesse
That it sounds more inviting to me than a "yes."

When you say "no" I don't know
Confused and going crazy that you say "no"
That you'll say "He didn't really want it!"
Perhaps tomorrow you'll complain "He's weak—
is he a man? He's just a freak
Hears no—and believes it."
And if I go perhaps you'll say "What a shame"
But if I stay maybe you'll say: "disgrace."

And when she says "no" what does she mean?
What does she mean when she says "no"?
Is it a completely final "No"
Or is it just a temporary "no"
Perhaps it's just "Ok, just not now"
Perhaps it's really just a "Well . . ."
But if all we say is "yes" and "no"
Well there's not much left to say . . .

When you say "no" what do you mean?
What do you mean when you say "no"?
Because if you really aren't interested at all at all
Then tell me to "go away" finally!
Tell me "Enough" or "Piss off!"
But please don't tell me "no"
Because you say "no" with such finesse
That it sounds even more inviting than "yes."

Translated by Rachel S. Harris

The song perpetuates a culture in which a woman's word is untrustworthy, and her expression of "no" may be regarded as fickle. Privileging persistence as a form of masculinity and denying it as harassment reflects the machismo that has been pervasive in Israeli culture. Moreover, the song establishes the real victim as the male who is rebuffed and forced to navigate the mixed signals of the clearly erratic female. Furthermore, it adds license to retroactive claims that the act of sex was consensual, despite what she may claim, since it is clear that her subsequent protests cannot be deemed trustworthy. The song enforces the idea that ultimately women tease men to the point of sexual frustration as part of a sexual game in which the man, in order to preserve his masculinity, must not back down.

In response to the Shomrat case, the lyricist Dan Almagor added another verse, which has since been cited by judges in response to the defendant's claims that the victim had offered a mixed message—however, the verse, which reiterates the popular slogan by antirape activists "No means no," is not always included in singers' renditions.

> When she says "no" she means it
> She means it when she says "no"
> That's why her "no" is final, absolute
> Only she decides, not a court
> So be a good cock[31]
> And don't be a smart ass
> She isn't hinting "yes" or "perhaps" or "try"
> When she says "no" she means "No"!

The portrayal of a rape victim in court and the often public trial in the press serve to construct a narrative. This performance tells a story in which a hero and a villain must be found. Yet the assigning of roles is unpredictable, as Alina Korn and Sivan Efrat discovered in their comparison of the "Ramat Hasharon rape" and the "countryside rape," two high-profile cases in which teenagers were gang-raped.[32] In a culture of victim blaming, moral judgements are passed on the victim of sexual assault through a series of inquiries into her behavior or manner that determine *her* guilt for the rape. These include questions about her previous sexual history, how she dressed, and her emotional state before and after the rape. In these two cases, "[t]he focus on the victims' prior sexual experience and on their reputations as sluts was used to disqualify their claims that they were raped and to imply that the girls were false accusers."[33]

While the way a woman presents herself, her previous behavior, and her behavior in relation to the rape are viewed as part of the victim's responsibility, other questions such as what the victim's age was (is she very young or very old), whether she previously knew the assailant, whether force (weapons or other forms of violence) was used, and what her social/ethnic background was, are also factors considered in the public judgment of the victim.

Ultimately, these questions seek to categorize the woman. If she is deemed innocent, then a cult of the virgin discourse emerges in which she is viewed as "holy" and as a "good girl," whereby her attack is conceptualized symbolically as an attack on the collective. If, however, she is deemed a "bad girl" or "whore," then she "asked for it" or "initiated it" or "encouraged it."[34] In this case, *she* drove him to it.[35] "By identifying the victims as bad girls who did not know how to behave, the papers sustained and reinforced the myth of the victim's contribution to the rape. According to this myth, it is extremely doubtful whether a young girl who is having consensual sex can ever be raped; if she is attacked, it is undoubtedly the result of her own behavior."[36] In these two particular cases, the girls were considered to be using sex "as a means of acquiring popularity or at least some semblance of social acceptability."[37] This kind of simplistic and stereotyped explanation pointed to the particular context of Israeli society, in which society was ready to believe that young women would offer up their bodies in order to gain social acceptance because of the high esteem with which belonging to the collective "or even the desire for being part of that collective," is viewed, and this would therefore provide a convenient narrative to explain motives for this in ways other than deviant social behavior.[38] Moreover, the press, in reporting these contested rape cases, delimits "legitimate female behavior and thus reinforce[s] conventional beliefs, values, and myths." As Korn and Efrat argue, "the depiction of contested trials encourages the inference that when women are not innocent virgins, they risk being raped. The message for female readers is to be careful not to enter male territory; otherwise, they might be held as contributors to their own rape and be perceived as asking for it."[39]

The press's focus on the victim, her person, and her behavior serves to indicate to women their responsibility for their attack and "displays the female body as an object that is in constant danger requiring masculine protection."[40] This kind of coverage reconfigures the question from "why was she attacked" to "why was it HER who was attacked," creating a culture in which the victim must prove her innocence. It also draws a distinction between those women who are attacked and those who are not—and validates the protection women who are not attacked receive—further accentuating the patriarchal role in "preserving" women's chastity. This line of reasoning promotes the Madonna/whore dichotomy and removes the possibility that women are complex human subjects. This dependency between the Madonna and her protector also isolates women who deny patriarchal rules, situating them as prey in an "open season" mentality that will not afford them social (or legal) protection. Thus an evaluation of the victim bases a reading of the "good woman" on her weakness and, in turn, makes a strong woman (or one who pursues her own interests) "bad."

The virgin/whore dichotomy also frames the attitude toward the assailant in the public consciousness. If the woman is innocent (the virginal Madonna), then the assailant is a guilty pervert, sexual deviant, unruly monster, deranged lunatic, sex addict, or animal—but if blame can be cast upon the woman's actions, then the assailant is viewed as an innocent victim of her provocations. In this case the male assailant must have been trapped, and he may even be regarded as the victim of a manipulative woman or as one who was seduced by a sexually precocious Lolita (young girl). The men's social standing is also brought to bear in these considerations, and men or boys from rich and politically powerful environments are viewed differently from poor ones—or more precisely, the ways in which they are defended differs. Rich men may be viewed as victims of an unscrupulous woman, while poor men (which may also reflect an ethnic element) are victims of circumstance who have not been educated to view sexual assault as criminal. When men are viewed as victims of society (or victims of women's malevolence), they cannot be held guilty for their crimes. This approach by which a man is "sick" or "weak" or suffers from social ills feminizes the rapist, thereby excluding him from the patriarchy. This, in turn, protects the patriarchy from responsibility for a culture of rape. Pathologizing the attack, or the attacker, means that the uniqueness of the sexual assault is preserved, thereby distancing each incident from any widespread sociocultural factors. The emphasis on male victimhood strengthens the tendency to blame women for their attack or to raise suspicion about women's complaints. In turn, this frames the public debate as "his word" against "her word." Journalism's pretense to objectivity, by which both sides must be heard equally, undermines the criminality of sexual assault by which one guilty party has committed a crime against another innocent party.

Mazali claims that Israel, as a "militarized, patriarchal society, led by its elites, in fact engenders and encourages violence against women in both covert and less covert ways. The girls and women who become the victims of this violence are forced into an exploitative 'mission' by group(s) with a vested interest in maintaining women's intimidation, in keeping them relatively frightened, hesitant, 'in their place.' The prevalence of such violence and the endemic fear of it keep not only the direct victims but the entire population of women intimidated and 'in place,' to some degree."[41] Many cinematic representations of rape uphold this culture of intimidation, serving as warning, modeling "correct" female behavior, and reminding woman of her victimhood. Projansky claims that "the structure of rape narratives varies historically, depending on cultural and national contexts."[42] In the Israeli context, the pervasive use of this trope can be seen in the frequency with which it appears in most chapters of this book, infiltrating every aspect of Israeli cinema and its depiction of Israeli society. As Sered claims, "Despite the deep ethnic, religious, and political cleavages found in so many areas of Israeli society, the theme of women's vulnerability and danger constitutes a commonality that can be seen as an Israeli metanarrative of gender. Public discourse reiterating and dramatizing the vulnerability and danger inherent in women's bodies legitimates surveillance and control of women, a process that puts out tentacles into various sexual and religious situations. . . . The interests of global capitalism, the secular state, and the religious establishment converge in legitimizing the intense and invasive focus on women's bodies."[43] Rape in Israeli cinema serves as a point of conflation between women's powerlessness, men's desire to control women, and the gendering of status in Israeli society. Largely, it paints the woman as victim, a role that dispossesses the woman of agency and aids in making her invisible, while offering multiple ways in which man's power as both perpetrator and savior occupies the central space on screen. These pervasive depictions of rape demonstrate female vulnerability and male hegemonic control, and rape culture in Israel repeats this discourse whereby rape serves as "a crime that dominates public fantasies regarding sexual and social difference"[44] and simultaneously reinscribes hierarchies of masculine power.

Miss Israel and the Perfect Rape

The rape of Linor Abargil, the reigning Miss Israel, weeks before she would be crowned Miss World was interpreted in the press and in the public in collective terms. "Whoever raped her, raped Israel."[45] Sered adopts Susan Jeffords's criticism that the co-opting of rape as a threat to the wider community means that there is little place in the discussion for considering women's violation, and she attributes the high visibility of Abargil's rape in the press partly to her symbolic representation of the nation as "Miss Israel"—thus the attack was viewed as an attack on the nation.[46] Moreover, Sered views the public's fascination with the case to be the result of society's identification of a beauty queen as an especially "rape-able" category due to "popular beliefs that beautiful women incite uncontrollable lust in men."[47] At the time, her bravery in coming forward offered her as a role model that could encourage other women to speak of their own experiences of rape. Later she would use the cultural capital she had gained as Miss World, and as a rape survivor, to advocate for women who had experienced sexual violence, a process chronicled in the American-Israeli coproduction documentary film *Brave Miss World*.

In the original media representation of the crime, and later in the discursive frame of the film, Abargil signified the ideal rape victim. At eighteen, she had little previous sexual history. She was a good student and epitomized the ideal of Israeli beauty. She was raped at knife point in a secluded wood in the middle of the night by an assailant who was a stranger to her and was assigned as her travel agent in Italy. No fault could be found in her dress, in her comportment, or in her previous history that could jeopardize her position as victim of a vicious and unprovoked violent crime. Moreover, the perpetrator was a serial rapist who had twice been arrested but had escaped conviction due to a lack of evidence. Furthermore, as an Egyptian Coptic with Israeli citizenship, he signified the "Arab other," which cast Abargil as "one more victim in the Israeli-Arab war."[48] Ironically, though Abargil's rape was co-opted by the collective, she reclaimed her narrative from its national symbolism whereby her rape could be viewed as an attack by one male group on the property of another male group, and instead recast sexual violence as a shared female experience. Thus, she created her own female sisterhood, a gendered collective, through which she reached out and championed women's rights and neutralized attempts to cast her as an object in a masculine conflict.

Abargil would eventually succeed in her attempts to have Uri Schlomo Nur imprisoned for his crimes, and he received a sixteen-year sentence. Forced to relive her trauma at the trial, Abargil experienced a figurative "second rape," which can be seen in her treatment in the media coverage of the original rape trial and in the emotional effect of attending another rape trial as a law student more than a decade later—affirming Horeck's contention that watching "a rape trial is to participate in, and to be an integral part of, the raped woman's ordeal."[49] Though Abargil would succeed in having her attacker imprisoned, she would have to offer evidence to the parole board every six months to ensure his continuing imprisonment. Rallying against a system that forced her to affirm his violence, she enlisted his other victims in her efforts to ensure that he served his full sentence.

Filming for *Brave Miss World* began ten years after the rape, and the documentary follows Abargil's international crusade to encourage rape victims to speak out about their abuse. The film demonstrates the ongoing difficulties that serve to dissuade women from coming forward and that maintain a culture of silence that ultimately furthers women's victimization. It also reveals the persistence of a culture that blames the victim and places the onus of proof upon her. The film includes the harrowing narratives of many rape survivors, and demonstrates the psychological impact provided by a positive support environment. As Abargil says of her own mother, "She didn't tell me to keep quiet. She didn't worry what the neighbors would say [sic]. She knew that the fault was his and not mine." This statement undergirds the film's mission to encourage women to speak out, so that the feelings of shame and disgust that many of the victims experienced can find cathartic release through the telling and retelling of their personal narrative. For those who experienced some form of legal justice, the capacity to heal, according to the film's economy, was far smoother than for those whose perpetrators remained unpunished. In its call for social and legal justice for victims of sexual violence, this conclusion serves as the film's defining feminist message.

Brave Miss World addresses a society in which a male fraternity condones male aggression and through which women are "slut-shamed" in a culture of victim blaming. Abargil's experiences constitute the "ideal" rape: an attack by a relative stranger, violently, in the middle of the night, while she was sober. She was sent to him, because of his work, by people responsible for her well-being. Moreover, he had previously committed similar offenses against at least two other women, and was generally viewed as a socially marginal figure. She is celebrated for keeping a cool head, and by promising the rapist that she would not report him she manages to save her life. Her keen account of the details of the crime enables Nur's successful prosecution where previous legal attempts by other victims had failed. Thus she constitutes a hero in two ways: as the unquestionable victim of a rape that she survived by maintaining a semblance of control (and by avoiding hysteria) in the moment of crisis, and as a woman who has used her fame to provide other women with a platform through which they may express their own experiences of rape and overcome a culture of silence. The film's testimonials by other women (and a single man) who discuss their rapes with Abargil reveal that, for many, rape and its aftermath are much less clear cut in apportioning blame, with the victims often experiencing recrimination while the rapist goes unpunished, exposing the unheroic experience of sexual violence that characterizes most victims' fate.

The clarity of Abargil's case, and the national consensus that she was the victim, protected her from the backlash that many other women face. In contrast to her successful identification and prosecution of her attacker, other victims were unable to identify their attackers, or, by turning against (or worse, not reporting) men who were considered local heroes, such as athletes or soldiers, appeared to fail in the journey from passive victim to active protagonist that marks the feminist experience of empowerment. Thus the film exposes the pervasive nature of gendered violence, the ways in which society maintains these abuses, the protections afforded to rapists, and the problematic nature of rape trials for the victim, whose trauma often serves as a second rape. But it also draws a line between successful and unsuccessful victims that is problematic in creating a hierarchy of victimhood and empowerment that further shames those victims who are unable to meet the rigorous standards of the ideal model.

The juxtaposition of Abargil's activism and her positive influence on rape survivors with her own struggles to overcome the trauma that she experiences reveals the trauma's persistent scar. Abargil argues that her turn to religion is her way "to do good," saying that it is "the only thing that counts," which her rabbi seconds, viewing her interest in religious observances as a path to healing her "deep wound" through a desire to do and be good. The physical transformation that takes place in her dress, and her increasing reluctance to be filmed in immodest garb, speak to a problematics of representation. In the first scene with the rabbi who is guiding her spiritual conversion (a move toward greater religious observance), we see him remark on the inappropriate display of her shoulder and request that she cover up when visiting him. For a woman who was once a high fashion model photographed all over the world in revealing and exposing poses, the change in her clothing illustrates the psychological barrier that develops between her current self and her former self. Like the physical separation that she begins to insist upon with her closest friend, a gay man who helped her through the recovery process, her clothes mark her adoption of the religious restrictions for female demeanor in the public space, and therefore her adoption of a patriarchal system of control. Though the topic is never addressed directly within the documentary, her newfound modesty bespeaks an acceptance of the religious tendency to announce the female body as profane and to demand its social abnegation or risk its violation. At the same time, it also references a psychological response to rape by which a woman might choose to remove her body from the mechanism of objectification and the voyeuristic penetrative gaze, which in a rape culture commodifies women and makes them available for rape.[50]

Ultimately, it is through a journey of return, where she, the camera crew, and her family visit Italy and physically walk through the night of her attack, that she finds a psychological release and appears to be finally at peace with her past, even in her newfound religious life. Yet, the ongoing legalities that require her to frequently correspond with the parole board highlight the ways in which the wound is systematically reopened. Moreover, the indignity by which she may only provide written evidence and is otherwise silenced, while the rapist has the opportunity to speak out at his parole hearing, demonstrates an enduring power imbalance between victim and assailant.

Abargil challenges the ways in which rape makes women invisible, to the perpetrators, to the legal system, and to themselves. Similarly, Michal Aviad's film *Invisible* (*Lo Roim Aleich*, 2011) is a conscious attempt to highlight the ways in which women's suffering following sexual violence can serve as an open-ended trauma, even as the legal system makes the victim invisible. In an experimental interweaving of fiction and history, the film combines real historical footage and court records about the "Polite Rapist," who raped sixteen women in the Tel Aviv area, including a thirteen-year-old girl, in the late 1970s, with the story of two fictional women who were raped by him. In interviews following the release of the film, Aviad frequently explained that she had been one of the victims of the original rapist, and while the film was not a factual account of the victims' lives, it explores the ways in which victims are affected by sexual violence long after the rapist is released from prison, thereby contrasting the psychological jail of the victim with the physical jail of the perpetrator.

Through the different media responses to the two female protagonists, Aviad teases out what Projansky refers to as the contradictions in the representations of women's vulnerability. "Specifically, two seemingly antithetical types of narratives are common: those that depict women's vulnerability as leading to rape and those that depict the rape of an independent woman as making her vulnerable."[51] Nira (Evgenya Dodina), a film editor, and Lily (Ronit Elkabetz), an aerobics instructor and political activist, meet at the site of a Palestinian olive harvest, where Israeli soldiers are harassing the local peasants and shouting violent sexist remarks at Lily, such as "Get her laid to calm her down." Both women had been victims of the same rapist and had been together at the lineup at which he was identified twenty years earlier. However, the introduction of this shared experience of the lineup is represented ambiguously, and at first implies that the women were in the lineup—thus the film's insinuation that it is they who were on trial provides a symbolic account of the ways in which rape victims are judged. Only when Nira asks if they caught him does it become clear that they were witnesses and victims identifying the perpetrator.

Through the friendship that develops between Lily and Nira, *Invisible* presents a sisterhood that accords with Horeck's contention that the depiction of rape as a moment of identification between women provides an important counterimage to the vision of rape as the site of civic identification between men. This recognition that rape can happen to any woman creates a means of sympathy that is not only dependent on the experience of rape—as *Brave Miss World* offers it—but is possible because of the potentiality of rape, a fear that women are taught, and that, according to Sered, facilitates the ongoing power of a male hegemony that offers to protect women from such violence.[52]

The conventions of this power structure in Aviad's film can be seen in the ways in which the original descriptions in the press cast woman as object. The women's treatment by doctors and policemen perpetuates a shield of male authority that sets up the victims as untrustworthy. Following her rape, Lily asks the doctor for an examination. He responds by charging her with deception by claiming consensual sex was rape. Only when she produces the newspaper article about her rape does he then give her antibiotics. His dependence on a second male authority (the journalist) to validate her claim of rape further undermines Lily's subjectivity following the attack. Other similar patterns are repeated in the treatment of all the victims. Nira interviews the head of the forensic lab to understand what took place, and all he can offer her is his personal memory, rather than scientific findings ("I remember you—you were beautiful") and his recollection that she said she was not a virgin. Another victim tells Nira that the police asked why she was out at night, thereby putting the onus on the victim, rather than the attacker. The women are remembered by single markers (not a virgin, out at night, student) that are contrasted with the extensive coverage the rapist received in the press. His nickname "The polite rapist" alludes to the ways in which he made the victims stroke his back and spend several hours with him as if they were on a date, a description that undermines the barbarity and violence of his attacks and the terror he inflicted on his victims. Furthermore, he is remembered by the head of the forensic lab, who was with a psychologist when each victim was interviewed, as having a thick penis and as someone who "drove *us* crazy, raping someone every few days." In press clippings of the events, Nira observes that the rape of a thirteen-year-old girl is described as a new way by which the rapist taunts and "punishes" the police. These descriptions from the past cast the victims as collateral damage in a conflict between the rapist and the police and make the women's suffering invisible.

The women display different aspects of post-trauma from the rape. Nira is revolted by sex, and her visceral reaction manifests in vomiting episodes. She is emotionally numb, has general trust issues, and rejects romantic entanglements. As a film editor, her work requires her to sit alone as a professional voyeur, viewing other people's experience of life while she is protected by the darkness of the editing room. Lily is emotionally distant with her family, a problem that is affecting her marriage and has created a tension in the relationship with her children. Her sudden starts in unexpected encounters display her almost constant sense of danger. Though Lily is at first reluctant to think about the original crime, Nira becomes obsessed with finding out about the rapist and begins investigating the way the crimes were reported in the media, police reactions to the victims, and the trial. When she finally sees the rapist, Nira, who is portrayed as emotionally repressed, breaks down and begins to cry. The shot in the car, in which the air conditioner does not work, conveys the claustrophobia of a woman trapped within her own trauma. Her filming of other rape victims, the investigation into the case, and the women's friendship constitute forms of rape therapy whereby the recovering of lost information and the empathy created in the shared rape survivor experience serve as a path to healing.

By repeatedly staging the women at the center of the film, Aviad reclaims a feminist space, in contrast to the women's previous marginalization and the dominant position afforded to the rapist in the press coverage and police reports. Though the rapist is convicted and sentenced to thirty years' prison for his crimes, the women discover, to their dismay, that he was released after ten years, technically serving only three months per victim, while they, twenty years later, continue to suffer from the crime. Aviad draws attention to the inequity of the legal system, particularly in the rapist's early release. According to the judge who released him, "a woman's body is not expendable, but there are other considerations," and he showed leniency because the rapist was a father of three, because his wife (a vice principal) stood by him, and because of the attribution of trauma due to his military service in the Yom Kippur War.

Through the two female characters, Aviad disrupts this passive acceptance of the patriarchal hegemony that forgives women's rape and is willing to displace blame on the trauma of military service. The ongoing post-trauma of rape is displayed time and again. Nira is divorced because she could no longer have sex with her husband and because the physical contact induced vomiting, and Lily is alienated from her husband and children, who treat her aggressively and dismissively. Nira, as a film editor, looks at others and through editing controls the gaze and the framing of narrative in the documentary, while Lily, through her activism, physically rejects an acceptance of the normative order. The tolerance of women's looked-at-ness is challenged repeatedly, shown in the women's modest dress (they are not exposed to a lascivious spectator), Nira's role as editor, and the victims' narratives of the rape (and their dismissive treatment by police and the media). Nira keeps the women's faces hidden in her footage of their narratives. Aviad's refusal to perpetuate women's public display occurs in multiple ways, such as Lily's one-night stand in a hotel room, whereby the scene is edited to keep viewers from seeing Lily's body, while, in a gratuitous inversion of the tendency to expose and flaunt the female body, Aviad tracks the lover in a long, lingering shot that exposes his sexual organs. This subversion of cinematic conventions also serves as a reminder of Nira's observation that the signs of rape are not visible on a woman—and that the penetrating gaze that cinematic representations of rape seek to somehow expose will produce nothing but another rape. Aviad denies the viewer this moment of crisis, substituting the primal trauma of the sexual attack for the women's trauma at reading about their case in the court records.

Lily's activism is shown as a way for her to take back power when in many other respects she is powerless, and this contrasts with both her husband's and her children's attitudes

Invisible: Lily (Ronit Elkabetz) and Nira (Evgenya Dodina) at the court photocopier.

toward her, shown in their descriptions of her as weak and their condemnations that she behaves like a victim. When Lily falls on the stairs at the gym, no one offers to help her up, and the act parallels the rape and her ultimate isolation. Nira's appearance and proffered assistance echoes the other ways in which this friendship serves to raise the women up and restore them from a place of humiliation and despair. At the same time, their friendship enables them to reject the role of victim and the requirement that they continue to conform to the role of "good girl," and together they drink beer in the street at night and vodka in Nira's apartment while smoking out of the window, transgressive acts that symbolize their refusal to continue to be compliant and virtuous.

In subtle ways the press and the police insinuate the women's responsibility for their own rape, for being out at night, for dressing provocatively, and for not being virgins. Aviad employs the reading of the newspaper articles, interviews with former officers and forensic experts, and the court reports as a way to confront male assertion of women's place. By focusing on the women's experiences, rather than the men's report of them, Aviad is able to reclaim the women's subjectivity. This occurs repeatedly throughout the film, as when showing Lily and Nira walking outside at night in a symbolic conquering of fear and the potential threats that exist under the cover of darkness. But even in this moment of empowerment, it is the women's togetherness that gives them courage. When the women walk off in different directions, a man suddenly appears behind Nira in the street and she takes a sharp turn and crosses the road to move away from him. The brief moment is symbolic both of the constant fear that continues to traumatize Nira and of the perpetual alertness and survival strategies that women are taught to use as they go about their daily lives.

Aviad's feminist agenda is also explicit in the ways she films Lily's lover. The shots of his naked genitals are Aviad's critique of the ways in which women are often represented on film. The image's jarring presentation highlights the degree to which women's nakedness has been normalized, while men's nakedness continues to remain taboo. The process of empowerment that the film depicts, and the criticism of the male anxiety over women's rapes (while marginalizing women's horrific experience of rape) set up Nira's guilt over causing her father's death by telling him about her rape as both ridiculous, since of course she is the victim, and realistic, since it plays into an internalization of societal expectations for females. Her consequent treatment by her family, which included blaming her for her father's death and isolating her at a time when she was already vulnerable following her sexual trauma, is explained as a source of the anxiety she develops and her tendency to take on social and professional roles that allow her to perpetuate her isolation. In overcoming her feelings of revulsion and alienation caused by the rape, and in the healing process that comes about through her friendship with Lily and her efforts to make the rape documentary, she is able to move past the initial trauma. In turn, this opens up the possibility of a romantic liaison with her Arab coworker.

The film empowers the female characters, but it also highlights the ways in which women exist in a perpetual sisterhood against all males, since all men have the capacity for violence. Many of the men in the film are bullies, including Lily's son, who appears in military uniform. The only exception is Nira's somewhat effeminate Arab coworker. His identity raises issues about the treatment of ethnicity in the film and the ways in which Arab males are emasculated. As symbolic "females," they can participate in the "sisterhood" of victimhood and do not offer the same threat as other males. This allying of the women and the Palestinians against Israeli male aggression is particularly potent in the paralleling of settings in which male violence manifests. The rapist took women to a grove, where he held them captive for several hours, while the Palestinians fight the Israeli military (and religious settlers) in the olive groves that constitute their livelihood. Lily's political activism on behalf of Palestinians against the Israeli state becomes a metaphor for her overcoming her previous rape. By going to the olive groves and standing up to the Israeli soldiers, she not only protects the Palestinians but also demonstrates her own empowerment. This is part of a continuum of activities she adopts that serve to reject her victimhood. At the same time, the acts of sexualized violence that are represented by the rape are reenacted in the soldiers' sexualization of her body in their attacks against her presence at these protests. Thus her rape is contextualized in a larger framework in which Israeli society and particularly the military is complicit in establishing women's rapeability and determining transgressive women as rapeable. The dominance of a masculine and militaristic society that positions itself as the guardian of women's bodies simultaneously normalizes attacks against women, a motif the film returns to frequently in the way Israeli society judges the raped women by considering why each was rapeable, thereby displacing responsibility from the rapist (or even society more broadly) onto the victim.

This connection that Aviad draws between male violence toward Palestinians (and the impact of the occupation) and the enactment of violence in civil society against women in her film is supported by Sered, Umanit, and Sharoni, who have shown in their sociological research that the veneration of the Israeli soldier propagates a culture of Israeli male privilege that ultimately leads to a permissive attitude toward the men's enactment of violence. The film makes this link apparent through the leniency shown by the courts to the rapist on the grounds that he was traumatized by his military service in the Yom Kippur War.

In the framework of the film, this paralleling of women and Palestinians as victims of Israeli male hegemony creates a problematic tension that remains unresolved. While Lily and Nira engage in acts that lead to their empowerment and demonstrate their resistance to being cast as victims by multiple layers of the Israeli establishment, the Palestinian is never given the opportunity to overcome Israeli acts of oppression. Even the protest is seen through Lily's presence and Nira's editing work—centralizing the Israeli females and making the Palestinian experience of conflict marginal within the film's diegesis. Ironically, this depiction, in turn, casts the Palestinian as perpetual victim, a position that shifts attention from male-female violence toward the Arab-Israeli conflict. By doing so, the film highlights rape in Israel as a social issue whose roots lie in the militarization of the country, but undermines women's gendered experience of hegemony and violence, even as the film ultimately marginalizes the experiences of Palestinian victims of the conflict.

Aviad's use of the conflict within a story that is ostensibly about women's rape points to the issues that can arise with activist filmmaking. The competing agendas of the politics surrounding the occupation, and the work of third-wave educated feminists, do at times overlap. However, there is also the risk that the macropolitics of national borders and wars, which are spheres that remain dominated by male authority figures and male-centered agendas, eclipse women's micropolitics and the advocacy on issues that focus on women's oppression—even when these are enacted against women by the same authorities that oppress other minorities.

The film's black/white aesthetic, in which the past is cast, serves as a metaphor for the binary nature by which rape is conceptualized. The women experience the rape in black and white (the white body pressing against them in the dark night), and Nira represents the white Ashkenazi (Russian) while Lily is the black Mizrahi (Moroccan). This black/white aesthetic also serves to describe the crime and the pursuit of the criminal, as these are divided into binaries: rapist/police, guilty/innocent, male/female. In introducing multiple women's testimonies the film disrupts this categorization and expands rape as a circle that includes multiple assailants (the forensic doctor, the judge, the police, the rapist), and offers rape as a communal problem with far-reaching effects on Israeli society. The banality of the rapist's home, which they find, and their decision not to confront him, deescalate the women's symbolic conflict. The transference of violence that is manifested in their desire to light a fire in the central square in Tel Aviv and conduct a public burning offers a ritualistic symbol of the social forces that perpetuate rape and the marginalization of women who are raped. The women wish to implicate the police, the media, and the legal system in gendered violence, but rather than offering yet another violent conflict, which symbolizes the male approach of protagonist/antagonist, they offer art as a healing response to the trauma. After filming the window of the rapist's home, Nira decides to use this as a shot in the documentary she is now making about the women who were victims of the polite rapist. Thus, in the final scenes, the film's fiction is conflated with the film's historical veracity, and the actresses are implicated in the director's personal experience of the rape and her artistic response to it.

Brave Miss World and *Invisible* both offer feminist agendas that criticize the ongoing victimization of rape survivors by the establishment and the court system. Through portraits of empowered females they seek to advocate for the importance of speaking out against rape, creating a sisterhood that can provide emotional and psychological support, and for the necessity of bringing the rapist to justice as part of the recovery process. While both films offer descriptions of the rapes, neither opts to screen reenactments of rape, a move that refuses to offer women up as spectacle for a voyeuristic audience. Their focus on clear-cut examples of rape, and particularly the examination of serial rapists, frees the filmmakers to address the institutionalization of rape culture and the social structures that continue to discriminate against women. But as the Ramat Hasharon and countryside rape case in Israel demonstrated, when the victims can be discredited, the very nature of a rape can be contested.

Gang Rape—And Other Ways Women Are Compelled into Sex

The Ramat Hasharon rape was not the first gang rape in Israel, nor was it the first rape of a teenager, but the affluent city, a commuter suburb for Tel Aviv, was envisaged as a model community, and the presence of a rape in what was deemed an upper-middle-class idyll, and the reaction to it, exposed the pervasive ways in which men continued to be protected in a patriarchal society that valued men more highly than women. While the victim received support "from the rape crisis center in Tel Aviv, the media, and Ezrat Nashim [an advocacy group of female celebrities and politicians],"[53] she was viewed as an outcast by her peers (male and female), by families associated with the school, and by the local community, who instead supported the teenage rapists. Thus, in a society in which belonging to the collective still maintains a powerful imaginative hold, the girl's civic death constituted a further attack.[54]

Susan Brownmiller has described gang rape as an act of male fraternity, and Horeck explains that in this sense, gang rape serves as a "homoerotic ritual that creates a collective identification between men."[55] As part of this male bonding, the disparagement of women is an "important ingredient of the mystical bond, and sexual aggression the means by which the bond is renewed."[56] Peggy Reeves Sanday has considered the ways fraternity culture on college campuses engages in gang rape to create male citizenship within a collective that reaches beyond the single institution or fraternity to the powerful alumni network that will later extend the brotherhood into wider society. While Israel does not have college campus fraternities, military units whose differing identities are part of a sociocultural code of identification and socialization serve as a substitute model for the ways in which male brotherhood is created. Sanday's conclusions in the American context can be applied not only to the military unit but to the heroic and militaristic youth culture that precedes conscription and that reflects the broader militarization of Israeli society. As Miri Talmon has shown in the Israeli context, young male bonding was a central feature of Israeli culture and the cinema that represented it.[57] This masculine community and its sense of privilege and idolization produced generations of men protected by a society that venerated their position and elevated them to the ruling tier of the hegemony. "The Gang," a recent popular song in Israel, captured this zeitgeist that continues to protect the "right" kind of men, highlighting their fraternity while disparaging the victim. For just as on college campuses in the United States, the girl who reports rape in Israel can often be blamed for destroying her attackers' futures, and she is shamed for denouncing their sexual violence.

The Whole Gang (Monica Sex) Words/Music Yali Sobol

The gang rode you like you were public transportation
But they're not the going to prison kind; they're the elite combat unit kind
The kind that raise the flag at school ceremonies and in youth movements.
In the Scouts they learn how to tie a knot
And it's much easier to tie up a girl.

The gang comes back each night to ride you,
The doctors listen for movement in your womb but they don't listen to your heart
Because there's no cure for a weight on your soul, you can't abort that
The doctors are satisfied, the operation succeeded, now you aren't ill.

The gang said they feel bad that things got complicated
regrets and all that shit, so why are they still smiling?
Because the judge gave a light sentence because you didn't cry out and weren't a virgin.
The dry letter of the law can't ever be dampened,
Not even by a girl's tears.

Translation Rachel S. Harris

The song's references to combat units and youth movements address the systemic issues within youth culture that create hierarchies of power. Dutiful participation in the collective is part of the metaphor that includes later military conscription. The codification of combat units as the military elite establishes the boys' socially privileged position. This translates into later, postmilitary life whereby men are advantaged in every avenue of society, including politics, industry, and the media. Gender inequality in Israel is rife, and men continue to hold most senior positions, women are paid less for the same work, and society is institutionally gendered. Sered has shown that gang rapes "parallel military operation in the male communal structure of the acts of violence," and "certain gang rapes" are forgiven precisely because of these military associations.[58] Feminist scholars point to the connection between training boys to aspire to commando units, male violence, and the abuse of women, a connection that is made explicit "in cases in which men's military accomplishments are cited in public and legal discourse as an 'excuse' for, or mitigating factor in, rape. The interpenetration of military and civilian violence is even clearer in cases in which weapons distributed by the IDF are used by men to carry out acts of violence, including sexual violence, against women,"[59] but this connection between a culture that promotes male violence and the enactment of this violence on women is rarely drawn in the press.

In the Ramat Hasharon case, the girl did not report the attacks (until she collapsed) because she knew she would be blamed for the rapes, and because the boys threatened to slander her as a "slut" if she did not accede to their demands. Similarly, the fourteen-year-old girl in the Kibbutz Shomrat case who was raped over a period of two weeks by three seventeen-year-old boys from the kibbutz and eight other men from elsewhere was threatened with retribution and violence if she told anyone. She remained silent until she finally broke down and told her family. Sered terms this "gender terrorism" that works because "the patriarchal system constructs women as vulnerable, and then offers to defend only those women who meet certain (sometimes ephemeral) standards."[60] The impacts of rape on women include a wide array of physical and mental illnesses, as well as pregnancy, that "intensify the reciprocal construction of femaleness and illness as inherently or 'naturally' coinciding conditions."[61] Thus, women's perceived (and actual) vulnerability creates a cycle that views women's bodies as weak and open to contamination and illness, due to which women require male protection, which therefore reaffirms male authority, an authority that is able to abuse the female body.

The song, "The Gang," like the Ramat Hasharon rape and the Shomrat rape, reveals the many levels at which Israeli society is complicit in a rape culture. The school principal, the head of the local council, and the boys' parents in Ramat Hasharon spoke out to defend the rapists and blamed the girl for her sluttish behavior. In the Shomrat rape, the girl was accused of not locking her dormitory door, not crying, and not resisting. The kibbutz members met and created a statement that referred to the rape only as a "serious incident."[62] Once she reported the incidents, she was hospitalized and then put under psychiatric care and deemed unable to make a statement, as a result of which the Haifa district attorney declined to prosecute the case. Later, in response to a public outcry, a trial was held during which the victim was questioned eight times, and the perpetrators were acquitted due to inconsistencies in her statements. Only after an appeal did four of the men serve jail time.

"The Gang" directs its attention to the immateriality of female suffering, shown in the doctor's medicalization of the female body, in which her only "sickness" can be cured with an abortion. The judge's verdict in the Shomrat case addressed the men's actions as "repulsive" and "perverse" and accused the men of using her as a mere tool, but their sentences were relatively light and only some of the men were convicted at all, while the victim was institutionalized and underwent severe psychological (as well as physical) trauma.[63] In the Ramat Hasharon case, the judge criticized the boys' ongoing claim that they were the real victims, and yet the sentences remained relatively lenient, with four of the seven perpetrators in the Ramat Hasharon case receiving community service and no prison time, while the victim was described by an evaluation of the court as "rarely leaving her house, unable to trust anybody, and suffering from acute insomnia and nightmares."[64]

In a 2013 hearing, Judge Nissim Yeshaya's statement that some women enjoy being raped shocked the courtroom, which descended into silence. As the judge responsible for deciding whether a teenage girl's rape by four Palestinian men could be considered an act of terror so that she could receive financial compensation from the government (as a victim of terrorism), he was responsible not only for protecting the victim and carrying out the letter of the law but for deciding on her position within the hierarchy of victimhood. Instead, his comments spoke to an active disavowal of the actual power dynamics of rape and women's victimization. The judge, apparently failing to understand the implications of his own words, continued to try and explain himself. Though he was positioned to be a leading figure for the judiciary in Prime Minister Netanyahu's government, activism by women's groups denouncing the statement and complaints from those within the courtroom, including negative press, led the prime minister to drop the judge from his professional favor. The judge's misogynistic comments reflect a culture that continues to oppress and marginalize women and derive from a long history of Jewish patriarchy. The song above invokes the biblical language of the prohibition against rape, whereby a woman who is raped in the city is assumed to be complicit, since "she did not cry out," and therefore she is punished by stoning, whereas a woman who is raped in a field is deemed innocent, an image that resonated in Linor Abargil's rape in a wood and the attacks by the "Polite rapist" in the groves outside Tel Aviv.[65] Thus, a parallel is drawn between contemporary treatment of rape victims by the legal system and the Jewish legal tradition, which also put the victim on trial, thereby highlighting a hegemony that continues to enact control over a woman's body.

Male sexual entitlement, at its most extreme, manifests in sexual assault. Its criminalization at least speaks to a culture that rejects unwanted sexual violence. However, the prioritization of male sexual needs (and the presumption that women will provide for these needs) continues to disadvantage women, even in a sex-positive culture whose only requirement is consent. "The game is rigged," as one American news article claimed, in speaking of campus cultures in which "men set the terms, host the parties, provide the alcohol, exert the influence."[66] Female worth is still judged according to male attention and male approval, "and women are still (perhaps increasingly) expected to look and fuck like porn stars—plucked, smooth, their pleasure performed persuasively."[67] In this culture, male climax remains the goal, while "a woman's orgasm is still the elusive, optional bonus round. Then there are the double standards that continue to redound negatively to women: A woman in pursuit is loose or hard up; a man in pursuit is healthy and horny. A woman who says no is a prude or a cock tease; a man who says no is rejecting the woman in question."[68] Abargil has been increasingly speaking out on college campuses against the prevalence of rape and the ways in which academic institutions often silence the victims and decline to prosecute the perpetrators. Her activism responds to a youth culture that has created a climate in which women are expected to be sexual, excel at sex, and prove always and ever available, while never making sexual demands for themselves. It is no wonder that rape cultures on campus and in high schools validate men's belief that they have consent, and that women are often made to feel that they cannot deny it. Horeck, citing Catharine Mackinnon, explains, "Rape law 'uniformly presumes a single underlying reality, not a reality split by divergent meanings, such as those inequality produces.' For the fact of the matter is that 'women are violated every day by men who have no idea of the meaning of their acts to women. To them, it is sex.'"[69] For those who defended the culprits in the Ramat Hasharon, Shomrat, and countrywide rape cases, the girls had willingly provided sex, and the men were innocent of any crime. Though the boys were eventually convicted by the courts, the media supported their divergent narrative and ultimately cast suspicion on the girls' testimony—a public framing that serves to reinforce a gender hierarchy that perpetuates men's ignorance of sex as rape.

S#x Acts brings together many of the narrative threads that pervade the representation of gang rapes of teenagers and the sexual culture that complicates the binary depiction of sexual consent as present or not present. The film considers other ways in which sex may be coercive, even if the act itself may not be legally considered rape, and speaks to a contemporary postfeminist culture in which the sex positive agenda of the feminist movement has in many ways silenced negative but technically consensual sex acts, thereby ignoring the ways in which men still control the sexual arena within which women continue to find themselves in subordinate positions. When Gili, a teenage girl from a low-income background living in an affluent suburb, joins a new high school, she wants to be part of the "in crowd," a group whose wealth, experience of international travel, and Ashkenazi identity situate them at the pinnacle of Israeli society. Viewing sexuality as the only commodity she has to trade, she posts sexually provocative pictures on a social network site in order to interest Tomer in her as a potential romantic opportunity. Tomer, who is ambivalent about Gili, is persuaded by his friend Omri to meet her in a parking lot and take her to a secluded overlook.

While Tomer serves as the reluctant foil, it is Omri whose wealth, charisma, and good looks place him at the center of a male fraternity preoccupied with sex. Not only will he use Gili's interest in Tomer to facilitate his own sexual encounter, he will begin to pimp her to his other friends and acquaintances and finally his preteen brother. On each occasion Gili's resistance and her repeated "no" are brushed aside through a barrage of compliments about her attractiveness and desirability and a social pivoting by Omri through which he accuses her of being a tease and tells her that not allowing him whatever sexual gratification he desires in the moment offends him. For the moments before and after the sexual acts, Gili is treated with kindness, included in future plans, and made to feel that she belongs to the group—but these promises of inclusion quickly evaporate, usually triggered by the boys' desire to spend time with girls from the "in group"—girls they treat differently, and whom they do not wish, at least immediately, to know about their relations with Gili.

Gili's treatment is positioned within a broader contextualization of the rape culture present in daily discourse that continually devalues intimacy and prizes sexual experiences. There are numerous examples of this male fraternity, including the communal viewing of porn, Omri's sharing of a video with his young brother Barel of Gili fellating him in the club's bathroom, and Omri's father's derogatory ways of speaking about women. Omri, his father, and his younger brother repeat the pattern of gaining access to sexual material and sharing it with their friends in acts of "pimping" that afford them higher social status within their respective peer groups. Omri's father desires to see the young girls on his son's and his son's friend's phones, images that he shares with other men his own age. Barel shares the video of Gili, while Omri shares Gili. The film also demonstrates female complicity within this culture of female sexualization. Omri's mother ignores the discussions of sex that she hears in her home, and later she ignores Gili's presence at a party in her son's bedroom.

In order to find social acceptance among a group of wealthy girls from school, a group who have already marked her out as otherwise different because of her poverty and poor dress, Gili uses her sexual encounters as a way to buy social influence. The girls' casual conversation with her before a party at a nightclub betrays the tensions that surround sexual knowledge within the female space. Gili exaggerates the extent of her experiences with Tomer and Omri in order to buy social capital with her female peers. Though they express concern that Gili is being used, thereby positioning them as "nice girls" who would not be similarly exploited, at the same time one of them briefly remarks to her friend, "See, it isn't that difficult." This small aside reveals their own anxiety about sexual experiences and their necessary participation in the high school sexual culture. In their discussion of what has so far transpired (a conversation echoed later with Shabat—the third of Omri's gang to partake of her, and the one who will finally force her in an act of penetration), the girls view Omri as untrustworthy and exploitative, but Gili denies that she is abused by the situation, claiming that she is using him. Her statements deny her victimization and are part of her need to "belong." She repeatedly denies to each of the men that she is serious or romantically interested in other members of the group, though her persistent calls and texts to first Tomer and then Omri suggest otherwise. Her attempts to claim control over the situation ring hollow for the audience, which has witnessed her abuse, and yet, she translates these experiences into social power—seen in her proposition to Omri of an orgy in the bathroom that ultimately allows her guest list access to the nightclub, which, in turn, facilitates an evening of dancing with the female peers who previously disregarded her. This apparent complicity in her sexualization and her rejection of victimhood unsettle the viewer and lead the audience to consider the complexity of attributing responsibility, by raising a distinction between collusion and culpability. In avoiding a single-position message, the film forces viewers to wrestle with the impossibility of a moral clarity that either blames or exonerates the victim.

On the DVD copy of the film, a "Behind the Scenes" short provides interviews with the director, writer, and actors about the making of the film. This material serves to create a distance between the film's pitiless rendition of a society preoccupied with sex, and the critical position that the film takes toward this rape culture. Discussing Gili's role as the class slut, the director claims that she is emblematic of Israeli youth culture and that there is such a girl in every year in every school in the country. While this generalization may be hyperbolic, the coercive sexual culture that the film portrays begins with the social discourse that the scriptwriter overheard while researching the script's dialogue. Observing high school students at restaurants, at hangouts, and sitting on the benches in the centers of affluent, middle- and upper-middle-class suburbs and cities, she noted that their language is filled with curses and is highly sexualized. Interviews with audience members after the screening of the film also described the "lifelike" quality of the film and the high degree to which it reflected the reality that they had encountered in high school.

The broader criticism of an abusive society that condones the commodification of women is seen in the only reference to schoolwork in the film. The students are studying the laws of Yibbum (levirate marriage), a Jewish legal condition in which a woman whose husband has died without issue is obligated to marry his brother. In this religious taxonomy the Rabbinut (rabbinical religious authority) pimps the woman as a way to ensure the continuation of the male line, serving as an overdetermined allusion to the three men of Omri's family and their shared objectification of Gili. Moreover, despite protests by other men, including Shabat, Eyal (the nightclub owner), and even Tomer about Omri's treatment of Gili, criticisms that lead to the men not talking (or having an argument), in the party at the end it is clear that the other men have forgiven Omri and have returned to being complicit in Gili's mistreatment.

In this final scene Omri offers Gili to his thirteen-year-old brother as a coming-of-age present, inverting the traditional Jewish rite of passage (bar mitzvah) in which a man becomes responsible for his own sins, into a rite of passage that repeats the sexual culture to which Barel is now being initiated. Finally, Barel will storm off, humiliated by his apparent rejection, and the party is shut down, but none of the youths are willing to defend Gili again or to take her home. Their failure to criticize Omri on this occasion indicates their return to a masculine hegemonic fold. Omri's father has already created a culture of sexual permissiveness in which the boys' actions appear not only acceptable but lauded. Hence his offer to drive Gili home, and his sexualized glances at her, suggest that he, too, will molest the young girl.

The problematics of making such a film are raised by the director, who explains that the only way in which the highly sexual scenes could be managed by the cast and crew was through detailed choreography, since only by making the interactions clinical could those on set manage to overcome the revulsion at what was taking place. He also stressed that for him, the most terrible aspect was the kissing scenes, as the actress had to kiss a different man every few days of filming. Though the sex scenes were simulated "acting," he described the kisses as "real." The lead actress who played Gili described the dissociative state that she had to enter into in order to be able to cope with the character's experiences, and she explained the gap she felt existed between how she might behave in the situations in which Gili found herself, and Gili's behavior, highlighting her internalized expectation of the ways in which a woman needs to behave in order to protect herself from male sexual aggression. The behind-the-scenes interviews seek to offer a serious consideration of the film's treatment of rape culture, but the jocularity and innuendo on set that the filming captures also demonstrate the dissonance between the presumed critical stance of the filmmaker and the young actors' tacit denial of the implications of male posturing in the creation of rape cultures.

The director's repeated disclaimer about the horror of the situation emphasizes the problematics of making films about rape—even ones that approach the subject critically. Gili's sexual encounters, and the violence (both emotional and physical) directed toward her, are viscerally displayed on the screen. But while the film takes a critical position, it does not overcome the eroticization of these problematic scenes. Gili is frequently seminaked or clad in very revealing clothes, as are Tomer, and particularly Omri, who is shirtless in a number of scenes (and bears a sexy tattoo on the side of his torso). Gili's clothes denote a low-class whorish quality, while Omri's suggest affluence—thus naked Omri elides the sexual commodification that dogs Gili, even when she is clothed. The highly charged sexual nature of the encounters and the ways in which they play into sexual fantasies of violence challenges Yosef's "enlightened viewer," who is repelled but may also become aroused.

Omri's pleasure is derived from his ability to make her yield and from his experiences of sexual gratification, but, more than that, from appearing as someone who can make things happen for others. His own internalization of the power of the collective means that he enjoys pimping her to the other boys. If Omri is concerned with power, Shabat's concern with Gili's well-being returns us to the medicalization of the female body—which is both vulnerable and abject. After he traps Gili by sitting on her and forcing her into a sexually compromising position, Shabat at first promises not to ejaculate inside her, and then when he does, insists that she take the morning-after pill. So concerned is he that she may become pregnant, and that she cannot be viewed as responsible enough to prevent this situation, that he insists on getting her the pill while driving her home. Gratuitously, he purchases two pills, so that she will have a spare, should she need it again. Thus the male takes responsibility for the female body that he has "made sick." Sered describes the "circular schema" by which "rape, violence, and the threat of rape and violence make women sick and weak" but through which "medical treatment does little more than disguise the true source of illness by training ever more attention upon women's 'pathological' bodies rather than upon the truly pathological cultural patterns that make violence and gender hierarchy seem inevitable."[70] The violence enacted upon Gili is ignored, trivialized, normalized, and joked about by the boys, exposing the ways in which a rape climate operates. The audience, disgusted by the boys' behavior and empathetic of the girl's pain, is nevertheless channeled into a moral judgment that also implicates Gili's behavior and therefore participates in rape culture's tendency to blame the victim. Despite the social disadvantages that Gili faces, her economic deprivation, and her abusive family environment, the audience regards her with antipathy. Yet, the false equivalence between her treatment and her behavior highlights the issue of agency (and lack thereof) in these rape films.

The sexualization of Gili in her naked display, the constant adjusting of her clothing, and the depictions of her participation in carnal acts also demonstrate the problematics of representation that *Brave Miss World* and *Invisible* consciously avoid. This pornographic display blurs the line between critical comment on sexual violence and the erotic representation of it. It also serves as a means to consider the issue of spectatorship, since the aroused audience becomes complicit in Gili's sexual commodification, patterning the very model the film denounces of watching the videoed recording of Gili performing sexual acts, for sexual pleasure. *Out of Sight* tackles this problem of representation by offering a blind protagonist, who, unable to see what took place, metaphorically provides the audience with a similar degree of blindness.

Out of Sight was among the first of several films to address the issue of childhood sexual abuse. Like *S#x Acts*, it moves beyond a criticism of the police handling of rape cases and the treatment of rape victims to confront the stereotype of rape as an act by a violent stranger. Instead, these two films reveal the ways in which society is complicit in the sexual violation of women, and the shroud of silence that protects the perpetrator. As with *S#x Acts,* it also considers the ways in which abuse creates an intergenerational cycle that perpetuates a legacy of abusers.

Ya'ara, a doctoral student studying in the United States, returns to Israel and her adoptive home, where she lived with her aunt and uncle and their two daughters, when she hears of her cousin Talia's death. Their close ages meant that they shared a room and went everywhere together, a friendship that Ya'ara remembers as the defining experience of her childhood, for Talia served as her eyes. During the week of mourning, she begins to uncover the sexual abuse that as a child she had failed to see, and slowly discovers the ways in which Talia abused Ya'ara's trust to trick her, humiliate her, and finally facilitate Ya'ara's own sexual attack. As Anat Zanger identifies the repeated patterns of abuse in Talia's response to Ya'ara's forced sexual encounter, "in a twisted role-play she abandons Ya'ara, just like her mother abandoned her to the hands of her own father."[71] Ya'ara's blindness is thus conveyed as both literal and figurative in her failure to see her friend's unhappiness, the sexual violence taking place within the family home, or the conditions of her own abuse.

As the investigation unfolds, Ya'ara discovers Talia's two pregnancies by her father Rafael and the abortions she underwent. In her public confrontation of Rafael at the swimming pool, Ya'ara directs us to the ways in which women are ongoing objects of the male gaze. Dressed in only her underclothes, she reveals her adult body, and this connects the present to childhood recollections of the two young girls learning to swim, their prepubescent bodies exhibited for the patriarch teaching them. In her blindness Ya'ara cannot gaze back, suggesting the impossibility of inverting the gaze, by which tactic women could occupy the uppermost point in a hierarchy. But she also rejects the passive role that her aunt adopted. Instead, she reveals her knowledge in the public space, removing the acts of abuse from the privacy of the domestic space where the crimes had been covered up and the perpetrator had been kept safe. Instead, "she makes her voice heard," asserting female power and offering up testimony.[72] By revealing the crimes to her aunt Hannah, Ya'ara creates a new kind of sisterhood, one that rejects complicity in patriarchal control of a woman's body and instead stakes control over the male body. Ya'ara uses this power to touch Rafael, invading his physical space as she reaches out for his sexual organs, and later Hannah, using Rafael's diabetic syringe, kills her husband.

Rafael's diabetes inverts the convention of presenting the sick and weak female body, offering instead a male whose pathology is both physical and psychological. Yet the film resists the implication that such a man is a social pariah. His sheer physical size (Assi Dayan dwarfs all the other actors in the film) and Talia's assertion in her suicide letter that he is very strong deny the emasculation that would traditionally absolve patriarchy by marginalizing the carbuncle in its midst. Ya'ara's central position in the film exemplifies the theme of blindness, and the metaphorical blindness of Talia's boyfriend, Hannah, and even Ya'ara's own father in failing to put together the things that they have seen and experienced about Rafael's role in Talia's suffering. Ya'ara speaks out in a series of episodes: in the kitchen she announces Talia's pregnancy; in the car she tells her father that she suspects Rafael of abusing his daughters;

and in carrying the letter to Hannah and proclaiming that she will go to the authorities, she reverses Talia's silence. Just as Talia had been her "eyes," she becomes Talia's mouth. As Zanger explains, "In the present feminist (or postfeminist) era, Israeli women have the 'right to speak' (not without difficulty, even so) and now that they have acquired it, they use it to create *lines of flight* for their voices."[73] Her claim refers to Ya'ara's speaking out, as much as it does to Noa Greenberg's screenplay in its excoriation of female sexual abuse.

Feminist Responses to Rape and Abuse

The criticism that Projansky has directed at films that consider rape from a feminist perspective is that "while they may offer a woman's *experience* of rape, even a feminist *perspective* on rape, they do not engage a particularly feminist *response* to rape."[74] In *Brave Miss World*, through the presentation of Abargil's activism, and through the provision of information about her dynamic website, which continues to accept and publish rape narratives, Cecilia Peck offers a film that not only substantially works to raise awareness about rape, the social and legal implications of rape, and the psychological and emotional trauma of rape but also displays ways in which feminists respond to rape and provides a resource for future feminist activism against rape. *Invisible*, by contrast, reveals the limits of engaging with the system that perpetuates a rape culture. By recording the testimony of rape victims and creating the mise-en-abyme documentary (within the film's diegesis), Aviad, like Peck, demonstrates the significance of bearing witness as a mode of feminist response. Moreover, her own experience of being assaulted by the Tel Aviv rapist, and this feature film that interweaves the real with the fictional, provides a feminist artistic response to rape. In *Out of Sight*, Ya'ara affords the role of witness the responsibility for also bringing her uncle to justice that ultimately turns it into a rape-revenge film. While many of the films analyzed in this book depict rape, this chapter confronts the idea that all rape representations are also feminist statements, even in films that otherwise seek to comment on the negative treatment of women and the power of patriarchy in Israeli society. The problematics of feminist portrayals of rape remain in the representational issues raised in the introduction of this book: that "a text that purports to be feminist can actually be hegemonic. While seeming to position women at the center, it can subvert this positioning through negative judgements and negative consequences."[75] When representations of rape uphold a culture that promotes women's fear—fear of being raped, fear of facing civic death, fear of not being believed, fear of serving as witness at a trial, fear of being put on trial, then while these films may continue to offer critical positions on the treatment of women or others in Israeli society, including the occupation, they nevertheless fail to adequately address the self-reflexive questions necessary for a feminist consideration of sexual violence.

The moral ethics of presenting rape scenes, and feeding rape culture, remain at the forefront of feminist issues in Israeli society. On September 30, 2015, a story broke in the press about the Allenby 40 nightclub, where "over the course of 4–5 hours dozens of men and women watched a number of men exploit a drunk woman, in order to use her body for their own wants and pleasure as if it were an object."[76] The scene was filmed by a number of people, and the videos were shared and uploaded online. Not one of the witnesses made any gesture to remove the woman from the bar, and several cheered on the men, chanting "Get on, work it" and "*Yalla*—more, more!"[77] In her article in the *Haaretz* newspaper, Irit Negbi, a professor of criminology, drew a direct correlation between the event and the rape scene in the American film *The Accused,* with its critical cinematic response to the real-life gang rape of a woman in a bar in New Bedford, Massachusetts. As Negbi argued, the scene in Tel Aviv was clearly one of rape, since the law considers a sexual act rape if a woman is unconscious or is otherwise unable to give consent, and the woman on the bar was evidently too drunk to assent to anything. She also addressed the witnesses' complicity, since in Israel it is unlawful to sit by while a criminal act is taking place without exerting efforts to stop it, and those who cheered on the rapists abetted in the criminal act. Furthermore, Israel's indecency laws forbid the filming and distribution of scenes of a sexual nature without the participants' consent, and those who recorded and distributed images of the event committed a crime.

Allenby 40 already had a seedy reputation in an area known for its sleazy bars and dance clubs. Police, aware of the club's actions in general, had opened an investigation after receiving footage of the woman being stripped on the bar and participating in acts of a sexual nature when it was circulated on the popular cell phone application "whatsap." *She* was brought in for questioning for "public disrobing," as the police believed she was committing a crime by being paid to strip in a venue that was not licensed for strippers. After several months the public indecency charges were dropped, thereby closing the case, and it was this report on Channel 10 that triggered the media frenzy. The ensuing public outcry and a request by the state's attorney led police to reopen the case, this time in order to examine charges of rape against the men involved.

But as details of the events emerged over the course of the following week, the woman's reputation became the central topic and would determine whether anyone would be held culpable. She had worked at the bar and on several previous occasions had taken part in "wet t-shirt competitions," until these events were closed down after public pressure by the journalist Orly Vilnai and the lawyer and social worker Assaf Rajan. Their activism led to police interest in underage drinking and unregulated "stripping" at the club, and, in turn, led its owners to cancel the competitions and instead repackage these events as "water-spraying" happenings where everyone in the bar participated.[78] Referred to in the press as "sexual acts," the display of her body on the bar in the context of the wet t-shirt competitions was used to cast the woman as sluttish, and later it was revealed that she had been part of two previous orgies on the bar. Moreover, the culture of public sex in nightclubs was defended in an opinion piece by Dana Golberg in *Haaretz* where she claimed only the cultural code about not filming such events had been transgressed.

The public furor eventually focused on whether the act was a gang rape, since the woman was so drunk that she was unable to consent to or prevent the acts being perpetrated on her, or whether it was consensual, as part of a sexually promiscuous climate in a trashy bar with a woman who had already displayed few reservations and had a history of indecent exposure. The woman's history, including the presence of hard drugs and alcohol in her system, the lies she told in the original investigation about acting of her own free will (in a context in which she was being accused of being paid to perform and risked imprisonment), and her participation in sexually provocative dancing in the bar on previous occasions, meant that the issue of consent was deemed murky, and no attempts were made to prosecute the men who participated in the sexual acts. However, the filming and distribution of the footage (such as putting the video online or sending it as a message by phone) were against Israel's decency laws, and public pressure led to the state's attorney's office making gestures to criminally prosecute those who filmed the act.

Falling back on victim-blaming and casting the woman as an immoral, libidinous slut is already a convention for the treatment of rape victims that disavows the accusation of rape and men's responsibility for it, but, curiously, a second front opened in the public rhetoric when Dana Goldberg accused feminists who determined the event to be a rape of "upholding the puritanical laws of a Victorian society" and disliking men and sex. She claimed that the woman was not a victim of rape because a woman can have sex with more than one man, despite what "prudish feminists" might think. Moreover, she disparaged the feminists' calls of rape, accusing them of disparaging the woman and turning her into a victim, saying, "feminists don't call other women 'weak' and then expect men to respect them."[79] In response, Tzafi Saar accused Goldberg of "adopting the well-worn argument that opposition to sexual violence is opposition to sex."[80] She accused Goldberg of collapsing the egalitarian ideals of a perfect world onto the imperfections of reality and pointed to the ongoing work by feminists to change a culture of masculine privilege and the concomitant violence enacted by men to see their needs met. That is, she addressed the existence of Israel's rape culture and the distinction between sex by means of consent and sex by means of violence, and called on the spectators' failure to intervene.

> Whoever sees a gang of men, one after another fucking one young woman, that some-one or some-many gave her more and more to drink, and someone untied the knot on her bathing suit and stripped her—and everyone around is cheering and filming and distributing the video—and whoever sees such an event and is able to say that we are talking about a woman's free will, and that she is fulfilling her sexuality, and isn't paying any attention to the alcohol she has drunk—has lost any connection to basic humanity.[81]

As Horeck has explained, the press surrounding the Big Dan rape and "the story of a group of men cheering, laughing and goading on a woman's gang rape threw the category of the witness into crisis. The act of viewing a spectacle of violence was revealed as participation in that violence, muddying a distinction between those who raped and those who watched."[82] The cinematic language of rape time and again offers up female disempowerment, and when rape is displayed on-screen, the audience, as witness, becomes implicated in the acts of violence. Rape on-screen is often presented uncritically, and therefore it directs a climate of fear that points to women's defenselessness and simultaneously their need to model culturally specific behavior that will keep them safe, thereby reinforcing the rape culture that already established a social difference between women and women-who-get-raped.

Rape and the representation of rape in Israel continue to demarcate lines of power. On one side lies male hegemonic control, expressed in the society's military culture and protection of male perpetrators of rape, who represent this patriarchy and are shielded from prosecution, are defended publicly, and receive light sentences if they are sentenced at all. On the other lies womankind. Any woman can be the victim of rape, and her social treatment post facto is an indication of her status within proscribed hierarchies of acceptable female positioning, which is governed by the patriarchy that rapes her and judges her. Feminist filmmaking in Israel has sought out ways to discredit the negative treatment of rape victims, to highlight the conspiracies of silence that continue to suppress rape reporting, and to speak out against a rape culture that denigrates women. Attributing blame to the militarization of Israeli culture underscores the pervasive nature of the conflict, as it infiltrates into the nation's psyche, but runs the risk of emphasizing Palestinian oppression, a move that returns the debate to the sphere of the Arab-Israeli conflict and, as a consequence, perpetuates the marginalization of women and female experience.

8

A Move to the Center

Foreign Workers, Arab Women, and the Shift from the Margins

Jellyfish, an avant-garde film that paralleled three separate story lines featuring women, won the 2007 Camera d'Or at the Cannes Film Festival. The film presents a variety of female interactions and relationships, which tease out a range of themes, including intergenerational dynamics, employer-employee relations, women's shared identification, jealousy, and competition, directing attention at the rich world of female socialization that is often invisible or marginalized within film culture. The opening scene at a wedding provides our first introduction to the three women who serve as the focus for each story line: Joy, a Filipina caregiver who longs to work with children but is repeatedly assigned elderly people who do not speak English and with whom she cannot communicate; Batya, a waitress who has a surrealist encounter with a little girl who emerges from the sea, and befriends the wedding photographer, who is fired from the same banquet hall on the same night; and Keren, whose broken leg prevents her from a dream honeymoon and who finds herself trapped in a colorless local hotel, embroiled in a poetic encounter with a lonely suicidal woman with whom her new husband becomes fascinated.

While the film speaks with a universalizing turn about the social and emotional life of women, all the characters except Joy are Israeli. As a Filipina caregiver, Joy is an interloper in the established dynamic of Israeli films, which tend to look inward at the society, and for whom the Palestinian conventionally retains the role of symbolic *other*. Her depiction establishes the pattern of treatment for foreign workers that developed in Israeli cinema toward the end of the first decade and into the second decade of the twenty-first century, and also reflects cultural attitudes toward migrant workers that were occurring during the same period within the artistic community in Israel.[1] Thus, Joy's depiction in this film can be seen as part of a feminist activist agenda that allied itself with the plight of caregivers and advocated, through consciousness raising, for better conditions for these women, by exploring their professional and legal situation. This chapter explores the sympathetic representation of female foreign workers, the relationship of women within the Israeli *polis* to them, and the political context in which the films *Jellyfish*, *Noodle*, and *Salsa Tel Aviv* sought to position foreign workers.

Joy's manpower agency moves her to different elderly people in need. Her necessary presence is a response to their children's absence, as they live in different locations, have careers,

Jellyfish: Joy (Ma-nenita De Latorre) cares for Malka (Zaharira Harifai) when she collapses in the street.

and are physically and emotionally disconnected from the elder parent. She first appears with the "grandmother" at a wedding, next with a deaf and housebound woman who dies, and finally with a woman who speaks only German and Hebrew, while Joy can speak neither. Joy's English is good, but useless here, since the caregiver and her charge cannot verbally communicate with one another. Hired by the woman's actress daughter, Joy is sent to collect the woman from the hospital and return her to her home. The difficult relationship between mother and daughter, a relationship without affection or physical contact, is contrasted with the bond that develops between the elderly woman and Joy, who learn to communicate nonverbally. Their deeply affective relationship culminates in a warm embrace for the tearful Joy, who is afraid that the ship she wanted to send her son has been sold. Instead, the elderly woman has purchased the gift to give to her, which speaks of a transcendent bond of motherhood. And yet, the mother-child relationship is problematic for both women, who have difficulty communicating with their children, the Israeli women because of the hostility and disappointment that saturates their interactions, the Filipina woman due to the distance and the difficulty of public telephone conversations with her five-year-old son in the Philippines.

As a caregiver, Joy stands in place of the elderly women's children, but her own child is far away, cared for by an aunt in a pattern common for female care workers in which a "'global care chain' develops in which women migrate to the receiving countries, leaving their own children and dependents in the care of unpaid family members or paid care workers in the sending countries."[2] Just as Joy's son begs her to return home, the Israeli women ask their own children to be more present. The film repeats this motif of absent parents and the impact on the children in Batya's story line (her own parents are absent in her life before her accident, they abandon her when she is in the hospital, the photograph album of her childhood is empty, and the five-year-old child she meets also has no parents). Even the eight-millimeter home movie that the photographer screens from her own childhood shows a little girl alone—revealing an intergenerational breakdown in emotional and material terms that addresses the disconnection of modern living.

Joy's presence within the family home, her intimate knowledge of family conflicts, and the elderly woman's abandonment place her within a domestic space that is a female economy of labor and emotions, constructing a "false kinship" characteristic of the lives of live-in migrant workers in Israel. Whereas domestic duties had primarily been viewed as the responsibility of women within the family, who shopped, cooked, cleaned, and cared for children and for the elderly, this work is now outsourced to the Filipina, who is seen in the film accompanying the women to public events (the theatre, a wedding), providing food, and performing other domestic duties in the homes of the elderly women for whom she is employed as caregiver. Meanwhile, the adult children are shown busy with their own nuclear family lives and with their careers. Thus the Filipina liberates the Israeli woman from the domestic space, enabling her upward mobility in a nondomestic labor force.

> While it is impossible to show a direct causal relation, it can generally be speculated that with the entrance of cheap unskilled labor into the country, Israeli women's level of (full-time) market participation has increased, as well as, presumably, their leisure time. This regime, however, does not necessarily imply greater gender equality. The gendered division of labor remains largely intact, given the fact that the majority of migrant care workers are women and that women in Israeli families are still regarded as responsible for managing dependent family members' care.[3]

At the expense of foreign labor, Israeli women across all sectors of the population have enjoyed a transformation in their own domestic roles, which has facilitated their pursuit of opportunities within the labor force, further encouraged by Ministry of Welfare subsidies for childcare, measures that traditionally afford women increasing social and economic power and thereby generally reduce the authority of patriarchy.

This narrative of the caregiver in Israel has occurred only since the 1990s, when the implementation of a health law that underwrote the cost of providing support services for the elderly and disabled living in their own homes, including laundry service, incontinence pads, and several hours of care per week, changed the ways in which many elderly were cared for in Israel. As Hila Shamir has shown, "The result has deeply affected the Israeli family: familial relations have changed due to the new availability of affordable, round-the-clock in-home care provision for the elderly, as have expectations in regard to caregiving for the elderly, intergenerational living arrangements, and the gendered division of care work in the Israeli household."[4] As part of a move toward the privatization of elderly provisions, the social security system introduced a Long-Term Care Benefit (*Gimlat Siuud*) by which migrant workers could be issued visas to "serve as in-home care workers for the elderly and disabled," and which also regulated "migrant workers' working conditions and life in Israel."[5] The measures reflected a recognition of the rapid aging of the Israeli population and a desire to keep the elderly within the community rather than in institutions. The costs of employing a migrant worker were significantly reduced, and subsidies that provided between five and eighteen hours of in-home care per week for those who met income tests reduced costs further.[6] Elderly deemed eligible may apply for permits to employ a caregiver, who is provided through an agency, and if the worker becomes "live-in" and is employed full-time (thereby exceeding the allocation of the Care Benefit), the "recipient pays the care-providing agency for the extra service hours. However, employing a live-in migrant care worker, under the current system, does not require increasing the worker's wage by a comparable ratio to the increase in work hours ... an amount that even upper-tier low-income households can afford when they are assisted by the Care Benefit."[7] Hence, the introduction of in-home care has changed the social role of many women. It has created "a relatively egalitarian apparatus for insiders (residents and citizens), whereby the middle class, as well as some low-income citizens, can purchase in-home care, but at the cost of employing a non-resident and therefore more vulnerable, unorganized, and often illegal workforce,"[8] thereby having a leveling effect on the ability of mostly Jewish women from different social strata to participate in the workforce.

Historically, the Israeli government has been strongly against hiring foreign migrants, concerned that, as has happened in other countries, the migrants would build lives in Israel and settle. Determined to prevent yet another non-Jewish population from affecting the ethnic makeup of the country, as part of the existential fear of the demographic threat (whereby a majority of non-Jews may change the "Jewish" status of the country), they have persistently denied requests from industry to allow a significant number of foreign worker visas. However, since 1993, when the government reluctantly responded to requests from the agricultural and building industries to issue visas for foreign workers in response to severe labor shortages, there has been a large influx of migrant workers into Israel, an influx that is increasingly reshaping low-rent urban areas and that provides approximately 10 percent of Israel's current workforce.

The intermittent closing of borders to Palestinians from Gaza and the West Bank following periods of violence and unrest resulted in an increasingly sporadic and undependable Palestinian workforce, who, since 1967, had traditionally been employed in these low-paid jobs. The difficulty with checkpoints, which, even when they were open, often included extensive waiting times, coupled with local Palestinian activism that discouraged working for Israelis, meant that industries dependent on Palestinian labor were under pressure to find alternative manpower. In an ethnically and nationally stratified process, foreign migrants began to arrive in the country, filtered into designated fields. Predominantly male and employed on two- or five-year work visas, Thai immigrants were sent to agricultural projects, mainly in the moshavim and kibbutzim in the country's periphery, while Turks, Romanians, and Chinese were employed in construction. Employers did not always honor agreements or treat the workers legally or fairly, and some left their original employers or overstayed the length of their visa, thereby becoming illegal. Despite the threat of deportation, the significant wage difference between Israel and the home country made remaining attractive. Moreover, for those hired through the legal process, broker fees and the cost of travel paid in advance in the home country (and often financed through high-interest loans) meant that many were debt slaves, responsible for paying back significant sums before they could view their foreign labor experience as profitable.

Unlike construction and agriculture, where visas were for a limited period and difficult to renew, in health care there was no quota on the number of migrants, and "care workers can apply for almost unlimited extensions of their visas. An extension can be given if a social worker has determined that the worker's departure will cause severe harm to the person in her or his care. As a result, some migrant care workers, especially those taking care of disabled children, can remain in Israel legally for decades yet not gain any legal rights toward residency or citizenship."[9] By contrast with the other industries, which have been dominated by men, the majority of foreign care workers are female migrants from the Philippines (later supplemented by Nepalese, Indian, and Sri Lankan women). Caregiving is the fastest growing sector in the Foreign Worker Program (FWP) "and the only one in which there is no formal cap on the numbers of permits that can be issued. In 2009, for example, 57,000 new permits were issued to prospective employers of caregivers, a sevenfold increase from the 8,100 permits that were issued in 1996, and the year permits for eldercare were first offered."[10] As Maya Shapiro observed in her anthropological research on the migrant worker program, "the sight of elderly Israelis with their migrant-worker employees was pervasive throughout Tel Aviv and had indeed become the prevailing icon of the FWP and of labor migration to Israel more generally.[11]

In an attempt to limit the migrants' opportunities to settle in Israel, along with restrictive visa policies, strict regulations tried to prevent the creation of family units. Workers could not be admitted if they had any other family members in the country (including partners, parents, or children) and were not permitted to remain if they married or had children (they had to leave the country with the child within ninety days and return alone) or they could lose their legal status.[12] In 2011, Supreme Court Justice Ayala Procaccia struck down this ruling by the Ministry of the Interior, using employment law to rule that it was illegal to discriminate against pregnant women or mothers, viewing such discrimination as against human rights law and calling for the protection of migrant workers' rights. However, the material reality has been that few women have been affected by these legal changes. Mya Guarinieri Jaradat, a journalist researching the situation of migrant workers in Israel, estimates as few as four to five women were actually affected by the ruling, since the reality has been that pregnant women or those with young infants are unable to work the long hours or perform the at times physically laborious tasks required in caring for the elderly and disabled, such that they will often lose their employment positions and, by extension, their rights.[13] As visas are held by the employer and not the employee, these grant the employers significant power and have often left the foreign migrants open to a range of abuses. In the first waves of the Foreign Worker Program, restrictive employment policies that limited the worker to the original visa applicant, known as the "binding agreement," meant that workers who left their employer lost their residency rights. "The binding arrangement provision sought to inhibit labor market mobility and to suppress the migrant workers' market power, making them reluctant to resist employers' exploitative behaviour for fear of losing their visas."[14] Later changes to the law reframed the binding agreement as sectorial, by allowing the migrant worker to change families and agencies on limited conditions (with restrictions to geographical areas and to the number of moves permitted).[15] But this does not help women who have become pregnant, and in general the unintended consequence of the binding agreement has been an incentive to work undocumented, in better-paid opportunities as nannies and domestics, and not as legally sanctioned caregivers. Yet illegal employment also exposes migrant workers to greater degrees of exploitation, and though they are subject to labor laws even when employed illegally, most do not report abuses due to the risk of deportation.

Along with those who have become illegal despite originally entering the country under legal means are those who arrived in Israel specifically to work illegally. Male immigrants from the former Soviet Union and from South America, who generally arrived on tourist visas but work illegally, often outstaying their allotted time in the country, have worked in construction. Female workers arriving on tourist visas are usually employed as nannies or domestics. These two groups often experience downward occupational mobility. Many have high levels of education, including advanced degrees. However, because of their undocumented status they cannot enter the professions in which they are qualified and therefore take on menial work, which is nevertheless paid at a higher rate than the professional employment opportunities available at home. Notwithstanding pride taken in the earning potential that work in Israel engenders, downward mobility is often traumatic, particularly among Latina workers who become live-in maids and are therefore disconnected from Latin American social networks, creating a very real experience of isolation.[16]

Filipina and Latina migrant workers may be dispersed during the week, but as part of Israeli law they are entitled to one day of rest a week, which usually begins on Saturday evening and runs through Sunday for the migrant workers.[17] On these days many meet to take part in religious and recreational activities. Churches are an important part of the community networking that takes place, "not only as a source of spiritual and moral support, but also as a place for exchanging vital information about jobs, housing, recreational activities, as well as useful information about remittances, health care, kindergarten, and schools."[18] The connection between Israel and Christianity adds to the country's desirability as a location for many Roman Catholic and Evangelical Christian migrant workers; thus the churches not only perform social functions but also reinforce the connection between religiosity and care service in Israel as a devotional act that may connect them to God.

> Filipino evangelicals are overrepresented in Israel due to evangelising in the diaspora and the attraction of Israel as a destination country for Christians proclaiming pro-Israeli attitudes and emphasising the Jewish roots of Christianity. They typically view being in Israel as part of a project of becoming proper Christians. For them, the term 'Christian' seems to signify an almost unattainable cultural ideal. Throughout their stays in Israel, women become increasingly devout or 'born again', gain strength from their faith or, alternatively, lose their uncritical belief in religious doctrines and rhetoric while discovering their own spiritual truth. Their stay in Israel not only allows Filipino Christians to obtain intimate access to highly esteemed spiritual knowledge, such as Judaism and Hebrew, but also enables them to undertake a Holy Land pilgrimage.[19]

For the migrants who place an important emphasis on religious participation, churches are often the only place that can marry undocumented foreign workers, and they will also baptize undocumented children. Claudia Liebelt's field research on Filipina workers revealed the importance of religious pilgrimages to major and minor holy sites as part of the social and religious identification with Israel and the West Bank.[20] Significantly, these religious connections are gendered responses to the experience of migration. It is women who establish new churches, fill the pews, rise in the institutions' ranks, and later translate this religious capital into high-status positions within the church in other migration countries or upon their return home. At the same time, the churches offer women practical support during the period in Israel through language lessons (Hebrew and English), sewing and hairdressing classes, social networks, and other activities that serve to create a sense of empowerment.

By the late 1990s, an estimated four hundred thousand foreign workers were in Israel, but mass deportations of undocumented foreign workers due to government crackdowns during the middle of the first decade of the twenty-first century have significantly reduced numbers.[21] An element of racism has informed these changing policies, and it is mostly those from the global south and Africa who are rounded up and sent home, while those from the former Soviet Union more often fly under the radar. As part of the policy to disrupt family units, men were frequently deported with the assumption that women and children would follow them. Instead, this has meant that women now constitute a majority of the foreign workforce generally, and in the urban centers particularly. According to the October 2015 bulletin of the Population, Immigration and Border Authority (PIBA), a publication that appears quarterly, at that time there were approximately 77,000 legal foreign workers and 16,000 illegal foreign workers (who originally arrived on legal work visas but no longer conformed to one or more of the criteria for their original employment), with a further 91,000 tourists who had overstayed, as well as 44,500 refugees. It must be noted that of this last group only 142 had entered in the first three-quarters of the 2015 calendar year, revealing a significant slowdown in this wave of migrants, which was at its height during 2010–2012, when 10,000 to 17,000 arrived per year. The majority of foreign workers were employed as caregivers, constituting around 61 percent, with 23 percent in agriculture and 8.6 percent in construction, with a further 7 percent in other industries, including skilled labor, hospitality, industry, and seasonal agriculture. A year later, the October 2016 bulletin shows similar numbers, with the greatest reduction being in tourists who have overstayed, now numbering 78,500, with only 18 refugees entering the country since January 2016, and with a growth in the number of legal foreign workers to 81,329.[22]

Filipina workers generally arrive legally on work visas, and *Jellyfish* focuses on the personal cost and the emotional issues, including the affective bond with the client, as well as the price of being apart from home and family. *Salsa Tel Aviv*, by focusing on a Mexican Latina, addresses the issues of illegal workers, who generally arrive on tourist visas with the aim of working (and overstaying). Unlike legal workers, they do not pay brokerage fees, but neither do they come for a specific employer, and they must find work within Israel. Commonly employed in domestic service as cleaners, maids, and nannies, these women, who may be educated and in their native countries may even have had servants themselves, often view the menial labor as a humiliating step down. Political reforms in South America that led to democratization (democratic elections, free press) after decades of repressive authoritarian regimes did not have corresponding socioeconomic reforms. "The increasing foreign debt, austerity plans dictated by the International Monetary Fund, high inflation, and consequent internal recession and economic stagnation widened social gaps and poverty rates. The combination of falling incomes, frustrated ambitions, and restructuring of many Latin American economies generated powerful pressures for emigration among both skilled blue-collar workers and the educated urban middle classes."[23] The arrival of large numbers of Latin Americans in Israel also reflected the country's relative tolerance (compared to North America), and patterns of transnational flow whereby previous workers extolled the virtues of life in Israel. For Latin Americans, as with most Christian immigrants, Israel's designation as the Holy Land and the birthplace of Christ also situates it in a unique position for attracting migrants.

In Israel, Latina women, like Filipina women, exist in an underground economy with their own social networks, clubs, and groups. Apartments are generally shared by several people, and these women constantly face the threat of deportation, which therefore leads to a greater likelihood of exploitation by employers. Moreover, by contrast with Filipina women, who are usually fluent in English and often pick up Jewish languages, including Hebrew and, less commonly, Ladino and Yiddish, Latina women are less likely to be able to communicate in Hebrew or English, thereby limiting their employment opportunities. With recent waves of Jewish immigration from Latin America, Christian Latinas often find employment in Jewish Spanish- and Portuguese-speaking homes.

Salsa Tel Aviv, written by Elisa Dor, is a film in the style of a Spanish *telenovela*, predominantly in Spanish with some Hebrew, about Vicki's illegal immigration to Israel in order to earn enough money to pay for the dental work her son needs in Mexico. The boy's father, Beto, who has been in Israel for some time, has failed to send home money. His established network, which includes a shared apartment in the downtrodden parts of south Tel Aviv, daily work as an office cleaner in the more upscale neighborhoods of the city, and evening work as a salsa instructor for the wealthy middle- and upper-middle-class Jewish Israelis, is similarly shared by a number of other women from Latin America, pointing to the existence of foreign worker networks. After receiving a temporary tourist visa, on the pretense of being the nun "Sister Victoria" who has come to Israel to visit the holy sites and work in a mission, Vicki joins Beto, working with him day and night, until she catches him carousing with another woman. Hurt, she leaves the apartment and therefore misses the arrival of the immigration police and the deportation of the apartment residents. The film interweaves a love story between Vicki and the Israeli Yoni, a Spanish-speaking professor she meets on the flight who helps her clear customs. Despite the persistence of Yoni's temperamental fiancé, Dafna, Vicki, the talented salsa dancer, eventually wins his heart but is deported. Finally, following the conventional romantic plot, he runs after her and together they live in Mexico with Vicki's son.

The film's comic turns, Vicki's bizarre and erratic behavior, and Yoni's overbearing Jewish mother, terrified that her son will fail to marry Dafna, work together to create a comedy reminiscent of the *bourekas* genre. In evoking this historic medium, the film supplants the Ashkenazi–Mizrahi romance with an Israeli–foreign worker one, thereby addressing the inequities in the treatment of non-Jewish workers in Israel and the institutionalized discrimination they face. The film's *telenovela* quality also points to the impact of foreign cultures on Israel's own cultural hegemony, and the transformation that is taking place is reflected in the metaparallel with the ways in which Latin American culture, through the salsa club and the use of Spanish, infiltrates and disrupts the traditions of Hebrew culture, such as the Hebrew language and the nationalistic folk dances. Though Israel has long departed from the days of Hebrewism's cultural hegemony, the experience of the foreign is usually portrayed in film through the Israeli's journey overseas or through its mediation by a returning Israeli in the local context. Thus, the presence of the Mexican woman, and the culture that she brings to Israel, serves as a metaphor for the significant cultural impact that the foreign worker has had on Israeli society and on its psyche. As Eran Riklis observes in connection to his film *The Human Resources Manager* (*Shlihuto shel HaMemuneh al Mash'abey Enosh*, 2010), in which the body of Yulia, a Romanian worker killed in a suicide bomb, is returned to her family in a journey of self-discovery for the human resources manager at the large bakery company where she once worked, the foreign worker phenomenon has "become a huge practical and moral issue" within Israeli society.[24]

In 2009, at the zenith of the government's deportation program, 1,200 children born to foreign workers in Israel were threatened with expulsion. Despite the government's aims to prevent women from developing family ties, the reality was the birth of hundreds of children in the two decades after Israel first opened its borders. Due to Israel's policy of citizenship by *jus sanguins* (right of blood), by which nationality is not determined by place of birth but by whether one or both parents are citizens of the country, children born to foreign workers have no right of residency, whereas the Law of Return grants a Jew an easy path to citizenship even without an Israeli-born parent. A quirk of Israeli law by which children above the age of three fall under the aegis of the Ministry of Education, as well as decisions by the Tel Aviv municipality, means that undocumented children may be enrolled in school in Israel. For many this has meant fluency in Hebrew and inculcation into the values of Israeli society. Thus the children present a humanitarian issue: though they are born and raised in Israel and many are fluent in Israeli culture, they have no rights. The efforts to deport these children to countries they did not know, to family they might never have met became controversial in Israeli politics. "[D]ue in large part to the efforts of committed Israeli and migrant activists, the rights of undocumented children became an especially popular cause in mainstream political circles. The White City's cosmopolitan set, including well-known musicians, actors, visual artists, producers, journalists, and politicians, demonstrated a particular eagerness to use their power and influence to promote an anti-deportation message, and indeed, to perform their own commitment to the so-called humanitarian issues in question."[25] Though the government still has no consistent policy for dealing with the naturalization of migrant workers' children, two one-time windows, in 2005 and 2010, offered periods of amnesty where children who met specific criteria became eligible to become citizens upon the completion of army service or when they turned twenty-one years of age. Few children met the stringent criteria, which was often prejudiced against children who had grown up in East Jerusalem in Christian schools, had aged out of the school system before the conclusion of the process, or were too young at the times of the amnesty, and only 700 of the children slated for deportation in 2009 were granted rights in 2010, with some still awaiting identity cards.[26]

Noodle: Miri (Mili Avital) explains the deaths of her husbands and her childlessness to the young Chinese boy (BaoQi Chen) in her care

Noodle centralizes the issues surrounding the question of undocumented children in its portrayal of a Chinese woman's deportation, and the problematic situation of her young son left behind in Israel in the accidental care of Miri, the air stewardess who had employed her as a domestic worker. As Miri and her sister begin to investigate the mother's disappearance, they discover the south Tel Aviv world of undocumented workers living in tight-knit quarters in the city's slums, and encounter an unsympathetic legal machinery of immigration police and bureaucratic institutions whose ability to help is limited, and where any possible measures will take an extended period of time. Born in Israel but without access to schooling, the child speaks no Hebrew, and his mother's illegal status means that he has no documents, such as a birth certificate or passport, that would facilitate his legal return home. He is recognized neither as an Israeli citizen nor as a Chinese citizen.

The film foregrounds the problem of the child's and mother's reunification, which is eventually resolved through Miri's plan to smuggle the child out of Israel and into China illegally, inverting the conventions of human smuggling that take place from the developing world to the developed world. But the child's presence facilitates a second narrative—that of the twice-bereaved war widow, left without children, who has become petrified and exists in a somnolent state. Flying above the world as an air stewardess, she is distanced from life on earth, in terms of not only the plight of foreign workers in Israel but also the breakdown in her sister's marriage, and the affair between her sister and a lover that took place soon after Miri's second husband died. Thus she remains blind to the realities of other people's lives in Israel and exists in a frozen state as the perpetual living tombstone.

In returning to the archetype of the war widow, the film draws on a convention for the representation of women's sacrifice within a nationalist context and the price that it exerts on women. Her emotional awakening through the child's presence, which, as Zerubavel has shown, emerges "out of the feminine base of the characters involved: the sisters' strong bonding, their female friends, the sensitive men who help them along the way (the brother-in-law and the sister's lover), and ultimately the child himself," disrupts the experience of sacrifice and despair, thereby facilitating Miri's sexual reawakening.[27] That it does so through the camaraderie of shared female space reflects the film's feminist message, which is extended to the universal sisterhood that exists in the women's determination to help return the boy, "Noodle," to his mother. The film's resolution poses a feminist problematic in its deployment of conventional orientalist paradigms—the upper-class white woman will save the child and aid the otherwise helpless lower-class *native* (although in this case not native to Israel). Miri's transformation by virtue of this experience also displaces the Chinese woman's voice, as she becomes merely the grateful recipient of the white woman's beneficence. At the same time, the now-shared child also signifies motherhood as an equalizing, and hence universalizing, experience that transcends the boundaries of ethnicity, color, and class to address a shared female narrative. From this perspective, women's shared plight in the face of a male hegemony in which women become the unintentional victims of war and *male* nationalistic concerns, transcends individual differences, creating a transnational sisterhood.

The film's exploration of female empowerment and its politically charged depiction of the plight of undocumented foreign workers and their children may portray a problematic situation within Israel relevant for many migrants. But the reality the film paints is tenuous. Israel's Chinese foreign labor force was predominantly male and in construction, and at its zenith constituted only 7 percent of the entire foreign labor force.[28] Today there are few Chinese laborers, and those who do live in Israel generally work in the food industry. It would have been extremely unusual for a Chinese woman to work in Israel, and unlikely that she would have been a domestic worker in an upper-middle-class Tel Aviv apartment, since the handful of Chinese women who did work in Israel were generally employed in factories in the more rural and impoverished development towns or in Be'er Sheva in the south. Moreover, the existence of a child meant that women were granted amnesty until their cases could be investigated and the child's status could be determined, knowledge that is shared among the informal networks of migrant workers. This changed in 2011, when Eli Yishai, former head of the Shas Party (associated with right-wing Mizrahi religious) and minister of the interior and therefore responsible for the legal situation of the foreign workers, ordered the government to begin deporting women with small children.[29] Nevertheless, it would be highly unusual for a woman to be deported without her child.

Salsa Tel Aviv shares a similar speciousness. Though many Latina migrants have arrived in Israel, they predominantly arrive from South, rather than Central, America, and Mexico is not well represented among foreign workers.[30] Rather, the largest group arrives from Colombia, while smaller populations have arrived from Bolivia, Peru, Chile, Uruguay, Argentina, Brazil, and Venezuela.[31] Though the paradigms that the two films portray offer critical pictures of the situation of foreign workers in Israel, their specifics do not. While this misrepresentation creates an orientalist prism that dissolves the differences between migrating groups in favor of a sociopolitical activist agenda and a metanarrative of female experience, it also reflects external pressures on the film industry in Israel. Funding for film is limited, and while government money pours into official film funds, these can usually provide only seed money, or finishing money, while other external resources are required to fully fund a film's production. *Noodle,* as a cultural document, signifies the burgeoning development of trade and political relations between Israel and China, whose hostility toward one another has been notorious since the 1950s. Similarly, recent developments in Mexican-Israeli relations, which have included the signing of a free trade agreement (2000); Mexican purchases of Israeli military equipment (2008); and a boom in tourism, with Mexicans providing one of the largest groups of tourists to the country (2013), have created both a local and an international market for a Mexican-Israeli film.

Despite the films' lack of verisimilitude, they are fictional, after all, and they share the representation of two major tropes: first, that foreign workers in Israel can never gain citizenship, and, knowing this, workers arrive with the intention of temporality, as a result of which they remain marginal within an Israeli society that has no interest in assimilating them or adding to the number of non-Jews in the country that could exacerbate the demographic threat; and second, that for many women the dominant experience is that of transnational motherhood. The women are shown to be dependent on other people to care for their children, usually in the home country, which creates a pressure that is articulated in the need to provide for a better life for their children at home. Thus they continue to fulfill their roles as mothers and caregivers, though they do so through other means. All the female foreign workers within the films eventually return home, either voluntarily or by deportation—even the deceased Romanian in *The Human Resources Manager* is returned to her home country, though when it emerges that none of her family wish to claim her body (demonstrating the ways transnational motherhood can also destroy family ties), she is brought back by the human resources manager and buried in Israel.

In *Noodle* the Chinese woman brings her child when she cleans Miri's apartment. This image reflects the film's broader activist agenda. In general, foreign workers who have children in Israel have to depend on black-market day care facilities for their children while they work until the children fall under the protection of the Ministry of Education at three years old, when they can be placed in government-funded preschool programs and then advance through primary and secondary schooling. The high-profile media attention surrounding the deportation of the children in 2009 revealed the ways in which Israeli society's established tropes for talking about women were deployed both for and against the government's policy. For those who framed activism in terms of human rights, the children's connection with Israel was phrased twofold as a love of the state and a willingness to serve it. Speaking Hebrew, participating in Israeli cultural rites, and being willing to serve in the army were framed as forms of Israeli identification. "As a defining principle of what it means to be the most loyal kind of Israeli, service in the army is implicitly understood as a necessary element of what children of migrant workers would be obliged to do in order to earn their citizenship rights."[32] For children who had known no other home, that they "felt" Israeli and were willing to take on the obligations of being Israeli, such as national or military service, was part of an emotional discourse that linked love and service in the oldest conventions of Zionism. "Months of demonstrations, media coverage, and a general mobilization of activity around what it means to be, and indeed feel Israeli have brought to light the ways that discourses of emotion and intimacy have become an integral part of current discussions about belonging and citizenship."[33] For those who objected to the presence of the foreign workers, particularly those in right-wing sectors, who feared the demographic threat, and residents in the south Tel Aviv neighborhoods, who believed that their own plight had been neglected, with little government investment in the area and no interest shown by affluent "White"Tel Aviv, while the situation of foreign workers had become a *cause célèbre,* they viewed the migrant laborers, in terms coined by Shapiro, as a "privileged underclass."[34] In response, those who supported deportation evoked the language of fear and defilement.

Yishai fomented dissent against the migrants, using every measure to discourage and to reject applications for residency. He evoked language that distinguished between "them" and "us," and in a famous instance he accused the migrants of bringing disease. Shapiro showcases an example in which a local resident in Tel Aviv questions the women's pregnancies, accusing them of abusing the nation's "kindness" toward children, and casting the women as promiscuous. "The man's presentation of migrant women as opportunistic, willing to craftily manipulate their bodies and indeed their entire lives in order to 'play' Israelis, exposes the deep sense of threat felt by Jewish Israelis living in south Tel Aviv."[35] The return to a female bodily discourse of unrestrained sexuality and disease that proved dangerous to the nation evoked a history of racialized female abjectification and the pathologizing of women's bodies. In these terms they revealed patriarchal patterns that had previously been deployed in the treatment of Jewish women by showing that they wanted to control women's bodies, that the bodies were ill or damaged, and that women's wombs were a threat to the nation. Thus they fell back on the already extant discourse about women's corporeality in Israel.

Most recently the entire public debate about foreign workers' human rights—that is, for women and their children—has been eclipsed in the hysteria surrounding the arrival of African asylum seekers from Eritrea, Sudan, and Somalia. The African asylum seekers crossing Israel's southern borders with Egypt are discouraged from working, but with the need to earn a living they have been mostly employed as day laborers or in menial work in hotels and restaurants, predominantly in Tel Aviv and Eilat, usually illegally.[36] They are generally denied anything except temporary residency visas that must be renewed every three months, and their presence has provoked race riots in south Tel Aviv. The restrictive legal measures that are aimed at preventing them from working (so that they don't become necessary to Israeli society and therefore likely to gain sympathy with the population) are enforced in myriad ways, particularly through financial penalties. These men have become the face of immigration. The presence of the African men in the public sphere is in contrast with the female foreign workers, who were invisible within their domestic employment as nannies, cleaners, and caregivers, and previous male foreign workers, who were in factories or fields in the country's periphery. The idea that they pose a physical threat which further encourages hostility towards them as a community is partly due to a small number of violent incidents but more generally due to a racist outlook by Israelis, who have provoked a fear discourse that these men will rape Jewish women, evoking the ultimate national and ideological threat. This has had a twofold impact, by reopening the debate about deportation and by silencing female foreign workers' legal activism and their experiences of abuse at the hands of individuals and of the government.

Dina Tvi Riklis's short film *The Ambassador's Wife* (*Eshet HaShagrir*, 2016) attempts to challenge the racially tinged violent rhetoric and fear-mongering in the discourse around the African refugees. Yerusalem, a poly-linguist with experience running nonprofits, is the beautiful and celebrated wife of the Eritrean ambassador to France. But when he is murdered as part of a political coup, she becomes a target for the rebel forces. After escaping Eritrea and fleeing across the border into Israel, she expects to find help with the current Eritrean ambassador to Israel (a personal friend) and assumes that her wealth and status will protect her. She herself views the other illegal immigrants and refugees around her as contemptible and eschews the menial labor they undertake. However, after she is robbed and the Eritreans deny her acquaintanceship, presumably to retain favor with the new government, she becomes a desolate refugee, dependent on menial labor for her very survival.

By tracing the story of a female refugee, and beginning before the point of immigration, Zvi-Riklis constructs a nonthreatening visual of the African asylum seeker, evoking the terrible suffering that led to her displacement and statelessness. She also highlights the Israeli government's failure to help refugees and provide protection. Finally, she challenges images of menial, lazy, and ill-educated migrants that govern Israeli perceptions about the African migrants. Furthermore, as a female, Yerusalem offers no threat of defilement or potential threat of rape to the Jewish body.

This newest response in the wave of films addressing foreign workers, and particularly females who serve in roles as caregivers and domestic workers, has been part of the feminist activist trend. These films position the Israeli woman at the center, highlighting her position in the hegemony and her social status, wealth, profession, independence, and often separation from men and contrast her with the foreign women who are marginalized as

The Ambassador's Wife: Yerusalem (Tehilla Yeshayahu) is forced to sell the only possession she has left, a watch given to her by her husband before he was murdered.

non-Hebrew, non-Jewish, poor, working in the lowest professions in roles that Israelis refuse, away from families and children, and often outside the protection of the law, if not directly in conflict with it. Whereas Israeli women were always afforded some degree of legal protection, were fully emancipated, and were fighting for women's rights and equality, the foreign worker experience reveals the degree to which feminist activities were traditionally concerned with first world issues of the upper and middle classes. Moreover, in raising this issue, the films situate the Israeli women as exploitative of the third world, and raise questions about Israeli women's independence from the social structures—or the ways in which they have internalized them.

The intersectionality of women's ethnicity, poverty, and subjugation in Israeli society addresses what many third-wave feminists saw as the failure of second-wave feminism: the need to consider "women's" issues in regard to class, income, and ethnicity. Poignantly, these films displace previously marginalized groups within Israel, such as Mizrahim, treating them as fully emancipated by comparison (though the reality reveals competition for resources between different marginalized sectors). Thus, the depiction of foreign workers (and now refugees) showcases the moving borders of feminist thinking and the new horizons addressed in feminist filmmaking. Among the general trends that have occurred with the increasing financial and artistic power women have garnered within the cinema industry has been this turn toward social issues. While in many cases feminist filmmakers have focused on the plight of women from economically disadvantaged communities, on women's issues such as rape and abuse, or on the effects of the occupation on Palestinians, to a lesser degree there has also been this move to represent the situation of foreign workers in Israel, often drawing a parallel between their situation and that of other disenfranchised communities such as Palestinians. Thus, feminist activism is often regarded as a way of creating a sisterhood built on shared female experiences (motherhood, intergenerational relationships, abuses by patriarchy) in order to advocate for social change in other spheres.[37]

That the feminist filmmakers of *Jellyfish*, *Noodle*, *Salsa Tel Aviv*, and *The Ambassador's Wife* were calling attention to the plight of female victims and female narratives, such as the experience of transnational motherhood, was part of a move toward the social consciousness raising shown toward Palestinians. "For some activists, establishing personal and emotional profiles for migrants and hosts that reinforced nationalistic, Zionist, and implicitly exclusionary frameworks, effectively harmed their broader and longer-term goals of challenging these ideologies and providing a space where rights could be granted regardless of emotional or sentimental compatibility with the host society."[38] A small percentage of activists resented the aligning of migrants' struggles with the established tropes of Zionism, "as opposed to aligning them with Palestinian's struggle for freedom and sovereignty."[39] As with films about the position of Palestinians that highlight the absolute marginalization of these two groups (foreign workers and Palestinians) and their abuses by patriarchy, the films demonstrate the impossibility of inclusion within Israeli society. In turn, this occupation of the social margins pushes Jewish Israeli women to the center, idealizing women as the benevolent establishment—who, through a universal sisterhood, can advocate for their fellow women or can exploit their social positions in order to maintain their status and thereby betray society's underlings and the activists' feminist causes.

Patterns of female marginalization in Israeli cinema that developed out of the nationalist rhetoric and its material enactment within Israeli culture, coupled with male dominance of the film industry, created a language that positioned women in socially inferior ways. This representation of Zionistic ideals made women accept their position in the hierarchy because they bought into the myths and national narratives that centralized the Zionist enterprise and men's role at the forefront of it. The ways that feminist filmmaking has sought to respond to these issues, by addressing social inequalities, ethnic marginalization, the employment of the gaze to keep women in their place, the suppression of female subjectivity, and the role that fear of rape plays in maintaining women in vulnerable and dependent positions, has confronted this cinematic past, leading to new forms of filmmaking. Women, and feminist filmmakers generally, have sought innovative responses to the militarization of Israeli society, the ongoing state of conflict, and the shared sidelining that both Israeli women and Palestinian women experience due to their positions within patriarchy (though their situations may be different, they have a shared female experience that transcends the male-positioned boundaries and that offers a path to interactions that are impossible for males). They respond to war differently, while the ways in which war takes place may also be changing. Feminism has resulted in increased spotlighting of women's gendered experience of military service, yet, simultaneously, the reactions to the representations reveal the ongoing and deep-seated influence of a male spectatorial position—thus audiences (both male and female) often respond to the screen through identification rather than through critical positions (and certainly reading against the grain is less common in these military films, precisely because in many ways they represent the normative situation of women). Thus the satire may serve as amusement, and even mockery of the system, but does little to challenge the reasons for patriarchy's marginalization of women—and may even serve to reinforce it. As with some rape representations, the context and the depiction may serve to reinforce women's objectification, rather than challenge it, thereby reinforcing a status quo that negatively situates women.

The stories of foreign workers provide a microcosm for the ways in which women's position is constantly in flux. That their representation in film takes place at a time in which women's narratives are finding space in Israeli cinema bespeaks the awareness of female subjectivity. But it also reveals the incongruity between the repetition of established tropes and resistance to the national culture through the transcendence of a female sisterhood. Furthermore, it exposes the ways in which feminist filmmakers operate politically, calling attention to social issues and using their own capital to advocate for women.

Afterword
The Effects of Feminist Activism on the Changing Cinematic Landscape

For a long time the Israeli film industry was viewed as a male enterprise. With a number of notable exceptions, almost every aspect of the film industry was controlled by men. Men served as directors, producers, leading actors, character actors, comedians, musicians, gaffers, cameramen, and engineers, and even composed music for the sound tracks. The film funds that financed productions were run by men, and men evaluated which films received the government's limited resources. Male critics would judge the male-centric plots that concerned male interests.

In reality, several women had been at the forefront of the industry, but their contributions had been forgotten and written out of Israeli cinema's historiography. Despite their limited representations on-screen and the highly masculine nature of filmmaking in Israel, these women shaped the development of cinema, both on-screen and behind the camera. In 1949, Margot Klausner, a pioneer of Hebrew cinema during the 1930s, established United Studios and, until her death in 1975, served as chairman and president of the company. More widely known as the Herzliya Studios, it housed the first film-processing laboratory, and under her directorship it would produce "over 1,000 documentary films, 850 daily advertising broadcasts, 390 daily news reels, 1,100 video productions for Israel television, 850 color satellite broadcasts to foreign countries, and no less than 100 different feature films."[1] Margot Klausner also wrote the screenplay for *The Hero's Wife* and played a direct role in several of the studio's productions. With the help of the recent documentary *Saga of a Photo* (*Sipur HaMathil BeTmuna*, 2013), her granddaughter Mooli Landesman has recovered Klausner's position in the lexicon of Israeli cinematic history. Lia Van Leer's contribution is captured in Taly Goldenberg's documentary *Lia* (2011). Van Leer's obsession with film, and her access to an 8mm projector, became the founding materials that established Israel's first cinema club in 1956, and would later help establish the Haifa Cinemateque. After a move to Jerusalem, Lia worked with Teddy Kollek, the city's mayor, and the Ostrovsky family to create the Jerusalem Cinemateque, which housed screening rooms, meeting spaces, a library, an archive, and the Israeli Film Archives in a dedicated building overlooking the Sultan's pool. There she instituted the annual Jerusalem International Film Festival and used her leverage to persuade the government to enact a law preserving Israeli film.

Other important foundational figures include Helga Keller (1922–2013), who made aliyah to Israel in 1958 after working in London with Lawrence Olivier. Her intention was to develop Israel's fledgling film industry, and she directed short documentaries, worked as a film editor, and later lectured in the film department at Tel Aviv University. Rachel Ne'eman and Orna Spector were screenwriters who worked on several features during the late 1960s and early 1970s. Elida Gera became Israel's first female feature film director in 1969. Working in the style of the "new sensitivity" cinema, her only feature film, the black-and-white *Before Tomorrow*, brought together two love stories, "Spring" and "Fall." Orna Ben Dor made documentary films and then served as the first director of the New Fund for Cinema and Television. Nelly Bogor was a film editor at Geva Studios responsible for most of the cinematic releases of the 1960s. Julie Shles and Tsipi Reibenbach made documentary films, and Nurith Aviv was one of Israel's first female cinematographers and would go on to become a documentary filmmaker herself, teaching filmmaking in Paris.

The rise of second- and third-wave feminism in Israel brought about systemic changes at every level of filmmaking. In 1994, Orly Lubin could still write that in the history of Israeli cinema only fourteen feature films had ever been made by women, and six of them by Bat-Adam.[2] Twenty years later, the 2014–15 Israeli film season alone could point to more than a dozen new films made by and about women. Women now serve in every field within the industry and make films that address a wide range of issues, feature both male and female leads, and receive funding from organizations on which women sit on the boards and serve as "readers," judging applicants and awards.[3] Female film critics have gained increasing visibility, and both audiences and awards flock to films made by and about women.[4] Moreover, men, too, have created strong female roles and have worked alongside female producers, scriptwriters, assistant directors, and actresses, reflecting the internalization of feminist advocacy about the need to offer women a place on the screen and behind the camera.

Though in many regards there has been a seismic change in the film industry, both in Israel and abroad, with greater attention paid to the representation of women and more nuance offered in women's portrayals, it is too early to say that the film industry has done away with female stereotypes, or that female actresses and filmmakers have full equality. Israeli set culture still reflects Israel's androcentric and militaristic norms. Run like a military operation, with the attendant male posturing, barking, and swearing, sets frequently continue to seem a hostile place for women. The salaries of traditionally male professions within the industry, such as grip, are higher than those of traditionally female professions, such as makeup artist, and women continue to share anecdotal tales of sexual harassment and male aggression on set. Feminism has taught us that women are entitled to equality and that the disparity and discrimination that women face within this—or any—profession needs to be addressed. Postfeminism has taught us to look out for essentialist representations and the trappings of binary models of he/she and them/us. It has made us aware of the ways in which some groups continue to be marginalized, even as other previously disenfranchised groups gain greater power. Postfeminism reminds us that representations of femininity can return us to a patriarchal vision of womanhood, that sexuality cannot be simply defined, and that feminists must continue to advocate for the changes they wish to see. This book has considered the ways in which these feminist and postfeminist debates have taken place on-screen, and, in turn, these films have reshaped the Israeli public sphere and the role of women within Israeli filmmaking.

This afterword considers the ways in which women's feminist activism within the industry is serving to change the contexts in which films are made and received. In 2013, the annual International Women's Film Festival in Rehovot celebrated its first decade. It had raised the profile of women's filmmaking in Israel and introduced international films made by and about women. The annual screenwriting grant for women that the festival organized not only exposed a variety of female writings but also the lack of resources that women were receiving from major funds. By fostering this talent, and by providing a venue in which to showcase women's work, the festival was part of efforts to raise the visibility of women in the Israeli film industry, to take films made by women into the mainstream, and to engage with women and world cinema. Despite strong attendance and making a significant impact on Israeli cinematic culture, the festival faced mounting pressure from the Rehovot municipality that had helped to fund it. The council's dominance by the religious Orthodox led to increasing attempts to censor aspects of the festival, such as the posters advertising the events—which were restricted from displaying women's figures. In 2014, using their money for leverage, the council demanded positions on the board commensurate with the funding they were offering—which would give them the capacity to impact the festival's annual theme and restrict the kinds of films screened. Their years of questioning the festival's decision to focus on such controversial topics as militarism, rape, and religious diversity, and their clashing conception with the festival's organizers that the films should be jovial and celebrate women, rather than offering critical artistic perspectives, meant their request was untenable. The municipality removed its financial support and instead offered a free public event with mass entertainment appeal—human statues. This three-day public festival had far higher attendance than the highbrow art of the Women's Film Festival, thereby appealing to a greater number of voters. It is a reminder that the intersection between politics, art, and commerce has competing agendas, ones that often leave women's issues and activism out in the cold. When no other municipality was willing to help support the festival, it closed its doors. Though the festival's original founder, Anat Shperling, has succeeded in awarding the women's screenwriting grants in 2015 and 2016 and has just secured funding for 2017, the future of this funding is uncertain. The festival's disappearance demonstrates the vulnerability of efforts toward full emancipation and the necessity of ongoing women's activism within the film industry. Good news emerged in December 2016, as this book was going to press, when the Tel Aviv Cinemateque organized "Women Filmmaker's Week: A Festival of Israeli Women's Filmmaking," which took place from December 18 to December 25, 2016, with screenings of television show episodes (for the coming season), documentaries, and feature films made by Israeli women. Whereas the Rehovot festival had focused on putting Israeli women into dialogue with international filmmaking, this festival is restricted to an internal conversation about women in the Israeli industry for local audiences and driven by industry rather than artistic concerns. Both the artistic director, Yacov Buaron, and the head of programming, Pini Schatz, are permanent staff at the Cinemateque (and male), but the festival coordinated two large public events with the Forum for Women Filmmakers and Television Artists, thereby linking the programing with the activism taking place within the industry.

The beginning of organized feminist activism within the profession might be traced to 2004 and the appearance of *Or, My Treasure* and *To Take a Wife*, two films made by the openly feminist filmmakers Keren Yedaya and Ronit Elkabetz, respectively. Along with other feminist directors, such as Michal Aviad, they would go on to form the Forum. Among the group's activities would be attempts at consciousness raising, highlighting the gender inequity on film fund boards (and raising the awareness of women who were judges), advocating for the inclusion of female film critics, and arguing for gender pay equity on set. They noticed that though women made up 40 to 50 percent of film course students, ten years later few were still working in the industry, and even fewer had made their own films. By contrast, many of the men had found work and had already made several features. Though some women were making documentaries, television programs, and promotional films, they were not writing, directing, or producing feature films. Seeking to understand this discrepancy, women in the Forum looked for ways to encourage and support female filmmakers in their debut features. Shperling's screenwriting grants were one part of the effort. Other activism included meeting with the directors of the major Israeli film funds to raise consciousness about the absence of women readers (lectors) in the decision-making process that awarded grants. They also noted that when women were among the readers but were in the minority on a decision, their voices were often silent, and thus the Forum encouraged women to speak out. Efforts to support female film critics, offer mentorship for filmmakers, and create a venue in which women could form a supportive peer group led to splinter projects such as a website for film reviews by women. *Mevakrot*, a blog by a group of women critics affiliated with the Forum, has created an online space to review the representation of women and to write about films by female filmmakers, who frequently receive less attention in the mainstream media.

These concrete examples of the Forum's productivity served as milestones in the organization's progress. But it was the very nature of the network itself that proved extremely important for many women involved in the film industry. In my interviews with many of the Forum's members and most of its current board, it emerged that the Forum served to dispel much of the isolation women experienced within Israel's filmmaking industry. Through the army, men develop extensive social networks that, after their discharge, become important social structures for professional advancement. Few women were included within this web, and it was only through the Forum that women were able to find female professionals working in technical areas (camera/sound/grips) to work on female-led projects. The Forum's active Facebook group serves as a place of discussion, recruitment, and marketing—such that women are able to publicize their films to one another, especially when these are often neglected by the wider media. In building trust, the network also became a safe space in which women began to open up to one another about sexual abuses on set and within the industry. This seedy underbelly had remained behind closed doors, and few women had spoken up out of fear of reprisals to their careers. Working together, the women exposed some of the worst crimes that had taken place. They alerted the media, which led to trial by journalism for a prominent Israeli actor, and reached out to members of the Knesset to rework the laws on sexual harassment, which offered no protection for contract workers. In some ways these measures are serving to make the industry less hostile to women who wish to participate in it.

Nonetheless, systemic inequalities remain. Few women hold faculty positions in the film schools spread throughout the country that are training the next generation of filmmakers. Instead, they serve as contingent labor, propping up required courses but having little power or influence over the direction of film education. At the Tel Aviv University School of Film and Television, Michal Aviad continues to be the only female director ever hired on faculty. As she observed in an interview with me, many students never meet a female director during their studies, and this perpetuates the sense that directing remains a male profession. Today, around 7 percent of female filmmakers in Israel are women, a percentage in line with worldwide statistics for the number of female filmmakers. Research in the United States has shown that a significant reason for the lack of growth in this area and for the maintenance of the status quo lies in the absence of women in positions of power within the industry.

> The lack of women making hiring decisions leads to a less diverse workforce. Evidence suggests that women in positions of power are more likely to employ other women. On films with female directors, women comprised 52% of writers, 35% of editors and 26% of cinematographers. When men directed, the number of female writers shrank to 8%, editors fell to 15% and cinematographers dropped to 5%. The same is true for directing opportunities. Women comprised 20% of directors on projects where at least a third of the producers were female, but just 7% of directors when the representation of female producers fell below that percentage.[5]

In Israel, women are still a minority within the power chambers of the film industry. In a country that depends on government funding for films to be made, it is likely that until there are changes in these areas, the percentage of women filmmakers will remain the same. This is also likely to result in male-centered plots and male-centric themes; for example, in 2013 more films were made about father-son relationships than all the films made by women that year. We are still counting the number of women nominated for different categories at the Israeli film awards (the Ophirs), the number of female-led films sent to international festivals, and the number of major film roles for women. Thus women's inclusion is still not a given.[6] Increasingly, there are limited efforts to support women's filmmaking, such as the Gesher Film Fund's special grant for religious women filmmakers in 2012, or the Women's Film Festival writing grants. The New Fund for Cinema and Television, established in 1993 to develop documentary filmmaking and which positions itself at the intersection between cinema and social change, recently introduced the Greenhouse Women's Program, which brings together Arab and Jewish filmmakers for a yearlong mentored crash course in peer-to-peer editing and pitching.[7] Begun in early 2014, it intended to award each of the participants a small grant that would enable them to "make a completed trailer and a 15-20 minute sample of their projects," and works with the filmmakers to help them apply to other film funds to complete their documentaries. "With 12 filmmakers participating, and representing a cross-section of religions and backgrounds, it offers a rare opportunity for Israel's female citizens to connect not on religious or social grounds, but simply on the basis of their shared creative dreams."[8] It is this kind of positive discrimination that can ultimately redress the imbalance within the industry (and its funding structures).

Among the activism in the Women's Film Forum has been the move by many to review films using the Bechdel test. Also known as the Bechdel-Wallace test, it was originally coined in a comic strip that was ridiculing the prevailing tendency to marginalize women. The critique was directed at the fact that women were often unnamed characters, that they were subordinate in every respect, and that if more than one token woman appeared and they interacted, they would still be discussing the absent man. This classification has since been adopted seriously by feminist critics as a way to measure the active presence of women in fiction and film, in order to call attention to gender inequality and sexism. The test evaluates whether a work of fiction features at least two women who talk to each other about something other than a man, and has become common shorthand for describing whether the film may be viewed as feminist (or at least female friendly). *Mevakrot* commonly uses this rating in its reviews.

The influence of this kind of rating can be seen in the response of the Swedish Film Institute (SFI), who supported an initiative in 2013 by several cinemas to rate film according to the Bechdel test as part of their development of a powerful feminist agenda in the ranking of films for funding. Anna Serner, the chief executive officer of SFI since 2011, has been working toward 50/50 gender equality for film funding, which was achieved in 2014. The funding of the film industry in Sweden is similar to that in Israel, in that it is based on government monies filtered through film funds. Invited to speak at the final year of the Rehovot film festival, Serner explained the concrete endeavors made in order to ensure equal representation, and explained that points in the funding system are explicitly awarded for having female characters or having a female writer, producer, or director. Creating a female positive climate has resulted in the production of more films by women and about women—films whose artistic quality has not been compromised by these positive discrimination agendas. While the Bechdel test has limitations—for example, it cannot account for a film about a powerful leading female who is discriminated against by men in which no other women appear—it nevertheless has raised awareness of the lack of films that address female issues or provide central female characters, which has been an important step on the road to improving female presence within cinema.

The diversity that women's filmmaking has brought, and the ways in which new topics are being addressed, demonstrates the extent to which the changes that have taken place are significant. In Israel, women now make every genre of film, they appear in a wide range of roles, and they offer complex characterizations that are a far cry from their positioning as eye candy for a male gaze. Increasingly, a cross-fertilization of genres and topics is evident in women's filmmaking as they reject the conventional boundaries and categories; for example, Yaelle Kayam's debut film *The Mountain* (*Hahar*, 2015) brings together a religious woman's lonely life with a cemetery filled with prostitutes. Hagar Ben-Asher's feature *The Burglar* (*HaPoretzet*, 2015) and Asaf Korman's *Next to Her* (*At Li Layla*, 2014) juxtapose the traditional role of female caregiver with a woman's search for independence and confront the transgressive implications that such pursuits traditionally implied. Moreover, several films combat the traditionally gendered intergenerational relationships of mother-daughter or father-son, to offer father-daughter films that examine the multifaceted tensions that intersect across gender, age, poverty, and war (*Ben Zaken* [Efrat Corem, 2015]; *Off-White Lies* [*Orlim LeRega*, Maya Kenig, 2012]). Some of these films also confront the taboo of sexual abuse, laying bare the issues of power and gender that are manifest in the increasing sexualization of society and its youth (*Princess* [*Nesicha*, Tali Shalom-Ezer, 2014]; *That Lovely Girl* [*Harchek Miheadro*, Keren Yedaya, 2014]).

The development of lesbian filmmaking has been slow, and by comparison with gay cinema, virtually nonexistent. Though shorts and some midlength films have received recognition, such as Tamar Glezerman's *The Other War* (*HaMilhama HaShniya*, 2008) and the feature film *Joe + Belle* by Veronica Kedar (2011), lesbian cinema is still in its infancy. As it begins to move out of the shadows, and as gay cinema and mainstream cinema create more lesbian characters (such as the lesbian couple in Eytan Fox's *Cupcakes* [*Bananot*, 2013]), the possibility of growth in this area is certain.

New films made by women also address political and social issues in Israeli society. Shira Geffen's latest film *Boreg* (2015) offers a look at the Arab-Israeli conflict through the eyes of two women who have switched identity and are living on the other side. While *A.K.A Nadia* (Nadia, 2015), Tova Ascher's film about a Palestinian woman passing as a Jewish Israeli for twenty years, like *The Mountain*, bares the deep-seated racism and fear of the Arab other that, in part, is a result of the ongoing conflict. *The Farewell Party* (*Mita Tova*, Tal Granit,

Sharon Maymon, 2014), as with the documentary *The Cemetery Club* (*Moadon Beit HaK'var-ot*, Tali Shemesh, 2006), offers a glimpse at the treatment of aging in Israeli society. Women's ongoing oppression by an institutionalized patriarchy maintained by the rule of religious law over matters of family life (marriage, divorce, burial) also continues to receive attention in films by Jewish and Palestinian women filmmakers.

Gett: The Trial of Viviane Amsalem (2014), the third part of Ronit and Shlomi Elkabetz's trilogy (the previous installments were *To Take a Wife* [2004] and *Shiva* [2008]), is a major national and international success. It shows the end of a marriage, after the other films have shown its ongoing breakdown, and displays a woman's attempt to procure a divorce from the religious legal courts (who are the only ones who have the power to force her husband to grant it to her) when her husband refuses. The film won Best Israeli Feature Film at the Jerusalem International Film Festival (2014) and would go on to win the award for Best Picture that year at the Ophir Awards (the awards given by the Israeli Academy of Film and Television, considered the Israeli "Oscars"). The Best Director and Leading Actress awards that year would go to *Zero Motivation*, which picked up six awards in total and had massive commercial success at the box office.

Though films by women are shown dominating the film industry where it matters, in national and international awards, and at the box office, the remarks by the jury in Jerusalem about *Gett* emphasize the ongoing inequality that women face. The jury observed that women continue to be denied their freedom by rabbinical tribunals, which is unthinkable for a modern society. Their observation that Vivianne wants to "stop being the object of a man's desire" parallels the film industry's own realization that women are no longer being offered up as an object, and that cinema should no longer cater exclusively to the male gaze. Yet, as with Vivianne, who "meets with the resistance of a powerful and invisible social machinery made of the various men who control her life and that of the women who appear in front of the tribunal court," a machinery whose "subtle continuity" can be seen in the patriarchal family (and society) that it serves, women filmmakers continue to battle the invisible strings that impact the films made, the stories told, and the women who appear on the screen.

Ronit Elkabetz, the lead actress, co-director, and scriptwriter of the film, began her career in the 1990s, playing several Mizrahi female characters on society's margins. Her success in *A Late Marriage*, which propelled her to international stardom, also provided her with the kinds of cultural capital that her predecessors, such as Almagor and Bat-Adam, had enjoyed, allowing her to shape a new kind of Mizrahi female protagonist. She would go on to work on feminist projects that worked to recover a female Mizrahi heritage in *Sh'Chur* and *Or, My Treasure* and serve as an iconic figure, conveying the social deprivation of Mizrahim trapped in Israel's periphery and of women's particular form of isolation and disenfranchisement. With the Viviane Amsalem trilogy that she wrote and directed with her brother (*To Take a Wife*, *Shiva*, and *Gett: The Trial of Viviane Amsalem*), she became the archetypal Moroccan

Gett: The Trial of Viviane Amsalem: Viviane (Ronit Elkabetz) faces an all-male tribunal to adjudicate her divorce.

Jewish woman facing a male establishment that has abandoned and disempowered women. Raya Morag described this as Elkabetz's "persona," so that even when playing characters from society's margins, her own identity shines through, enabling her to assert "the existence of an educated modern secular Mizrahi woman who controls her body, sexuality and decisions."[9] In her many and varied roles she has shown the ways in which women have created their own homes, livelihoods, and emotional independence despite social and economic limitations, and perhaps it is only through the range and the plurality of roles that this fundamental intersectional paradox can be overcome.

Her roles on-screen became part of her larger project of fighting for women's rights, such as her work as president of Ahoti. In March 2016, for International Women's Day, Elkabetz wrote a column in *Yediot Aharonot* that set out a feminist manifesto. In it she proclaimed the importance of being faithful to oneself, claiming that she had recognized that life is an ongoing battle in which progress can be achieved only by vigilance, determination, and the recognition of a woman's quintessential essence. She spoke about beauty ("you're fabulous in trainers, and in 20cm heels; you're beautiful dressed and naked"), about women's freedom and independence to create their own identity, and of the obligation not only to oneself but to the legions of women who had bravely advocated for women's rights, demanding better treatment and better conditions.[10] It was one of her last public acts, and unbeknownst to her fans, she was fighting the cancer that would kill her barely a month later. The obituaries following her death elevated her to the pantheon of Israeli cinematic greats for her "immense emotional vulnerability" on-screen.[11] Her coffin was displayed publicly at the Tel Aviv Cinemateque before her burial, and the former Israeli president Shimon Peres described her as a cultural ambassador of the Jewish State.

This reification belied years of insults hurled at her performances of the Mizrahi identity for which she was later celebrated. Yaron Shemer chronicled this criticism, mostly by male reviewers, such as Uri Klein's accusation that "her expressive, exotic and largely eccentric presence ... is precisely why Elkabetz needs someone to guide and especially to restrain her," or claims that her performance was "unrestrained" and at times shrill and showy, or, as Gidi Orsher suggests, "A devouring, shrilling, vulgar, and hysterical vulture.... In the case of Elkabetz ... there can happen an ecological disaster." Shemer adds Meir Schnitzer's review, in which "he cautions the viewer that an hour after the beginning of the film, 'for [a] long 11 minutes, she [Elkabetz] screams, whispers, groans, suffers, twists, begs, contorts, twitches her fingers, rolls her heavily mascaraed eyes. Some might call it acting.'"[12] Shemer addresses the gendered nature of these reviews, which ignore similar expressions of hysteria by men in the films and point to the reviewers' discomfort in a woman's demeanor when it falls outside the bounds of the recognized and established language of Israeli cinema's expectation of women—that of a restrained, Ashkenazi silence. Elkabetz's cinematic comportment was the polar opposite of what was regarded as the appropriate form of suffering, epitomized in Mooli Landesman's documentary about Margot Klausner, *Saga of a Photo*, with its repeated refrain, "Yekki's don't cry." What distinguished Elkabetz's career was not a change in her carriage but the ways in which she increasingly educated an audience to tolerate, if not enjoy, a different model of Israeli womanhood. The final chapter in her trilogy, *Gett: The Trial of Viviane Amsalem*, which appeared the year before her death, showed a woman beaten down by the constant and oppressive power of Israeli patriarchy. Her silent acceptance of the religious divorce documents appears to be acquiescence to the male authorities by a woman who no longer has the energy to fight for what is rightfully hers. At the same time, the film became a powerful feminist statement about the ongoing systems of injustice enacted against women.

It was an expression of what had become her legacy: the transformation of women's representation on-screen, and efforts to radically change the ways in which the Israeli film industry had controlled and censored women by limiting their access to the industry and by devastatingly critiquing female expressions they did not understand, that threatened the traditional order, or that posed a threat to the hegemony of the Ashkenazi male narrative. Her involvement with the film forum, her public manifesto, and her award-winning career offered important battles in feminist activist efforts against the status quo.

In some regards, *Gett* returns us to *Tel Aviv Stories* and Tikva's determination to be granted a divorce and bring her husband to justice. Twenty years after feminist cinema first broke out on the Israeli screen, *Gett* reminds us that despite the progress that has been made for women due to the persistent efforts of feminists, and despite the ways in which cinema has responded and recorded these battles on-screen, feminist filmmaking continues to have a political agenda, because for feminism there is still work to be done.

Notes

Introduction

1. Ella Shohat, "Making the Silences Speak in Israeli Cinema," in *Israeli Women's Studies: A Reader*, ed. Esther Fuchs (New Brunswick, NJ: Rutgers University Press, 2005), 295.

2. Yael Zerubavel, *Recovered Roots: Collective Memory and the Making of Israeli National Tradition* (Chicago: University of Chicago Press, 1995), xviii.

3. Oz Almog, *The Sabra: The Creation of the New Jew*, trans. Haim Watzman (Berkeley: University of California Press, 2000).

4. Nurith Gertz, "Space and Gender in the New Israeli and Palestinian Cinema," *Prooftexts* 22, no. 1–2 (2002): 157–58.

5. Anat Helman, *Becoming Israeli: National Ideals and Everyday Life in the 1950s*, Schusterman Series in Israel Studies (Waltham, MA: Brandeis University Press, 2014), 115.

6. Rachel S. Harris "Gender & Land: The Israeli Western," in *Casting a Giant Shadow: The Transnational Shaping of Israeli Cinema*, ed. Rachel S. Harris and Dan Chyutin (unpublished manuscript under consideration).

7. Molly Haskell, *From Reverence to Rape: The Treatment of Women in the Movies* (New York: Holt, Rinehart and Winston, 1974).

8. See also Marjorie Rosen, *Popcorn Venus: Women, Movies, and the American Dream* (New York: Coward, McCann and Geoghegan, 1973).

9. Charlotte Brunsdon, "Crossroads: Notes on Soap Opera," *Screen* 22, no. 4 (1981).

10. Laura Mulvey, "Visual Pleasure and Narrative Cinema," in *The Sexual Subject*, ed. Laura Mulvey and Mandy Merck (New York: Routledge, 1992), 32.

11. E. Ann Kaplan, *Women and Film: Both Sides of the Camera* (New York: Routledge, 2013), 31.

12. Ibid., 6–7.

13. Mary Devereaux, "Oppressive Texts, Resisting Readers and the Gendered Spectator: The New Aesthetics," *Journal of Aesthetics and Art Criticism* 48, no. 4 (Fall 1990): 339.

14. Orly Lubin, "The Woman as Other in Israeli Cinema," in *Israeli Women's Studies: A Reader*, ed. Esther Fuchs (New Brunswick, NJ: Rutgers University Press, 2005), 303.

15. Linda Williams, "'Something Else Besides a Mother': *Stella Dallas* and the Maternal Melodrama," in *Feminism and Film*, ed. E. Ann Kaplan (Oxford: Oxford University Press, 2000), 143.

16. Zerubavel, *Recovered Roots*.

17. Kaplan, *Women and Film*; E. Ann Kaplan, "Is the Gaze Male?," in *Feminism and Film*, ed.

E. Ann Kaplan (Oxford: Oxford University Press, 2000).

18. Mary Ann Doane, "Film and the Masquerade: Theorising the Female Spectator," in *Feminism and Film*, ed. E. Ann Kaplan (Oxford: Oxford University Press, 2000).

19. Laura Mulvey, "Afterthoughts on 'Visual Pleasure and Narrative Cinema' Inspired by King Vidor's *Duel in the Sun*," *Framework*, no. 15 (Summer 1981): 12.

20. Claire Johnston, "Women's Cinema as Counter-Cinema," in *Notes on Women's Cinema*, ed. Claire Johnston (London: Society for Education in Film and Television, 1973).

21. Oz Almog, "From Blorit to Ponytail: Israeli Culture Reflected in Popular Hairstyles," *Israel Studies* 8, no. 2 (Summer 2003): 93.

22. Harareet's most famous role was as Esther in *Ben Hur*, but by 1964 she had retired from acting. See the forthcoming article from Julie Grimmeisen in *Casting a Giant Shadow: Transnational Shaping of Israeli Cinema*, ed. Rachel S. Harris and Dan Chyutin (unpublished manuscript under consideration).

23. Gila Almagor, interview, *A Feast for the Eyes—The Story of Israeli Cinema* [Hagigah Leeynaim—Sipuro Shel Hakolnoa Hayisre'eli], episode 3, July 5, 2015, Channel 1.

24. *Casablan* was a Greek-Israeli-American coproduction directed by Larry Frisch that adopted Yigal Mossinsohn's stage play of the same name to the screen in a black-and-white production that today is little known. It has been overshadowed by the later musical version *Kazablan* (1974) filmed in color.

25. Almagor proposed the story of *Queen of the Road* to Menahem Golan, but in her original incarnation the prostitute was to be played as an Ashkenazi. Golan argued that the role needed to be Mizrahi, and when Almagor discussed the role with the police she was told that an Ashkenazi prostitute would not be believable. See Almagor, interview.

26. 6 Yosefa Loshitzky, *Identity Politics on the Israeli Screen* (Austin: University of Texas Press, 2001).

27. Gilberto Tofano was an Italian director who had become fascinated with Zionists. When he met with Gila Almagor, who suggested the story of a widow to him, he transformed her narrative into a film (*Siege*) that explored the experience of an entire nation living in a postwar society, with a feeling of besiegement. Though he was not a member of the *Kayitz* group (an acronym for Young Israeli Cinema), his work shared their sensibility, helped in part by the cast and crew, who belonged to the young Israeli cinema scene.

28. Lubin, "The Woman as Other in Israeli Cinema," in *Israeli Women's Studies*, 303.

29. Ibid., 304.

30. While Jewish female characters were not the only women in the films, they were the major category represented. A greater ambivalence—and a more respectful distance—was generally taken in the representation of Christian female characters, such as in *Nini* and

On a Narrow Bridge, possibly influenced by the depiction of Katherine "Kitty" Fremont (Eva Marie Saint) in *Exodus* (1960). Arab women, by contrast, were usually represented as background or extras, and were functionally invisible.

31. Orly Benjamin, "Don't Wanna Be Nice Girls: The Struggle for Suffrage and the New Feminism in Israel," *Nashim: A Journal of Jewish Women's Studies & Gender Issues*, no. 13 (2007); Hanna Herzog, "Re/Visioning the Women's Movement in Israel," *Citizenship Studies* 12, no. 3 (June 2008); *Hannah Naveh, ed., Gender and Israeli Society: Women's Time* (United Kingdom: Vallentine Mitchell & Company, 2003).

32. Kaplan, *Women and Film*, 10.

33. Ibid.

34. Johnston, "Women's Cinema as Counter-Cinema."

35. See, for example, Caroline Bainbridge, *A Feminine Cinematics: Luce Irigaray, Women and Film* (United Kingdom: Palgrave Macmillan, 2008).

36. Judith Mayne, *Cinema and Spectatorship* (New York: Routledge, 2002).

37. Devereaux, "Oppressive Texts, Resisting Readers and the Gendered Spectator"; Doane, "Film and the Masquerade." Janet Staiger takes a deconstructivist approach to the issues of spectator, arguing that meaning within film is not fixed, but rather determined through their interaction with the film. Thus meaning is culturally (and contextually) produced. Janet Staiger, *Perverse Spectators: The Practices of Film Reception* (New York: NYU Press, 2000).

38. Cultural sensitivity emerged only after the white British feminist theories of the 1970s were critiqued for their narrow—but universalizing—perspective. See, for example, Bell Hooks's essay on black spectatorship: Bell Hooks, "The Oppositional Gaze: Black Female Spectators," in *The Feminism and Visual Culture Reader*, ed. Amelia Jones (New York: Routledge, 2003).

39. Stuart Hall, "Encoding/Decoding," in *Culture, Media, Language: Working Papers in Cultural Studies, 1972–79*, ed. Centre for Contemporary Cultural Studies (London: Hutchinson, 1980).

40. Laura Mulvey, "The Oedipus Myth: Beyond the Riddles of the Sphinx," *Public*, no. 2 (1989). See also, Pam Cook and Claire Johnston, "The Place of Woman in the Cinema of Raoul Walsh," in *Issues in Feminist Film Criticism*, ed. Patricia Erens (Bloomington: University of Indiana Press, 1990); Johnston, "Women's Cinema as Counter-Cinema."

41. The first department of film and television in Israel was created at Tel Aviv University in 1972, now the Steve Tish School of Film and Television, though it still does not offer PhD accreditation. Many Israeli filmmakers have studied abroad, particularly in the United States, Britain, and France, and they were often exposed to film theory in these courses even before gender and film theory made its way into the Israeli academy.

42. Interview with Michal Bat-Adam in *Israeli Cinema-Herstory* a documentary film and webseries directed by Smadar Zamir (not yet released).

43. Lubin, "The Woman as Other in Israeli Cinema," in *Israeli Women's Studies*.

44. Amy Kronish and Costel Safirman, *Israeli Film: A Reference Guide* (Westport, CT: Praeger Publishers, 2003), 18.

45. They had previously screened their separate shorts *Crows* and *Big Girl* together. There was a third writing credit for Shemi Zarhin in *Tel Aviv Stories*.

46. This image of the heroic soldier-hero, which became associated with Hollywood in the late 1970s and 1980s, particularly through *Rambo* and *Delta Force*, was actually created by Menahem Golan, who had first used it in his adaptation of the raid on Entebbe story (which also had several American films made of it) *Mivtza Jonathan*.

47. Palestinian male filmmaking has shown an increasing respect in its representation of women but has not yet elevated to the level of feminist filmmaking (which includes advocating for women on-screen) in the ways in which some Israeli filmmaking has.

48. See Eylem Atakav, *Women and Turkish Cinema: Gender Politics, Culture, Identity and Representation* (London: Routledge, 2012); Gönül Dönmez-Colin, "Women in Turkish Cinema: Their Presence and Absence as Images and as Image-Makers," *Third Text* 24, no. 1 (2010); Lina Khatib, "The Voices of Taboos: Women in Lebanese War Cinema," *Women: A Cultural Review* 17, no. 1 (2006); Ziba Mir-Hosseini, "Negotiating the Forbidden: On Women and Sexual Love in Iranian Cinema," *Comparative Studies of South Asia, Africa and the Middle East* 27, no. 3 (2007).

49. In response, Labaki would return to the conflict and its pervasive impact on Lebanese society in her second film, *Where Do We Go Now?* (*Et maintenant on va où*, 2011), a comedy in which the Muslim and Christian women of a village work together to distract the men to prevent them going to war.

50. Debra Kamin "Female Arab Directors Are Breaking Out of Region," *Variety*, October 16, 2013.

51. Yael Munk, "Ethics and Responsibility: The Feminization of the New Israeli Documentary," *Israel Studies* 16, no. 2 (Summer 2011): 155.

52. Ibid.

53. Regine Mihal Friedman, "Between Silence and Abjection: The Film Medium and the Israeli War Widow," *Filmhistoria online*, 3, no. 1–2 (1993); Anat Zanger, "Women, Border, and Camera: Israeli Feminine Framing of War," *Feminist Media Studies* 5, no. 3 (2005); Yael Zerubavel, "Coping with the Legacy of Death: The War Widow in Israeli Films," in *Israeli Cinema: Identities in Motion*, ed. Miri Talmon and Yaron Peleg, Jewish History, Life, and Culture (Austin: University of Texas Press, 2011); . Anat Zanger, *Place, Memory and Myth in Contemporary Israeli Cinema* (London: Vallentine Mitchell, 2012);. Nurith Gertz, "Gender and Space in the New Israeli Cinema," *Shofar: An Interdisciplin-*

ary Journal of Jewish Studies 22, no. 1 (Fall 2003); Nurith Gertz, "Woman—the Image of the 'Other' in Israeli Society," *Literature Film Quarterly* 24, no. 1 (1996).

54. Raz Yosef, *The Politics of Loss and Trauma in Contemporary Israeli Cinema*, Routledge Advances in Film Studies Series, 8 (New York: Routledge, 2011);. Yosefa Loshitzky, *Identity Politics on the Israeli Screen* (Austin: University of Texas Press, 2001);. Yaron Shemer, *Identity, Place, and Subversion in Contemporary Mizrahi Cinema in Israel* (Ann Arbor: University of Michigan Press, 2013);. Dan Chyutin, "'The King's Daughter Is All Glorious Within': Female Modesty in Judaic-Themed Israeli Cinema," *Journal of Jewish Identities* 9, no. 1 (January 2016).

55. Orly Lubin, "Body and Territory: Women in Israeli Cinema," *Israel Studies* 4, no. 1 (Spring 1999); Orly Lubin, "The Woman as Other in Israeli Cinema," in *Israeli Women's Studies;* Yael Munk, "The Privatization of War Memory in Recent Israeli Cinema," in *Israeli Cinema: Identities in Motion*, ed. Miri Talmon and Yaron Peleg, Jewish History, Life, and Culture (Austin: University of Texas Press, 2011); Munk, "Ethics and Responsibility"; and the forthcoming essay by Yael Munk in *Casting a Giant Shadow: Transnational Shaping of Israeli Cinema*, ed. Rachel S. Harris and Dan Chyutin (unpublished manuscript under consideration).

56. E. Ann Kaplan, "Introduction," in *Feminism and Film*, ed. E. Ann Kaplan (Oxford: Oxford University Press, 2000). See also, Sue Lees, "Media Reporting of Rape: The 1993 British 'Date Rape' Controversy," in *Crime and the Media: The Post-Modern Spectacle*, ed. David Kidd-Hewitt and Richard Osborne (London: Pluto Press, 1995).

Chapter 1

1. Nir Cohen, *Soldiers, Rebels, and Drifters: Gay Representation in Israeli Cinema* (Detroit: Wayne State University Press, 2011), 42.

2. Shanna Swendson, "The Original Chick-Lit Masterpiece," in *Flirting with Pride and Prejudice: Fresh Perspectives on the Original Chick-Lit Masterpiece*, ed. Jennifer Crusie (Dallas: BenBella Books, 2005).

3. Cohen, *Soldiers, Rebels, and Drifters*, 42–49.

4. Ibid., 44.

5. Ibid., 43.

6. Yaron Peleg, *Israeli Culture between the Two Intifadas: A Brief Romance* (Austin: University of Texas Press, 2008), 88, 89.

7. Yael S. Feldman, "From the Madwoman in the Attic to the Women's Room: The American Roots of Israeli Feminism," *Israel Studies* 5, no. 1 (Spring 2000); Yael S. Feldman, *No Room of Their Own: Gender and Nation in Israeli Women's Fiction* (New York: Columbia University Press, 1999), chapters 5, 6 (see notes for chapters 5 and 6 and bibliography, 306–7).

8. Peleg, *Israeli Culture between the Two Intifadas*, 90.

9. Cohen, *Soldiers, Rebels, and Drifters*, 48.

10. Peleg, *Israeli Culture between the Two Intifadas*, 90.

11. Cohen, *Soldiers, Rebels, and Drifters*, 47.

12. Kelly A. Marsh, "Contextualizing Bridget Jones," *College Literature* 31, no. 1 (December 2004): 52–72; Alison A. Case, *Plotting Women: Gender and Narration in the Eighteenth-and Nineteenth-Century British Novel* (Charlottesville: University of Virginia Press, 1999) ; Justine Ashby, "Postfeminism in the British Frame," *Cinema Journal* 44, no. 2 (Winter 2005): 127–33.

13. *Time* magazine, June 25, 1998.

14. Nurith Gertz, "The Medium That Mistook Itself for War: Cherry Season in Comparison with Ricochets and Cup Final," *Israel Studies* 4, no. 1 (1999): 154.

15. *Bridget Jones' Diary* plays continually with this character. Bridget is obsessed with the six-part BBC adaptation of the novel starring Colin Firth. The hero of the Diary is Mr. Darcy, a connection of which both the character and the audience are well aware—but this link became highly postmodernist when, in the film adaptation, Mr. Darcy was played by Colin Firth. See Swendson, "The Original Chick-Lit Masterpiece." In the sequel, this became considerably more complicated when Bridget, now working as a journalist, is supposed to interview the real "Colin Firth." This hyperrealist complexity, more suitable for a Paul Auster novel than the romantic-comedy genre, meant that the scene was cut from the film but inserted as an extra for viewers in the DVD release. This "meta" postmodernist experience is echoed similarly in *The Song of the Siren*. The musical intertext is a cinematic adaptation of a written text that disappears in the film adaptation of Linor's own novel.

16. Gertz, "The Medium That Mistook Itself for War," 170.

17. Nurit Gertz, *Captive of a Dream: National Myths in Israeli Culture* (Tel Aviv: Am Oved, 1995). English edition. Chapter 8 deals specifically with the Gulf War.

18. Gertz, "The Medium That Mistook Itself for War," 170.

19. Gertz, "Captive of a Dream," 135–36.

20. See films such as *Lemon Tree*, *Close to Home*, and *Free Zone*.

21. Meira Weiss examines the unique role played by nurses in the Gulf War. While others dove for cover, these women rushed to hospitals, surrendering themselves to danger and inverting the traditional gender order hierarchy in times of war, where women seek shelter while men are at the battlefront. Danny Kaplan, "'Cyclic Interruptions': Popular Music on Israeli Radio in Times of Emergency," in *Narratives of Dissent: War in Contemporary Israeli Arts and Culture*, ed. Rachel S. Harris and Ranen Omer-Sherman (Detroit: Wayne State University Press, 2012).

22. Jean Baudrillard, "The Gulf War Did Not Take Place," trans. Paul Patton (Sydney: Power Institute of Fine Arts, 1995.) Originally published in French as "La Guerre du Golfe n'a as eu lieu." Steve Redhead, *The Jean Baudrillard Reader* (Edinburgh: Edinburgh University Press, 2008),108.

23. Morbidly, one of the reasons for wearing bright colors was to increase the likelihood of being discovered if the building was shelled and people were buried in the rubble.

24. This situation was exacerbated for men by the gas masks, which were carried like women's handbags, and by the fact that facial hair had to be removed so that the masks fitted properly, both acts of emasculation.

25. Kaplan, ""Cyclic Interruptions," 68.

26. Ibid., 69.

27. Olga Gershenson and Dale Hudson, "Absorbed by Love: Russian Immigrant Woman in Israeli Film," *Journal of Modern Jewish Studies* 6, no. 3 (2007): 304.

28. Valerie Begley and Olga Gershenson, "Introduction: Volumes," *Journal of International Women's Studies* 6, no. 2 (2005): 2.

29. Gershenson and Hudson, "Absorbed by Love," 304.

30. Ibid., 309.

Chapter 2

1. Anat Zanger, "Filming National Identity," in *The Military and Militarism in Israeli Society*, ed. Edna Lomsky-Feder and Eyal Ben-Ari (Albany: SUNY Press, 2012).

2. Zerubavel, "Coping with the Legacy of Death."

3. The Border Trilogy is a set of three films by Israeli director Amos Gitai: *Promised Land* (2004), *Free Zone* (2005), and *Disengagement* (*Hitnatkoot*, 2007).

4. Anat Zanger, "Blind Space: Roadblock Movies in the Contemporary Israeli Film," *Shofar: An Interdisciplinary Journal of Jewish Studies* 24, no. 1 (Fall 2005): 39.

5. Kuhu Tanvir, "Interview: Eran Riklis," *Wide Screen* 1, no. 1 (April 2009).

6. Ibid.

7. Laura Mulvey, "Visual Pleasure and Narrative Cinema."

8. Dorit Naaman, "The Silenced Outcry: A Feminist Perspective from the Israeli Checkpoints in Palestine," *NWSA Journal* 18, no. 3 (Fall 2006): 174.

9. Ibid., 177.

10. Ibid., 178.

11. Esther Fuchs, "Images of Love and War in Contemporary Israeli Fiction: A Feminist Re-Vision," in *Arms and the Woman: War, Gender, and Literary Representation*, ed. Helen

M. Cooper, Adrienne Auslander Munich, and Susan Merrill Squier (Chapel Hill: University of North Carolina Press, 1989), 276. Man's military service is one of the most important rites of passage creating his social value, yet the fraternal framework not only excludes women from the military, it continues long after into Israeli society, creating a very powerful social network that women cannot infiltrate either politically, professionally, or personally.

12. Naaman, "The Silenced Outcry," 178.

13. Ilan Pappe, "'Mada V'alila Bsherut Haleumiyout: Historiographia V'kolnoa Bsichsuch Haaravi-Yisraeli" (Science and Plot in the Service of Nationalism: Historiography and Film in the Arab-Israeli Conflict)," in *Mabatim Fictiviyim: Al Kolnoa Yisraeli* (*Fictive Looks:On Israeli Cinema*), ed. Nurith Gertz, Orly Lubin, and Judd Ne'eman (Tel Aviv: Open University Press, 1998), 108; quoted in Loshitzky, *Identity Politics on the Israeli Screen*, 112–14.

14. Loshitzky, *Identity Politics on the Israeli Screen*, 113.

15. See ibid.

16. Though the Israeli woman does not appear in *The Syrian Bride*, Amal's ability to join mainstream Israeli society by studying for a degree in social work offers her the dual role of being the possible Israeli woman within this internal discourse.

17. Ralph Donald and Karen MacDonald, *Women in War Films: From Helpless Heroine to G.I. Jane* (Lanham, MD: Rowman & Littlefield, 2014), 1.

18. Ibid., 7.

19. Fuchs, "Images of Love and War in Contemporary Israeli Fiction," 276.

20. Ibid., 275.

21. Ibid., 274.

22. Zanger, "Filming National Identity," 266–70.

23. Nurith Gertz and George Khleifi, *Palestinian Cinema: Landscape, Trauma and Memory* (Edinburgh: Edinburgh University Press, 2008).

24. Ella Shohat, "The Cinema of Displacement: Gender, Nation, and Diaspora," in *Dreams of a Nation on Palestinian Cinema*, ed. Hamid Dabashi, intro. by Edward Said (London: Verso, 2006). However, this has been changing since 2007, and there is now a small body of films with a feminist agenda made by Palestinian women filmmakers.

25. Yael Ben-Zvi-Morad, "Borders in Motion: The Evolution of the Portrayal of the Israeli-Palestinian Conflict in Contemporary Israeli Cinema," in *Israeli Cinema: Identities in Motion*, ed. Miri Talmon and Yaron Peleg, Jewish History, Life, and Culture (Austin: University of Texas Press, 2011), 284, 286.

26. Benny Ben-David, "The Siege Syndrome: The Six Day War and Israeli Cinema," *Journal of Israeli History* 28, no. 2 (2009).

27. Nitzan S. Ben-Shaul, "Fellow Traveler: The Cinematic-Political Consciousness of Judd Ne'eman," *Shofar: An Interdisciplinary Journal of Jewish Studies* 24, no. 1 (Fall 2005): 96.

28. Ibid., 96–97.

29. Janet Burstein, "Yehuda 'Judd' Ne'eman," *Bomb* 95 (Spring 2006).

30. Ben-Shaul, "Fellow Traveler," 106.

31. Ibid.

32. During the late 1990s, the rise of filmmaking dealing with the individual and focusing on Tel Aviv culture fed into a new discourse in the first decade of the twenty-first century whereby Palestinians were shown interacting within the same urban sphere, but such films are more focused on the role of minorities within the state than on the situation of the conflict.

33. Zanger, "Filming National Identity," 268.

34. Nurith Gertz, "The War That Wasn't: Comparing the Cherry Season with Final Cup and Two Steps from Zidon," in *Fictive Looks: On Israeli Cinema*, ed. Nurith Gertz, Orly Lubin, and Judd Ne'eman (Tel Aviv: Open University, 1998), 67–91. Republished in English in a slightly different version as "The Medium That Mistook Itself for War: Cherry Season in Comparison with Ricochets and Cup Final."

35. Ella Shohat, *Israeli Cinema: East/West and the Politics of Representation*, rev. ed. (London: I. B. Tauris, 2010), 252–53.

36. Ben-Zvi-Morad, "Borders in Motion," 278.

37. Gertz, "Gender and Space in the New Israeli Cinema"; Gertz, "The Medium That Mistook Itself for War."

38. Eran Kaplan, "From Hero to Victim: The Changing Image of the Soldier on the Israeli Screen," in *Israeli Cinema: Identities in Motion*, ed. Miri Talmon and Yaron Peleg, Jewish History, Life, and Culture (Austin: University of Texas Press, 2011).

39. Ben-Zvi-Morad, "Borders in Motion."

40. Zanger, "Filming National Identity," 269.

41. Loshitzky, *Identity Politics on the Israeli Screen*, 151.

Chapter 3

1. Yoffi Tirosh, "'Efes Beyahasei Enosh'? Al Hakav Hamehaber Beyn M16 Le-Ekdah Sikot" [Zero Motivation: The Connection between an M16 and a Staple Gun], *Te'oriya U-bikoret* 43 (Fall 2014).

2. The image of the Jew as victim was immortalized in a poem about the Kishniev pogrom *Ir Ha'hariga* H. N. Bialik. For further discussion of modern Hebrew writing about war see Glenda Abramson, *Hebrew Writing of the First World War* (United Kingdom: Vallentine Mitchell & Company, 2008).

3. Zerubavel, "Coping with the Legacy of Death."

4. Lubin, "The Woman as Other in Israeli Cinema," in *Israeli Women's Studies; Naveh, Gender and Israeli Society;* and Orit Rozin, "The Struggle over Austerity Policy: Israeli Housewives and the Government" [in Hebrew] *Israel* 1 (2002).

5. Sachlav Stoler-Liss, "'Mothers Birth the Nation': The Social Construction of Zionist Motherhood in Wartime in Israeli Parents' Manuals," *Nashim: A Journal of Jewish Women's Studies & Gender Issues* 6 (Fall 2003); Susan Starr Sered, *What Makes Women Sick? Maternity, Modesty, and Militarism in Israeli Society* (Waltham, MA: Brandeis University Press, 2000); Meira Weiss, *The Chosen Body: The Politics of the Body in Israeli Society* (Stanford, CA: Stanford University Press, 2004); and Meira Weiss, "Mother, Sister and Soldier: Recollections from the Gulf War" [in Hebrew], *Te'oriya U-bikoret* 3 (Winter 2005).

6. Yael S. Feldman, "From Essentialism to Constructivism? The Gender of Peace and War—Gilman, Woolf, Freud," *Partial Answers: Journal of Literature and the History of Ideas* 2, no. 1 (2004); Michael Feige, "Peace Now and the Legitimation Crisis of 'Civil Militarism,'" *Israel Studies* 3, no. 1 (1998).

7. Sered, *What Makes Women Sick?*, 76, 78, 80–81, and 86.

8. Ibid., 86.

9. Ibid.

10. Orna Sasson-Levy, "Feminism and Military Gender Practices: Israeli Women Soldiers in 'Masculine' Roles," *Sociological Inquiry* 73, no. 3 (August 2003).

11. Orna Sasson-Levy, "Gender Performance in a Changing Military," in *Israeli Women's Studies: A Reader*, ed. Esther Fuchs (New Brunswick, NJ: Rutgers University Press, 2005), 266–67.

12. Ibid., 269.

13. Esther Fuchs, *Israeli Mythogynies: Women in Contemporary Hebrew Fiction* (Albany: SUNY Press, 1987), 28.

14. Ibid., 29.

15. Ibid.

16. Ibid.

17. Ibid., 30.

18. Ibid.

19. Sered, *What Makes Women Sick?*, 69.
20. Hilary Neroni, *The Violent Woman: Femininity, Narrative, and Violence in Contemporary American Cinema* (Albany: SUNY Press, 2012), 19.
21. Ibid., 16.
22. Dafna N. Izraeli and Ephraim Tabory, "The Perception of Women's Status in Israel as a Social Problem," *Sex Roles* 14, no. 11/12 (1986): 675.
23. Almog, "From Blorit to Ponytail," 89–90.
24. Ella Shohat, *Israeli Cinema*, 144.
25. Shohat, Making the Silences Speak in Israeli Cinema, 297.
26. Lubin, "The Woman as Other in Israeli Cinema," in *Israeli Women's Studies*.
27. Shemer, *Identity, Place, and Subversion in Contemporary Mizrahi Cinema in Israel*, 197.
28. For more on the symbolism of suicide in the military unit see Rachel S. Harris, "The IDF: Training Base Four with all the Cripples," in *An Ideological Death: Suicide in Israeli Literature* (Evanston, IL: Northwestern University Press, 2014).
29. *The Debt* (2007) was an Israeli film starring Gila Almagor and was remade as *The Debt* (2010) with Helen Mirren in the lead role.

Chapter 4

1. Chyutin, "'The King's Daughter Is All Glorious Within.'"
2. Lubin, "The Woman as Other in Israeli Cinema," in *Israeli Women's Studies*.
3. Similarly, the Muslim and Christian communities control the rules of marriage and divorce within their own religious groups. This division is derived from the Ottoman millet system. Though Israeli filmmaking is generally more advanced and has had a number of documentaries and feature films that consider the masculinity of the Israeli religious courts and its impact on women, Ibtisam Mara'ana-Menuhin's *3 Times Divorced* (2008) provides the first examination of the Muslim legal court system's control over women, who are denied divorce without their husband's approval but can be divorced in absentia by them. Following a Bedouin woman trapped in an abusive relationship with a husband who keeps divorcing her (but whom she is unable to leave because she has no protections from the Israeli authorities, as her immigration status is contingent on her marriage), it highlights the bind Muslim women who wish to divorce face in Israel.
4. Galeet Dardashti, "Televised Agendas: How Global Funders Make Israeli TV More 'Jewish,'" *Jewish Film and New Media: An International Journal* 3, no. 1 (Spring 2015): 82.
5. Ibid., 89.
6. Yael Friedman Hakak and Yohai Hakak, "Jewish Revenge: Haredi Action in the Zionist Sphere," *Jewish Film and New Media* 3, no. 1 (Spring 2015).

7. Debra Kamin, "Filmmakers Who Are Ultra-Orthodox and Ultracommitted," *New York Times*, October 18, 2012.

8. Dardashti, "Televised Agendas," 94.

9. See Nurith Cohn and Emanuel Cohn, *The Little Dictator* (*HaDiktator HaKatan*, 2015); Shira Gabai, *The Gravedigger's Daughter* (*HaBat Shel Hakavran*, 2016); Tehila Raanan, *Wall, Crevice, Tear* (*Kir, Sadak, Dima'ah*, 2015); Anat Zuria, *Purity* (*Tehora*, 2002), *Sentenced to Marriage* (*Mekudeshet*, 2004), *Black Bus* (*Sorreret*, 2010), and *The Lesson* (*HaShiur*, 2012); Eliezer Shapiro, *Srugim* (2008–10); Lihi Sabag, *The Girl* (*HaYelda*, 2016); and Hadar Friedlich *Voices from the Heartland: Slaves of the Lord* (*Shiur Moledet: Avdei Hashem*, 2002).

10. An acronym for Dati LeSheavar (DatLaSh)—the formerly religious, contrasted with the "secular," the *datlash* community remains interested in traditional ideas about Judaism and its members often seek out the company of other *datlash*.

11. Atakav, *Women and Turkish Cinema*, 98.

12. The very recent and hotly contested debates over women's education by the traditional yeshiva method that have resulted in female ordination within the Orthodox movement may reveal signs of change but are viewed as a marginal movement within mainstream Orthodoxy, and are entirely absent from the *Haredi* community.

13. This is a false dichotomy, since eligibility for marriage is often governed by interests beyond the prospective bride's control that have significant weight in the intended suitors offered by a matchmaker, including father's learning, reputation, and wealth, or other advantageous relationships (and marriages) within the family.

14. Shai Ginsburg, "Love in Search of Belief, Belief in Search of Love," in *The Modern Jewish Experience in World Cinema*, ed. Lawrence Baron (Waltham, MA: Brandeis University Press, 2011), 371.

15. I have written on this topic extensively elsewhere. See Harris, *An Ideological Death*, 185–88.

16. Mulvey, "Visual Pleasure and Narrative Cinema," 23.

17. Ibid., 24.

18. Jyoti Sarah Daniels, "Scripting the Jewish Body: The Sexualized Female Jewish Body in Amos Gitai's *Kadosh*," in *Jews and Sex*, ed. Nathan Abrams (Nottingham: Five Leaves, 2008), 78–79.

19. Ibid., 84.

20. John Berger, *Ways of Seeing* (United Kingdom: Penguin UK, 2008).

21. Chyutin, "'The King's Daughter Is All Glorious Within,'" 40.

22. The film also circulated in the religious community, often in illicit ways through illegal

downloads, as many *Haredim* do not attend the cinema but wanted to see the film. Recognizing that this had become a problem of piracy that deprived the Rands of income, *Haredim* found ways to send the couple money through public collections or by ordering cinema tickets and then not showing up at the screenings. Avishai Ben Haim, "Vetodah leshem yitbarech" (With Thanks to God), *Ma'ariv* February 3, 2005, www.nrg.co.il/online/11/ART/864/285.html.

23. Ginsburg, "Love in Search of Belief, Belief in Search of Love," 174.

24. Mary Ann Doane, *The Desire to Desire: The Woman's Film of the 1940s* (Washington, DC: Georgetown University Press, 1987), chapter 2.

25. Yael Israel-Cohen, *Between Feminism and Orthodox Judaism: Resistance, Identity, and Religious Change in Israel* (Leiden, The Netherlands: Brill, 2012), 81.

26. Shira Wolosky, "Foucault and Jewish Feminism: The *Meḥitzah* as Dividing Practice," *Nashim: A Journal of Jewish Women's Studies & Gender Issues* 17 (Spring 2009): 23.

27. Chyutin, "'The King's Daughter Is All Glorious Within,'" quoting Wolosky, "Foucault and Jewish Feminism: The *Meḥitzah* as Dividing Practice," 23.

28. Avi Shafran, "How Ultra-Orthodoxy Is Most Feminist Faith," February 2, 2015, http://forward.com/opinion/213671/how-ultra-orthodoxy-is-most-feminist-faith/.

29. The name takes the feminine form, indicating its identity as a "woman's" party.

30. Motti Inbari, *Jewish Fundamentalism and the Temple Mount: Who Will Build the Third Temple?* (Albany: SUNY Press, 2009); Motti Inbari, *Messianic Religious Zionism Confronts Israeli Territorial Compromises* (Cambridge: Cambridge University Press, 2012); Michael Feige, "One Space, Two Places: Gush Emunim, Peace Now, and the Construction of Israeli Space" [in Hebrew] (Jerusalem: Magnes Press, 2002); Michael Feige, *Settling in the Hearts: Jewish Fundamentalism in the Occupied Territories* (Detroit: Wayne State University Press, 2009).

31. David Newman, "From Hitnachalut to Hitnatkut: The Impact of Gush Emunim and the Settlement Movement on Israeli Politics and Society," *Israel Studies* 10, no. 3 (Fall 2005): 196–97.

32. Yaakov Herskovitz, "Settlers Versus Pioneers: The Deconstruction of the Settler in Assaf Gavron's *The Hilltop*," *Shofar: An Interdisciplinary Journal of Jewish Studies* 33, no. 4 (Summer 2015).

33. Lubin, "The Woman as Other in Israeli Cinema," in *Israeli Women's Studies*, 302.

34. Philip Hollander. Association for Israel Studies presentation (unpublished manuscript, 2011).

35. Ibid.

36. Since 2013 the title of yoetzet halakhah has been used in Israel for graduates of Nishmat, while more controversy has surrounded a similar program in the United States in

which women are ordained by Yeshivat Maharat as a maharat (or rabbah).

37. Daniels, "Scripting the Jewish Body," 78.

38. Ibid., 79

Chapter 5

1. Robert Alter, "Magic Realism in the Israeli Novel," *Prooftexts* 16, no. 2 (1996): 151.

2. Fredric Jameson, "On Magic Realism in Film," *Critical Inquiry* 12, no. 2 (1986): 320.

3. Jean Franco, *The Decline and Fall of the Lettered City: Latin America in the Cold War* (Cambridge, MA: Harvard University Press, 2009).

4. Dorit Naaman, "Orientalism as Alterity in Israeli Cinema," *Cinema Journal* 40, no. 4 (Summer 2001): 37.

5. Shohat, *Israeli Cinema*, 78, particularly chapter 3, "The Representation of Sephardim/Mizrahim," 105–61, and revisited in the "Postscript" to the second edition.

6. Naaman, "Orientalism as Alterity in Israeli Cinema," 40.

7. See Justine Ashby for a discussion of *Shirley Valentine, Educating Rita, Wish You Were Here, Letter to Brezhnev,* and *Pink Pyjamas.* Justine Ashby, *"It's Been Emotional": Reassessing the Contemporary British Woman's Film* (London: Routledge, 2009).

8. Ibid., 153.

9. Ibid.

10. Ibid., 155.

11. Yael Munk, "The Postcolonial Function of Television's Virtual Space in '90s Israeli Cinema," *Framework: The Journal of Cinema and Media* 49, no. 1 (Spring 2008): 85.

12. Shemer, *Identity, Place, and Subversion in Contemporary Mizrahi Cinema in Israel*, 200.

13. Tova Gamliel, "Performed Weeping: Drama and Emotional Management in Women's Wailing," *TDR/The Drama Review* 54, no. 2 (2010): 73.

14. Ibid., 77.

15. Tova Gamliel, *Aesthetics of Sorrow: The Wailing Culture of Yemenite Jewish Women* (Detroit: Wayne State University Press, 2014).

16. Shemer, *Identity, Place, and Subversion in Contemporary Mizrahi Cinema in Israel,* 209.

17. Gamliel, "Performed Weeping."

18. Tova Gamliel has argued that a social contract exists between wailers in the Yemenite-Jewish community, who have learned their skill as a craft often handed off between generations, and the audience, who is obliged to be moved by the words and music of the professional mourners' performance. This, however, assumes that the audi-

ence has the cultural knowledge to understand and appreciate this ritual. For an Ashkenazi viewing public among whom quiet crying or restraint is the expected response in grief, these mourning rituals may seem alien, barbaric, and staged. Gamliel, "Performed Weeping," 70–90.

19. Ariela Popper-Giveon and Jonathan J. Ventura, "Blood and Ink: Treatment Practices of Traditional Palestinian Women Healers in Israel," *Journal of Anthropological Research* 65, no. 1 (Spring 2009): 32.

20. Ibid.

21. Carol Bardenstein, "Cross/Cast: Passing in Israeli and Palestinian Cinema," in *Palestine, Israel, and the Politics of Popular Culture*, ed. Rebecca L. Stein and Ted Swedenburg (Durham, NC: Duke University Press, 2005),100.

22. Ibid., 102.

23. Ibid., 101.

24. Popper-Giveon and Ventura, "Blood and Ink," 37. See also, Yehouda Shenhav and Hannan Hever, "'Arab Jews' after Structuralism: Zionist Discourse and the (De) Formation of an Ethnic Identity," *Social Identities* 18, no. 1 (January 2012) ; Nina Toren, "Intersection of Ethnicity, Gender and Class: Oriental Faculty Women in Israel," *Gender Issues* 26, no. 2 (June 2009) ; Moshe Shokeid Minkovitz, "Social Networks and Innovation in the Division of Labour between Men and Women in the Family and in the Community: A Study of Moroccan Immigrants in Israel," *Canadian Review of Sociology/Revue Canadienne de Sociologie* 8, no. 1 (February 1971); Daniel J. Schroeter, "The Shifting Boundaries of Moroccan Jewish Identities," *Jewish Social Studies* 15, no. 1 (Fall 2008).

25. Popper-Giveon and Ventura, "Blood and Ink," 32.

26. Yaron Shemer, "Identity, Place, and Subversion in Contemporary Mizrahi Cinema in Israel" (doctoral dissertation, University of Texas at Austin, 2005), 310.

27. Alter, "Magic Realism in the Israeli Novel,"161.

28. http://self-help.sheatufim.org.il/detail-orgeng.php?id=127&idtop=25 (accessed April 8, 2013).

29. With the possible exception of Enrique Rottenberg's *The Revenge of Itzik Finkelstein* (1993), which does portray a ghost with a mission of vengeance, though not exactly in the format of Hollywood films, the usual image of ghosts evoked in Jewish literature (and particularly performance) are *Dybbuk* possessions, which were a staple of Yiddish theatre.

Chapter 6

1. Tamar Mayer, "From Zero to Hero: Masculinity in Jewish Nationalism," in *Israeli Women's Studies: A Reader*, ed. Esther Fuchs (New Brunswick, NJ: Rutgers University Press, 2005), 100. The notion that women should remain in traditional roles already informed the first aliyah. "Just as Hovevei Zion took a conservative approach, preferring to preserve the traditional role of women, the Jewish maskilim continued to see women as mothers and housewives, leaving them outside public life." Margalit Shilo, "The Double or Multiple Image of the New Hebrew Woman," *Nashim: A Journal of Jewish Women's Studies & Gender Issues*, no. 1 (Winter 1998): 77.

2. Mayer, "From Zero to Hero," 100.

3. Julie Grimmeisen, "Halutzah or Beauty Queen? National Images of Women in Early Israeli Society," *Israel Studies* 20, no. 2 (Summer 2015): 30.

4. Shohat, *Making the Silences Speak in Israeli Cinema*, 292.

5. Lynne Attwood and Maya Turovskaya, *Red Women on the Silver Screen: Soviet Women and Cinema from the Beginning to the End of the Communist Era* (London: Rivers Oram Press, 1993).

6. Boaz Neumann, *Land and Desire in Early Zionism* (Waltham, MA: Brandeis University Press, 2011).

7. Grimmeisen, "Halutzah or Beauty Queen?"

8. Ibid., 38.

9. Aliza Gur won Miss Israel in 1960 and was a runner-up in Miss Universe that same year. Her success translated into a Hollywood acting career that included some television credits and a role in *From Russia with Love* (1963). Haya Harareet, whose acting career started in *Hill 24 Doesn't Answer*, had a short-lived film career but famously appeared in *Ben Hur*; Daliah Lavie featured in *Holot Lohatim* (*Blazing Sands*, 1960), one of the major films in the heroic-nationalist genre. Her fluency in several languages led to a very successful international career, and she would appear in a large number of European and American films, including Vincente Minnelli's *Two Weeks in Another Town* (1962) and Mario Bava's gothic classic *La Frusta e il corpo*, or *The Whip and the Body* (1963), in the role of The Girl in *Lord Jim*, and in the first Matt Helm film, *The Silencers* (1966), opposite Dean Martin, though her best-known role would be in *Casino Royale*.

10. Almog, "From Blorit to Ponytail," 93.

11. Ibid.; Oz Almog, *Farewell to "Srulik": Changing Values among the Israeli Elite* (Tel Aviv: Zmora Bitan, 2004).

12. Grimmeisen, "Halutzah or Beauty Queen?," 41.

13. Ibid., 39; also quoting footnote 86.

14. Almog, "From Blorit to Ponytail," 90.

15. Almog, *Farewell to "Srulik."*

16. Mary Ann Doane, *Femmes Fatales: Feminism, Film Theory, Psychoanalysis* (New York: Routledge, 2013), 35.

17. Lubin, "The Woman as Other in Israeli Cinema," In *Israeli Women's Studies*, 304.

18. I have written extensively about the issues surrounding the expectation of procreation and its representation in literature and culture elsewhere. See Harris, *An Ideological Death*; Rachel S. Harris, "Introduction Sex, Violence, Motherhood and Modesty: Controlling the Jewish Woman and Her Body," *Nashim: A Journal of Jewish Women's Studies & Gender Issues* 23, no. 1 (2012): 5–10.

19. Elizabeth Cowie, *Representing the Woman: Cinema and Psychoanalysis* (Minneapolis: University of Minnesota Press, 1997), 19.

20. Zerubavel, "Coping with the Legacy of Death," 85.

21. Ibid.

22. Ibid.

23. Friedman, "Between Silence and Abjection," 80; Pierre Nora, "Between Memory and History: Les Lieux De Mémoire," *Representations* 26 (Spring 1989): 7–24.

24. Friedman, "Between Silence and Abjection," 84.

25. Zerubavel, "Coping with the Legacy of Death," 88.

26. Shohat, *Making the Silences Speak in Israeli Cinema*, 298.

27. Loshitzky, *Identity Politics on the Israeli Screen*, 98.

28. Ibid., 93.

29. Sarah Projansky, *Watching Rape: Film and Television in Postfeminist Culture* (New York: NYU Press, 2001), 53.

30. Loshitzky, *Identity Politics on the Israeli Screen*, 104.

31. Ibid.

32. Ibid., 123.

33. Grimmeisen, "Halutzah or Beauty Queen?," 30, discussing the work of Deborah Bernstein in *Women on the Margins: Gender and Nationalism in Mandate Tel-Aviv*.

34. Doane, *The Desire to Desire*, chapter 2.

35. Ram A. Cnaan, "Notes on Prostitution in Israel," *Sociological Inquiry* 52, no. 2 (1982); Delila Amir and Menachem Amir, "The Politics of Prostitution and Trafficking of Women in Israel."

36. Russell Campbell, *Marked Women: Prostitutes and Prostitution in the Cinema* (Madison: University of Wisconsin Press, 2006), 3.

37. Ilana Szobel, "'Lights in the Darkness': Prostitution, Power and Vulnerability in Early Twentieth-Century Hebrew Literature," *Prooftexts* 34, no. 2 (Spring 2014): 171, quoting from David Vogel's *Married Life* [*Haiyei Nesuim*], 1929.

38. The conventions of the genre would become so well established that in Assi Dayan's film *An Electric Blanket Called Moshe* (1996), Malka would code as Mizrahi—through her name, curly hair, red heels and long nails and the décor in her apartment—particularly the image of the hayeled haboheh picture, cartoon pajamas, and childish wallpaper—despite identifying herself as Romanian in the final moments of the film.

39. Szobel, "'Lights in the Darkness,'" 174; Thomas Heise, *Urban Underworlds: A Geography of Twentieth-Century American Literature and Culture* (New Brunswick, N.J.: Rutgers University Press, 2011), 9.

40. Szobel, "'Lights in the Darkness,'" 174.

41. Amir and Amir, "The Politics of Prostitution and Trafficking of Women in Israel," 145.

42. Gershenson and Hudson, "Absorbed by Love," 303.

43. Israel began addressing its human trafficking problem with a law in 2006. After years of negligence, the government measures, coupled with increases in prosecutions, a public campaign against trafficking, and the building of a fence across the Egyptian-Israeli border, reduced the number of women smuggled in and broke up many criminal rings. In 2012 and 2013, Israel was ranked in Tier 1 by the U.S. State Department's "Trafficking in Person's Report," the highest rating given to a government that has acknowledged the problem of trafficking and taken active measures to address the problem and protect the victims.

44. Yosef, *The Politics of Loss and Trauma in Contemporary Israeli Cinema*, 83.

45. Ibid.

46. Menahem Golan, in an interview about *Eldorado* for *The First Israeli Films*, a program about the history of Israeli cinema, claimed that it was Herzl who said it, and he made a film about these characters to show the country's normalization. An article in *Haaretz* attributes it to Bialik and Ben-Gurion, though with no reference to its origins. The phrase is most often attributed to Ben-Gurion while he was in office. Joel Braunold, "Jewish Prostitutes, Jewish Thieves, Jewish Supremacists," *Haaretz* [English edition], May 15, 2014, www.haaretz.com/jewish/the-jewish-thinker/.premium-1.590920.

47. Campbell, *Marked Women*, 3.

48. Amir and Amir, "The Politics of Prostitution and Trafficking of Women in Israel," 150.

49. Cnaan, "Notes on Prostitution in Israel."

50. Amir and Amir, "The Politics of Prostitution and Trafficking of Women in Israel," 150.

51. Yosef, *The Politics of Loss and Trauma in Contemporary Israeli Cinema*, 84.

52. Ibid.

53. Campbell, *Marked Women*, 6.

54. Bat-Sheva Margalit Stern, "Who's the Fairest of Them All? Women, Womanhood, and Ethnicity in Zionist Eretz Israel," *Nashim: A Journal of Jewish Women's Studies & Gender Issues* 11 (2006).

55. Yosef, *The Politics of Loss and Trauma in Contemporary Israeli Cinema*, 85.

56. Ibid., 91.

57. Ibid., 94.

58. Lubin, "The Woman as Other in Israeli Cinema," In *Israeli Women's Studies*, 305.

59. Ibid.

60. Ibid., 314.

61. Ibid., 315.

62. A woman who has a child with a man, while married to another, forfeits the child's right to marriage within Judaism (at least without serious constraints).

63. Lubin, "The Woman as Other in Israeli Cinema," In *Israeli Women's Studies*, 305.

64. Hagar Ben-Asher's previous short film *Pathways* (*Mish'ulim*, Hagar Ben-Asher, 2007) shares similar themes and plot.

65. In many ways the staging evokes Judy Chicago's landmark feminist art instillation "The Dinner Party" (1979), famous for its evocation of women's genitalia on the plates' decoration and its mission to represent silenced women of history.

66. *Yellow Asphalt* (Dan [Nokyo] Verete, 2000), three interwoven shorts examining women in the Bedouin community in the Judean desert, follow women trapped within patriarchy and tribal justice. Though the films focused on the situation of women, they are in many ways trapped within the historical conventions of prefeminist Israeli film, whereby they ultimately become the vehicle by which the Jewish and Bedouin men interact.

Chapter 7

1. Projansky, *Watching Rape*, 3.

2. Tanya Horeck, *Public Rape: Representing Violation in Fiction and Film* (New York: Routledge, 2013), 155.

3. Irit Umanit, "Violence against Women," in *Jewish Feminism in Israel: Some Contemporary Perspectives*, ed. Kalpana Misra and Melanie S. Rich (Waltham, MA: Brandeis University Press, 2003), 133.

4. Projansky, *Watching Rape*, 9.

5. Sered, *What Makes Women Sick?*, 91.

6. Simona Sharoni, "Homefront as Battlefield: Gender, Military Occupation, and Violence against Women," in *Israeli Women's Studies: A Reader*, ed. Esther Fuchs (New Brunswick, NJ: Rutgers University Press, 2005), 232.

7. Horeck, *Public Rape*, 81.

8. Lubin, "The Woman as Other in Israeli Cinema," in *Israeli Women's Studies*, 302.

9. Projansky, *Watching Rape*, 2–3, italics in original.

10. Horeck, *Public Rape*, 8.

11. Umanit, "Violence against Women," 133.

12. Ruth Halperin-Kaddari, *Women in Israel: A State of Their Own* (Philadelphia: University of Pennsylvania Press, 2004), 192.

13. Isabel Kershner, "Former President of Israel Is Convicted in Rape Case," *New York Times*, December 30, 2010, A4.

14. Gili Cohen, "Four Israeli Soldiers Arrested for Suspected Gang Rape," *Haaretz*, April 30, 2015, www.haaretz.com/israel-news/.premium-1.654196.

15. Ibid.

16. Kershner, "Former President of Israel is Convicted in Rape Case," A4.

17. Umanit, "Violence against Women," 134.

18. Ibid.

19. Halperin-Kaddari, *Women in Israel*, 198.

20. Umanit, "Violence against Women," 139.

21. Sered, *What Makes Women Sick?*, 69.

22. Rela Mazali, "'And What About the Girls?' What a Culture of War Genders out of View," *Nashim: A Journal of Jewish Women's Studies & Gender Issues* 6 (Fall 2003), 46.

23. Recently feminists have responded by staging "slut walks" in Israel (there have been four so far), in which scantily clad women march in public streets in protest against domestic violence and sexual assault. The marches have received significant public attention but have, as yet had little impact on social attitudes as can be seen in the coverage of the Allenby 40 rape.

24. Lees, "Media Reporting of Rape," 107–30.

25. Maria Los and Sharon E. Chamard, "Selling Newspapers or Educating the Public-Sexual Violence in the Media," *Canadian Journal of Criminology* 39, no. 3 (July 1997): 293.

26. Lees, "Media Reporting of Rape"; Alina Korn and Sivan Efrat, "The Coverage of Rape in the Israeli Popular Press," *Violence Against Women* 10, no. 9 (2004): 1062.

27. Hagar Lahav, "The Defendant, the Nightmare, and the Clockwork Strawberry: A Case Study of Rape Coverage in the Israeli Press," *Megamot 46*, no. 1/2 (2009).

28. Catharine A MacKinnon, *Feminism Unmodified: Discourses on Life and Law* (Cambridge, MA: Harvard University Press, 1987) ; Susan Brownmiller, *Against Our Will: Men, Women and Rape* (New York: Simon and Schuster, 1975).

29. Lahav, "The Defendant, the Nightmare, and the Clockwork Strawberry."

30. Halperin-Kaddari, *Women in Israel*, 312, in note 19.

31. The original term "male chicken," which I have translated here as "cock," is a play on the name of the band "The Chickens" that originally released the song.

32. Korn and Efrat, "The Coverage of Rape in the Israeli Popular Press." In the first case a sixteen-year-old girl was raped by several peers over a six-week period. The affluence of the neighborhood and the boy's social standing played a prominent role in the coverage of the incident. In the second case a thirteen-year-old girl was raped by several men, including adults (not all of whom were known to her), and the ethnicity of the boys involved was highlighted in the coverage.

33. Ibid., 1070.

34. Lahav, "The Defendant, the Nightmare, and the Clockwork Strawberry," 90.

35. Korn and Efrat, "The Coverage of Rape in the Israeli Popular Press," 1072.

36. Ibid., 1074.

37. Ibid., 1071.

38. Ibid.

39. Ibid., 1059.

40. Lahav, "The Defendant, the Nightmare, and the Clockwork Strawberry," 91.

41. Mazali, "And What About the Girls?," 46.

42. Projansky, *Watching Rape*, 3.

43. Susan Sered, "Replaying the Rape of Dinah: Women's Bodies in Israeli Cultural Discourse," in *Jews and Gender: The Challenge to Hierarchy*, ed. Jonathan Frankel (Oxford: Oxford University Press, 2000), 193.

44. Horeck, *Public Rape*, 4.

45. Sered, *What Makes Women Sick?*, 100.

46. Susan Jeffords, "Rape and the New World Order," *Cultural Critique* 19 (Autumn 1991): 212.

47. Sered, *What Makes Women Sick?*, 100.

48. Ibid.

49. Horeck, *Public Rape,* 89.

50. It is Abargil's mother who sees her daughter's religious transformation as a direct response to the rape experience. She frames it as one possible response, and a preferred one to becoming anorexic or turning to drugs.

51. Projansky, *Watching Rape,* 46.

52. Sered, *What Makes Women Sick?,* 128.

53. Umanit, "Violence against Women," 137.

54. Horeck, *Public Rape,* 70. Horeck addresses the "Big Dan" rape trial in New England, in which the victim of a gang rape in a bar was accused of bringing shame on a community of Portuguese immigrants who were already marginalized. The woman's rape also reveals the "utter violence of civic identification," as the woman's violation was transferred in the media into the violation of New Bedford.

55. Ibid., 113, 114.

56. Peggy Reeves Sanday, *Fraternity Gang Rape: Sex, Brotherhood, and Privilege on Campus* (New York: NYU Press, 2007), 48.

57. Miri Talmon, *Blues Latzabar Haavud: Havurot Venostalgia Bakolno'a Israeli* [Blues for the Lost Sabra: Community and Nostalgia in Israeli Cinema] (Tel Aviv: Open University, 2001).

58. Sered, *What Makes Women Sick?,* 96.

59. Ibid., 88.

60. Ibid., 97.

61. Ibid., 88.

62. Lital Levin "This week in Haaretz 1988 11 Men Accused of Raping Kibbutz Shomrat Girl." *Haaretz,* August 26, 2010, www.haaretz.com/print-edition/features/this-week-in-haaretz-1988–11-men-accused-of-raping-kibbutz-shomrat-girl-1.310280.

63. "Acquittal in Israeli Rape Case Draws Protests." *New York Times.* November 15, 1992, www.nytimes.com/1992/11/15/world/acquittal-in-israeli-rape-case-draws-protests.html.

64. Sered, *What Makes Women Sick?,* 98, citing *Haaretz,* December 16, 1999.

65. Deuteronomy 22:24–25. If she had cried out in the city it is assumed that she would have been heard and either this would have been a deterrent to the man or help would have come, whereas in the field it is assumed that he took her there to kill her and she is not deemed complicit—and is therefore not subject to punishment.

66. Rebecca Traister, "The Game is Rigged," *New Yok Magazine*, October 19, 2015, http://nymag.com/thecut/2015/10/why-consensual-sex-can-still-be-bad.html.

67. Ibid.

68. Ibid.

69. Horeck, *Public Rape*, 146, citing Catherine McKinnon, "Feminism, Marxism, Method and the State: Toward Feminist Jurisprudence," *Signs* 8, no. 4 (Summer 1983): 652.

70. Sered, *What Makes Women Sick?*, 103.

71. Zanger, *Place, Memory and Myth in Contemporary Israeli Cinema*, 87.

72. Ibid.

73. Ibid., 94.

74. Projansky, *Watching Rape*, 58.

75. Lubin, "The Woman as Other," in *Israeli Women's Studies*, 303.

76. Irit Negbi, "We Were Like Sodom," *Haaretz [Hebrew edition]*, October 6, 2015 www.haaretz.co.il/news/law/1.2750041 (though other reports would debate the number of hours and number of men involved); Yaniv Kobovitch, "What Really Happened at Allenby 40: New Revelations," *Haaretz [Hebrew edition]*, October 12, 2015, www.haaretz.co.il/news/law/1.2745264.

77. "Yalla" is a slang term of encouragement best translated in this context as "get on with it."

78. See Vilnai's original investigative article about the competitions at Allenby 40 that were part of the pressure that led to the closing down of the competitions when she pointed out that the girls were drunk, and made drunker when they refused to comply, and were probably underage. Orly Vilnai, "Wet T-Shirt Competitions: On the Bar Without Free Will," *Haaretz* [Hebrew edition], November 27, 2013.

79. Dana Goldberg, "In the Name of Feminism," *Haaretz*, October 8, 2015, www.haaretz.co.il/opinions/.premium-1.2747310.

80. Tzafi Saar. "Feminists Don't Hate Men and Sex." *Haaretz*. October 9, 2015, www.haaretz.co.il/opinions/.premium-1.2748162.

81. Ibid.

82. Horeck, *Public Rape*, 87.

Chapter 8

1. Other films include *James' Journey to Jerusalem*, *What a Wonderful Place*, *Promised Land*, *My Neighbor the Assassin*, and Boaz Armoni's short film *Trains in the Desert*.

2. Hila Shamir, "Migrant Care Workers in Israel: Between Family, Market, and State," *Israel Studies Review* 28, no. 2 (Winter 2013): 203.

3. Ibid., 200–201; see also Hila Shamir "The State of Care: Rethinking the Distributive Effects of Familial Care Policies in Liberal Welfare States," *American Journal of Comparative Law* 58, no. 4 (Fall 2010): 953–86.

4. Shamir, "Migrant Care Workers in Israel," 192–93.

5. Ibid., 192.

6. Ibid., 194.

7. Ibid., 195.

8. Ibid., 203.

9. Ibid., 199.

10. Maya Shapiro, "The Development of a 'Privileged Underclass,' Locating Undocumented Migrant Women and Their Children in the Political Economy of Tel Aviv, Israel," *Dialectical Anthropology* 37, no. 3–4 (December 2013): 429–30.

11. Ibid.

12. Shamir, "Migrant Care Workers in Israel," 199; Claudia Liebelt concluded from her field research that the need for annual renewal and the attendant bureaucratic hassles meant that between "employers' neglect and frequent contradictory institutional practice, migrants were typically 'illegalised' within the first years of their stay in Israel and subsequently threatened with deportation." Claudia Liebelt, "Becoming Pilgrims in the Holy Land: On Filipina Domestic Workers' Struggles and Pilgrimages for a Cause in Israel," *Asia Pacific Journal of Anthropology* 11, no. 3–4 (2010): 260.

13. This chapter owes a great deal to Mya Guarnieri Jaradat's field research in south Tel Aviv in the summer of 2015. The changing situation on the ground has meant that legal rulings, patterns of deportation, the ethnic makeup of the migrant population, and the treatment of migrants' children in Israel is dynamic, and scholarly research (and the statistics on which it is often based) can quickly become dated. Much of the most recent, detailed information about the situation and experiences of migrant workers is thanks to the insights that Guarnieri Jaradat shared with me from her research before her book *The Unchosen: The Lives of Israel's New Others* (London: Pluto Press, 2017) was published, and data from the Population, Immigration and Border Authority that is published quarterly online at https://www.gov.il/he/Departments/publications/.

14. Shamir, "Migrant Care Workers in Israel," 198.

15. Mya Guarnieri Jaradat has observed that the restriction of movement, like the patrolling of south Tel Aviv by the border guards, is reminiscent of the ways in which the government responds to Palestinians. To some degree, both populations share the demographic threat, and thus their parallel treatment is indicative of government attitudes.

16. Rebeca Raijman, Silvina Schammah-Gesser, and Adriana Kemp, "International Migration, Domestic Work, and Care Work: Undocumented Latina Migrants in Israel," *Gender & Society* 17, no. 5 (2003).

17. By contrast with the official Israeli day of rest, which runs from Friday afternoon through Saturday.

18. Silvina Schammah-Gesser et al., "'Making It' in Israel? Latino Undocumented Migrant Workers in the Holy Land," *Estudios Interdisciplinarios de America Latina y el Caribe (EIAL)* 11, no. 2 (2000).

19. Liebelt, "Becoming Pilgrims in the Holy Land," 260–61.

20. Claudia Liebelt, "On Sentimental Orientalists, Christian Zionists, and Working Class Cosmopolitans: Filipina Domestic Workers' Journeys to Israel and Beyond," *Critical Asian Studies* 40, no. 4 (2008).

21. Turkish and Chinese workers have all but returned, and those that remain generally work in Asian restaurants. Numbers of Poles and Romanians have been significantly reduced, and many of the undocumented Filipino workers were deported or moved on to other places. For many, Israel is viewed as one stop on a path of multiple migrations, situated above the Arab world but below Western Europe and North America. Liebelt, "Becoming Pilgrims in the Holy Land."

22. The official statistics provide a breakdown of documented and undocumented workers in these industries, which I have combined for the purposes of these statistics. Approximately 58 percent of documented foreign workers are employed as caregivers, while 75 percent of undocumented workers are caregivers (and in 2016, 73 percent of undocumented workers were caregivers). PIBA October 2016, Third-Quarter Report Actual figures for October 2016: 81,329 documented foreign workers, 16,736 undocumented foreign workers, 40,721 refugees, and 78,500 tourists who overstayed their visas or are working illegally on tourist visas.

23. Schammah-Gesser et al., "'Making It' in Israel?," accessed November 30, 2015, http://eial.tau.ac.il/index.php/eial/article/view/1003. They, in turn, cite Arend Lijphart and Carlos Waisman, eds., *Institutional Design in New Democracies: Eastern Europe and Latin America* (Boulder, CO: Westview Press, 1996) and Mario Sznajder, "Legitimidad y Poder Políticos frente a las Herencias Autoritarias: Transición y Consolidación Democrática en América Latina," *Estudios Interdisciplinarios de América Latina y el Caribe*, 4, no. 1 (1993): 27–55.

24. Susan King, "Israel's Immigrant Wave Has Personal Side in 'The Human Resources Manager,'" *Los Angeles Times*, March 14, 2011.

25. Shapiro, "The Development of a 'Privileged Underclass,' Locating Undocumented Migrant Women and Their Children in the Political Economy of Tel Aviv, Israel," 433.

26. For those who were granted rights of residency and a path to naturalization, their moth-

ers were granted resident visas that must be renewed annually. Mya Guarinieri Jaradat has reported that despite the fact that women have not had trouble renewing these documents, they live in a state of anxiety at the precariousness of their situation and remain concerned that a change in law or regime will result in their potential separation.

27. Zerubavel, "Coping with the Legacy of Death," 92–93.

28. Li Minghuan, "Making a Living at the Interface of Legality and Illegality: Chinese Migrant Workers in Israel," *International Migration* 50, no. 2 (April 2012).

29. Dana Weiler-Polak, "Israel Begins Long-fought Deportation of Foreign Workers' Kids on Yishai's Orders," *Haaretz* [English edition], March 15, 2011.

30. In 2014, Mexicans made up 3.6 percent of the migrants who entered on tourist visas and stayed.

31. Raijman, Schammah-Gesser, and Kemp, "International Migration, Domestic Work, and Care Work."

32. Maya Shapiro, "The Politics of Intimacy, (Re)Defining Class through Migrant Elder Care Relationships," in *When Care Work Goes Global: Locating the Social Relations of Domestic Work*, ed. Mary Romero, Valerie Preston, and Wenona Giles (Abingdon: Routledge, 2014), 189.

33. Ibid., 178.

34. Shapiro, "The Development of a 'Privileged Underclass,' Locating Undocumented Migrant Women and Their Children in the Political Economy of Tel Aviv, Israel," 425.

35. Shapiro, "The Politics of Intimacy," 189.

36. During the 1990s these migrants from Ghana and Nigeria came in search of economic opportunity, and can be distinguished from those seeking asylum, who arrived as refugees predominantly since the second half of the first decade of the twenty-first century from Sudan, Eritrea, Ethiopia, and the Ivory Coast. Granted temporary visas that must be renewed every three months, they are not allowed to work, or face financial penalties if they do. Though the Israeli government originally tolerated the African migrants, and many worked in menial, low-paid jobs in hotels and restaurants, the significant increase in the number of migrants raised alarm, and the government began to refer to them as "infiltrators." Though the illegal workers can be rounded up and deported, the refugees—due to international agreements about the protection of asylum seekers—are not returned, though their applications for asylum, in general, have not been processed. Thus they exist in a holding pattern, discouraged from working and living in a state of temporary settlement.

37. However, it is necessary to note that foreign workers continue to be a partisan issue, and their support by the white liberal elite is not necessarily shared by Mizrahi women

activists.

38. Shapiro, "The Politics of Intimacy, (Re)Defining Class through Migrant Elder Care Relationships," 197. Though the activists on the ground, and the foreign workers, saw these parallels, most generally tried to avoid drawing these connections in their advocacy, as they recognized that appealing to the Israeli public (and the government) on human rights issues, and particularly the situation of children, was less threatening and more likely to be accepted positively than allying with the toxicity surrounding the conflict and the situation of Palestinians in Israel.

39. Ibid.

Afterword

1. Information from the history section of the studio's website, accessed May 18, 2016, www.hsil.tv/about-us/our-company/.

2. This is the original publication date of her article. See Orly Lubin, "The Woman as Other in Israeli Cinema," in *The Other in Jewish Thought and History* (New York: New York University Press, 1994). I have been citing from its 2005 republication in Esther Fuchs, ed., *Israeli Women's Studies: A Reader* (New Brunswick, NJ: Rutgers University Press, 2005).

3. In Israel the term for a "reader" is a "lector."

4. Yuval Avivi, "Israel's Women Filmmakers Move to Center Stage," Al-Monitor, posted March 12, 2015, www.al-monitor.com/pulse/originals/2015/03/israel-movie-industry-women-director-actresses-awards.html#.

5. Brent Lang, "Women Comprise 7% of Directors on Top 250 Films (Study)," *Variety*, October 27, 2015, http://variety.com/2015/film/news/women-hollywood-inequality-directors-behind-the-camera-1201626691/.

6. With thanks to Michal Aviad, interview with the author, May 11, 2015.

7. Debra Kamin, "Israel's New Fund for Cinema and TV Cultivates Directors with Greenhouse Program," *Variety*, April 24, 2015.

8. Ibid.

9. Raya Morag, "Ronit Elkabetz's Persona," *Haaretz*, April 24, 2016, www.haaretz.co.il/literature/study/.premium-1.2925886.

10. Ronit Elkabetz, "I'm a Fighter," *Yediot Aharonot*, written for International Women's Day, March 8, 2016, republished after her death April 20, 2016, http://yedioth.ynet.co.il/articles/0,7340,L-4793985,00.html.

11. Debra Kamin, "Ronit Elkabetz, Actress and Filmmaker, Dies at 51," *Variety*, April 19, 2016, http://variety.com/2016/film/news/ronit-elkabetz-dead-actress-israeli-french-cancer-1201756261/.

12. From Shemer, *Identity, Place, and Subversion in Contemporary Mizrahi Cinema in Israel*, 208–9.

Filmography

All films were produced in Israel, unless otherwise stated. Coproductions with Israel are usually not marked. Where Palestinian films were not made in conjunction with Israel, other participants have been listed. Where they were made in conjunction with Israel, both Palestine and Israel are listed.

The Accused Jonathan Kaplan (USA), 1988

A.K.A. Nadia [*Nadia*] Tova Ascher, 2015

The Ambassador's Wife [*Eshet HaShagrir*] Dina Tvi Riklis, 2016

The Assassin Next Door [*Kirot*] Danny Lerner (Israel, France, USA), 2009

Atalia Tzvika Kertzner, 1984

Aunt Clara [*Doda Clara*] Avraham Hefner, 1977

Aviva My Love [*Aviva Ahuvati*] Shemi Zarhin, 2006

Aviya's Summer [*HaKayitz Shel Aviya*] Eli Cohen, 1988

Avodah [*Labor*] Helmar Lerski, 1935

The Ballad of the Weeping Spring [*Balada LeAviv HaBohe*] Benny Toraty, 2012

The Band's Visit [*Bikur HaTizmoret*] Eran Kolirin, 2007

Banot (a.k.a. *You're in the Army Now*, a.k.a. *Girls*) Nadav Levitan, 1985

Barash Michal Vilnk, 2015

Beaufort Joseph Cedar, 2007

Before Tomorrow [*Lifnei Mahar*] Elida Gera, 1969

Ben Zaken Efrat Corem, 2015

Beyond the Walls [*MeAhorai HaSoragim*] Uri Barbash, 1984

Black Bus [*Sorreret*] Anat Zuria, 2009

Big Girl [*Yalda Gdola*] Nirit Yaron, 2008

Blazing Sands [*Holot Lohatim*] 1960

Boreg Shira Geffen, 2014

Braids [*Tzamot*] Yitzhak Halutzi, 1989

Brave Miss World Cecilia Peck, 2013

Bread [*Lehem*] Ram Loevy, 1986

Bread [*Le Pain*] Hiam Abbas, 2001

Bridget Jones' Diary Sharon Maguire (UK, USA, France), 2001

Bruriah Avraham Kushnir, 2008

The Burglar [*HaPoretzet*] Hagar Ben-Asher, 2015

Bye Bye to Love [*Bye Bye L'Ahava*] Ayelet Dekel, 2006

Campfire [*Medurat HaShevet*] Joseph Cedar, 2004

Caramel [*Sukkar Banat*] Nadine Labaki (France, Lebanon), 2007

The Cemetery Club [*Moadon Beit HaK'varot*] Tali Shemesh, 2006

Circles [*Ma'agalim Shel Shishi Shabat*] Idit Shehori, 1980
Close to Home [*Karov La Bayit*] Vardit Bilu and Dalia Hager, 2005
Colombian Love [*Ahava Colombianit*] Shay Kanot, 2004
Crows [*Orvim*] Ayelet Menahemi, 1988
Cupcakes [*Bananot*] Eytan Fox, 2013
Cup Final [*G'mar Gaviya*] Eran Riklis, 1991
Dalia and the Sailors [*Dalia VeHamalahim*] Menahem Golan, 1964
Day after Day [*Yom Yom*] Amos Gitai 1998
The Day We Met [*Neshika BaMetzah*] Sam Firstenberg, 1990
Dead End Street [*Kvish L'lo Motzah*] Yaki Yosha, 1982
The Debt [*HaHov*] Assaf Bernstein, 2007
The Debt John Madden (USA), 2010
Der Tel-Aviv-Krimi (television series) (Germany), 2016
Desperado Square [*Kikar HaHalomot*] Benny Toraty, 2000
Disengagement [*Hitnatkoot*] Amos Gitai, 2007
Dizengoff 99 Avi Nesher, 1979
Dolls [*Duma*] Abeer Zeibak Haddad, 2011
Don't Tell Morgenstein [*Af Milah L'Morgenstein*] 1963
Eastern Wind [*Hamsin*] Daniel Wachsmann, 1982
The Edge of Danger 1955
Educating Rita Lewis Gilbert (UK), 1983
Eldorado Menahem Golan, 1963
An Electric Blanket Named Moshe [*Smicha Hashmalit U'Shema Moshe*] Assi Dayan, 1994
The Eternal Dance [*La Danse éternelle*] Hiam Abbas (France) 2004
Every Bastard a King [*Kol Mamzer Meleh*] Uri Zohar, 1968
Exodus Otto Preminger (USA) 1960
Eyes of a Thief [*Ayoun al-Haramiya*] Najwa Najjar (Palestine/France/Algeria), 2014
Eyes Wide Open [*'Eynaim Petukhot*] Haim Tabakman, 2009
The Farewell Party [*Mita Tova*] Tal Granit, Sharon Maymon, 2014
Fellow Travelers [*Magash Hakesef*] Judd Ne'eman, 1983
Fever at Dawn [*Hajnali làz*] Peter Gardos (Hungary/Israel), 2015
Fictitious Marriage [*Nisui'im Fictivim*] Haim Bouzaglo, 1988
Fill the Void [*Lemaleh et HaHalal*] Rama Burshtein, 2013
Fire Birds [*Tziporey Hol*] Amir Wolf, 2015
5 and 5 [*Hamesh Hamesh*] Shmuel Imberman, 1980
Fortuna Menahem Golan, 1966
Free Zone [*'Ayzor Hofshei*] Amos Gitai, 2005
The General's Daughter Simon West (USA), 1999
Gett: The Trial of Viviane Amsalem [*Gett*] Ronit and Shlomi Elkabetz, 2014

Ghost Jerry Zucker (USA), 1990

G. I. Jane Ridley Scott (USA, UK), 1997

The Girl [*HaYelda*] Lihi Sabag, 2016

The Gravedigger's Daughter [*HaBat Shel Hakavran*] Shira Gabai, 2016

Here Comes Mr. Jordan Alexander Hall (USA), 1941

The Hero's Wife [*Eshet HaGibor*] Yoseph Millo, 1963

Hill 24 Doesn't Answer Thorold Dickinson, 1955

Hole in the Moon [*Hor B'Levana*] Uri Zohar and Amos Kenan, 1964

The Human Resources Manager [*Shlihuto shel HaMemuneh al Mash'abey Enosh*] Eran Riklis, 2010

I Love You Rosa [*Ani Ohev Otach Rosa*] Moshé Mizrahi, 1972

Infiltration [*Hitganvut Yehidim*] Dover Kosashvili, 2010

Inheritance [*Héritage*] Hiam Abbas, 2012

Invisible [*Lo Roim Aleich*] Michal Aviad, 2011

Jaffa [*Kalat HaYam*] Keren Yedaya, 2009

Jellyfish [*Meduzot*] Shira Geffen and Etgar Keret, 2007

Jenin, Jenin Mohammed Bakri, 2002

Joe + Belle Veronica Kedar, 2011

Julia Mia Yuval Granot, 2007

Kadosh Amos Gitai, 1999

Kazablan Menahem Golan, 1973

Khirbet Khizeh Ram Loevy, 1978

Kippur Amos Gitai, 2000

Lady Kul El Arab Ibtisam Salh Mara'ana, 2008

A Late Marriage [*Hatuna Meuheret*] Dover Kosashvili, 2001

Late Summer Blues [*Blues Lahofesh Hagadol*] Renen Schorr, 1987

Lebanon [*Levanon*] Samuel Maoz, 2009

Lemon Popsicle [*Eskimo Limon*] Boaz Davidson, 1978

Lemon Tree [*Etz Limon*] Eran Riklis and Suha Arraf, 2008

The Lesson [*HaShiur*] Anat Zuria, 2013

Lia Taly Goldenberg, 2011

Light Out of Nowhere [*Or Min HaHefker*] Nissim Dayan, 1973

A Little Bit of Luck [*Tipat Mazal*] Ze'ev Revach, 1990

The Little Dictator [*HaDiktator HaKatan*] Nurith Cohn, 2015

The Lover [*HaMe'ahev*] Michal Bat-Adam, 1985

Madame Rosa [*La Vie devant soi*] Moshé Mizrahi (France), 1977

May in the Summer Cherten Dabis (Jordan, Qatar, USA), 2013

Miral Julian Schnabel (France/Israel/Italy/India/USA), 2010

Moments [*Moments de la vie d'une femme*] Michal Bat-Adam (France/Israel), 1979

The Mountain [*Ha-har*] Yaelle Kayam, 2015

My Father My Lord [*Hofshat Kaitz*] David Volach, 2007

My Lovely Sister [*Ahoti HaYafa*] Marco Carmel, 2011

My Michael [*Michael Sheli*] Dan Wolman, 1974

My Mother the General [*Imi HaGeneralit*] Joel Silberg, 1979

Next to Her [*At Li Layla*] Asaf Korman, 2014

Nini Shlomo Suriano, 1962

Noa at 17 [*Noa bat 17*] Isaac Zepel Yeshurun, 1981

Noodle [*Noodel*] Ayelet Menahemi, 2007

Nurith George Ovadiah, 1972

Off-White Lies [*Orhim LeRega*] Maya Kenig, 2011

On a Narrow Bridge [*Gesher Tzar Me'od*] Nissim Dayan, 1985

On the Third Day [*Be Yom HaShlishi*] Moshe Ivgy, 2010

One of Us [*Ahad MiShelanu*] Uri Barbash, 1989

Orange People [*Anashim Ketumim*] Hannah Azoulay Hasfari, 2013

Or, My Treasure [*Or*] Keren Yedaya, 2004

The Other War [*HaMilhama HaShniya*] Tamar Glezerman, *2008*

Out of Sight [*Lemarit Ain*] Danny Syrkin, 2006

The Paratroopers [*Masa Alunkot*] Judd Ne'eman, 1977

Pathways [*Mish'ulim*] Hagar Ben-Asher, 2007

Peeping Toms [*Metzizim*] Uri Zohar, 1972

A Place by the Sea [*Makom L'yad Hayam*] Rafael Revivo, 1988

Princess [*Nesicha*] Tali Shalom-Ezer, 2014

Promised Land [*Ha'eretz Hamuvtachat*] Amos Gitai, 2004

Purity [*Tehora*] Anat Zuria, 2002

Queen of the Road [*Malkat Hakvish*] 1971

Repeat Dive [*Tzlila Hozeret*] Shimon Dotan, 1982

Ricochets [*Shetei Etzbaot Mi'Tzidon*] Eli Cohen, 1986

Rock the Casbah [*Rock BaCasba*] Yariv Horowitz, 2012

Room 514 [*Heder 514*] Sharon Bar Ziv, 2012

S#x Acts [*Shesh Peamim*] Johnathan Gurfinkel, 2012

Saga of a Photo [*Sipur HaMathil BeTmuna*] Mooli Landesman, 2013

Sallah [*Sallah Shabbati*] Ephraim Kishon, 1964

Salsa Tel Aviv Yohanan Weller, 2011

Salt of this Sea [*Milh Hadha al-Bahr*] Annemarie Jacir (Palestine/Belgium/France/Spain/Switzerland), 2008

Sarit George Obadiah and Shimon Herma, 1974

The Secrets [*HaSodot*] Avi Nesher, 2007

Sentenced to Marriage [*Mekudeshet*] Anat Zuria, 2004

77 Steps [*77 Dragot*] Ibtisam Salh Mara'ana, 2010

Sex, Lies and Dinner [*Sex, Shkarim Va'Arukhat Erev*] Dan Wolman, 1996

Sh'chur Shmuel Hasfari, 1994

She's Coming Home [*Hahi She Hozeret HaBayta*] Maya Dreifuss, 2013

Shirley Valentine Lewis Gilbert (UK), 1989

Shiva [*Shiva*] Ronit and Shlomi Elkabetz, 2008

Shoah Claude Lanzmann (France/UK), 1985

Shuli's Boyfriend [*Ha Bachur Shel Shuli*] Doron Tsabari, 1997

Siege [*Matzor*] Gilberto Tofano, 1969

Sixtieth Street [*Rehov Shishim*] George Ovadiah, 1976

The Slut [*HaNotenet*] Hagar Ben-Asher, 2011

The Song of the Siren [*Shirat HaSirena*] Eytan Fox, 1994

Srugim (television series) Eliezer Shapiro, 2008–10

Stairway to Heaven Michael Powell and Emeric Pressburger (UK), 1946

Stella Dallas King Vidor (USA), 1937

Sweet Mud [*Adama Meshuga'at*] Dror Shaul, 2006

The Syrian Bride [*HaKalah HaSurit*] Eran Riklis, 2004

Tel Aviv Stories [*Sipurei Tel Aviv*] Ayelet Menahemi and Nirit Yaron, 1992

That Lovely Girl [*Harchek Miheadro*] Keren Yedaya, 2014

Three Mothers [*Shalosh Imahot*] Dina Zvi-Riklis, 2006

3 Times Divorced [*Shalosh Pe'amim Megureshet*] [*Talaq bil-thalath*] Ibtisam Salh Mara'ana, 2008

3000 Nights [*3000 Layla*] Abeer Zeibak Haddad, 2015

A Time for Cherries [*Onat HaDuvdevanim*] Haim Bouzaglo, 1990

Time of Favor [*HaHesder*] Joseph Cedar, 2000

To Know a Woman [*Mikra Ishe*] Jacques Katmor, 1969

To Take a Wife [*Lakahat Isha*] Ronit and Shlomi Elkabetz, 2004

A Touch Away [*Merhak Negiah*] (television series) 2006

The Troupe [*HaLahaka*] Avi Nesher, 1978

Truly Madly Deeply Anthony Minghella (UK), 1990

Turn Left at the End of the World [*Sof Ha'Olam Smola*] Avi Nesher, 2004

Ushpizin [*HaUshpizin*] Giddi Dar, 2004

Villa Touma Suha Arraf (Israel/Palestine), 2014

Voices from the Heartland: Slaves of the Lord [*Shiur Moledet: Avdei Hashem*] Hadar Friedlich, 2002

Wall, Crevice, Tear [*Kir, Sadak, Dima'ah*] Tehila Raanan, 2015

Waltz with Bashir [*Valtz im Bashir*] Ari Folman, 2008

The Wanderer [*HaMeshotet*] Avishai Sivan, 2010

Wedding in Galilee [*Hatunah B'Galil*] [*Urs Al-Jalil*] Michel Khleifi (Palestine/Belgium/France), 1987

What a Gang [*Havura SheKazot*] Ze'ev Havatzelet, 1962

What a Wonderful Place [*Eize Makom Niflah*] Eyal Halfon, 2005

When I Saw You [*Lamma Shoftak*] Annemarie Jacir (Palestine/Jordan/Greece/United Arab Emirates), 2012

Where Do We Go Now? [*Et maintenant on va où*] Nadine Labaki (France/Lebanon/Egypt/Italy), 2011

The Witch Sima Vaknin [*Sima Vaknin Machshefa*] Dror Shaul, 2003

Women of Hamas [*Nashot Hamas*] Suha Arraf, 2010

The Women Pioneers [*Nashim Halutzot*] Michal Aviad, 2013

Write Down, I am an Arab [*Sajil Ana Arabi*] Ibtisam Salh Mara'ana (Israel/Palestine), 2014

Yana's Friends [*HaHaverim Shel Yana*] Arik Kaplun, 1999

Yellow Asphalt-Three Desert Stories [*Asfalt Tzahov*] Dan (Nokyo) Verete, 2000

Yossi and Jagger [*Yossi VeJagger*] Eytan Fox, 2002

Zero Motivation [*Efes BeYahasei Enosh*] Talya Lavie, 2014

Bibliography

Abramson, Glenda. *Hebrew Writing of the First World War*. United Kingdom: Vallentine Mitchell, & Company, 2008.

Almagor, Gila. Interview. *A Feast for the Eyes—The Story of Israeli Cinema [Hagigah Leeynaim—Sipuro Shel Hakolnoa Hayisre'eli]*, episode 3, July 5, 2015, Channel 1.

Almog, Oz. *Farewell to "Srulik": Changing Values among the Israeli Elite*. Tel Aviv: Zmora Bitan, 2004.

———. "From Blorit to Ponytail: Israeli Culture Reflected in Popular Hairstyles." *Israel Studies* 8, no. 2 (Summer 2003): 82–117.

———. *The Sabra: The Creation of the New Jew*. Translated by Haim Watzman. Berkeley: University of California Press, 2000.

Alter, Robert. "Magic Realism in the Israeli Novel." *Prooftexts* 16, no. 2 (May 1996): 151–68.

Amir, Delila, and Menachem Amir. "The Politics of Prostitution and Trafficking of Women in Israel." In *The Politics of Prostitution: Women's Movements, Democratic States and the Globalisation of Sex Commerce*, edited by Joyce Outshoorn, 144–64. Cambridge: Cambridge University Press, 2004.

Ashby, Justine. *"It's Been Emotional": Reassessing the Contemporary British Woman's Film*. London: Routledge, 2009.

———. "Postfeminism in the British Frame." *Cinema Journal* 44, no. 2 (Winter 2005): 127–33.

Atakav, Eylem. *Women and Turkish Cinema: Gender Politics, Culture, Identity and Representation*. London: Routledge, 2013.

Attwood, Lynne, and Maya Turovskaya. *Red Women on the Silver Screen: Soviet Women and Cinema from the Beginning to the End of the Communist Era*. London: Rivers Oram Press, 1993.

Bainbridge, Caroline. *A Feminine Cinematics: Luce Irigaray, Women and Film*. (United Kingdom: Palgrave Macmillan, 2008).

Bardenstein, Carol. "Cross/Cast: Passing in Israeli and Palestinian Cinema." In *Palestine, Israel, and the Politics of Popular Culture*, edited by Rebecca L. Stein and Ted Swedenburg, 99–125. Durham, NC: Duke University Press, 2005.

Begley, Valerie, and Olga Gershenson. "Introduction: Volumes." *Journal of International Women's Studies* 6, no. 2 (2005): 1–6.

Ben-David, Benny. "The Siege Syndrome: The Six Day War and Israeli Cinema." *Journal of Israeli History* 28, no. 2 (2009): 175–93.

Ben-Shaul, Nitzan S. "Fellow Traveler: The Cinematic-Political Consciousness of Judd Ne'eman." *Shofar: An Interdisciplinary Journal of Jewish Studies* 24, no. 1 (Fall 2005): 94–106.

Ben-Zvi-Morad, Yael. "Borders in Motion: The Evolution of the Portrayal of the Israeli-Palestinian Conflict in Contemporary Israeli Cinema." In *Israeli Cinema: Identities in Motion*, edited by Miri Talmon and Yaron Peleg. Jewish History, Life, and Culture, 276–93. Austin: University of Texas Press, 2011.

Benjamin, Orly. "Don't Wanna Be Nice Girls: The Struggle for Suffrage and the New Feminism in Israel." *Nashim: A Journal of Jewish Women's Studies & Gender Issues*, no. 13 (Spring 2007): 265–69.

Berger, John. *Ways of Seeing*. United Kingdom: Penguin UK, 2008.

Brownmiller, Susan. *Against Our Will: Men, Women and Rape*. New York: Simon and Schuster, 1975.

Brunsdon, Charlotte. "*Crossroads*: Notes on Soap Opera." *Screen* 22, no. 4 (1981): 32–37.

Burstein, Janet. "Yehuda 'Judd' Ne'eman." *Bomb* 95 (Spring 2006): 78–84.

Campbell, Russell. *Marked Women: Prostitutes and Prostitution in the Cinema*. Madison: University of Wisconsin Press, 2006.

Case, Alison A. *Plotting Women: Gender and Narration in the Eighteenth- and Nineteenth-Century British Novel*. Charlottesville: University of Virginia Press, 1999.

Chyutin, Dan. "'The King's Daughter Is All Glorious Within': Female Modesty in Judaic-Themed Israeli Cinema." *Journal of Jewish Identities* 9, no. 1 (January 2016): 39–58.

Cnaan, Ram A. "Notes on Prostitution in Israel." *Sociological Inquiry* 52, no. 2 (1982): 114–21.

Cohen, Nir. *Soldiers, Rebels, and Drifters: Gay Representation in Israeli Cinema*. Detroit, MI: Wayne State University Press, 2011.

Cook, Pam, and Claire Johnston. "The Place of Woman in the Cinema of Raoul Walsh." In *Issues in Feminist Film Criticism*, edited by Patricia Erens, 19–27. Bloomington: University of Indiana Press, 1990.

Cowie, Elizabeth. *Representing the Woman: Cinema and Psychoanalysis*. Minneapolis: University of Minnesota Press, 1997.

Daniels, Jyoti Sarah. "Scripting the Jewish Body: The Sexualised Female Jewish Body in Amos Gitai's *Kadosh*." In *Jews and Sex*, edited by Nathan Abrams. Nottingham: Five Leaves, 2008, 77–87.

Dardashti, Galeet. "Televised Agendas: How Global Funders Make Israeli TV More 'Jewish.'" *Jewish Film and New Media: An International Journal* 3, no. 1 (Spring 2015): 77–103.

Dekel, Tal. "From First-Wave to Third-Wave Feminist Art in Israel: A Quantum Leap." *Israel Studies* 16, no. 1 (Spring1 2011): 149–78.

Devereaux, Mary. "Oppressive Texts, Resisting Readers and the Gendered Spectator: The New Aesthetics." *Journal of Aesthetics and Art Criticism* 48, no. 4 (Fall 1990): 337–47.

Doane, Mary Ann. *The Desire to Desire: The Woman's Film of the 1940s*. Bloomington: Indiana University Press, 1987.

———. *Femmes Fatales: Feminism, Film Theory, Psychoanalysis*. New York: Routledge, 2013.

———. "Film and the Masquerade: Theorising the Female Spectator." In *Feminism and Film*, edited by E. Ann Kaplan, 418–36. Oxford: Oxford University Press, 2000.

Donald, Ralph, and Karen MacDonald. *Women in War Films: From Helpless Heroine to G.I. Jane*. Lanham, MD: Rowman & Littlefield, 2014.

Dönmez-Colin, Gönül. "Women in Turkish Cinema: Their Presence and Absence as Images and as Image-Makers." *Third Text* 24, no. 1 (2010): 91–105.

Feige, Michael. *One Space, Two Places: Gush Emunim, Peace Now, and the Construction of Israeli Space* [in Hebrew]. Jerusalem: Magnes Press. 2002.

———. "Peace Now and the Legitimation Crisis of' Civil Militarism.'" *Israel Studies* 3, no. 1 (1998): 85–111.

———. *Settling in the Hearts: Jewish Fundamentalism in the Occupied Territories*. Detroit: Wayne State University Press, 2009.

Feldman, Yael S. "From Essentialism to Constructivism? The Gender of Peace and War—Gilman, Woolf, Freud." *Partial Answers: Journal of Literature and the History of Ideas* 2, no. 1 (2004): 113–45.

———. "From the Madwoman in the Attic to the Women's Room: The American Roots of Israeli Feminism." *Israel Studies* 5, no. 1 (Spring 2000): 266.

———. *No Room of Their Own: Gender and Nation in Israeli Women's Fiction*. New York: Columbia University Press, 1999.

Franco, Jean. *The Decline and Fall of the Lettered City: Latin America in the Cold War*. Cambridge, MA: Harvard University Press, 2009.

Friedman, Regine Mihal. "Between Silence and Abjection: The Film Medium and the Israeli War Widow." *Filmhistoria online* 3, no. 1–2 (1993): 79–89.

Fuchs, Esther. "Images of Love and War in Contemporary Israeli Fiction: A Feminist Re-vision." In *Arms and the Woman: War, Gender, and Literary Representation*, edited by Helen M. Cooper, Adrienne Auslander Munich, and Susan Merrill Squier, 268–82. Chapel Hill: University of North Carolina Press, 1989.

———. *Israeli Mythogynies: Women in Contemporary Hebrew Fiction*. Albany: SUNY Press, 1987.

———, ed. *Israeli Women's Studies: A Reader*. New Brunswick, NJ: Rutgers University Press, 2005.

Gamliel, Tova. *Aesthetics of Sorrow: The Wailing Culture of Yemenite Jewish Women*. Detroit: Wayne State University Press, 2014.

———. "Performed Weeping: Drama and Emotional Management in Women's Wailing." *TDR/The Drama Review* 54, no. 2 (2010): 70–90.

Gershenson, Olga, and Dale Hudson. "Absorbed by Love: Russian Immigrant Woman in Israeli Film." *Journal of Modern Jewish Studies* 6, no. 3 (2007): 301–15.

Gertz, Nurith. *Captive of a Dream: National Myths in Israeli Culture* [in Hebrew]. Tel Aviv: Am Oved, 1995.

Gertz, Nurith. "Gender and Space in the New Israeli Cinema." *Shofar: An Interdisciplinary Journal of Jewish Studies* 22, no. 1 (Fall 2003): 110–16.

———. "The Medium That Mistook Itself for War: Cherry Season in Comparison with Ricochets and Cup Final." *Israel Studies* 4, no. 1 (1999): 153–74.

———. "Space and Gender in the New Israeli and Palestinian Cinema." *Prooftexts* 22, no. 1–2 (2002): 157–85.

———. "The War That Wasn't: Comparing the Cherry Season with Final Cup and Two Steps from Zidon." In *Fictive Looks: On Israeli Cinema*, edited by Nurith Gertz, Orly Lubin, and Judd Ne'eman, 67–91. Tel Aviv: Open University Press, 1998.

———. "Woman—the Image of the 'Other' in Israeli Society." *Literature Film Quarterly* 24, no. 1 (1996): 39.

Gertz, Nurith, and George Khleifi. *Palestinian Cinema: Landscape, Trauma and Memory*. Edinburgh: Edinburgh University Press, 2008.

Ginsburg, Shai. "Love in Search of Belief, Belief in Search of Love." In *The Modern Jewish Experience in World Cinema*, edited by Lawrence Baron, 371–76. Waltham, MA: Brandeis University Press, 2011.

Grimmeisen, Julie. "Halutzah or Beauty Queen? National Images of Women in Early Israeli Society." *Israel Studies* 20, no. 2 (Summer 2015): 27–52.

Hakak, Yael Friedman and Yohai. "Jewish Revenge: Haredi Action in the Zionist Sphere." *Jewish Film & New Media* 3, no. 1 (Spring 2015): 48–76.

Hall, Stuart. "Encoding/Decoding." In *Culture, Media, Language: Working Papers in Cultural Studies*,

1972–79, edited by the Centre for Contemporary Cultural Studies, 128–38. London: Hutchinson, 1980.

Halperin-Kaddari, Ruth. *Women in Israel: A State of Their Own*. Philadelphia: University of Pennsylvania Press, 2004.

Halperin-Kaddari, Ruth, and Yaacov Yadgar. "Between Universal Feminism and Particular Nationalism: Politics, Religion and Gender (In)Equality in Israel." *Third World Quarterly* 31, no. 6 (2010): 905–20.

Hansen, Miriam Bratu. "The Mass Production of the Senses: Classical Cinema as Vernacular Modernism." *Modernism/modernity* 6, no. 2 (April 1999): 59–77.

Harris, Rachel S. "Gender and Land: The Israeli Western." In *Casting a Giant Shadow: Transnationalism and the Shaping of Israeli Cinema*, edited by Rachel S. Harris and Dan Chyutin. Unpublished manuscript under consideration.

———. *An Ideological Death: Suicide in Israeli Literature*. Evanston, IL: Northwestern University Press, 2014.

———. "Introduction Sex, Violence, Motherhood and Modesty: Controlling the Jewish Woman and Her Body." *Nashim: A Journal of Jewish Women's Studies & Gender Issues* 23, no. 1 (2012): 5–10.

Haskell, Molly. *From Reverence to Rape: The Treatment of Women in the Movies*. New York: Holt, Rinehart and Winston, 1974.

Heise, Thomas. *Urban Underworlds: A Geography of Twentieth-Century American Literature and Culture (New Brunswick, NJ: Rutgers University Press, 2010)*.

Helman, Anat. *Becoming Israeli: National Ideals and Everyday Life in the 1950s*. Schusterman Series in Israel Studies. Waltham, MA: Brandeis University Press, 2014.

Herskovitz, Yaakov. "Settlers Versus Pioneers: The Deconstruction of the Settler in Assaf Gavron's *The Hilltop*." *Shofar: An Interdisciplinary Journal of Jewish Studies* 33, no. 4 (Summer 2015): 173–89.

Herzog, Hanna. "Re/Visioning the Women's Movement in Israel." *Citizenship Studies* 12, no. 3 (June 2008): 265–82.

Hooks, Bell. "The Oppositional Gaze: Black Female Spectators." In *The Feminism and Visual Culture Reader*, edited by Amelia Jones, 94–104. New York: Routledge, 2003.

Horeck, Tanya. *Public Rape: Representing Violation in Fiction and Film*. New York: Routledge, 2013.

Inbari, Motti. *Jewish Fundamentalism and the Temple Mount: Who Will Build the Third Temple?* Albany: SUNY Press, 2009.

———. *Messianic Religious Zionism Confronts Israeli Territorial Compromises*. Cambridge: Cambridge University Press, 2012.

Israel-Cohen, Yael. *Between Feminism and Orthodox Judaism: Resistance, Identity, and Religious Change in Israel*. Leiden, The Netherlands: Brill, 2012.

Izraeli, Dafna N., and Ephraim Tabory. "The Perception of Women's Status in Israel as a Social Problem." *Sex Roles* 14, no. 11/12 (1986): 663–78.

Jameson, Frederic. "On Magic Realism in Film." *Critical Inquiry* 12, no. 2 (Winter 1986): 301–25.

Jaradat, Mya Guarnieri. *The Unchosen: The Lives of Israel's New Others*. London: Pluto Press, 2017.

Jeffords, Susan. "Rape and the New World Order." *Cultural Critique* 19 (Autumn 1991): 203–15.

Johnston, Claire. "Women's Cinema as Counter Cinema." In *Notes on Women's Cinema*, edited by

Claire Johnston. London: Society for Education in Film and Television, 1973.

Kaplan, Danny. "'Cyclic Interruptions': Popular Music on Israeli Radio in Times of Emergency." In *Narratives of Dissent: War in Contemporary Israeli Arts and Culture*, edited by Rachel S. Harris and Ranen Omer-Sherman, 65–77. Detroit: Wayne State University Press, 2012.

Kaplan, E. Ann. "Introduction." In *Feminism and Film*, edited by E. Ann Kaplan, 1–18. Oxford: Oxford University Press, 2000.

———. "Is the Gaze Male?" In *Feminism and Film*, edited by E. Ann Kaplan, 119–38. Oxford: Oxford University Press, 2000.

———. *Women and Film: Both Sides of the Camera*. New York: Routledge, 2013.

Kaplan, Eran. "From Hero to Victim: The Changing Image of the Soldier on the Israeli Screen." In *Israeli Cinema: Identities in Motion*, edited by Miri Talmon and Yaron Peleg, 59–69. Jewish History, Life, and Culture. Austin: University of Texas Press, 2011.

Khatib, Lina. "The Voices of Taboos: Women in Lebanese War Cinema." *Women: A Cultural Review* 17, no. 1 (2006): 65–77.

Klein, Shira. "An Army of Housewives: Women's Wartime Columns in Two Mainstream Israeli Newspapers." *Nashim: A Journal of Jewish Women's Studies & Gender Issues* 15, no. 1 (Spring 2008): 88–107.

Korn, Alina, and Sivan Efrat. "The Coverage of Rape in the Israeli Popular Press." *Violence Against Women* 10, no. 9 (2004): 1056–74.

Kronish, Amy, and Costel Safirman. Israeli Film: A Reference Guide. Westport, CT: Praeger Publishers, 2003.

Lahav, Hagar. "The Defendant, the Nightmare, and the Clockwork Strawberry: A Case Study of Rape Coverage in the Israeli Press" [in Hebrew]. *Megamot* 46, no. 1/2 (2009): 86–108.

Lees, Sue. "Media Reporting of Rape: The 1993 British 'Date Rape' Controversy." In *Crime and the Media: The Post-Modern Spectacle*, edited by David Kidd-Hewitt and Richard Osborne, 107–30. London: Pluto Press, 1995.

Liebelt, Claudia. "Becoming Pilgrims in the Holy Land: On Filipina Domestic Workers' Struggles and Pilgrimages for a Cause in Israel." *Asia Pacific Journal of Anthropology* 11, no. 3–4 (2010): 245–67.

———. "On Sentimental Orientalists, Christian Zionists, and Working Class Cosmopolitans: Filipina Domestic Workers' Journeys to Israel and Beyond." *Critical Asian Studies* 40, no. 4 (2008): 567–85.

Los, Maria, and Sharon E. Chamard. "Selling Newspapers or Educating the Public? Sexual Violence in the Media." *Canadian Journal of Criminology* 39, no. 3 (July 1997): 293–328.

Loshitzky, Yosefa. *Identity Politics on the Israeli Screen*. Austin: University of Texas Press, 2001.

Lubin, Orly. "Body and Territory: Women in Israeli Cinema." *Israel Studies* 4, no. 1 (Spring 1999): 175–87.

———. "The Woman as Other in Israeli Cinema." In *Israeli Women's Studies: A Reader*, edited by Esther Fuchs, 301–16. New Brunswick, NJ: Rutgers University Press, 2005.

———. "The Woman as Other in Israeli Cinema." In *The Other in Jewish Thought and History: Constructions of Jewish Culture and Identity*, edited by Laurence J. Silberstein and Robert L. Cohn, 305–25. New York: New York University Press, 1994.

MacKinnon, Catharine A. *Feminism Unmodified: Discourses on Life and Law*. Cambridge, MA:

Harvard University Press, 1987.

Marsh, Kelly A. "Contextualizing Bridget Jones." *College Literature* 31, no. 1 (December 2004): 52–72.

Mayer, Tamar. "From Zero to Hero: Masculinity in Jewish Nationalism." In *Israeli Women's Studies: A Reader*, edited by Esther Fuchs, 97–117. New Brunswick, NJ: Rutgers University Press, 2005.

Mayne, Judith. *Cinema and Spectatorship*. New York: Routledge, 2002.

Mazali, Rela. "'And What About the Girls?': What a Culture of War Genders Out of View." *Nashim: A Journal of Jewish Women's Studies & Gender Issues* 6 (Fall 2003): 39–50.

Minghuan, Li. "Making a Living at the Interface of Legality and Illegality: Chinese Migrant Workers in Israel." *International Migration* 50, no. 2 (April 2012): 81–98.

Minkovitz, Moshe Shokeid. "Social Networks and Innovation in the Division of Labour between Men and Women in the Family and in the Community: A Study of Moroccan Immigrants in Israel." *Canadian Review of Sociology/Revue Canadienne de Sociologie* 8, no. 1 (February 1971): 1–17.

Mir-Hosseini, Ziba. "Negotiating the Forbidden: On Women and Sexual Love in Iranian Cinema." *Comparative Studies of South Asia, Africa and the Middle East* 27, no. 3 (2007): 673–79.

Mulvey, Laura. "Afterthoughts on 'Visual Pleasure and Narrative Cinema' Inspired by King Vidor's *Duel in the Sun*." *Framework*, no. 15 (Summer 1981): 12–15.

——. "The Oedipus Myth: Beyond the Riddles of the Sphinx." *Public*, no. 2 (1989): 19–43.

——. "Visual Pleasure and Narrative Cinema." In *The Sexual Subject: A Screen Reader in Sexuality*, edited by Laura Mulvey and Mandy Merck, 22–34. New York: Routledge, 1992.

Munk, Yael. "Ethics and Responsibility: The Feminization of the New Israeli Documentary." *Israel Studies* 16, no. 2 (Summer 2011): 151–64.

——. "The Postcolonial Function of Television's Virtual Space in '90s Israeli Cinema." *Framework: The Journal of Cinema and Media* 49, no. 1 (Spring 2008): 83–92.

——. "The Privatization of War Memory in Recent Israeli Cinema." In *Israeli Cinema: Identities in Motion*, edited by Miri Talmon and Yaron Peleg, 96–109. Jewish History, Life, and Culture. Austin: University of Texas Press, 2011.

Naaman, Dorit. "Orientalism as Alterity in Israeli Cinema." *Cinema Journal* 40, no. 4 (Summer 2001): 36–54.

——. "The Silenced Outcry: A Feminist Perspective from the Israeli Checkpoints in Palestine." *NWSA Journal* 18, no. 3 (Fall 2006): 168–80.

Naveh, Hannah, ed. *Gender and Israeli Society: Women's Time*. United Kingdom: Vallentine Mitchell, 2003.

Neroni, Hilary. *The Violent Woman: Femininity, Narrative, and Violence in Contemporary American Cinema*. Albany: SUNY Press, 2012.

Neumann, Boaz. *Land and Desire in Early Zionism*. Waltham, MA: Brandeis University Press, 2011.

Newman, David. "From Hitnachalut to Hitnatkut: The Impact of Gush Emunim and the Settlement Movement on Israeli Politics and Society." *Israel Studies* 10, no. 3 (Fall 2005): 192–224.

Nora, Pierre. "Between Memory and History: Les Lieux De Mémoire." *Representations* 26 (Spring 1989): 7–24.

Pappe, Ilan. "'Mada V'alila Bsherut Haleumiyout: Historiographia V'kolnoa Bsichsuch Haaravi-Yisraeli' (Science and Plot in the Service of Nationalism: Historiography and Film in the Arab-Israeli Conflict)." In *Mabatim Fictiviyim: Al Kolnoa Yisraeli (Fictive Looks:On Israeli Cinema)*, edited by

Nurith Gertz, Orly Lubin, and Judd Ne'eman, 92–119. Tel Aviv: Open University Press, 1998.

Peleg, Yaron. *Israeli Culture between the Two Intifadas: A Brief Romance*. Austin: University of Texas Press, 2008.

Popper-Giveon, Ariela, and Jonathan J. Ventura. "Blood and Ink: Treatment Practices of Traditional Palestinian Women Healers in Israel." *Journal of Anthropological Research* 65, no. 1 (Spring 2009): 27–49.

Projansky, Sarah. *Watching Rape: Film and Television in Postfeminist Culture*. New York: NYU Press, 2001.

Raijman, Rebeca, Silvina Schammah-Gesser, and Adriana Kemp. "International Migration, Domestic Work, and Care Work: Undocumented Latina Migrants in Israel." *Gender & Society* 17, no. 5 (2003): 727–49.

Redhead, Steve. *The Jean Baudrillard Reader*. Edinburgh: Edinburgh University Press, 2008.

Rimalt, Noya. "From Law to Politics: The Path to Gender Equality." *Israel Studies* 18, no. 3 (Fall 2013): 5–18.

Rosen, Marjorie. *Popcorn Venus: Women, Movies, and the American Dream*. New York: Coward, McCann and Geoghegan, 1973.

Rozin, Orit. "The Struggle over Austerity Policy: Israeli Housewives and the Government" [in Hebrew]. *Israel* 1 (2002): 81–118.

Safir, Marilyn P., Jessica Nevo, and Barbara Swirski. "The Interface of Feminism and Women's Studies in Israel." *Women's Studies Quarterly* 22, no. 3–4 (1994): 116–31.

Sanday, Peggy Reeves. *Fraternity Gang Rape: Sex, Brotherhood, and Privilege on Campus*. New York: NYU Press, 2007.

Sasson-Levy, Orna. "Feminism and Military Gender Practices: Israeli Women Soldiers in 'Masculine' Roles." *Sociological Inquiry* 73, no. 3 (August 2003): 440–65.

———. "Gender Performance in a Changing Military: Women Soldiers in 'Masculine' Roles." In *Israeli Women's Studies: A Reader*, edited by Esther Fuchs, 265–76. New Brunswick, NJ: Rutgers University Press, 2005.

Schammah-Gesser, Silvina, Rebeca Raijman, Adriana Kemp, and Julia Reznik. "'Making It' in Israel? Latino Undocumented Migrant Workers in the Holy Land." *Estudios Interdisciplinarios de America Latina y el Caribe (EIAL)* 11, no. 2 (2000): 94–119.

Schroeter, Daniel J. "The Shifting Boundaries of Moroccan Jewish Identities." *Jewish Social Studies* 15, no. 1 (Fall 2008): 145–64.

Sered, Susan Starr. "Replaying the Rape of Dinah: Women's Bodies in Israeli Cultural Discourse." In *Jews and Gender: The Challenge to Hierarchy*, edited by Jonathan Frankel, 191–208. Oxford: Oxford University Press, 2000.

———. *What Makes Women Sick? Maternity, Modesty, and Militarism in Israeli Society*. Waltham, MA: Brandeis University Press, 2000.

Shamir, Hila. "Migrant Care Workers in Israel: Between Family, Market, and State." *Israel Studies Review* 28, no. 2 (Winter 2013): 192–209.

———. "The State of Care: Rethinking the Distributive Effects of Familial Care Policies in Liberal Welfare States," *American Journal of Comparative Law* 58, no. 4 (Fall 2010): 953–86.

Shapiro, Maya. "The Development of a 'Privileged Underclass,' Locating Undocumented Migrant Women and Their Children in the Political Economy of Tel Aviv, Israel." *Dialectical Anthropology*

37, no. 3–4 (December 2013): 423–41.

———. "The Politics of Intimacy, (Re)Defining Class through Migrant Elder Care Relationships." In *When Care Work Goes Global: Locating the Social Relations of Domestic Work*, edited by Wenona Giles, Valerie Preston and Mary Romero, 177–201. United Kingdom: Routledge, 2013.

Sharoni, Simona. "Homefront as Battlefield: Gender, Military Occupation, and Violence against Women." In *Israeli Women's Studies: A Reader*, edited by Esther Fuchs, 231–46. New Brunswick, NJ: Rutgers University Press, 2005.

Shemer, Yaron. "Identity, Place, and Subversion in Contemporary Mizrahi Cinema in Israel." Doctoral dissertation, University of Texas at Austin, 2005.

———. *Identity, Place, and Subversion in Contemporary Mizrahi Cinema in Israel*. Ann Arbor: University of Michigan Press, 2013.

Shenhav, Yehouda, and Hannan Hever. "'Arab Jews' after Structuralism: Zionist Discourse and the (De) Formation of an Ethnic Identity." *Social Identities* 18, no. 1 (January 2012): 101–18.

Shilo, Margalit. "The Double or Multiple Image of the New Hebrew Woman." *Nashim: A Journal of Jewish Women's Studies & Gender Issues* 1 (Winter 1998): 73–94.

Shohat, Ella. "The Cinema of Displacement: Gender, Nation, and Diaspora." In *Dreams of a Nation: On Palestinian Cinema*, edited by Hamid Dabashi, introduction by Edward Said (London: Verso, 2006), 100.

———. *Israeli Cinema: East/West and the Politics of Representation*. Austin: University of Texas Press, 1989).

———. *Israeli Cinema: East/West and the Politics of Representation*. Revised edition. London: I.B. Tauris, 2010.

———. "Making the Silences Speak in Israeli Cinema." In *Israeli Women's Studies: A Reader*, edited by Esther Fuchs, 291–300. New Brunswick, NJ: Rutgers University Press, 2005.

Staiger, Janet. *Perverse Spectators: The Practices of Film Reception*. New York: NYU Press, 2000.

Stern, Bat-Sheva Margalit. "Who's the Fairest of Them All? Women, Womanhood, and Ethnicity in Zionist Eretz Israel." *Nashim: A Journal of Jewish Women's Studies & Gender Issues* 11 (Spring 2006): 142–63.

Stoler-Liss, Sachlav. "'Mothers Birth the Nation': The Social Construction of Zionist Motherhood in Wartime in Israeli Parents' Manuals." *Nashim: A Journal of Jewish Women's Studies & Gender Issues* 6 (Fall 2003): 104–18.

Swendson, Shanna. "The Original Chick-Lit Masterpiece." In *Flirting with Pride and Prejudice: Fresh Perspectives on the Original Chick-Lit Masterpiece*, edited by Jennifer Crusie, 63–69. Dallas: BenBella Books, 2005.

Swirski, Barbara, and Marilyn P. Safir, eds. *Calling the Equality Bluff: Women in Israel*. Oxford: Pergamon Press, 1991.

Szobel, Ilana. "'Lights in the Darkness': Prostitution, Power and Vulnerability in Early Twentieth-Century Hebrew Literature." *Prooftexts* 34, no. 2 (Spring 2014): 170–206.

Talmon, Miri. *Blues Latzabar Haavud: Havurot Venostalgia Bakolno'a Israeli* [Blues for the Lost Sabra: Community and Nostalgia in Israeli Cinema]. Tel Aviv: Open University, 2001.

Tanvir, Kuhu. "Interview: Eran Riklis." *Wide Screen* 1, no. 1 (April 2009).

Tirosh, Yoffi. "'Efes Beyahasei Enosh'? Al Hakav Hamehaber Beyn M16 Le-Ekdah Sikot" [Zero Motivation: The Connection between an M16 and a Staple Gun]. *Te'oriya U-bikoret* 43 (Fall

2014): 301–13.

Toren, Nina. "Intersection of Ethnicity, Gender and Class: Oriental Faculty Women in Israel." *Gender Issues* 26, no. 2 (June 2009): 152–66.

Umanit, Irit. "Violence against Women." In *Jewish Feminism in Israel: Some Contemporary Perspectives*, edited by Kalpana Misra and Melanie S. Rich. Waltham, MA: Brandeis University Press 2003.

Weiss, Meira. *The Chosen Body: The Politics of the Body in Israeli Society*. Stanford, CA: Stanford University Press, 2004.

———. "Mother, Sister and Soldier: Recollections from the Gulf War" [in Hebrew]. *Te'oriya U-bikoret 3* (Winter 2005): 235–46.

Williams, Linda. "'Something Else Besides a Mother': *Stella Dallas* and the Maternal Melodrama." In *Feminism and Film*, edited by E. Ann Kaplan. Oxford: Oxford University Press, 2000.

Wolosky, Shira. "Foucault and Jewish Feminism: The *Mehitzah* as Dividing Practice." *Nashim: A Journal of Jewish Women's Studies & Gender Issues* 17 (Spring 2009): 9–32.

Yosef, Raz. *Beyond Flesh: Queer Masculinities and Nationalism in Israeli Cinema*. New Brunswick, NJ: Rutgers University Press, 2004.

———. *The Politics of Loss and Trauma in Contemporary Israeli Cinema*. Routledge Advances in Film Studies Series 8. New York: Routledge, 2011.

Zanger, Anat. "Blind Space: Roadblock Movies in the Contemporary Israeli Film." *Shofar: An Interdisciplinary Journal of Jewish Studies* 24, no. 1 (Fall 2005): 37–48.

———. "Filming National Identity." In *The Military and Militarism in Israeli Society*, edited by Edna Lomsky-Feder and Eyal Ben-Ari, 261–79. Albany: SUNY Press, 2012.

———. *Place, Memory and Myth in Contemporary Israeli Cinema*. London: Vallentine Mitchell, 2012.

———. "Women, Border, and Camera: Israeli Feminine Framing of War." *Feminist Media Studies* 5, no. 3 (2005): 341–57.

Zerubavel, Yael. "Coping with the Legacy of Death: The War Widow in Israeli Films." In *Israeli Cinema: Identities in Motion*, edited by Miri Talmon and Yaron Peleg, 84–95. Jewish History, Life, and Culture. Austin: University of Texas Press, 2011.

———. *Recovered Roots: Collective Memory and the Making of Israeli National Tradition*. Chicago: University of Chicago Press, 1995.

Index

3 Times Divorced, 20, 259n3, 281
5 and 5, 67–68, 278
3000 Layla, 20, 281

Abargil, Linor, 33, 198–201, 210–11; legal case, 200. See also *Brave Miss World*
Abbas, Hiam 20, 22, 25, 49–50, 52, 55–56, 59, 61, 182, 277, 278, 279. *See also* Palestinian woman
Abecassis, Yaël, 22, 172
abject, 140, 161–62, 169–70, 215
abortion, 47, 136, 167, 210, 216
absence, 7, 12–13, 17, 33, 39, 42, 46, 66, 85, 242–43; structured, 21
absolution, 114, 117–18
abuse, act of, 57, 85, 104, 113–15, 134, 161–62, 166, 171, 174, 184, 189, 199–209, 213–17, 226, 235–37, 259n3
abuses: domestic, 181, 191; human rights, 56
Academy Awards, Palestinian entry, 61
accented cinema, 20
accordion, 106
activism, 27–28, 34, 63, 105, 203, 210–11, 218, 233, 237, 241–42, 244, 275n38; Abargil's, 200, 217; antirape, 195 (*see also* rape); Palestinian, 63, 224; political, 85, 201, 205
activist filmmaking, 206
activists: citizen rights, 11; gay rights, 33; migrant, 230
actors, 15, 19, 94, 152, 167, 169, 172, 175, 180, 207, 213–14, 216, 239–40; as activists, 230, 275n38; comic, 116; as influential figures, 9, 16, 22, 25, 49, 61, 182, 246–47, 250n25, 250n27; turned directors, 22, 246; religious, 104; theatre, 8, 19
Adama Meshuga'at. See *Sweet Mud*
adaptation, *Song of the Siren*, 33, 35–36, 38
adoption, 3, 200, 216
adulthood, 52, 178–79

advancement: professional, 70, 168, 242; of women, 27, 78
advertising broadcasts, daily, 239
advocacy, 191, 206–7, 275n38; GLBT, 33
aesthetics (feminist), 15, 27, 96, 180
affluence, 213–14, 234
Af Milah L'Morgenstein. See *Don't Tell Morgenstein*
Agency: advertising, 32, 34–35; care-providing, 221, 224, 226; religious men's, 99; women's, 49, 55–56, 106, 109, 114, 179, 190; women's lack of, 11, 17 55, 59, 61, 76, 83, 96, 101, 158, 198, 215
Agenda: Mizrahi feminist, 12; religious feminism, 94, 105, 122; feminist, 27–28, 182; film-making, 28, 182; gay, 35; Gesher Film Fund, 93; male-centered, 206; peace, 86; political, 187, 248; positive discrimination, 245; progressive, 26
aggression, 18, 174–75, 177, 199, 205, 240
aging, 120, 175, 177, 224, 246
agricultural community, 173. *See also* kibbutz; moshavim
agricultural labor, 3, 67, 74, 77, 149, 225, 228
agriculture, seasonal, 228
Agudath Israel, 106
Ahad Mi Shelanu. See *One of Us*
Ahava Colombianit. See *Colombian Love*
Ahi, 142
Ahoti, 142, 247
Ahoti HaYafa. See *My Lovely Sister*
airbrushed models, 183
air raids, 40
air stewardess, 231
alarm sirens, 37
alcohol, 176, 211, 219
Alfred Lord Tennyson, 99
Alice in Wonderland, 167
alienation, 69, 96, 123, 205
Allenby 40, 218, 268n23, 271n78. *See also*

rape cases
allure, suggested sexual, 4, 103, 152, 160, 178, 188
Ally McBeal, 36–38
Almagor, Gila, 8–9, 16, 135, 155–56, 163–64, 167, 169, 195, 246, 250n25, 250n27 259n29
Almodovar, Pedro, 146
Aloni, Shulamit, 11
Alter, Robert, 123
Alterman, Nathan, 154
The Ambassador's Wife, 235–37, 277
American Cinema, 188, 218, 252n46, 264n9. *See also* Hollywood
American culture, Latin, 229
American high school experience, 67. *See also* youth culture
American-led feminism, 191
American peace movement, 67
American slang, 142
Amir, Yigal, 108–9
amnesty (undocumented children), 230, 232
Amotz, Dan Ben, 155
Amsallem, Reymond, 22, 145
amulet, 134, 141–42, 144
anal stage, 177
Anashim Ketumim. See *Orange People*
androcentrism, 91
androgeneity, 155
androgynous, 150, 158
anger, 102, 115, 133, 142, 158, 171
Anglo-American romance (heroine), 32, 36. *See also* chick-flick
Ani Ohev Otach Rosa. See *I Love You Rosa*
Ankari, Etti, 127
Annihilation: national, 3, 41, 44; women's, 98, 165, 181
Anthony, Susan B., 37
anti-Arab sentiment, 108
anti-deportation message, 230
antiestablishment, 158
anti-heroes, 19
antinational, 137
antirape activists, 195. *See also* rape
anti-Semitism, 3, 149

anti-war, 70
anti-Zionist, 92
anxiety, 149, 156–57, 165, 177, 205, 212: castration, 5; existential, 21, 34; male, 98, 157, 183, 205
apparition, 143–44
apron, 55, 120
Arab, 10, 14, 20, 25, 50, 54, 63–64, 83, 87, 118, 123, 138, 144–45, 157–58, 205, 244–45
Arab authority, 53
Arab citizens, 54, 66, 82–83, 87; profiling, 83
Arab directors, female, 201, 216, 252n47. *See also* Palestinian women filmmakers
Arab feminists, 12
Arabi, Sajil Ana, 20, 282
Arab-Israeli conflict, 24, 34, 39, 49, 56, 64, 85, 134, 189, 206, 220, 245
Arab-Israeli woman, 17
Arab-Jewish relationships, 57
Arab-Jewish societies, 132. *See also* Mizrahi
Arab-Jewish women filmmakers, 21. *See also* Mizrahi women filmmakers
Arab Jews, 126, 142, 146. *See also* Mizrahi
Arab males, 66, 205
Arab masculinity, 10
Arab peasants, female, 86
Arab populations, 135
Arabs, cast as antagonists, 4, 16, 86, 139, 198
Arab Women, 61, 82–83, 221, 251n30. *See also* Palestinian women
Arab world, 20–21, 63, 125, 134, 145, 273n21
Arak, 141
Aramaic, 54
Ardent, Fanny, 117
Argov, Sasha, 194
Armoni, Boaz, 271n1
army, 66–68, 70–78, 81–82, 85–87, 140, 154, 168, 230, 234, 242, 277. *See also* militarism; military
army base. *See* military base

army fatigues, 25
army unit. *See* military unit
Arraf, Suha, 20, 22, 60–61, 279, 281, 282
art films, 17–18
artistic community, 14, 18, 169, 221
artistic expression, 21, 61, 65, 207, 217
Ascher, Tova, 245, 277
Asfalt Tzahov. See *Yellow Asphalt*
ashamnu bagadnu, 114
Ashby, Justine, 128
Ashkenazi (Ashkenazim), 9–10, 20, 27, 56–57, 76, 124-25, 130-133, 135, 138, 140, 142, 146, 158–60, 163-64, 248, 250n25; comedies, 126; feminists, 12; hegemony, 10, 20, 76, 165, 169; hero complex, 10, 76, 86, 158–61, 166
Ashkenazification, 128–29, 140. *See also* Lehitashknez
Ashkenazi Judaism, 9, 137, 146
Ashkenazi-Mizrahi romance, 9, 125–26, 134, 229. *See also* bourekas films
Ashkenazi prostitute, 250n25. *See also* prostitute; prostitution
Ashkenazi women, 9, 140, 159–60
assailant, 195–98, 201, 206
assassination (of Yizhak Rabin), 108
Assassin Next Door, 25, 86, 161, 187, 277
assassins, female, 86
assault, 70, 113, 192–93
assimilation, 20, 86, 128, 140, 146, 168, 233; cultural, 129
asylum seekers, African, 234–35, 274n36
Atakav, Eylem, 252n48
Atalia, 10, 156, 173
Atlas Mountains, 132
At Li Layla. See *Next to Her*
atmosphere: hypersexual, 70; magical, 143
attacker, 80, 102, 188, 190, 197, 199–200, 202, 208
Atzmon, Anat, 169
Atzmon, Shmulik, 169
audience, 3, 9–10, 14–16, 33, 38, 55–56, 68, 80, 83–85, 93, 98, 104, 112–16, 121, 125, 132, 141, 146, 164–67, 174, 178–79, 207, 213, 215; European, 38; feminist, 15; Hebrew-speaking, 64, 145–46; international, 3, 13–14, 105; male, 93, 97, 100, 189
Aunt Clara, 10, 277
Auster, Paul, 254n15
auteur status, 33
authorities, 5, 52, 63–64, 78–79, 83–85, 87, 107, 132, 150, 167, 172, 206, 209, 217, 223; British, 5; Israel's military, 68; male, 53, 64, 111, 157, 202, 209, 248; rabbinical, 172
auxiliaries, 57, 59, 69, 72, 159
avant-garde film, 26, 221
Avdei Hashem. See *Voices from the Heartland: Slaves of the Lord*
Aviad, Michal, 22, 85, 149, 153, 201–6, 217, 242–43, 275n6, 279, 282
Avi Chai Foundation, 92–93
Avital, Mili, 231
Aviv, Nurith, 240
Aviva Ahuvati. See *Aviva My Love*
Aviva My Love, 20, 277
Aviya's Summer, 16–18, 277
Avodah. See *Labor*
awakening, women's, 18, 117
awards, 93–94, 240, 244, 246; Ophir, 31
ayin hara, 135
Ayoun al-Haramiya. See *Eyes of a Thief*
Ayzor Hofshei. See *Free Zone*
Azoulay Hasfari, Hanna, 20, 22, 182, 280

---

ba'alat tshuva, 118
babies, 40, 106, 167
Babylonia, 120
Bachur Shel Shuli. See *Shuli's Boyfriend*
Bakhtin, Mikhail, 133
Bakri, Mohammed, 63
Balada LeAviv HaBohe. See *Ballad of the Weeping Spring*
Ballad of the Weeping Spring, 138, 277
Bananot. See *Cupcakes*
The Band's Visit, 38, 127–28, 138, 145, 277
Banot, 17, 25, 27, 70, 73, 75–78, 80, 82, 84, 86–87, 127, 187–88, 277
Barash, 277
Barbash, Uri, 62

Barda, Meital, 99–100
Bardenstein, Carol, 138
Barkan, Yehuda, 183
bar mitzvah, 214
barrenness, 96–97, 106
Bar Ziv, Sharon, 280
basic training, 41
Bat-Adam, Michal, 15–16, 22, 240, 246, 252n42
bathing, 96, 171, 177, 219
bathrooms, 176, 212–13
battered women, 181, 191
battle, 33, 40, 42, 50-52, 60, 65–66, 69, 83, 113, 132, 246, 248: demographic, 154, 272n15
battle fatigues, 42
battlefield, 24, 39, 50, 59–60, 69, 80, 254n21
battle scene, 76
Baudrillard, Jean, 38–39, 42, 46–47
Beaufort, 69, 277
beauty, women's, 5, 8, 153, 183
beauty pageants, 8, 152
beauty parlor culture, 152
beauty queen, 151–53, 158–59, 165, 198, 264n9
Bechdel-Wallace test, 244–45
Bedouin, 66, 267n66
Bedouin woman, 259n3, 267n66
Beeri Case, 190. *See also* rape cases
Before Tomorrow, 15–16, 240, 277
Begley, Valerie, 43
behavior, 46, 63, 86, 95, 110–11, 118, 162, 175–76, 189, 192–93, 195–96, 215, 220: army's, 85; community's, 76, 115–16; correct female 75, 101–2, 106, 135, 182, 196–97; deviant, 6, 94, 112, 118, 129, 133, 146, 162, 173, 175, 209, 229
behind the Scenes, 213–14
Beit Din, 120
belief, 41, 135, 196, 211
Ben-Asher, Hagar, 173–74, 245, 267n64, 277, 280, 281
Ben Dor, Orna, 240
Ben-Gurion, David, 154, 162, 266n46

Ben Hur, 250n22, 264n9
Ben-Shaul, Nitzan, 62
Ben Zaken, 245
Ben-Zvi-Morad, Yael, 60, 63
Berber, 118, 139
bereavement, 111
besiegement, 155–56, 250n27
betrayal, 64, 108, 129, 181; sexual, 119, 144
betrothal, 105–6
Beyond the Walls, 17, 277
Bialik, Haim Nachman, 162, 258n2, 266n46
bias, male, 23, 103
Big Dan rape trial, 270n54. *See also* rape cases
Big Girl, 17, 252n45, 277
Bikel, Einat, 32
Bikur HaTizmoret. See *The Band's Visit*
Bilu, Vardit, 278
birth, 27, 70, 97, 104, 164, 181, 230
black-and-white, 206, 240, 250n24
Black Bus, 260n9, 277
black magic, 132, 136, 144
black panthers (American), 127. *See also* identity politics, black
black panthers (Israeli), 127. *See also* Mizrahi
Blazing Sands, 8, 51, 264n9, 277
blindness, 40, 215–16
blood, 140, 230
Bluebeard, 177
Blue Mountain, 124
Blues Lahofesh Hagadol. See *Late Summer Blues*
Bnei Akiva, 112
board games, 25, 46
body, *See* female body. *See also* Mizrahi body
body politic, 157–59, 162
Bogor, Nelly, 240
bomb, 108–9, 180
bomb shelter, 41, 45–46
bond, 170, 207, 222: affective, 228; female, 118
bonfire celebration, 112
border crossings, 51, 56, 64, 82

border guards, 272n15
borders, 49, 51–52, 54, 67, 115, 134, 224, 230, 235: Jordanian, 51; national, 25, 206; shifting, 24, 236; southern, 234
Boreg, 245, 277
born again (*baal tshuva*), 227
bourekas films, 9, 125–27, 133–34, 138, 146, 229
Bouzaglo, Haim, 62–63, 68, 278, 281
boys, 67, 74, 101, 111–15, 146, 197, 209–12, 214–15, 232; religious, 101; young, 157; young Chinese, 231
Bradshaw, Carrie, 36
braids, 74–75, 83
Braids, 17, 83, 277
Brandeis, Yochi, 34
Brave Miss World, 27, 198–201, 207, 215, 217, 277. *See also* Abargil, Linor
bravery, 39, 76, 198
Brazil, 233
Bread, 126–28, 277
breakdown, intergenerational, 223
breakups, 174, 180–81
breast cancer, 12
breasts, 98, 112, 153; exposed, 77. *See also* nudity
Brener, Baruch, 122
Brenner, Rachel, 86
Bridget Jones' Diary, 36–38, 254n15
British cinema, 5, 12, 127–28, 143
British colonial history, 138
British cultural theory, 15. *See also* Hall, Stuart
British feminist film scholars, 15, 251n38
British Mandate, 161
British police, 2
broker fees, 225, 228
brothels, 142, 161, 163. *See also* massage parlor
brother, 135, 142, 158–59, 168, 189, 212–14, 246
brotherhood, 191, 208
brother-in-law, 35, 232
brothers-in-arms, 151
brother's widow, 107

Brownmiller, Susan, 193, 207
Bruriah, 26, 116, 119–22, 277
Bruriah, Ma'aseh, 119, 121
brutality, 67, 72, 83, 86, 162
Buaron, Yacov, 242
Buhbut Case, 190. *See also* rape cases
Bukstein, Ania, 119
bureaucracy, 78, 163
The Burglar, 245, 277
burial, 246–47
burned-out settlement, 49
burning, public, 206
burning trees, 39
Burshtein, Rama, 21, 94, 105, 278
Burstein, Janet, 62
bus, 85, 127
bus stop, 101, 143
Bye Bye L'Ahava. See *Bye Bye to Love*
Bye Bye to Love, 27, 149, 180–82, 277
B'Zhutan, 107, 261n29. *See also* religious feminism

cable programming, 18
camaraderie, 17, 50, 55, 65, 67, 73–75, 232; homoerotic, 151; male, 69, 170
camera, 3–6, 18, 22, 24, 43, 55, 98, 102, 105, 110, 113, 121, 163, 166–68, 170–71, 176, 180, 239–40
camera crew, 113, 180, 200, 239-40
Campbell, Russell, 159, 162, 164–65
Campfire, 26, 94, 108–16, 188, 277
campus culture, 211
cancer, 132, 162, 247
candid camera films, 183
Cannes Film Festival, 221
Caramel, 21, 277
care, psychiatric, 210
Care Benefit, Long-Term, 224
care chain, global, 222. *See also* caregiving
careers, 8, 21-22, 33–34, 168, 179, 221, 223, 243, 246, 248, 264n9
care facilities, 233
caregiving, 107, 221–25, 227–28, 233, 235, 245, 273n22; Filipina, 221, 226
Carmel, Marco, 123, 146, 279

carnivalesque, 47
Carroll, Lewis, 167
Casablan, 250n24. *See also* Kazablan
Casbah, 69, 280
Casino Royale, 264n9
Castel-Bloom, Orly, 34
casting, 27, 67, 130, 179, 219, 234
castrating bitch, 60
castration, male anxiety, 5, 97
Cedar, Joseph, 26, 66, 108–9, 111–16, 277, 281
cemetery, 144–45, 245
The Cemetery Club, 246, 277
censorship, 21, 93, 104: intracommunity, 21
ceremony, 99, 117-118; incantation, 118; memorial, 68; public, 47
Chagall, Marc, 103
characters, 6, 22–23, 34, 36–37, 58, 69, 103, 105, 133, 135, 142, 144, 146, 162, 168, 183: lesbian, 17, 245; marginalized, 126; religious, 93
central female, 2, 4, 10, 17, 19, 21–22, 24, 28, 36, 43, 47, 69, 174, 183, 203, 205, 244–46, 250n22, 250n25. *See also* protagonists, female
central male, 3, 158, 183
chastity, 10, 27, 99, 135, 155, 158, 173, 196
chattel, 9, 69
chauvinism, male, 18
chavruta, 95. *See also* yeshiva
checkpoints, 51, 56–57, 224
CHEN (women's corp), 70, 75
Chen, BaoQi, 231
Chicago, Judy, 267n65
Chicago Palestine Film Festival, 61
chicken, male, 269n31
chicken farmer, 173
chicken house, 150
The Chickens, 193–94, 269n31
chick-flick, 31–32, 35, 38, 44, 46–47, 173, 254n15. *See also* Song of the Siren; Yana's Friends
chick lit, 31, 254n15
child, 11, 96–97, 104–5, 118, 151, 155, 157, 160, 175, 180–81, 216, 222–23, 225, 231–33; illegitimate, 267n62; male, 97; naïve, 126; now-shared, 232; retarded, 164
childbirth, 97, 105, 150
childhood, 20, 52, 62, 135, 176, 178, 215–16, 223; reenacts, 176
childhood home, 174-175, 179
childhood recollections, 216
childhood synagogue, 120
childlessness, 231
children, 40, 51–53, 60–61, 95–98, 117, 125, 129, 133, 150–51, 180–82, 202–3, 221–23, 225, 230–34, 272n13; disabled, 225; undocumented, 227, 230–31 (*see also* amnesty)
Chopin, Frederic, 80
Christ, 228
Christian, 10, 114, 227, 250n30; Evangelical, 227–28; Filipino, 227–28; Latinas 227–29
Christianity, 227
Christian schools, 230
Chyutin, Dan, 23, 91, 103
cinema club, 239
cinema industry, 236, 239–48
cinema's historiography, 15, 239–41
Cinemateque, 15, 242. *See also* Jerusalem Cinemateque; Haifa Cinemateque
cinematic history, 8, 20, 24, 239–41. *See also* historiography
Cinéma vérité, 43, 68
Circles, 17, 277
circumcision, 141
citizen rights activist, 11. *See also* activists
citizens, 39, 42, 54, 190, 224, 244, 230
citizenship, 27, 207, 225, 230, 233–34
city, 37–38, 40, 43, 46, 173, 210, 213, 229, 270n65; partitioned, 156; white, 230
cityscape, 156, 173
city's slums, 231
civilian violence, 209
civil law, 108
civil marriage, 92. *See also* marriage
civil rights movement, 12
Cixous, Hélène, 13

class (social), 125, 157–58, 163
classical cinema, 13. *See also* Hollywood
claustrophobia, 16, 42, 174, 202
cleanliness, 81, 152, 162
Close to Home, 25, 72, 82–87, 278
clothes, 74, 77, 80, 98, 117, 120, 131, 142, 166, 175, 192, 200, 214
cock, 195, 269n31. *See also* chicken, male
cock tease, 211
coercive sexual culture, 213; coffee, 69; making, 67, 78, 84
Cohen, Eli, 175
Cohen, Nir, 33–35
Cohn, Emanuel, 94
Cohn, Nurith, 94, 260n9, 279
Collective (women as), 181
collectivism, 7, 9–10, 13, 16, 42, 44, 64, 67, 70, 75, 84, 109, 126, 139, 150–51, 153–55, 165, 187, 196–98, 207–9, 214
college campuses, 66, 207–8, 211
college campus fraternities, 208
Colombia, 232
Colombian Love, 161, 278
colonialism, 60, 139
colonization, 160
color, 103, 126, 136, 138, 159, 163, 180, 182, 232; bright clothing, 42, 255n23; men of, 157; women of, 158, 160, 170
colorless, 126, 221
color satellite broadcasts, 239
combat, 38–39, 42, 59, 62, 71, 74, 76, 83–84
combat soldiers, 71, 74
combat units, 68, 77, 83, 87, 209
comedy, 11, 32, 67, 77, 94, 125–26, 146, 229; Askhenazi, 126; musical, 67; rape, 80
comic actor, 116
comic strip, 244
coming-of-age, 214
commanding officer, 2, 70, 73, 82, 85. *See also* mefakedet
commemoration practices, 131, 155
commodification, 168, 177, 213: sexual, 213–15
community, 91, 93, 95–97, 99, 103–9, 111, 113, 119–21, 125–26, 130, 133, 145–46. (*see also* Haredi and Ultra-Orthodox); agricultural, 173 (*see also* kibbutz and moshavim); artistic, 169, 221; datlash, 260n10 (*see also* dati lesheavar); disadvantaged, 142, 236
community networks, 147, 227
community service, 210
commuter suburb, 207
competitions, wet t-shirt, 218, 271n78
computer games, 42, 70, 78
condoms, 101–2
confession, 111–12, 114–15
conflict, 21, 25, 27, 29, 33–35, 40–42, 44, 47, 49–64, 85–87, 125, 128, 130–31, 206, 236–37; internal national, 39; Israeli-Palestinian, 49, 62
Conquest (sexual), 100
Consciousness (public), 39, 61, 196
consciousness raising, 190, 221, 237, 242
conscription, 54, 65, 67–68, 70, 73, 78, 192, 208. *See also* military service
consent, 49, 80, 211, 218–19; sexual, 96, 193, 196, 211
contingent labor, 243
control: patriarchal, 175, 216; sexual, 158, 174, 177
cooking, 35–36, 120
coproductions, 277
Corem, Efrat, 245, 277
corruption, 118, 126, 133–34, 157, 161–62
cosmetic services, 74. *See also* beauty parlor culture
costumes, 35, 39
counter-cinema, 12, 250–51
countryside rape case, 195, 207. *See also* rape cases
courthouse, 55–56, 59
courtroom, 210
courts, 52, 114, 117, 190, 192–93, 195, 206, 210–11
Cowie, Elizabeth, 154
cows, 111, 158
credit, screenwriting, 9
cricket, 139

crimes, 9, 126, 128, 160–61, 163–65, 171, 191, 193, 197–99, 202–3, 206, 211, 216, 218; petty, 163; sexual, 192 (*see also* rape cases); unprovoked violent, 198
criminality, 146, 151, 160, 163, 197
criminalization, 211
criminal underworld, 129, 158
criminology, 218
critics: female film, 240, 242 (*see also* Hamevakrot); male film, 239
Crows, 17, 252n45, 278
cultural context, 15, 188
cultural elite, 146
cultural hegemony, 229–30
culture, 65–66, 70, 72, 74, 146, 188–89, 195–97, 199, 209–12, 217–19; campus, 211; cinemateque, 15; contemporary, 190; drugs, 9, 76, 129, 160, 171, 219, 270n50 (*see also* drug culture); IDF, 65, 189, 191; Israeli set, 240; phallocentric, 96 107, 132, 153; popular, 71, 152, 159; religious Zionist, 109; secular Jewish, 114; sex-positive, 211
culture of silence, 199
Cupcakes, 245, 278
Cup Final, 63–64, 278
curly hair (coded Mizrahi), 266n38

Dabis, Cherten, 61
Dalia and the Sailors, 10, 278
Dalia VeHamalahim. See *Dalia and the Sailors*
Damari, Shoshanna, 2
Daniels, Jyoti Sarah, 98, 117
Danse éternelle. See Eternal Dance
Dar, Giddi, 281
Darcy, Mr. (*Bridget Jones' Diary*), 254n15
Dardashti, Galeet, 92–93
dati lesheavar, 95, 260n10. See also datlash
daughters, 17, 26, 60, 109, 111–13, 115, 117, 119–21, 126, 132, 140, 174–75, 179–80, 216, 222
Davidson, Boaz, 9, 126, 173, 183, 279
Day After Day, 64, 278
Dayan, Assi, 3, 70, 160, 216, 266n38, 278

Dayan, Nissim, 126, 279–80
Dayan, Tikva, 169
The Day We Met See also rape comedy
Dead End Street, 27, 160, 166–69, 278
death, 103, 126, 129–30, 132, 134–35, 138, 143, 145, 155, 168, 171, 247–48; civic, 207, 217
The Debt (2007), 25, 86–87, 259n29, 278
The Debt (2010), 259n29, 278
decency laws, 219
Deevon, Hava, 94
Dekel, Ayelet, 277
Delta Force, 252n46
deportation, 225–26, 229–35, 272n12, 272n13
De Quincy, Thomas, 114
Der Tel-Aviv-Krimi, 8, 278
desert, 4, 58, 65, 78–79, 82, 124, 136, 145, 267n66, 271n1
desertion, 40, 62
desk jockeys, 74
Desperado Square, 138, 278
Deuteronomy, 270n65
development (psychosexual), 176–78. *See also* Electra complex
development towns, 76, 78, 124–28, 133, 145, 164, 232
Devereaux, Mary, 6
deviance, 7, 91, 103, 118–19, 146, 159; sexual, 116, 161, 196; diaspora, 17, 65, 227
Director, Best, 246. See also *Zero Motivation*
directors, 10, 15–16, 22, 60, 63, 65, 68, 91–92, 94, 174, 180, 207, 213–14, 239–40, 242–44; artistic, 242; female, 15, 18–19, 22, 28, 61, 240, 243, 252n47 (*see also* Palestinian women filmmakers); Italian, 250n27 (*see also* Tofano, Gilberto)
dirty dishes, 78. See also washing dishes
disadvantaged communities, 142, 236
discrimination, 12, 19–21, 28, 70, 87, 116, 125, 135, 159, 191, 225, 240; institutionalized, 229; positive, 244; Repeating, 10; sexual, 73
disenfranchisement, 27, 65, 86, 96, 236, 246

300 - Index

Disengagement, 278
dishonorable conduct, 109
divorce, 18, 20, 92, 96, 98, 105, 107, 120, 129, 172, 180, 182, 246–48, 259n3
Dizengoff 99, 118, 173, 278
Doane, Mary Ann, 7, 105, 153, 159
documentary, early Zionist, 3, 41, 65
documentary films, 22, 55, 85, 94, 166, 187, 199–200, 203, 207, 239–41, 244, 246, 259n3
Doda Clara. See *Aunt Clara*
Dodina, Evgenya, 22, 85, 201, 204
Dolls, 20, 278
domestic labor, 126
domestic violence, 100
Dönmez-Colin, Gönül, 252n48
Don't Tell Morgenstein, 8, 278
Dor, Elisa, 229
Dorit Rabinyan, *Persian Brides*, 34
Dotan, Shimon, 280
drama, 4, 11, 16, 58, 130, 144, 157, 161
Dreifuss, Maya, 176–77, 179
dress, 8, 35, 75, 91, 95, 102, 120, 137–38, 144, 175, 180–81, 198, 200, 203, 212; black evening, 35, 180; civilian, 75; drug addict, 75, 270n50
drug culture, 9, 76, 129, 160, 171, 219
drunk, 126, 144, 218–19
drunken woman, 26, 102, 218, 271n78
Druze, 2, 22, 51, 53–54, 58
Duma. See *Dolls*
duties, 67, 70, 75, 82, 84, 86, 102, 129, 150–51, 155; domestic, 117, 167, 223; marital, 25, 104; women's, 78, 83, 154; women's military, 78
Dybbuk possessions, 263n29

earth, 114, 143, 231
earth mother, 150
Eastern Wind, 57, 157–58, 278
Educating Rita, 127
education, 12, 23, 73, 92–93, 95, 117, 121, 125, 127–28, 146, 226, 230, 233; limited, 125; religious, 116; women's, 91, 116, 119, 260n12

Efes BeYahasei Enosh. See *Zero Motivation*
Efrat, Sivan, 195–96
egalitarian ideals, 4, 35, 121, 173, 187, 219, 224
eggs, 173–74
Ein Harod, 153
Eize Makom Niflah. See *What a Wonderful Place*
Eldorado, 9, 160, 163–64, 167–69, 266n46, 278
Electra complex, 176–77. *See also* genital stage
An Electric Blanket Named Moshe, 160, 266n38, 278
Elizabeth Bennet, 38
Elkabetz, Ronit, 22, 85, 129–30, 135, 169–70, 182, 201, 204, 242, 246–48, 275n10, 278, 281; persona, 275n9
Elkabetz, Shlomi, 129, 246, 278, 281
Elon, Emuna, 34
emancipation, 21, 37, 150, 241
employment, 12, 86, 95, 226, 229, 235–37. *See also* Foreign Worker Program (FWP)
employment law, 225
employment policies, restrictive, 226
empowerment, 46, 56, 71, 173, 181, 200, 204–6, 227; female, 28, 47, 64, 76, 87, 95, 119, 232
Encoding/Decoding, 14, 68
equality, 4, 8, 11–12, 66, 104, 105, 107, 116, 149–50, 159, 236, 240
Eritrea, 234–35, 274n36
Eritrean ambassador, 235. See also *The Ambassador's Wife*
Eros, 59–60
erotica, 119, 193
eroticism, 98, 139, 150–51, 157, 164, 170, 178–79, 183, 188, 214–15
Eshet, Michaela, 110
Eshet HaGibor. See *The Hero's Wife*
Eshet HaShagrir. See *The Ambassador's Wife*
Eskimo Limon. See *Lemon Popsicle*
establishment, 9, 21, 57, 65, 80, 109, 116, 125, 137, 153, 172–73, 191, 207, 247;

religious, 92, 104, 116, 139, 197
Eternal Dance, 278
ethnic-feminist filmmaking, 26, 182. *See also* Mizrahi women filmmakers; Palestinian women filmmakers
ethnic filmmaking, 20. *See also* Mizrahi filmmaking; New Mizrahi Cinema; Palestinian Cinema
ethnicity, 2, 9, 12, 15, 19, 23, 25–26, 34, 62, 86, 89, 129–31, 158–61, 232–36
ethnic melodramas, 32
ethnic stereotypes, 9, 182
ethos, national, 7, 9, 41, 160
Etz Limon. See *Lemon Tree*
European Jewry, 3
Evangelical Christian, 227
Every Bastard a King, 40, 66, 69, 278
evil eye, 135, 141, 143
excise duties, 51
exclusion, 19, 109, 116, 127, 159
excommunication, 107, 121
execution, 32, 76
exile, 32, 119, 126; symbolic, 121
Exodus, 251n30, 278
exotic, 26, 157, 248
exoticism, 8, 61, 123, 129, 132
eye candy, 74, 245
Eyes of a Thief, 61, 278
Eyes Wide Open, 92, 121, 278
Eynaim Petukhot. See *Eyes Wide Open*

Facebook group, 243. *See also* The Women's Film Forum
factories, local, 125, 135
factory worker, 136
faith, 26, 67, 104, 227
faithlessness, 69
family, 41–42, 58, 60, 110, 112–13, 115, 129, 131–33, 135–37, 141–44, 146, 175–76, 181, 230; Moroccan, 134 (see also *Sh'chur* and *Shiva);* nuclear, 111, 223; traditional, 9, 167
family home, 167, 216, 223
family life, 21, 246
family purity, 95, 97. *See also* mikveh

fanaticism (religious), 108–9, 114; religious settler's, 134
fantasy: forbidden, 178; Hollywood escapist, 3; Oriental, 160, 165; rape-revenge, 72, 164, 217; sadomasochistic, 71, 157
The Farewell Party, 245, 278
farming, 124, 157–58
farming collectives, *See* kibbutz; moshavim. *See also* agricultural community
father, 51, 54, 101, 109–10, 115–16, 118, 121, 133, 135–36, 138, 140, 144, 174–77, 212, 216
A Feast for the Eyes: The Story of Israeli Cinema, 250n23
fecundity, 70, 136, 151, 170, 173; land's, 150–51
Fellow Traveler, 62–63, 68, 278
female body, 98, 105, 116–17, 136, 140, 149, 152–55, 159–62, 169–73, 175–76, 179, 183–84, 187–89, 196, 200, 203, 206, 209–10, 215–16. *See also* nudity
female experience, 12–13, 16, 61, 121, 123, 173, 181, 183, 188–89, 220, 233; shared, 19, 21, 198, 237
female exploitation, 173
female-focused stories, 17
female sexuality, 37, 149, 157–58, 160, 162, 174, 183, 212
female spaces, 24, 26, 75, 91, 119, 130–31, 140, 173, 180, 212, 232
female spectatorial pleasure, 7
female spectators, 4, 7–8, 13, 160; black, 251n38
female stereotypes, 68, 84, 240
female subjectivity, 16, 26, 28, 31, 73, 165, 168, 173, 179, 182–83, 237–38
feminine gaze, 55
femininity, 6–7, 12, 25, 43, 46–47, 50, 72–73, 75, 85– 86, 98, 107, 139, 150–52, 155, 157, 165, 174–75, 180, 190–91, 240
feminism, 12, 14, 16, 18–19, 21, 23–24, 28, 84, 106–7, 185, 187, 190–91, 248: American-led, 191; religious (Haredi/Ultra Orthodox), 12, 21, 105–7; second-wave, 4, 11, 105, 236; third-wave, 34, 182,

206, 236, 240; feminist activism, 11–12, 19, 24, 28, 87, 191, 217, 235–36, 239, 240–41; organized, 221, 240–42, 248
feminist filmmakers, 10–13, 15–16, 21–24, 26, 56, 62, 64, 87, 91, 94, 126, 128, 149, 183–84, 207, 214, 237–38, 239–48. *See also* Haredi women filmmakers; Mizrachi women filmmakers; Palestinian women filmmakers
feminist film theory, 5–7, 11, 13–16, 22–24, 42–44, 55–56, 76, 91, 97, 105, 113, 153, 159–61, 168–72, 178, 187–89, 209, 240
feminist manifesto, 247
feminist movement, 21, 33, 190, 211; Israel's, 12. *See also* feminist activism
feminists, 19–20, 25–26, 28, 73, 77, 79, 164, 166, 217, 219, 237, 240–41, 244: Jewish-Israeli, 20–21; liberal, 33; pioneering, 37; religious, 12, 21, 105; third-wave, 206, 236
fertility, 96–97, 136, 265n18
fertility treatment, 97
fetish, 137, 153
fetishization, 26, 98, 119, 157–58; scopophilic, 105
Fever at Dawn, 8, 278
Fiction: Israeli war, 71; women's, 34
Fictitious Marriage, 17, 62, 278
Filipina migrant workers. *See* Christian, Filipino; migrant workers
Fill the Void, 26, 93–94, 103-107, 278
film department, 240
film editor, 201–3, 240
film festivals, 18. *See also* Cannes Film Festival; Jerusalem International Film Festival; Rehovot Women's Film Festival); international, 94
film funds, 233, 239, 242–44 Gesher film fund; New Fund for Cinema and Television
film industry, 8, 19, 21, 23–24, 92, 233, 237, 239–44, 246; Haredi, 93
filmmaking, 14, 16, 21, 27–28, 33, 49–50, 56, 59, 62, 92, 123, 127-129, 174, 180, 183, 237, 239–41, 245; protofeminist, 17–18, 23, 166. *See also* documentary filmmaking; feminist filmmakers; Haredi women filmmakers; lesbian cinema; Mizrahi women filmmakers; Palestinian filmmakers
film schools, 18, 243
First World War. *See* World War I
Firth, Colin, 254n15
flâneur, 46
flirtation, 69, 159–60, 175, 177
fluids, bodily, 140, 162
folk religion, 26, 117–18, 123, 129–30, 136, 139. *See also* witchcraft; witches
Folman, Ari, 281
food, 36, 40, 151, 174, 176, 223
food engineer, 34–35, 45
football, 139
Foreign Worker Program (FWP), 225–26
foreign workers. *See* migrant workers
Fortuna, 9, 278
Fox, Eytan, 33, 35–36, 38, 245
Franco, Jean, 124
fraternity, 199
Freedman, Marcia, 11
freedom, 12, 59, 103, 150, 182, 237, 246; women's, 247
freedom fighters, 63
Free Zone, 25, 49–51, 58, 61–64, 278
Freud, Sigmund, 5
Friedan, Betty, 37
Friedlich, Hadar, 94, 260n9, 281
Friedman, Regine-Mihal, 23, 155
friendship, 69, 82, 104, 113, 182, 201, 204–5, 216; female, 113, 203
Frisch, Larry, 250n24
frontier life, 51, 74, 151
Fuchs, Esther, 57, 59–60, 71
funding (for filmmaking), 14, 18, 21, 28, 92–93, 126, 233, 240–41, 244
funeral, 132, 138, 143
funeral wailer, 123, 125, 127, 129–33, 135, 137, 139, 141, 143, 145, 147, 262–63n18
Furstenberg, Hani, 110

Gabai, Shira, 94, 260n9, 278
Galei Tzahal, 77

Galilee, 40, 157, 281
Galron, Hadar, 122
Gamliel, Tova, 130–31, 262–63n18
gang, the, 8, 208–9
Gang, The, 208–9
gang rape (*see also under* rape), 27, 164–65, 190, 207, 209, 211, 218–20, 270n54
gangster's moll, 9
Gaon, Yehoram, 3, 66, 155, 166–68, 193
garbage dump, 170
garbage truck, 171–72
gas masks, 39–40, 42, 44–45, 47, 132, 255n24
gay cinema, 31, 33, 35–36, 200, 245
gay homeless teens, 17
gay rights activists, 33
Gaza, 224
gaze, 3, 6, 22, 41, 49, 55–56, 98, 108, 110, 113–14, 168, 171, 203, 216, 237; historical, 14; male, 5–6, 11, 55, 77, 91, 97, 119, 160, 170–71, 173, 178, 189, 216, 245–46; occidental, 136; scopophilic, 98; secular, 10; voyeuristic, 178
Geffen, Shira, 245, 279
gender, 10, 12, 26, 33, 35, 42–43, 76, 84, 129–31, 165–66, 245
gender roles, 26, 38, 44, 84, 150
gender segregation, 121. *See also* Mehitzah
The General's Daughter, 73
genitalia (female), 176–77 180, 267n65
genitalia (male), 183
genital stage, 177. *See also* Electra complex
genre, 9–10, 23, 32, 36, 43–44, 59, 62, 67, 82, 87, 103, 124, 168, 173, 245: bourekas, 126, 138, 229; chick-flick, 35, 46, 254n15; heroic-nationalist, 41, 170, 264n9; Israeli war film, 39, 62, 65-87
Gera, Elida, 15–16
Gershenson, Olga, 42–44, 161
Gertz, Nurit. *See* Gertz Nurith
Gertz, Nurith, 3, 23, 63
Gesher Film Fund, 93, 244
Gesher Tzar Me'od. See *On a Narrow Bridge*
Gett. See *Gett: The Trial of Vivianne Amsalem*
Gett: The Trial of Viviane Amsalem, 129, 246–48, 278
Geva Studios, 240
Ghost, 143, 278
ghosts, 80, 141, 143–44, 263n29
Gibert, Lewis, 281
G. I. Jane, 73, 75
Gimlat Siuud. *See* Long Term Care Benefit
Ginsburg, Shai, 96, 105
The Girl, 260n9, 278
Gitai, Amos, 49, 61, 63–64, 69, 92, 97, 100, 161, 178
glass ceilings, 70, 78
GLBT advocacy, 33
G'mar Gaviya. See *Cup Final*
God, 104–5, 114, 117, 154, 227
Golan, Menahem, 3, 15, 250n24, 252n46, 266n46, 278
Golan Heights, 51, 53–54, 62
Golberg, Dana, 218–19
Goldenberg, Taly, 239, 279
Golden Globe, 9, 126
Goldstein, Baruch, 108
Gothic romance, 31
Gov, Gidi, 193
government, 39, 54, 99, 108, 161, 163, 224, 230, 232, 235, 239, 266n43, 272n15, 274n36; Iraqi, 17
government coalitions, 94; right-wing, 92
government-funded preschool programs, 233
government funding, 93, 243
government's deportation program, 230
Granit, Tal, 245, 278
Granot, Yuval, 161
grant, annual screenwriting, 241–42
graphic sex, 94
The Gravedigger's Daughter, 260n9, 278
Greek mythology, 37
Greenberg, Noa, 217
Greenhouse Program, 244
Grimmeisen, Julie, 152
Grossman, David, 123
grotesque, 133, 145, 175

Gulf War, 31–47, 132, 254n21
guns, 25, 39, 72, 80–82, 86–87; women wielding, 86
Gur, Aliza, 264n9
Gur, Batya, 34
Gur-Lavi, Boaz, 45
Guttman, Amos, 33

HaBat Shel Hakavran. See *The Gravedigger's Daughter*
Hadassi, Esther, 66
Haddad, Abeer Zeibak, 20, 278, 281
HaDiktator HaKatan. See *The Little Dictator*
Ha'eretz Hamuvtachat. See *Promised Land*
Hagigah Leeynaim. See *A Feast for the Eyes*
Hagoel, Evelin, 22, 145
HaHar. See *The Mountain*
HaHaverim Shel Yana. See *Yana's Friends*
HaHesder. See *A Time of Favor*
Hahi SheHozeret HaBayta. See *She's Coming Home*
HaHov. See *The Debt* (2007)
Haifa Cinemateque, 239
hairdressing classes, 227
hairstyles, 74
Haiyei Nesuim. See *Married Life*
Hajnali làz. See *Fever at Dawn*
HaKalah HaSurit. See *The Syrian Bride*
HaKayitz Shel Aviya. See *Aviya's Summer*
Halakha. *See* religious law
HaLahaka. See *The Troupe*
Halfon, Eyal, 161, 281
Hall, Stuart, 14, 23–24
Halutzah, 152
Halutzi, Yitzhak, 17, 277
HaMe'ahev. See *The Lover*
Hamesh Hamesh. See *5 and 5*
HaMeshotet. See *The Wanderer*
HaMevakrot, 242, 244. *See also* critics, female film
HaMilhama HaShniya. See *The Second War*
Hamsin. See *Eastern Wind*
Hannah Gonen, 11, 156, 158
HaNotenet. See *The Slut*
HaPoretzet. See *The Burglar*
Harareet, Haya, 2, 5, 8, 250n23, 264n9
harassment, 70, 192, 195
Harchek Miheadro. See *That Lovely Girl*
Haredi, 66, 91–96, 102–8, 120–21, 260n12, 260n13
Haredi film industry, 93–96, 103-108
Haredi rules, strict, 93
Haredi women filmmakers, 21, 26, 93–94, 103–7, 278. *See also* Burshtein, Rama
Harifai, Zaharira, 222
Harris, Rachel S., 194, 208, 259n3, 265n18
Hasfari, Shmuel, 20, 134
HaShiur. See *The Lesson*
Hasidism, 98. *See also* Haredi
Haskell, Molly, 4
HaSodot. See *The Secrets*
Hassidic fairy tales, 103
Hatarnegolim. See The Chickens
Hatunah B'Galil. See *Wedding in Galilee*
Hatuna Meuheret. See *A Late Marriage*
Hatzerim Air Base, 190
HaUshpizin. See Ushpizin
Havura SheKazot. See *What a Gang*
HaYelda. See *The Girl*
hayeled haboheh, 266n38
head coverings, 91
head scarf, 55
head teacher, 68, 176
healers, male, 135
healing, 200, 203, 205, 207
health, 21, 141, 153, 159
health care, 225, 227
health law, 223
Hebrew, 3, 49, 52, 131, 142, 145, 159, 222, 227, 229–31; religious, 131
Hebrew audiences, 64, 145–46
Hebrew cinema, 239
Hebrewism, 13, 17, 128, 152, 229–30
Hebrew literature, 123, 160
Hebron, 108
Heder 514. See *Room 514*
Hefner, Avraham, 277
Heise, Thomas, 160

Helm, Matt, 264n9
helpmates, accommodating, 67
Hendel, Yehudit, 34
Here Comes Mr. Jordan, 143
Héritage, 20, 279
Herma, Shimon, 280
hero, 3–4, 9, 18–19, 31, 47, 65, 67, 87, 133, 165, 195, 199–200; male, 7, 66, 160; national, 86, 153; heroic-nationalist genre, 41, 170, 264n9
heroine, 31, 36, 38, 41, 167, 179; advertising executive, 32; chick-lit, 31; modern urban, 38
heroism, 2, 4, 16–17, 39, 45, 67, 75–76, 158, 187; women's, 86
The Hero's Wife, 10, 239, 279
Herzl, Theodor, 149, 162, 266n46
Herzliya studios, 15, 239
Hesder, 66, 94, 108
hierarchies, 26, 66, 131, 138, 146, 159, 192, 198, 200, 209–10, 216, 220, 237; ethnic, 58, 138, 161; gendered, 70, 101, 124, 131, 254n21
highways, 161, 170
Hill 24 Doesn't Answer, 1–2, 4–6, 8, 13–14, 22, 41, 66, 264n9, 279
historical drama, 17, 183
Hitganvut Yehidim. See *Infiltration*
Hitnatkoot. See *Disengagement*
Hofshat Kaitz. See *My Father My Lord*
Hogg, James, 114
A Hole in the Moon, 151–52, 279
Hollander, Philip, 115, 261n34
Hollywood films, 3–4, 7, 13, 27, 31–33, 152, 157, 252n46, 263n29, 264n9
Hollywood's Golden Age, 4, 13
Hollywood starlets, 8, 264n9
Hollywood's war films, 59
Holocaust, 6, 16–17, 34, 114, 123–24, 154
Holocaust films, 18, 23
Holocaust memorialization, 142
Holocaust survivor, 2
Holot Lohatim. See *Blazing Sands*
holy days, high, 114
Holy Land, 227–28

holy sites, 227, 229
home, 25, 39–41, 52–53, 69, 71–72, 76, 82, 84–87, 95, 144–45, 173–74, 178–79, 214–15, 222–23, 226–28
homecoming, 40, 61
Homefront woman, 60
Home Guard, 89
homeland, 3, 60, 66, 69, 109, 149
homemakers, traditional, 71, 126. *See also* housewife
homoerotic interactions, 151, 157–58, 188, 207
homosexuality, 95
homosocial bonding, 11
honey trap, 69
Hor B'Levana. See *A Hole in the Moon*
Horeck, Tanya, 190, 207, 211, 220
Horn, Shifra, 34
Horowitz, Yariv, 69, 280
hospital, 101, 170, 222–23, 254n21
hospitality, 228
hotel, 40–41, 163, 176–77, 179, 203, 221, 234, 274n36
house, 53, 126, 131, 139, 144, 158, 161, 174–76, 179, 210; abandoned, 76; chicken, 150; children's, 150
housewife, 8, 46, 81, 152–53. *See also* homemaker
housing, 92, 125, 227
housing plans, 126
Hovevei Zion, 38, 264n1
Hudson, Dale, 161
humanitarian issues, 230
The Human Resources Manager, 230, 233, 279
human rights, 56, 85, 233–34
human rights abuses, 56
human rights law, 225
human trafficking, 161, 231, 266n43. *See also* white slave trade
husband, 51–55, 58–59, 63–64, 69–70, 95–98, 101–2, 104, 110–11, 120–21, 139–41, 144, 154–55, 172, 203, 246
husband cheating, 139, 181
husband's authority, 64, 259n3

husband's death, 155
husband's identity, 51
hysteria, 11, 45, 79, 129, 131–32, 171, 181, 199, 234, 248

identity, 51, 128–29, 138, 140, 154, 156, 177–78, 180, 205, 208; female, 158, 180; intersectional, 140; women's, 49, 182
idenity cards, 82
identity politics, 12, 14, 23, 33, 47, 123; black, 191
IDF, 57, 65, 70–71, 73–74, 87, 189–90, 209, 259n28. *See also* army; militarism; military
idyll, rural, 37, 124
I Love You Rosa, 10, 279
images, photographic, 69
Imberman, Shmuel, 67, 278
Imi HaGeneralit. See *My Mother the General*
incantation, 44, 117–18, 134
Indian Jews, 138–40, 225
Indians, Native American, 4
infertility, 105. *See also* fertility
Infiltration, 79, 279
ingénue, 117, 179
interethnic conflict, 38
international competitions (Miss World), 152
International Women's Day, 247, 275n10
International Women's Film Festival, 241
intersectionality, 76, 129, 140, 236, 247; Mizrahi female's, 129–31, 247. *See also* Ronit Elkabetz
intifada, 47, 69; Second, 82
investigator, female military, 72, 83
Invisible, 27, 85, 188, 201–7, 279
Iranian Cinema, 126, 252n48
Iranian culture, 20
Iranian Jews, 138
Iraqi missile attacks, 37–38, 43
Irigaray, Luce, 13
Islamic world, 9, 20–21
Israeli authorities, 20, 52, 108, 259n3
Israeli Cinema-Herstory, 252n42

Israeli Film Archives, 239
Israeli film awards. *See* Ophirs
Israeli government, 38, 52, 58, 92, 224, 235, 274n36
Israeli law, 226, 230
Israeli masculinity, 10, 41, 69
Israeli nationalists, 54
Israeli-Palestinian Conflict, 24, 34, 39, 49–64, 85, 108, 134, 189, 206, 220, 245
Israeli-Palestinian peace process, 108
Israeli soldiers, 82, 201, 205–6 (*see also* soldiers; IDF); captured, 68
Israeli soldier's humanity, 69
Ivgy, Dana, 22, 169
Ivgy, Moshe, 161, 280

Jacir, Annemarie, 20, 61, 280, 281
Jaffa, 38, 163, 279
Jameson, Frederic, 124
Jaradat, Mya Guarinieri, 226, 272n13, 272n15, 273–74n26
jealousy, 144, 167, 221; mother's, 179
Jeffords, Susan, 198
Jellyfish, 27, 221–23, 228, 237, 279
Jenin, Jenin, 63, 279
Jerusalem, 37, 40–41, 72, 82, 93, 127, 141, 156, 239, 246; East, 230
Jerusalem Cinemateque, 239
Jerusalem International Film Festival, 239
Jerusalem zoo, 120
Jesus, 114
Jewish, 7, 92, 96, 131, 141, 149, 154, 157, 210, 213, 246, 250n30, 259n3 (*see also* Haredi); American, 11
Jewish-Arab ethnicity, 2. *See also* Mizrahi
Jewish learning, informal, 92
Jewish liturgy, 97
Jewish Underground, 108
Jews: attacked, 65; Diaspora, 2, 65, 74; Haredi (*see* Haredim); Indian, 138; Iranian, 138; national-religious, 66; nonobservant, 97; North African, 126, 143–47 (*see also under* Mizrahi); Oriental, 123, 128–30, 137–39, 142, 160, 165, 182 (*see also under* Mizrahi); religious, 99 (*see*

Index - 307

also under Haredi); Yemenite, 131
Jezreel Valley, 40
jobnicks, 74, 80
Joe + Belle, 245, 279
Johnston, Claire, 12
Jordan, 51, 143, 156, 279
Jordanian border, 51
Jordanian landscape, 49
journalist, 202, 226, 230; CNN, 39; female, 64
Judaism, 103, 227, 260n12
Judea, 108
Judean desert, 267n66
Judeo-Arabic, 146
judges, 210
judgment, 210, 183
Julia Mia, 161, 279
junior officer, 75
jury, 246
jus sanguins, 230
justice, 47, 183, 191, 199, 207, 210, 217, 248; tribal, 267n66

Kabbalah, 116–17
Kadosh, 26, 91–93, 96–105, 116–17, 120–21, 178, 187, 279
Kafka, Franz, 78
Kahan, Dalit, 45
Kahane, Meir, 108. *See also* makhteret
Kalat HaYam. See *Jaffa*
Kanot, Shay, 161, 278
Kaplan, Danny, 42, 254n15
Kaplan, E. Ann, 6–7, 12, 27
Karov La Bayit. See *Close to Home*
Karp Report, 191
Katmor, Jacques, 183, 281
Katzav, Moshe, 190
Katzir, Yehudit, 34
Kayam, Yaelle, 245, 279
Kayitz group, 250n27
Kazablan, 9, 250n24, 279. See also *Casablan*
Kedar, Veronica, 279
Keller, Helga, 239
Kenan, Amos, 279
Kenig, Maya, 245, 280

Keret, Etgar, 279
Khatib, Lina, 252n48
Khelifi, Michel, 60, 281
Khirbet Khizeh, 68, 279
kibbutz, 40, 67, 69, 78, 150, 153, 173, 209, 225
kibbutz (in film), 67–69, 126, 153, 156, 163, 173. See also *Atalia; Sweet Mud; The Slut*
kibbutz movement, 126, 163, 173
Kibbutz Shomrat case, 190, 209. *See also under* rape cases
Kikar HaHalomot. See *Desperado Square*
kindergarten, 227
Kippur, 40, 279
Kir, Sadak, Dima'ah. See *Wall, Crack, Tear*
Kirot. See *My Neighbor the Assassin*
Kishniev pogrom, 258n2
Kishon, Ephraim, 3, 15, 126, 280
kisses, 32, 75, 82, 101, 112, 118, 146, 176, 214
kissing scenes, 214
kitchen, 2, 35, 78, 110, 216
Klausner, Margot, 15, 239, 248
Klein, Shani, 79
Klein, Uri, 248
klezmer, 118
Knesset, 243
Kollek, Teddy, 239
Kolirin, Eran, 127, 277
Kol Mamzer Meleh. See *Every Bastard a King*
Korman, Asaf, 245, 280
Korn, Alina, 195–96
Kotel. *See* Wailing Wall
Kristeva, Julia, 13, 140, 161
Kushnir, Avraham, 120
Kvish L'lo Motzah. See Dead End Street

Labaki, Nadine, 21, 252n49, 277, 281
Labor, 277
labor (Zionist ideology), 3, 67, 157, 160, 162. *See also* Labor Zionism
labor (foreign). *See* Foreign Worker Program (FWP); migrant workers
labor laws, 226
labor rights, 142

labor shortages, 224–26
Labor Zionism, 3–4, 20
Lacan, Jacques, 5
Ladino, 229
Lady Kul el Arab, 20, 279
Lag Ba'Omer, 112
Lahav, Hagar, 192–93
Lakahat Isha. See *To Take a Wife*
Lamma Shoftak. See *When I Saw You*
land, 2–3, 26, 40–41, 52, 60–62, 67, 82, 86, 109, 111, 149, 151–52, 157–58
Landesman, Mooli, 239, 248, 280
land mines, 156
landscape, 37–38, 46, 69, 82, 111, 124, 126, 135, 138–39, 142–43, 145–46, 152, 170; nostalgic, 20; urban, 40; Western frontier, 4
languages, biblical, 210
Lanzmann, Claude, 281
A Late Marriage, 26, 38, 140, 246, 279
Late Summer Blues, 68–69, 77, 86, 279
Latina, 229
Latin America, 123, 229
Latin American culture, 229
Latina migrant workers. *See* migrant workers
Latorre, Ma-nenita De, 222
laundry, 38, 139, 150, 223
Lavie, Arik, 3
Lavie, Daliah, 264n9
Lavie, Efrat, 11
law, 64–66, 85, 95, 97, 108, 114, 159, 161, 190–91, 193, 199, 208, 210, 213, 221–25, 235–36, 239, 259n3, 266n43; biblical, 107–8; Israel's decency, 219; religious, 26, 95, 104, 107, 111, 116, 129, 131, 246
lawyer, 163, 218
Lazslo, Hannah, 22, 49–50
Lebanese society, 252n49
Lebanese War Cinema, 252n49
Lebanon, 69, 279
Lebanon, 9, 63, 68–69, 277, 279
legal system, 201, 203, 207, 210
Lehem, 126-127, 277
Lehitashknez, 128. *See also under* Ashkenazification
Leibrecht, Savyon, 34

Lemaleh et HaHalal. See *Fill the Void*
Lemarit Ain. See *Out of Sight*
lemon grove, 52, 60
Lemon Popsicle, 173, 279
lemons, pickling, 60
Lemon Tree, 25, 49–50, 52–56, 59–61, 63–64, 279
Lerski, Helmar, 277
lesbian cinema, 245
The Lesson, 260n9, 279
Letters to Brezhnev, 262n7
Levant, 54
levirate marriage, 107, 213
Levitan, Nadav, 17, 70, 277
Lia, 239
Liebelt, Claudia, 227
life-cycle events, 130
Lifnei Mahar. See *Before Tomorrow*
Light Out of Nowhere, 126, 279
liminal time, 130
liminal spaces, 25, 49, 51–52, 55, 128
Linor, Irit, 31–35, 38, 254n15
Lipaz-Michael, Rona, 54, 56, 59
lipstick, 35, 46, 75, 176–77
A Little Bit of Luck, 9, 279
The Little Dictator, 260n9, 279
live-in migrant workers, 223–26. *See also* migrant workers
livelihood, 58, 60, 205, 247
local community, 207
local councils, 163, 209
local film industry, 3
Loevy, Ram, 68, 126, 277
Long-Term Care Benefit, 224
looked-at-ness, 167, 203
Lord Jim, 264n9
Lo Roim Aleich. See *Invisible*
Loshitzky, Yosefa, 23, 57, 138, 157–58
Love: forbidden, 32, 57, 64, 118; homoerotic, 151, 157; sexual, 146; True, 34; unrequited, 99. *See also* love stories
love affair, 40; aborted, 129; enduring, 67
love nest, 158
The Lover, 57, 279
lovers, 2, 9, 43, 57, 79–80, 84, 129, 179,

203, 231, 279; long lost, 43; star-crossed, 58, 129
love stories, 57, 64, 152, 229, 240. *See also* love
luftmenschen, 149
lust, 102, 130, 136

Ma'agalim Shel Shishi Shabat. See *Circles*
Ma'aleh school, 94
Ma'aseh Bruriah. *See* Bruriah, Ma'aseh
MacDonald, Karen, 59
Machsom Watch, 56–57
Mackinnon, Catharine, 193, 211
Madame Rosa, 161, 279
madness, 16, 97–99, 130, 156; female, 156; mother's, 17
Madonna, 132, 150, 196
Magash Hakesef. See *Fellow Travelers*
magazine, 152, 163; Laisha, 152
magazine aid, 101
magazine culture, 152
Magdalene, Mary, 102
magic, 49, 134–36, 139, 141, 143
magical potion, 139
magical realism, 123–24, 141, 145–46
magic ritual, 136
maids, 226, 228
Makhteret. *See* Jewish Underground
Makom L'yad Hayam. See *A Place by The Sea*
male fantasies, 26, 153, 158, 182
Malkat Hakvish. See *Queen of the Road*
manifesto, 32, 248
Al-Mansour, Haaifa, 21
Maoz, Samuel, 279
Mara'ana-Menuhin, Ibtisam Salh, 20, 259n3, 280, 281, 282
marat ayin, 111
marginalization, 11, 26, 76, 80, 87, 107, 109, 115, 123, 130, 145, 156, 207, 220; ethnic, 128, 166, 237; female, 22, 136, 139, 237
marginalized place, 7, 68, 87
marital infidelity, 177
Maron, Hanna, 169

Maron, Maya, 110
marriage, 32, 36, 38, 95–98, 100–101, 107, 116, 118, 156, 159, 171–72, 175, 181–82, 246, 259n3, 260n13; arranged, 99; levirate, 107, 213
marriage bed, 98
married life, 173. *See also* marriage
married woman, 66, 91, 159
Martin, Dean, 264n9
martyr (female), 1–3, 156
martyr (male), 102, 119
Masa Alunkot. See *The Paratroopers*
masculine women, 60
masculinity, 2–3, 6, 8, 10, 14, 17, 25, 32, 35, 39, 43, 63, 66, 70, 72–73, 75, 78, 81–84, 87, 154, 174, 180, 193, 195, 205
masks, 37, 40, 42, 45–46; gas, 39–40, 42, 44–45, 47, 132, 255n24
masochistic, 164
masquerade, 39, 84, 180, 192
massage parlors, 161. *See also* brothels
mass media, 42. *See also* media
masturbation, 101, 177–79
Matalon, Ronit, 34
matchmakers, 95, 260n13
matriarch, 34, 60–61, 119, 123, 127–29, 131–32
Matzor. See *Siege*
May in the Summer, 279
Maymon, Sharon, 246, 278
Mayne, Judith, 7
Mazali, Rela, 192
MeAhorai HaSoragim. See *Beyond the Walls*
no means no, 195. *See also* antirape activists
media, 14, 32, 42–43, 161, 163, 192–93, 201–4, 207, 209, 211, 243, 270n54. *See also* press
media coverage, 198–99, 234
mediation, 50, 64, 230
medicalization, 210, 215
medical treatment, 215
medics, 74, 77
medieval romance, 31, 47
Mediterranean Sea, 145. *See also* sea

Mediterranean island, 134
Medurat HaShevet. See *Campfire*
Meduzot. See *Jellyfish*
mefakedet, 73–75, 78–79, 82–83
mehitzah, 91, 107. *See also* gender segregation
Meir, Golda, 11, 78
Mekudeshet. See *Sentenced to Marriage*
melancholia, 11
melodrama, 44, 126, 146, 156
mémoire, 155
memorial, 156; living, 22, 51, 66, 154–55
memorial duty, 171
memorialization, 131, 155
memory, 23, 43–44, 141, 143, 155, 175; collective, 42; cultural, 15; national, 2, 155
Menahemi, Ayelet, 17, 22
menial labor, 226, 228, 234–35
menstruation, 96
mental illnesses, 16, 209
mentorship, 16–17, 172, 242
Merhak Negiah. See *A Touch Away*
Metz, Christian, 5
Metzizim. See *Peeping Toms*
Mexican-Israeli relations, 233. See also *Salsa Tel Aviv*
Mexican Latina, 228
Michael Sheli. See *My Michael*
Michelle Ezra Safra, 126
microaggressions, 175
middle classes, 150, 224, 228, 236
middle-class women, 12
Middle Eastern Cinema, 8, 10, 20–21
Middle Eastern feminist cinema, 20–21
midrasha, 95, 116, 119, 121
migrant activists, 230
migrant care workers, 223, 225, 272n12–15. *See also* Foreign Workers Program (FWP); migrant workers
migrant worker program. *See* Foreign Worker Program (FWP); *see also* migrant workers
migrant workers, 134, 161, 221–30, 232–35, 237, 272n12–15
migration, 126, 136–37, 146, 227

Mikra Ishe. See *To Know a Woman*
mikveh, 96–98, 117–19, 121–22. *See also* family purity
Milh Hadha al-Bahr. See *Salt of this Sea*
militarism, 3, 6, 21, 24, 29, 32, 35–37, 39, 42, 62, 65, 68, 70–73, 75, 79
militaristic culture, 35, 60, 65, 71, 87, 191, 220
militaristic society, 83, 152, 205, 240
militarization, 64, 81, 86, 188, 206, 208, 220, 237
military, 44, 54, 57, 60–62, 66–67, 70, 73, 75–77, 79–84, 86–87, 189–90, 205, 209, 240. *See also* army; IDF
military base, 25, 39, 67–69, 74–75, 78–80, 82
military police, 74, 83, 190
military service, 65–72, 80–83, 85, 92, 94, 99, 108–9, 127, 174, 203, 206, 234, 237, 256n11. *See also* national conscription
military slang, 142
military training, women's, 60, 65–87
military unit, 50, 63, 66–67, 74, 173, 187, 205, 208, 259n28; religious, 66. *See also* Hesder
Millais, Sir John Everett, 99
Millo, Yoseph, 279
Minghella, Anthony, 143
Minnelli, Vincente, 264n9
minor holy sites, 227
minorities, 54, 206, 242–43; political, 125
minors, protecting, 162
Miral, 279
Mirren, Helen, 259n29
mirror, 58, 98–100, 112, 126, 178–79
miscarriage, 136
miscegenation, 86
Mish'ulim. See *Pathways*
misogyny, 11, 92, 115, 160
missiles, 39. 41–42, 44–46
Miss Israel, 152, 198, 264n9
Miss Universe, 152, 264n9
Miss World; crowned, 198; international competitions, 152
Mita Tova. See *The Farewell Party*

Mivtza Jonathan. See *Raid on Entebbe*
Mizrachiut, 123
Mizrahi, 2, 9, 10, 20, 27, 39, 69, 75–77, 80, 108–9, 113, 123–28, 130–36, 138–40, 142, 146–47, 159, 163–64, 167–68, 187, 191, 206, 232, 236, 246, 250n24
Mizrahi Cinema, 10, 20, 124, 137–40
Mizrahi, Moshé, 16, 161, 183, 279
Mizrahi women, 2, 10, 14, 19, 22, 27, 75–78, 118, 123–47, 158, 160–62, 168–70, 182, 206, 250n25. *See also* Mizrahi prostitutes
Mizrahi women filmmakers, 20, 182, 246–49
Mizrahi prostitutes, 9, 27, 80, 129, 149, 158–71, 187, 206, 246
Mizrahi women, rape of, 27, 187. *See also* Mizrahi prostitutes
Moadon Beit HaK'varot. See *The Cemetery Club*
mockery, 77–78, 134, 238
modernity, 137, 142
modesty, 8, 26, 95–96, 102–3, 106, 110, 120. *See also* mehitzah
Moldova, 161
Moments, 15–16, 118, 279
Moments de la vie d'une femme. See *Moments*
Morag, Raya, 247
morality, 43, 160
Moroccan-Jews, 9, 123, 129, 131, 134, 138–40, 147, 163, 206, 246, 262–63n18. *See also* Mizrahi
moshavim, 124, 225
Mossad agents, 86
Mossinson, Yigal, 163, 250n24
mother, 10–11, 16, 84–85, 101, 110–12, 134–36, 139, 141–44, 151–52, 169–70, 172–73, 175–77, 180, 231–33
mother-child relationship, 222
mother-daughter, 17, 245
mother earth, 158
motherhood, 25–26, 70, 73, 98, 105, 117, 164, 168, 170, 173, 182, 222, 232, 236; transnational, 233, 237

motherless, 117
mother's jealousy, 179
mother's prostitution, 170
The Mountain, 245, 279
mourning, 11, 130–32, 142–44, 155, 216, 262–63n18
movement: civil rights, 12; national, 65; religious youth, 112; settler, 94–95, 108–9, 112, 188
movies, eight-millimeter home, 223
Mulhare, Edward, 5
Mulvey, Laura, 5–7, 13, 43, 97, 178. *See also* to-be-looked-at-ness
municipal services, 172
Munk, Yael, 22–23
murder, 117, 124, 165
musical troupe, 69, 77
musicians, 15, 230, 239
Muslims, 10, 108, 259n3
Muslim holy sites, 109
My Father My Lord, 92, 279
My Lovely Sister, 26, 123–24, 137, 140–47, 279
My Michael, 10–11, 156–58, 279
My Mother the General, 10, 280
My Neighbor the Assassin, 25, 271n1, 277
mystical bond, 207
mystical powers, 129, 137. *See also* witchcraft
mystical practices, 135
mysticism, 116–17
myths, 11, 40, 68, 75, 126, 174, 196, 237, 252. *See also* national myths

Naaman, Dorit, 56–57
Naficy, Hamid, 20
Nahal outpost, 77
Nails (painted), 140, 176, 266n38
Najjar, Najwa, 61, 278
naked bodies, 77, 178, 215
naked genitals, 205
nakedness, 11, 77, 98, 102, 205; women's, 100, 153, 205
nannies, 226, 228, 235
narratives, 12, 21, 24, 32, 39, 44, 46–47, 51,

53–55, 58, 61, 66, 72, 93, 124, 182, 190, 201, 203, 237–38
Nashim Halutzot. See *The Women Pioneers*
Nashot Hamas. See *Women of Hamas*
nation, 60, 150, 153–54, 156–57, 162, 165, 188, 191, 198, 234; birthing the, 70
nationalism, 1–4, 9–11, 17–18, 26, 35–37, 60, 66, 86, 108, 124, 150, 155, 229
nationality, 10, 230
national memory, 2, 155
national myths, 63
national project, 8, 86, 109, 154, 156, 158, 183
national womb, 71, 154, 171
Native American Indians, 4
naturalization, 230, 273n26
Navon, Israel, 52
Nazi, 86
Nazi atrocity, 123
neck, 83, 99
Ne'eman, Judd, 62–63, 68, 278, 280
Ne'eman, Rachel, 240
Negbi, Irit, 218
Negev, 4, 58, 65
Neroni, Hilary, 72
Nesher, Avi, 118
Nesicha. See *Princess*
Netanyahu, Benjamin, 134, 210
networks, 18, 208, 242–43; social, 226–27, 229, 242, 256n11. *See also* Women's Film Forum
New Bedford, 218, 270n54
New Fund for Cinema and Television, 240, 244. *See also* Greenhouse Program
New Jew, 2, 65, 149, 152, 162, 183. *See also under* sabra
New Mizrahi Cinema, 20, 137. *See also* Mizrahi cinema
new sensitivity cinema, 155, 240
news reels, daily, 239
Newton-John, Olivia, 67
nightclubs, 37, 212–13, 218
nightmares, 210
Nini, 10, 250n30
Nirgad, Liron, 67

Nishmat, 260n12, 261n36
Nisui'im Fictivim. See *Fictitious Marriage*
Noa at 17, 10, 280
Noa bat 17. See *Noa at 17*
no-man's-land, 51
non-Jewish sex worker, 161
non-Jewish workers, 224, 229–33. *See also* migrant workers
nonprofits, running, 235
Noodel. See *Noodle*
Noodle, 27, 221, 231–33, 237, 280
Nora, Pierre, 155
North African, Jewish community, 126, 143, 145, 147. *See also* Mizrahi; Moroccan Jews
nostalgia, 104, 122–23, 182
nuclear family, 111, 223
nuclear submarine, 35
nudity, 11, 77, 98, 119, 153. *See also* female body
Nurith, 280

object; nonmilitary, 43; Oriental, 130; sexual, 26, 57, 113
objectification, 4, 6, 10, 19, 55, 61, 70, 96, 130, 183, 189, 238, 192, 200. *See also* to-be-looked-at-ness
objectivity, 197
obligations, 65, 95, 102, 152, 234, 247; male, 95; national, 80; religious, 95; reproductive, 101
observance, religious, 92, 103, 108, 116, 120–21, 129, 200
obsession, 98, 117, 171–72
occidental gaze, 136–37. *See also* gaze
occupation (the), 33, 39, 54, 57, 63, 85–87, 206, 217, 236–37
occupied territories, 72
odalisque paintings, 178
Oedipus, 105, 251
offenders, 190, 192–93, 199
office politics, 70
officer training, 74, 77
offstage (violence), 110, 115
Off-White Lies, 245, 280

olive groves, 205
Olivier, Lawrence, 239
On a Narrow Bridge, 57, 251n30, 280
Onat HaDuvdevanim. See *A Time for Cherries*
One of Us, 68, 280
On the Third Day, 161, 280
opening scene, 110, 143–44, 174, 221
opening shots, 110, 113
opening title sequence, 36
Operation Cat, 172. See also *Tel Aviv Stories*
Ophir Awards, 31, 244, 246
oppressed groups, 34
oppressed heroines, 10
oppression, 26, 54, 76, 86, 98, 100, 103, 120, 134, 168, 184, 206; women's, 9, 11, 165, 168, 184, 206
oral fixation, 176
oral traditions, 139
Orange People, 20, 280
Organizations; political, 126; women's, 163. See also Ahoti
organs, sexual, 153, 192, 203, 216. See also genitalia
orgasm, 118, 177, 211
orgies, previous, 218
Orhim LeRega. See *Off-White Lies*
Orient, 129, 136
Oriental, 9, 76, 128–29, 136–37
orientalist, 2, 58, 123, 157, 182, 232–33
Orientalist fantasy, 160, 165
orientalization, traditional, 61
orientalized past, 137
Oriental Jews, 139
Or Min HaHefker. See *Light Out of Nowhere*
Or, My Treasure, 27, 149, 161, 169–71, 246, 281
Orsher, Gidi, 248
Orthodox Jewish community, 91–94, 105–6, 108–9, 120–22, 260n12, 261n36
Orvim. See *Crows*
Oscars, 246
Ostrovsky family, 239

othering, 20, 26, 91, 157, 161, 173
Ottoman millet system, 259n3
Out of Sight, 27, 215–17, 280
Ovadiah, George, 10, 126, 161, 280, 281
Oz, Amos, 156–57

pageants, 152, 165
pain, 77, 100–101, 277
paints, 69, 167, 198
pairing, 110, 181
palace intrigue, 165
Palestine, 5, 65, 124, 149; pre-state, 65. See also British Mandate
Palestinian authority, 52, 109, 115
Palestinian Cinema, 60, 138, 256n24
Palestinian nationalism, 14
Palestinian olive harvest, 85, 201
Palestinian oppression, 86, 206, 220
Palestinian territories, 33, 87
Palestinian woman, 49, 52, 55, 57, 61, 245
Palestinian women filmmakers, 20–22, 25, 60–61, 182, 246, 256n24. See also Abbas, Hiam; Arraf, Suha
Palestinian women's experience of conflict, 49–64
Palmach, 70
pantheon, national, 150
parachutist, 45
The Paratroopers, 68, 280
parents, 101, 130, 142, 144, 167, 174–76, 179, 209, 223, 225, 230
Paris, 136, 240
parody, 9, 35, 78, 132–33, 151–52
parole board, 199, 201
passing, 57, 123, 128, 142, 176–77; in Israeli and Palestinian cinema, 138
passion, 111, 118, 129, 142, 146
Passover, 93
passport, 51, 231
pastoral scenes, 2, 103, 124
pathology, 160, 163, 197, 216, 234
Pathways, 267n64, 280
patriarchy, 6–7, 9–12, 20, 32–33, 35, 54, 58–60, 65, 76, 96, 108, 125, 128, 132, 143, 153–54, 157–59, 165, 168, 175, 191,

196–97, 207, 216–17, 220, 223, 236–37, 246
patriotism, 2
peace, 47, 52–53, 108, 143, 191, 201
peace movements, 12, 70
peasant shirts, simple, 74
Peck, Cecilia, 27, 217
pedophilia, 157
Peeping Toms, 161, 173, 280
peers, 37, 82, 86, 112, 116, 178, 192, 207, 212–13
Peleg, Yaron, 34
penetration, 213
penis, 112
Peres, Shimon, 190, 247
periphery, 73, 125, 133, 142, 145 (*see also* development towns); Israel's, 124–25, 135, 164, 225, 235, 246; social, 162, 182
perpetrators, 76, 115, 193, 198–99, 201, 210–11, 215–16, 220
Persian tribes, 54
phallic stage, 176
phallus, 16, 118, 189, 193
photograph album, 223
pictures, provocative, 212
pietistic mode, 132
pilgrimages, 141
pimp, 102, 159, 165–66, 168, 187, 212–13, 215. *See also* prostitution
pioneer, 4, 74, 111, 124, 149–54, 158–59, 170, 239
pioneering, 9, 26, 150–53
pioneering feminists, 37
piracy (video), 261n22
A Place By The Sea, 160, 280
police, 86, 134, 191, 202–3, 206–7, 218, 250n25; British, 2
policewomen, 19, 72, 172
polite rapist (the), 193, 201, 207, 210
political coup, 235
political critique, 58, 140, 188
political disenfranchisement, 27
political satire, 35, 132
politics, 12, 33, 36–38, 42, 92–94, 116, 125, 206, 209

poltergeists, 39
ponytail, 74–75, 83. *See also* hairstyles
pool halls, 163
Popper-Giveon, Ariela, 139
population, 3, 53, 65, 123, 197, 223, 228, 232, 235
pornography, 26, 146, 193, 215
porn stars, 211
Portman, Natalie, 49–50
Portuguese-speaking homes, 229
possession, demon, 135
post-Bourekas, 138. *See also* New Mizrahi cinema
postcolonial discourse, 157
Postfeminism, 185, 187, 190, 211, 217, 240
post-Lebanon Israeli war films, 60. *See also* progressive war films
postmenopausal woman, 130
post-trauma, 202–3
poverty, 16, 36, 96, 104, 125–26, 128, 143, 146, 163–64, 166–67, 169, 212, 236, 245
Powell, Michael, 143
power, 3, 6, 55, 57, 71–72, 83–84, 116, 118–19, 134–37, 139–40, 158, 168–69, 174, 191, 193, 214–17, 223, 243, 245–46; telekinetic, 135
prayer, 141, 154
pregnancy, 234
Preminger, Otto, 278
pre-Raphaelite, 99
press, 50, 192–93, 195–96, 198, 202, 204, 209, 217–18, 220, 228, 241, 269n32. *See also* media
primal trauma, 188, 203
primitivism, 9, 117, 123, 132, 135, 139, 182
princess, 8, 152
Princess, 245, 280
prison violence, 39
The Private Memoirs and Confessions of a Justified Sinner, 114
privatization, 224
privilege, male, 16, 206, 208, 219
Procaccia, Ayala, 225
procreation, 154, 265n18
producers, 3, 15–16, 32, 60, 94, 230, 239,

243–44; female, 240, 243
progressive war films, 60, 62–63
progressive tribal activism, 34
Projansky, Sarah, 188, 190, 197, 201, 217
Promised Land, 65, 161, 187, 271n1, 280
promotional films, 187, 242
prosthetics, 44
prostitute, 22–23, 27–28, 69, 80, 85, 102, 111, 113, 120, 129, 150, 153, 158–71, 175, 177, 182, 191, 196, 245, 250n25
prostitute's killing on-screen, 165
prostitution, 9, 149, 159–66, 168–69, 171, 177, 184; on beaches, 161, 170
protagonists, female, 18, 32–34, 36–38, 44, 47, 60, 84, 86, 128, 201, 246. *See also* characters, central female
protofeminist filmmaking, 17–18, 23, 166
Purim, 165
Purity, 260n9, 280

Queen of the Road, 9, 160, 163–68, 187–88, 250n25, 280

Raanan, Tehila, 94, 260n9, 281
Rabbi Hananiah, 119
Rabbi Meir, 119–21
rabbinical authorities, 94, 120, 172, 213, 246. *See also* rabbis
rabbinic sources, 109, 120. *See also* religious sources
rabbinut. *See* rabbinical authorities
rabbis, 93, 106–9, 117, 120, 172, 200 (*see also* rabbinical authorities); Yesha, 108
rabbi's daughter, 109, 116
Rabbi Shmuel Halevi, 121
Rabbi Yaacov, 120
Rabin, Yitzhak, 108–9
racial inequity, 125
racism, 108–9, 125–27, 134, 142–44, 227, 245
Raid on Entebbe, 252n46
Rajan, Assaf, 218
Ramat Hasharon rape, 192, 195, 207, 209–11. *See also under* rape cases
Rambo, 18, 252n46

Rand, Michal, 104
Rand, Shuli, 94, 104, 261n22
rape, 26–27, 80, 113, 115, 164–65, 187–220, 238, 270n50, 270n54, 270n65
rapeability, establishing women's, 192, 205
rape cases, 80, 150, 190, 192–93, 195–96, 198–200, 203, 207, 209–11, 218, 269n32
rape comedy, 80
rape crisis centers, 191
rape culture, 27, 80, 164, 189–90, 192, 197–98, 200, 207, 209, 211–14, 217, 219–20
rape hotlines, 191
rape-revenge fantasies, 72, 164, 217
rape survivors, 198–200, 207
rape victims, 27, 191, 195, 198–99, 201, 203, 210, 215, 217, 219–20
rapist, 80, 187, 190, 197–203, 205–7, 209, 218
rapist's home, 206–7
rapist taunts, 202
Rashi, 120
refugees, 228, 235–36; African, 235
Rehovot International Women's Film Festival, 15, 28, 241–42, 244
Rehovot municipality, 241
Rehov Shishim. *See Sixtieth Street*
Reibenbach, Tsipi, 240
relationship (abusive), 162, 166, 259n3. *See also* abuse (act of); abuses, domestic
religion, 10, 25–26, 34, 89, 95, 109, 118, 150, 200, 244
religious community, 23, 26, 66, 91–97, 103–5, 107–9, 112–13, 115–16, 120–22, 260n12. *See also* Haredi
religious community's settlement project, 115
religious divorce documents (gett), 248
religious establishment, 92, 104, 139, 197
religious feminism, 12, 21, 105, 107, 261n29. *See also* B'Zhutan
religious garb, 168
religious law, 26, 95, 105, 107, 111, 116, 129, 131, 246. *See also* rabbinical authorities; rabbinical sources
religious observance, 91–92, 95–96, 103,

108, 110, 116, 120–21, 129–32, 200–201
religious parties, 92
religious sources (*see also* rabbinic sources); parsed, 95; traditional, 97, 117–18
religious women (representation of), 26, 91–115
religious women filmmakers, 244. *See also* Haredi women filmmakers; Ma'aleh school
religious youth movement, 112
religious Zionism, 94, 108–10, 115
Repeat Dive, 10, 280
reporter, 50, 172. *See also* media; press
reproduction, 14, 96
reproductive inadequacy, 102
reproductive obligations, 101
reputations, woman's, 112, 218
rescue fantasy, 164, 166
reserve call-up, 39
residency rights, 226
Revach, Ze'ev, 10
revenge, 136, 157, 263n29
Revivo, Rafael, 160, 280
Ricochets, 63, 68, 280
rights, 52, 70, 86, 96, 142, 150, 225–26, 230, 237; human, 56, 85, 96, 233–34; legal, 225
right-wing government coalitions, 92
right-wing Mizrahi, 232
Riklis, Eran, 49, 53–55, 58, 60–61, 63–64, 230, 278, 279, 281
rite (of passage), 51, 65–66, 68, 81, 117, 128–31, 189, 214, 256n11
ritual bath. *See* mikveh. *See also* family purity
rituals, 83, 95, 108, 130–32, 135–38, 170, 263n18. *See also* rite; *Shiva*
Rock BaCasba. See *Rock the Casbah*
rocket, incoming, 133
Rock the Casbah, 69, 280
Roman Catholic, 227
romance, 8, 31–32, 34, 46, 129, 141, 175; Anglo-American, 32; Askenazi-Mizrahi, 229; Gothic, 31; interracial, 58; medieval, 47; sexual, 40

romance films, 31–32, 34, 174
Romanian (deceased), 233. *See also The Human Resources Manager*
Romanian worker, 225, 230, 273n21
Roman Russi. See *Blue Mountain*
romantic, 6–7, 34, 36–37, 44, 47, 67, 77, 109, 111, 134, 171–72, 178, 202, 205
romantic comedy, 31–32, 36–37, 43–44, 254n15
romantic rival, 175
romantic women's fiction, 32
Romeo and Juliet, 32, 64
Ron-Feder, Galila, 17
roofs, 42, 125
room (sealed), 41, 43–44, 47
Room 514, 25, 72, 83–87, 280
roommates, 36, 116
Rottenberg, Enrique, 263n29
Rubinstein, Amnon, 17
Russian (Israeli/Jewish), 22, 69, 77, 80, 83–84, 118, 163, 206; hard-drinking, 85
Russian immigrants, new, 41, 75, 78, 161
Russian literature, 84
Russian mafia, 161, 163
Russian socialist pioneers, 149
Russian women, 22, 42, 84–85, 149, 161, 187

S#x Acts, 27, 211–15, 280
Saar, Tzafi, 219
Sabag, Lihi, 94, 260n9, 278
Sabbath, 129
sabra, 84. *See also* New Jew
sabra-soldier, 75
sackcloth garment, 118
sacrifice, 4, 41, 69, 75, 154–56, 170, 232
sacrificial, 68, 115, 153
sadomasochistic fantasies, 71, 157
Safir, Marilyn P., 11
Saga of a Photo, 239, 280
Saint, Eva Marie, 251n30
Sallah, 9, 126, 133, 280
Sallah Shabbati. See *Sallah*
salsa club, 229
salsa instructor, 229
Salsa Tel Aviv, 27, 221, 228–29, 232–33,

237, 280
Salt of this Sea, 20, 61, 280
Sanday, Peggy Reeves, 207
Sarit, 9
Sasson-Levy, Orna, 71
satire, 78, 125, 134, 146, 152, 238; political, 35, 132
satiric newspapers, 32
Saudi Arabia, 21
scenes; final, 51–52, 58, 83–84, 115, 118, 125, 168, 170, 207; kissing, 214; opening, 110, 143–44, 174, 221; sexual, 153, 177, 214
Schatz, Pini, 242
school, 42, 52, 94, 120, 176, 207, 209, 212–13, 227, 230 (*see also* education); boarding, 17, 137
school ceremonies, 208
school corridors, 176
school dance, 176
schooling (secondary), 231, 233
Schorr, Renen, 68, 279
Schultz, Bruno, 124
scopophilia, 5, 98, 105
Scouts, 208
screening rape, 188
screenings, 38, 93–94, 213, 241, 261n22; public, 94
screenplay, 33, 239
screenwriters, 9, 31, 240
screenwriting grant, 241–42
scriptwriter, 213, 240, 246
Scud missiles, 34, 39
sea, 20, 61, 134, 145–46, 160, 221, 280
sealed rooms, 41, 43–44, 47
The Second War, 245, 280
Second World War. *See* World War II
secretaries, 57, 67, 69, 79, 83–84
The Secrets, 26, 92, 116–21, 280
secular world, 93, 95, 98–99
security, 12, 49, 52–53, 59, 72
security forces, 52, 55–56
seduction, 45, 75, 80, 120–21, 171, 176, 192; sexual, 151
self, 124, 177, 200

self-castration, 99
self-discovery, 176, 230
semen (stolen), 140
seminary, women's, 66, 95, 116, 260n12, 261n36
senior officer, 82. *See also* mefakedet
senior ranks, 73
Sentenced to Marriage, 260n9, 280
Sephardi, woman, 76. *See also under* Mizrahi women
Sered, Susan Starr, 27, 70, 197–98, 202, 206, 209, 215
serial killer, 165
serial rapists, 190, 198, 207
Serner, Anna, 244
service: domestic, 228; laundry, 223; national, 66, 94, 189 (*see also* conscription); prayer, 114; public, 54
settlement, 38, 65, 110–12, 114–16, 129, 174
settler movement, 94–95, 108–9, 112, 188
settlers, religious, 115, 205
sex, 37–38, 41, 59–61, 68, 72, 78, 129–30, 140–41, 149, 164–65, 168, 182–83, 195–96, 202–3, 211–13, 219, 280; graphic, 94; lesbian, 119
Sex, Lies and Dinner, 156, 280
Sex, Monica, 208
Sex, Shkarim Va'Arukhat Erev. See *Sex, Lies and Dinner*
sexism, 22, 65, 134, 244
sex-positive culture, 211
sex scenes, 153, 174, 177, 183, 214
sexual abuse. *See* abuse (act of). *See also* sexual assault
sexual acts, 98, 112, 170, 188, 192, 212, 215, 218–19
sexual aggression, male, 207, 214
sexual appeal, 67
sexual assault, 70, 74, 113, 176, 188, 190–92, 195, 197, 203, 211, 216. *See also* abuse (acts of)
sexual awakening, 101, 158, 179
sexual behavior, 103, 112, 159–60, 176, 183, 214, 218. *See also* sexual pleasure
sexual betrayal, 119, 144

sexual commodification, 214–15. *See also* prostitution
sexual conquest, 100
sexual consent, 211
sexual culture (coercive), 160, 211–14
sexual deviance, 116, 196
sexual exploitation, 17, 158, 161, 192. *See also* prostitution
sexual fantasies, 2, 11, 25, 157–58, 214
sexual fetishes, male, 26
sexual harassment, 12, 70, 189–91, 240, 243. *See also* sexual assault
sexual intercourse, 17, 101–3, 136, 146, 157–58, 170, 174, 252n49. *See also* sexual pleasure
sexuality, 12, 15, 23, 25–26, 61, 70–71, 89, 91, 98, 117, 142, 149, 151, 157–62, 171–75, 177, 183, 205, 212–13, 215
sexual liberation, 34, 111, 153
sexually explicit, 119
sexual maturity, 178
sexual offenders, 193. *See also* rapists
sexual organs, 153, 192, 203, 216. *See also* genitalia
sexual paraphernalia, 146
sexual pleasure, 5, 153, 158, 179, 182, 212, 214–15. *See also* sexual behavior; sexual intercourse
sexual promiscuity, 159
sexual proposition, 80
sexual reawakening, 11, 232
sexual response. *See* orgasm
sexual subject, 71, 171
sexual tension, 102
sexual violence, 26–27, 80, 108, 113–15, 165, 189, 193, 198–201, 205, 208–9, 211, 215–17, 219. *See also* sexual assault; sexual harassment; abuse (acts of)
Shakespeare's Kate, 38
Shakespeare's Ophelia, 99
Shakespearian fool, 126
Shalev, Meir, 124
Shalom-Ezer, Tali, 245, 280
Shalosh Imahot. See *Three Mothers*
Shalosh Pe'amim Megureshet. See *3 Times Divorced*
Shamir, Hila, 223
Shapiro, Eliezer, 260n9, 281
Shapiro, Maya, 225, 234
Sharon, Tali, 178–79
Sharona Honey, 171. *See also Tel Aviv Stories*
Sharoni, Simona, 206
Shas Party, 107, 232
Shatila refugee camps, 68
Shaul, Dror, 133, 156, 281, 282
Sh'chur, 20, 26–27, 132, 134–38, 140, 143–45, 246, 280
Shehori, Idit, 277
Shemer, Yaron, 20, 23, 76–77, 129–31, 137–38, 140, 248
Shemesh, Tali, 246, 277
Shenhav, Yehouda, 26
Sheor Meoded, Israela, 15
She's Coming Home, 27, 149, 174–80, 280
Shesh Peamim. See *S#x Acts*
Shiloach, Joseph, 10
Shirat HaSirena. See *Song of the Siren*
Shirley Valentine, 127, 141
Shiva, 130–33, 138, 143–45, 246, 281
Shles, Julie, 240
Shoah, 114
Shohat, Ella, 2, 23, 63, 76–77, 125–26, 128, 133, 150, 157
Shomrat case, 190, 195, 209–11. *See also* rape cases
shot/reverse-shot technique, 170
Shperling, Anat, 241–42
Shtamler, Michal, 119
Shuli's Boyfriend, 20, 281
siege, 42
Siege, 10, 42, 155–56, 250n27, 281
siege mentality, 61
Silberg, Joel, 280
Sima Vaknin Machshefa. See *The Witch Sima Vaknin*
Sippurei Tel Aviv. See *Tel Aviv Stories*
Sipur HaMathil BeTmuna. See *Saga of a Photo*
Sipuro Shel Hakolnoa Hayisre'eli, 250n23

Index - 319

siren, 40, 44–45, 133
sirens (alarm), 37
sisterhood, 25, 113, 181, 198, 201, 205, 207, 216, 236, 238; transnational, 232; universal, 232, 237
sisters, 26, 110, 112, 116, 123, 135, 140, 142–45, 231–32
Sivan, Avishai, 101, 281
Six-Day War, 43, 61, 66
Sixtieth Street, 161, 281
skills, culinary, 35
skin ailment, 142, 144
skirts, simple, 74
slogans, national, 37, 134, 195
slut, 27, 100, 149, 173, 175, 195, 209, 281
The Slut, 27, 149, 173–75, 281
slut, libidinous, 219
slut walks, 268n23
Smicha Hashmalit U'Shema Moshe. See *An Electric Blanket Names Moshe*
smoking, 101, 175–76, 179, 181, 204; transgressive, 175
smuggling, human, 231
social violence, 104, 193
social work, 64, 163, 225, 256n16
society: Arab-Jewish, 132; francophone, 139; Lebanese, 252n49; modern, 136, 161, 246; patriarchal, 162, 197, 207; religious, 104, 117
Sof Ha'Olam Smola. See *Turn Left at the End of the World*
soil, 60, 151
soldiers, 2, 4, 38–39, 65–68, 70–72, 75, 77, 79–80, 82–86, 154, 187, 189–90, 192, 252n46; auxiliary, 72; fallen, 155; female, 27, 29, 61, 65–67, 73, 76, 80–81, 83, 87, 152, 190; frontline, 189; Hesder, 108; male, 69, 71, 74, 78–81, 189; professional, 74; rebellious, 82
song, 25, 31–34, 37–38, 40, 42–43, 45, 47, 49, 67–68, 107, 173, 193, 195, 209–10; popular, 193, 208
Song of the Siren, 25, 31–47, 173, 254n15, 281
Sorreret. See *Black Bus*
soundtrack, 38, 52, 96, 102, 239

South American literature, 124
South American migrants. *See* migrant workers
Space; domestic, 20, 25, 57, 70, 91, 123, 139, 216, 223; public, 91, 96, 137, 139, 170, 200, 216
Spanish-speaking, 229
Spanish telenovela, 229
spectatorial position, 7–8, 237. *See also* gaze
spectators, 5, 8, 13–14, 105, 153, 158, 183, 188–89, 215, 219, 251n37
Spector, Orna, 240
spell, 135–36, 140
sperm sample, 101
spies, 72, 172, 175
sportswear, 42
Sri Lankan migrant worker. *See* migrant workers
Srugim, 93–94, 260n9, 281
Staiger, Janet, 251n37
Stairway to Heaven, 143, 281
star-crossed lovers, 58, 129
Steinem, Gloria, 37
Stella Dallas, 279
sterility, 97
Steven Spielberg's Holocaust Archives, 114
Steve Tish School. *See* Tel Aviv University
streetwalker, 170. *See also* prostitutes
striptease, 178–79, 181, 218
Studlar, Gaylyn, 13
subaltern, 2, 58
subculture, 13, 129
subjectivity, 4–6, 12, 55, 110, 157, 160, 165–84
subversion, 11, 60, 71, 178, 203
Succot, 93, 104
suicide, 79–80, 84–85, 99, 120, 171, 259n28
suicide bombings, 72, 82–83, 230
suicide letter, 216
suitors, 95
Sukkar Banat. See *Caramel*
Sultan's Pool, 239
supernatural, 26, 118, 135, 137, 139
superstitions, 117, 141, 143, 145

support roles, 86, 183
support services, 223
Supreme Court, 52, 64
Suriano, Shlomo, 280
surveillance, 46, 58
survival, 41, 162, 235; national, 35, 44
Sweden, film industry, 244
Swedish Film Institute (SFI), 244
Sweet Mud, 156, 173, 281
Syria, 9, 51, 54, 56, 59–62
The Syrian Bride, 25, 49–58, 61, 63–64, 256n16, 281
Syrkin, Danny, 280
Szobel, Ilana, 159–60

Tabakman, Haim, 92, 278
taboos, 104, 188, 205, 245, 252n48; sexual, 157
Tagar, Nelly, 79, 81
Talaq bil-thalath. See *3 Times Divorced*
Talmon, Miri, 208
teaching filmmaking, 240
tearjerkers, 9
Tehora. See *Purity*
Tel Aviv, 11, 32, 34, 37–40, 135, 159, 174, 201, 232, 234, 257n32
Tel Aviv Cinemateque, 241, 247
Tel Aviv landscape, 43
Tel Aviv municipality, 230
Tel Aviv rapist, 217. *See also* polite rapist (the)
Tel Aviv Stories, 18–19, 23, 37, 171–73, 182, 187, 248, 252n45, 281
Tel Aviv undocumented workers, 231
Tel Aviv University Steve Tish School of Film and Television, 240, 243, 251n41
Tel Aviv yuppie, 75
telekinetic power, 135
television, 17–18, 42, 67, 92–94, 240–41, 243–44, 246
television dramas, 33, 161
television serials, 122
television stations, 18, 94
Temple (the), 141
Temple Mount, 109
terrorists, 157

Thai immigrants, 134, 225
Thanatos/Eros, 59, 134
Thatcher, Margaret, 78
That Lovely Girl, 245, 281
Three Mothers, 20, 281
time bomb, 180
A Time for Cherries, 63, 68, 281
Time of Favor, 66, 108, 116, 281
Tipat Mazal. See *A Little Bit of Luck*
Tirosh, Yoffi, 65
to-be-looked-at-ness, 5, 178
Tofano, Gilberto, 250n27, 281
To Know a Woman, 183, 281
tombstone, living, 231
Topol, Haim, 3, 133
Torah study, 116
Toraty, Benny, 138, 277, 278
To Take a Wife, 129, 131, 242, 246, 281
tourists, 228, 233, 273n22, 274n30
tragedy, 58, 129; Greek, 168
training base, 73, 259n28
trauma, 35, 188, 201–5, 114, 217
travel agent, 198
Travolta, John, 67
Tribeca Film Festival, New York, 65
tribunal, all-male, 247
tribunal court, 246
triumphalism, 66–67; Israel's military, 68
Trojan horse, 54
tropes, anti-Semitic, 3
The Troupe, 67–68, 77–78, 86, 281
troupe, musical, 77
Truly Madly Deeply, 143
Tsabari, Doron, 20, 281
Turkish Cinema, 9, 103, 126, 138, 252n48
Turkish workers, 225
Turn Left at the End of the World, 26, 38, 127, 132, 138, 140, 145, 281
Tvi Riklis, Dina, 235, 277
Tzamot. See *Braids*
tzav shmoneh, 8, 39, 278
Tzlila Hozeret. See *Repeat Dive*

Ultra Orthodox. *See* Haredi
underworld, 160

undocumented children, 227, 230–31
undocumented foreign workers, 232
United States, 41, 208, 216, 243
upper-class white woman, 232
upper-middle-class idyll, 207
upper-middle-class Jewish Israelis, 229
urban planning solutions, motivated, 127
urban war zones, 42
Urs Al-Jalil. See Wedding in Galilee
Ushpizin, 26, 93–94, 103–5, 116, 261n22, 281

vaginal emissions, 95
Valtz im Bashir. See *Waltz with Bashir*
Van Leer, Lia, 15, 239. See also *Lia*
Ventura, Jonathan J., 139
victim blaming, 195, 199, 219. *See also* rape
victimhood, 174, 197, 200, 205, 210
victimization, 76, 213
victims, 65–66, 76, 80, 114, 161–62, 164, 167, 188, 190, 192–93, 195–208, 210–11, 213, 215; Palestinian, 206
Victorian art, 99
Victorian society, 219
video, 93, 212, 218–19
video art, 180
Vidor, King, 281
village elders, 52
Villa Touma, 20, 61, 281
Vilnai, Orly, 218, 271n78
violence, 12, 71–72, 85–87, 96, 99, 104, 108 160, 164–66, 188–89, 191, 193, 197, 202, 205–6, 209, 214–15, 219–20
violence against women, 200, 206–7. *See also* rape; sexual assault
violent woman, 72
virgin, 196
virginity, 80, 99, 158; violated, 111
virgin/whore, 149, 151, 196
visas, 224–26, 273n22; temporary residency, 235, 273n26; tourist, 226, 228–29, 273n22, 274n30
Visual Pleasure and Narrative Cinema, 5, 13, 97, 183
Voices from the Heartland, Slaves of the Lord, 260n9, 281
Volach, David, 92, 279
vomiting, 81
voyeurism, 7, 26, 42, 46, 97–98, 102, 202, 207, 118, 171, 193, 200; mother's, 112
voyeuristic gaze, 178
voyeuristic pleasure, 100, 167, 179. *See also* scophophilia

Wachsmann, Daniel, 157, 278
wailers, funeral, 123, 125, 127, 129–33, 135, 137, 139, 141, 143, 145, 147, 262–63n18
wailing culture, 130–32, 143, 262–63n18
Wailing Wall, 141
Wall, Crack, Tear, 260n9, 281
Walsh, Timothy, 21
Waltz with Bashir, 69, 281
The Wanderer, 26, 92, 96, 101–3, 187, 281
war, 24–25, 32, 34–35, 37–47, 59–62, 65, 67–70, 72, 77–78, 126, 188–89, 237, 245, 252n49
warfare, 45–47, 65
war films, 39–40, 50, 59–60, 62–63, 67
War of Attrition, 68
War of Independence, 65, 71, 126
warriors, 23, 28, 43, 188
wartime, 37, 47, 70
war widow, 10–11, 36, 50–51, 59, 66, 69, 155–56, 173, 231
washing, 85, 95, 178
washing dishes, 35, 170. *See also* dirty dishes
Waterhouse, John William, 99
Waxman, Anat, 22
weapons, 25, 41, 43, 71, 81, 83, 86, 193, 195, 209
wedding, 47, 99–100, 126, 180, 221–23, 281
wedding dance, 118
Wedding in Galilee, 281
wedding list, 35
wedding photographer, 221
wedding planner, 35
wedding videographer's lens, 56

Weiss, Meira, 254n21
welfare state, 92
welfare subsidies, 223
Weller, Yohanan, 280
West Bank, 83, 108–9, 115, 189, 224, 227
Western feminist film theory, 13
What a Gang, 8, 281
What a Wonderful Place, 161, 271n1, 281
When I Saw You, 61, 281
White City (intelligentsia), 230. *See also* activists
white liberal elite, 182, 274n37
whiteness, 58, 138, 157–58, 232
white slave trade, 22, 163. *See also* human trafficking
The Whole Gang, 208
whores. *See* prostitutes. *See also* prostitution
widow archetype, 23, 53, 139, 156. *See also* war widow
wig, 95, 120
Williams, Linda, 7
wisdom, 119–20, 126, 133; folk, 118, 130, 136. *See also* folk religion
witch, 23, 28, 123, 125, 127, 129–35, 137, 139, 141, 143, 145, 147
witchcraft, 26, 117–18, 129–30, 135–37, 139–41, 143, 145–46. *See also* folk religion; mystical powers
witch-crone, 132
witch curses, 134
The Witch Sima Vaknin, 133–34, 138, 145, 282
witness, 47, 114, 201, 217–18, 220
wives, 4, 71–72, 96, 105, 140, 154
Wolman, Dan, 11, 156, 279, 280
womanhood, 4, 8, 19, 98, 151–52, 159, 175–77, 220, 240
woman's beauty, 5
woman's charity, 142. *See also* Ahoti
woman's films, 7, 32, 105, 173
womb, 234; collective, 151; national, 71, 154, 171
women healers, 139
Women of Hamas, 20, 61, 282
The Women Pioneers, 149, 282

Women's Film Forum, 244
women's funerary lamentations, 131
women's literature, 31
women's magazines, 8
women's roles, 63–64, 69–71, 77, 97, 103, 153, 170, 177
women's screenwriting grants, 241
women's seminary, 66, 95, 116
women's servility, 153
women's wailing, 130, 262–63n18
workers, 126, 224–27, 233 (*see also* migrant workers); Romanian, 225, 230, 273n21 (*see also* Foreign Worker Program [FWP]); skilled blue-collar, 228
work visas, 228. *See* Foreign Worker Program (FWP)
world cinema, 241
World War I, 65
World War II, 43, 65

Yalda G'dola. See *Big Girl*
Yamit, 58
Yana's Friends, 25, 31–32, 37–38, 40–47, 173, 282
Yaron, Hadas, 106
Yaron, Nirit, 17–18, 277, 281
Yedaya, Keren, 22, 182, 242, 245, 279, 280, 281
Yellow Asphalt, 267n66, 282
Yemen, mourning culture, 130. *See also* wailing culture
Yemenite-Jewish community, 131, 262–63n18
Yerushalmi, Esti, 135
Yesha, 108
Yeshaya, Nissim, 210
Yeshayahu, Tehilla, 236
yeshiva, 66, 95–97, 108, 116, 119, 137; rosh, 118
Yeshivat Maharat, 261n12, 262n36
Yibbum, 107, 213
Yiddish, 104, 120, 229
Yiddish fables, 103
Yiddishpiel, 169
Yiddish Theatre, 169, 263n29

Yishai, Eli, 232, 234, 274n36
Yishuv, 67, 149
yoetzet halachah, 261n36. *See also* Yeshivat Maharat; Nishmat
Yom HaShlishi. See *On the Third Day*
Yom Kippur War, 67, 191, 203, 206
Yosef, Raz, 23, 161, 164, 169–70
Yosha, Yaki, 278
Yossi and Jagger, 69, 282
Yossi VeJagger. See *Yossi and Jagger*
Young Israeli Cinema, 250n27
young women, 83, 117, 127, 139, 163, 196
youth, 52, 116, 157, 175, 214, 245; radicalized, 108
youth culture, 209, 211; militaristic, 208
youth movements, 17, 208

Zamir, Smadar, 252n42
Zarhin, Shemi, 20, 252n45, 277
Zero Motivation, 25, 27, 65, 69–70, 72, 78–82, 84, 86–87, 187, 246, 282
Zerubavel, Yael, 2, 23, 66, 155–56, 232
Zionism, Labor, 3–4, 20
Zionist, 2, 9, 18, 35, 38, 77, 94, 109, 124, 149, 152, 170, 237. *See also* religious Zionism
Zohar, Uri, 3, 15, 66, 152, 161, 278, 279, 280
Zuria, Anat, 94, 260n9, 277, 279, 280

www.ingramcontent.com/pod-product-compliance
Lightning Source LLC
Chambersburg PA
CBHW080633230426
43663CB00016B/2855